DATE DUE

W. B. YEATS AND THE TRIBES OF DANU
Three Views of Ireland's Fairies

IRISH LITERARY STUDIES

1. *Place, Personality & the Irish Writer.* Andrew Carpenter (editor)
2. *Yeats and Magic.* Mary Catherine Flannery
3. *A Study of the Novels of George Moore.* Richard Allen Cave
4. *J. M. Synge the Western Mind.* Weldon Thornton
5. *Irish Poetry from Moore to Yeats.* Robert Welch
6. *Yeats, Sligo and Ireland.* A. Norman Jeffares (editor)
7. *Sean O'Casey, Centenary Essays.* David Krause & Robert G. Lowery (editors)
8. *Denis Johnston: A Retrospective.* Joseph Ronsley (editor)
9. *Literature & the Changing Ireland.* Peter Connolly (editor)
10. *James Joyce, An International Perspective.* Suheil Badi Bushrui & Bernard Benstock (editors)
11. *Synge, the Medieval and the Grotesque.* Toni O'Brien Johnson
12. *Carleton's Traits & Stories & the 19th Century Anglo-Irish Tradition.* Barbara Hayley
13. *Lady Gregory, Fifty Years After.* Ann Saddlemyer & Colin Smythe (editors)
14. *Woman in Irish Legend, Life and Literature.* S. F. Gallagher (editor)
15. *'Since O'Casey', & Other Essays on Irish Drama.* Robert Hogan
16. *George Moore in Perspective.* Janet Egleson Dunleavy (editor)
17. *W. B. Yeats, Dramatist of Vision.* A. S. Knowland
18. *The Irish Writer and the City.* Maurice Harmon (editor)
19. *O'Casey the Dramatist.* Heinz Kosok
20. *The Double Perspective of Yeats's Aesthetic.* Okifumi Komesu
21. *The Pioneers of Anglo-Irish Fiction 1800-1850.* Barry Sloan
22. *Irish Writers and Society at Large.* Masaru Sekine (editor)
23. *Irish Writers and the Theatre.* Masaru Sekine (editor)
24. *A History of Verse Translation from the Irish, 1789-1897.* Robert Welch
25. *Kate O'Brien: A Literary Portrait.* Lorna Reynolds
26. *Portraying the Self: Sean O'Casey & The Art of Autobiography.* Michael Kenneally
27. *W. B. Yeats and the Tribes of Danu.* P. Alderson Smith

W. B. YEATS AND THE TRIBES OF DANU
Three Views of Ireland's Fairies

Peter Alderson Smith

1987
COLIN SMYTHE
Gerrards Cross, Bucks

BARNES AND NOBLE BOOKS
Totowa, New Jersey

Copyright © 1987 by Peter Alderson Smith

All rights reserved

First published in 1987 by Colin Smythe Limited Gerrards Cross, Buckinghamshire

British Library Cataloguing in Publication Data

Alderson Smith, Peter
W.B. Yeats and the tribes of Danu: three
views of Ireland's fairies. — (Irish
literary studies. ISSN 0140-895X; 27)
1. Yeats, W.B. — Knowledge — Folklore,
mythology 3. Folklore — Ireland
I. Title II. Series
821'.8   PR5908.F64

ISBN 0-86140-257-X

First published in the United States of America
by Barnes & Noble Books, 81 Adams Drive, Totowa,
N.J. 07512

Library of Congress Cataloging in Publication Data

Alderson Smith, Peter, 1947–
W.B. Yeats and the tribes of Danu.
(Irish literary studies; 27)
Bibliography: p.
1. Yeats, W.B. (William Butler), 1865–1939 — Knowledge
— Folklore, mythology. 2. Fairies in literature.
3. Fairy poetry, English — History and criticism.
4. Mythology, Celtic, in literature. 5. Folklore in
literature. 6. Folklore — Ireland. 7. Ireland in
literature. 8. Celts in literature. I. Title.
II. Series.
PR5908.F33A43   1987   821'.8   86-22332

ISBN 0-389-20696-2

Produced in Great Britain

To
Larry Friedman
and
K. R. Sands,
who like the things that I like;
and to
Eric Paff,
who dislikes the people that I dislike

*"Ah, faeries, dancing under the moon,
A Druid land, a Druid tune."*

CONTENTS

Introduction		13
Part One		14
Part Two		18
Part Three		19
Acknowledgements		21

PART ONE: NA TUATHA DÉ DANANN   23

1. Before the Celts Left the Land of Summer   25
    - I   The Invasion of Nemed   25
    - II   The Fomorians   26
    - III   The Battle of Torinis and the Invasion of the Fir Bolg   28
    - IV   The Invasion of the Tuatha Dé Danann and the First Battle of Moytura   31
    - V   The Second Battle of Moytura   33
    - VI   The Invasion of the Sons of Mil   36
    - VII   The Feast of Age   37

2. The Ever-Living   39
    - I   The Appearance of the Tuatha Dé Danann   39
    - II   The Domain of the Tuatha Dé Danann   40
    - III   The Powers of the Tuatha Dé Danann   46

3. Dramatis Personae   52
    - I   Áine   52
    - II   The Dagda   56
    - III   Angus Óg   58
    - IV   Midhir of Brí Leith   59
    - V   Ogma   59
    - IV   Lugh   60
    - VII   Manannan   61
    - VIII   The Morrigu   63

4. The People of Peace   67
    - I   Narrative Evidence   68
    - II   The *Lebor Gabála*   70
    - III   Kinship   71

IV	The Lord of the Dead	71
V	Linguistic Evidence	73

5. Dei Terreni   76
   I   Linguistic Evidence   76
   II Evidence from Abroad   79
   III The Pantheon   81
   IV The Worship of Elves   84
   V   Crom Cruach and Crom Dubh   88

6. The Tribes of the Goddess Danu   92
   I   The Tuatha Dé Danann and the Sídhe   92
   II The Charm of Iron   95
   III Gold   97
   IV The Sídhe   97
   V   The Tuatha Dé Danann   99
   VI Fairy Speech   100

PART TWO: NA DAOINE SÍDHE   103

7. The Fairy Faith in Transition   105
   I   The Immortality of the Sídhe   107
   II The Stature of the Sídhe   108
   III The Domain of the Sídhe   109

8. A First Census of Fairyland   112
   I   The Leprechaun   112
   II The Cluricaun   115
   III The Mermaid   116
   IV The Banshee   118

9. A Second Census of Fairyland   122
   I   Omens   122
   II Swans and Hares   123
   III Cats   124
   IV Weasels   124
   V   Frogs and Fishes   125
   VI Psychic Powers of Animals   125
   VII Pigs   126
   VIII The Black Dog   126
   IX Water-Horses   127
   X   The Pooka   128

10. The Quick and the Dead   130
   I   Angels   130

Contents

II	Eschatology	131
III	Ghosts	133
IV	The *Cóiste Bodhar*	135
V	Burials	136
VI	Changelings	137

11. The Host of the Air — 145
    I   The Costume of the Solitary Fairies — 145
    II The Costume of the Trooping Fairies — 146
    III The Disposition of the Solitary Fairies — 147
    IV The Disposition of the Trooping Fairies — 147
    V   The Stray Sod — 149
    VI The *Féar Gortach* — 150
    VII The Homogeneity of the Fairies — 150
    VIII The *Sluagh Gaoithe* — 151

PART THREE: THE UNAPPEASABLE HOST — 153

12. *The Countess Cathleen*: "Longing for a Deeper Peace" — 155
    I   Yeats and the Fairies — 155
    II *The Countess Cathleen* — 158
    III The Context — 160
    IV The Imagery — 163
    V   The Scenery — 164
    VI Conclusions — 171

13. The Rose and Her Servants — 174
    I   The Rose — 175
    II   The Fairies — 178
    III Nature (i) — 180
    IV   *The Land of Heart's Desire* — 181
    V   Optimistic Poems — 185
    VI   Fallen Vision — 186
    VII The Eternal Gospel — 188
    VIII The Seekers — 190
    IX   Fergus — 190
    X   Cuchulain and "Out of the Rose" — 193
    XI   The Countess Cathleen, "The Man Who Dreamed of Faeryland," and the First Person Persona — 194
    XII The Sin Against the Rose — 195
    XIII The Prince of Failure — 197
    XIV Nature (ii) — 199
    XV   The Meaningless Universe — 201
    XVI "The White Birds" and "The Heart of the Spring" — 203

14. "The Cauldron, the Stone, the Sword, the Spear": *Stories of Red Hanrahan* — 205
   I   1897 — 205
   II   The Symbol — 208
   III   The Tarot — 210
   IV   The Grail Quest — 211
   V   The Nation — 212
   VI   The Fairies — 213

15. "The Flaming Door": *The Wind Among the Reeds* as Psychic Narrative — 218
   I   The Irresistible Call — 219
   II   The Recognition of the Moods — 221
   III   Earth's Inadequacy — 223
   IV   Ambivalence — 224
   V   Acceptance — 227
   VI   The Apocalyptic Cycle — 229
   VII   "Mongan laments the Change that has come upon him and his Beloved" — 231
   VIII   "Hanrahan laments because of his Wanderings" — 232
   IX   "Michael Robartes bids his Beloved be at Peace" — 233
   X   "Hanrahan reproves the Curlew" and "To my Heart, bidding it have no Fear" — 236
   XI   "Michael Robartes remembers Forgotten Beauty" — 237
   XII   "The Valley of the Black Pig" (i): The Sexual Content — 238
   XIII   "The Valley of the Black Pig" (ii): The Tradition — 239
   XIV   "The Valley of the Black Pig" (iii): The Apocalypse — 242
   XV   "The Travail of Passion" — 246
   XVI   "Aedh hears the Cry of the Sedge" — 247
   XVII   "Mongan thinks of his Past Greatness" — 248
   XVIII   "The Blessed" — 249
   XIX   "The Secret Rose" — 251
   XX   "Aedh wishes his Beloved were Dead" — 253

16. *The Shadowy Waters*: "What the World's Million Lips are Thirsting For" — 255
   I   Solipsism — 256
   II   The *Imram* Tradition — 257
   III   The Land of the Dead — 258
   IV   Fairyland — 261
   V   The Ground of Being — 263
   VI   Imagination — 263

17. "I have No Happiness in Dreaming of Brycelinde"		267
I	"Under the Moon"	268
II	"The Withering of the Boughs"	269
III	"Running to Paradise"	270
IV	"The Two Kings"	271
V	"The Hour Before Dawn"	272
VI	"The Cold Heaven"	274
VII	Conclusion	277

Appendix A. Mortal Protégés of the Tuatha Dé Danann		281
I	The Dagda and Angus Óg	281
II	Manannan	282
III	The Problem of the Avatar	283

Appendix B. Additional Notes on *The Countess Cathleen*   288

Notes   291

Glossary   323

Bibliography   325

Index   337

INTRODUCTION

The early literature of any nation reveals more clearly than the later literature does, and perhaps more clearly than it can, the pure nature of the world-view that supplies that nation with its primary and perennial imaginative stimulus. Thus, the great majority of the Icelandic and Norwegian sagas reveal even more clearly than Ibsen the down-to-earth outlook of the Scandinavian people. Anglo-Saxon literature reveals a world in which monsters and marvels occur only rarely, and in which the emphasis is on human heroism. In Early Irish literature, on the other hand, no story seems worthwhile unless it is replete with wonder. The supernatural may take many forms, but the most abundant and enduring source of wonder is the fairies. They populate the earliest Irish tales, they persist through the centuries in Irish folklore, and, even when the belief in them has faded, they retain through art their power to fascinate.

A fairy may be defined as a member of a mysterious and magical race of people who inhabit the same world as common men but inhabit it, somehow, on different terms. The image invoked by the word 'fairy' in most minds today derives from Charles Perrault and J. M. Barrie. Even the *OED* is not immune, for it defines fairies as 'diminutive', which is not necessarily the case. The achievement of Perrault and Barrie in distorting the popular image of the fairy is not less remarkable than it is baleful, for the fairies as we first meet them, the Tuatha Dé Danann, are noble, splendid, and mighty beyond the dreams of humanity. However, it is not only through Perrault and Barrie that the fairies have degenerated. They are the mirror of their believers, and the Irish fairies have changed with the changing fortunes of Ireland. The fairies of folklore may be helpful or mischievous, but it would be too much to call them 'noble'; in appearance, they are seldom more splendid than the peasantry themselves; and, although they retain their magical powers, they are more cunning than mighty. In the literature of the Irish Renaissance they regain much of their splendour, but now they are at the service of the artist. What is most important in the poetry of W.B. Yeats is not where or what fairyland is, but how he responds to its allure. In this book, I mean to trace the early and modern stages of the fairy faith and examine the use made of it by Yeats, to whom I confine myself for reasons of space. There is naturally a good deal of interplay involved, and a certain amount of cross-reference is an essential part of the process of analysis.

I. Part One

The first three chapters of Part One are essentially descriptive, and the last three theoretical. The first three, in other words, mainly set forth what we are actually told about the Tuatha Dé Danann: their 'history', their appearance, their habitat, and their powers. Other races involved in the 'history' of the Tuatha Dé include the Fir Bolg; the Nemedians, who are common ancestors of the Tuatha Dé and the Fir Bolg; the Fomorians; and the Milesians. The Milesians are the ancestors of the Gael, and therefore not fairies, but the same cannot be categorically stated of the Fir Bolg and the Fomorians, who consequently receive their own share of attention.

Chapters four, five, and six examine the three main theories that have been advanced to explain the identity of the Tuatha Dé and, *ipso facto*, to account for the origin of the fairy faith. The first holds that the Tuatha Dé Danann are spirits of the dead; the second that they are gods, perhaps in a degraded form; and the third that they are a folk-memory of a very ancient race of mortals. None of these theories is altogether ridiculous. There is a certain amount of truth in all of them. By and large, however, I believe that the first is the weakest; the second is strong, but ultimately misleading; and the third is closest to the truth. It remains to be said, though, that in the final analysis the Tuatha Dé Danann are simply themselves. Already, in the earliest texts available to us they deserve to be considered as an independent creation. The Ancient Irish, in other words, had neither gods nor ghosts, but fairies.

The Early Irish literature which provides the source material for Part One may be divided into four cycles: the Mythological Cycle, so called; the Ulster Cycle; the Fenian Cycle: and the Royal Cycle. In addition, there are the Lives of the Saints and a good many stories which do not properly belong to any cycle. In terms of narrative time, the oldest cycle is the Mythological. It tells the 'history' of Ireland until the invasion of the Milesians. The Royal Cycle, which deals with the Kings and High Kings of the Milesians, takes up the story with very little interruption and continues well into authentic historical time. Even Brian Boru (d. 1014) is included. The Ulster and Fenian Cycles may be considered as extended episodes within the Royal Cycle. The first is concerned with the reign of Conchobar mac Nessa, King of Ulster around the beginning of the Christian era. Its great hero is Cúchulainn, a warrior in the service of Conchobar. The Fenian Cycle is supposed to take place

Introduction

approximately two centuries later. It concerns Finn mac Cumhail and his *fianna*, or followers, comprising a body often roughly styled a militia. Finn is the not particularly loyal servant of a series of High Kings, chief among them Cormac mac Airt.

The texts that preserve these cycles are contained in several massive collections of miscellaneous material, such as the *Book of Leinster*, the *Book of Lecan* and the *Yellow Book of Lecan*, the *Book of Ballymote*, and the *Book of Lismore*, as well as in a vast profusion of shorter manuscripts of very various date. The dating of Early Irish materials is, in fact, a matter of great difficulty. Because of the highly conservative nature of Irish calligraphy, even the manuscripts are not easily dated. The great majority, however, are in Middle, rather than in Old, Irish, and cannot, therefore, be of extreme antiquity. For surviving manuscripts, in fact, the fourteenth century would seem to have been a high watermark of production. It is very seldom safe to assume that the texts which these manuscripts contain are not copies from older manuscripts, sometimes faithful copies and sometimes adapted to Middle Irish. Therefore, the dating of the texts as distinct from the manuscripts verges on the impossible. I think there is not a single Early Irish text whose dating is not the subject of controversy, and often the dates proposed vary widely, although it is probably true that no story which we now possess existed in recognisable form before the fifth century A. D.

The process of manuscript transmission has, in fact, given rise to some anomalies. For instance, the main portion of the Mythological Cycle is contained in the *Lebor Gabála*, or *Book of Invasions*. The oldest surviving manuscript of the *Lebor Gabála* is probably that in the *Book of Leinster*, which may with some certainty be ascribed to the fourteenth century. That is more recent than the earliest manuscripts of the Ulster Cycle, and yet style and content suggest that the Mythological Cycle is certainly the earlier of the two. Furthermore, the ninth century *Historia* of the British writer Nennius contains passages which clearly originate in the *Lebor Gabála*. Whether Nennius had a copy or translation of the *Lebor Gabála* before him, or whether the words were transmitted to him through still older British sources, is a question that further complicates the matter.

Clearly, then, the dating of Early Irish texts will long remain a task for specialists. I do not claim to be among those specialists, and I do not intend to involve myself in a controversy that I am not qualified to pursue. In general, though, it seems safe to say that the order of production of the four cycles parallels the chronological order of their contents. The Mythological Cycle is the oldest, followed by the Ulster Cycle. The Royal Cycle must have been written sporadically over a long period of time. With a very few exceptions, the oldest texts of the Fenian Cycle are not very old, while the latest texts are not old at all. It is just possible that original Fenian oral literature is still being produced in remote, Irish-speaking areas; it certainly was as recently as a hundred years ago.

The Fenian Cycle, in fact, presents problems of its own. Its appeal has always been to the peasantry, not to the nobility. It must have existed orally before it was admitted to the literary canon, and its end has paralleled its beginning. As literature, in the true sense, therefore, it fades in and out of existence. Its misty beginnings are not so important, and anyway we can do little about them; but as for its end, it would be desirable if there were some point at which we could say, 'Here Early Irish literature ends and folklore begins'. As far as the adjective 'Early' is concerned, of course, we can draw the line where we wish, but the distinction between literature and folklore is not so easily made. It is important, because folklore constantly transmutes its material, whereas conscious artists, at least in Ireland, are far more conservative. For instance, the Fenian poem *Laoi Oisín ar Thír na nÓg* (*The Lay of Oisín in the Land of Youth*), by the antiquary Micheál Coimín, actually dates from the eighteenth century, but its content clearly ranks it, paradoxical as it may sound, with Early Irish literature, not with folklore. In plain terms, its fairies belong to the Tuatha Dé Danann, not to the later *daoine sídhe*. In the end, we must fall back on our own judgment in the case of every text, and that judgment may well be subjective.

Though the originals of nearly all the primary sources of Part One are in Irish (the few exceptions being in Latin), this book is intended for readers of English. I have therefore kept Irish quotations to a minimum. Where reliable translations exist, I have relied on them, and fortunately reliable translations are now abundant. Only one translator has caused me any misgivings, and that is Lady Gregory. Her errors, both of omission and of commission, are fairly notorious. She is capable of simple mistranslations that are sometimes very elementary indeed. She is also capable of combining without warning passages from two or more texts that in the original are quite separate, and, worst of all, of inserting in what purports to be a translation from Early Irish passages in fact derived from oral folklore. On the other hand, it is possible to exaggerate her sins. Herbert V. Fackler is quite within his rights to note Lady Gregory's words that 'I am not enough of a scholar to read the old manuscripts from which these stories were taken', but apparently infers that she could not read printed Irish texts either, even though he refers himself to her reliance on them, 'If we accept her word'. 'That her retelling of the Irish legends is not literal translation' entirely overstates the case.[1] On the whole, I think, Lady Gregory is a sufficiently reliable authority. Although her books do not include parallel Irish texts, the careful reader can generally spot her departures from strictly accurate translation.

When the Irish text has been available, I have occasionally quoted the odd word when it is ambiguous, or when the translation seems arguable or tentative, or when for some other reason it has seemed advisable. In the case of poetry, I have sometimes added the original in the text or in a footnote simply because readers of Irish might like to know it. In Part Two I have had to deal with some untranslated materials. Here I have made my own translation but have invariably quoted the original in a footnote.

The spelling of Irish words and names constitutes another problem, as Irish orthography, even now, is scarcely settled, and in past centuries has been almost haywire. The attempted introduction of a new, simplified orthography after the War of Independence, subsituting simple vowels for those long concatenations of letters that seem so strange and unpronounceable to English readers, having been only partially successful, has if anything only further complicated the situation. When quoting or referring to a particular work, be it a text or a commentary, I have followed the practice of that work, except in the case of lenited consonants. These are indicated in Irish, when indicated at all, either by a point superscript or by a following h. I have converted all points superscript to h, except in the case of a few lenited s's, where the editors whose texts I am following have apparently thought it important to preserve the point. When not making reference to a specific work, I have used consistently the spelling that I myself prefer, which is generally the most popular. Naturally, then, there are some diversities of spelling, but none which should cause any confusion. I have generally avoided anglicisations, but one to which I should call attention is 'Maeve'. I have used this spelling in Parts Two and Three, as against 'Medhbh' in Part One, to conform to popular usage and avoid the appearance of pedantry. For the same reason, I have spelt the site of the great battle between the Tuatha Dé Danann and the Fomorians 'Moytura' thoughout.

My documentation does not deviate from accepted procedure in any important particulars, but I should mention that in Part Two, especially, the source material is extremely repetitive, and I have not thought it worthwhile or helpful to list every occurrence of a particular motif or observation where one or two are sufficient.

II. Part Two

Part Two of this work deals with the fairies of folklore, *na daoine sídhe*. By far the greater portion of the source material for this Part has been collected within the last 150 years. I should here emphasise that I am concerned with *Irish* fairies and *Irish* foklore. Some form of fairy is to be found in almost every country, but it is nowhere precisely the same. The fairy faith of the British Isles presents a special case, and the Irish fairy faith a special case of that special case: special, not least, in that the folklore embodying it is so abundant. As a rule, then, it is sufficient for me that a story or a belief exists in Ireland: I have not called attention to parallel stories or beliefs in Scotland, or Wales, or Norway, or anywhere else. Still less have I called attention to stories and beliefs of other countries that are not paralleled in Ireland. However, where the belief of another country, especially a neighbouring country, helps to explain an Irish belief, I have mentioned it. In particular, to exclude Robert Kirk's *Secret Commonwealth* from the evidence would be absurd. This work hails from Scotland, whose fairy faith is the nearest relative of Ireland's, and dates from the seventeenth century, which may be called the heyday of the fairy faith. Its evidential value is very great.

The greatest difference between the fairy faith of Early Irish literature and the fairy faith of folklore is the diversity of the latter's fairy population. Whereas before we had essentially only the Tuatha Dé Danann, we now have everything from the leprechaun to the pooka. One task of Part Two, then, will be to undertake a census. Every fairy phenomenon must be judged on its own merits. Some are more explicable than others: for example, the Black Dog. There have been attempts to bring order to this chaos, chiefly by distinguishing between solitary and trooping fairies. These theories will be examined, but they are, I believe, misguided, and unjustified by the evidence. As capriciousness is a great part of the faries' nature, their cosmos is bound to be unpredictable, and we must accept the chaos we find.

That does not, however, preclude us from questioning the nature of the fairy faith itself. The questions that we shall have to ask will be much the same as in Part One, but the answers will differ. The fairies of modern Ireland have had to live with the Christian faith of many centuries. It is chiefly through the influence of the priests, I believe, that the Sídhe have come to be confused with ghosts and fallen angels. Essentially they are, like the Tuatha Dé Danann, nothing but themselves. However, much of the confusion surrounding the nature of the Sídhe is better attributed to folklorists than to the folk themselves.

III Part Three

Part Three is critical part of this book. W. B. Yeats was not, of course, the only writer of the Irish Renaissance to deal with fairies. His work, however, is the most interesting, because it has very deep roots in tradition and is yet intensely personal. In other words, he stands pre-eminent, perhaps even unique, in the creative use of tradition. On the one hand, Yeats is a believer in the fairies. He is sensitive to the spirit as well as to the letter of mythology and folklore. On the other hand, he has thought so much about the fairies that his dialogue with them has become almost synonymous with his inner life. The fairies dwell as much in Yeats's imagination as in the world, and he would have been the first to admit it.

Part Three does not concern all of Yeats's works, but only those, from his early period, which are most involved with the fairies. Even then, it excludes the rather immature *Wanderings of Oisin* and 'Crossways', and begins with *The Countess Cathleen* and 'The Rose'. Fairyland for Yeats represents an escape from the fallen world, but the escape itself is difficult and of questionable desirability. The price of escape is complete alienation from the quotidian world. In *The Countess Cathleen* the dilemma is more a question asked than a question answered. In 'The Rose', Yeats sees himself as striving for escape but recoiling in horror. The *Stories of Red Hanrahan* in a sense reversed the perspective of 'The Rose'. Hanrahan is the outcast of fairyland, not the beggar at its gates. He suffers from the alienation that the personae of 'The Rose' only fear. The stories end on an optimistic note, however, which perhaps emboldens Yeats for the reckless and self-deluding plunge into fairyland of *The Wind Among the Reeds*. *The Shadowy Waters* shows evidence of exhaustion, and finally, in *Responsibilities*, having worn out his obsession, Yeats is able to bid farewell to the fairies.

In the course of my research a number of people have objected to me that Yeats could have known nothing of Early Irish literature as he knew no Irish. As it is apparently widespread, this objection must be answered, and now is the time. Even if the objection were sound, Early Irish literature and the work of Yeats would remain two related depositories of fairy lore, each of them interesting for its own sake. They could not help but be related, even if the relationship were indirect. As it happens, though, the premise of the objection is false. Yeats knew no language besides English very well, but he was not entirely ignorant for all that. Even though he says in 'The Trembling of Veil' (1922) that 'We had no Gaelic', his letters belie him. He wrote to Lily Yeats on July 11, 1898, that he was learning Irish and to the editor of *The Gael* (New York) in (probably) November 1899 that he had 'taken up Gaelic again'. His works contain more than 400 Irish words. Though most of these are either proper nouns or words like 'colleen' that are in common English circulation, others, like 'gluggerabunthaun', though authentic, are not even in common Irish circulation.[2] Also, Yeats speaks of translating Douglas Hyde,[3] and, in his long essay on *The Irish Dramatic Movement*, refers to several plays in Irish. In general, therefore, it is clear that Yeats was not entirely baffled by the Irish plays which he produced, or helped to produce.[4]

It is true that Yeats did not claim to be learning Irish until after he had written *The Wind Among the Reeds*, but, on the other hand, it is the output of his first ten years of publication that is richest in Irish words.[5] This is partly, no doubt, affectation, all of a piece with Yeats's hinting, falsely, that he had read *Laoi Oisín ar Thír na nÓg* in the original,[6] and quoting and 'translating,' with perfect accuracy, a verse of Irish at the end of 'The Adoration of the Magi' (1897) that he could not have pronounced, much less understood, without someone else's assistance.[7] Until the end, Yeats's spelling of Irish remained eccentric, and what we know, or can gather, of his pronunciation worse: for instance, pronouncing 'Emer' as if it were English and stressing the second syllable of 'Dectora'. Sometimes, indeed, Yeats invented the Irish language as he went along. Thomas MacDonagh, the martyr of 1916, remarked of 'Red Hanrahan's Song about Ireland' that 'nothing is gained, surely, by that extraordinary perversion of the Irish name of the Old Woman of Beare, *Cailleach na Béara*. The word *clooth* is not Irish; it has no meaning.'[8] On the other hand, Yeats's early use of Irish cannot be all affectation. He may have had no systematic knowledge of the language, but he had picked up the word 'gluggerabunthaun' somehow. And the pronunciation of Irish did vary greatly in diferent parts of the country.

Yeats's knowledge of Irish, in any case, has little bearing on his knowledge of Early Irish literature. He had ample access to translations and, indeed, to translators. His own work is surely the best proof that he was well acquainted with Early Irish literature.

There is a problem of textuality with Yeats as well as with Early Irish literature. He was so given to revision that the texts by which much of his early work is best known were actually written in his old age. These are the texts of *Collected Poems* and *Collected Plays*. I have, nonetheless, generally relied on these texts. They are at least Yeats's own revisions, whereas the early texts, he tells us, were often high-handedly revised by W. E. Henley.[9] More importantly, Yeats never revises the content of his poems. There is no attempt to force his later philosophy upon his earlier poems. Thus one may say that his late texts are simply the best expression of his early thought. However, when early texts have

Introduction

something to add, I have not ignored them. In the cases of *The Countess Cathleen* and *The Shadowy Waters*, indeed, my preference for the final text is so marginal that it may be truer to say that I have considered all texts promiscuously. In the case of the *Stories of Red Hanrahan*, I have considered the 1897 text before the 1907 text. *The Wind Among the Reeds* is a definite exception to my normal practice, though I had not at first intended that it should be. I found myself quoting the 1899 text so often that it soon became apparent that that should be my primary text.

IV. Acknowledgements

The first and warmest of my acknowledgements must surely go to my informants in the Co. Sligo, whom an absurd American law prevents me from naming. In the same breath, I must thank the staff of Roinn Bhéaloideas Éireann, University College, Dublin, for the unfailing warmth and courtesy with which they helped me to inspect their vast collection of manuscripts, and Professor Bo Almqvist, Director of Roinn Bhéaloideas Éireann, for permission to quote from these manuscripts. I must also thank the administrators of the University of Arizona Graduate Student Program Development Fund for a generous grant, without which I could neither have met my informants, nor visited Roinn Bhéaloideas Éirean, nor attended the Yeats International Summer School at Sligo. I am indebted to Prof. Thomas Dillon Redshaw and the editors of *Éire-Ireland* for permission to include in this book the chapter on *The Countess Cathleen*, which is founded upon two articles published in that journal. Professors George J. Bornstein, Henry Goodman, Michael P. Goldman, and Sister M. Rosalie Ryan have kindly allowed me to quote from their unpublished doctoral dissertations. It has unfortunately proved impossible to contact Drs. Thomas L. Dume and Frederick Stewart Colwell. Should they ever have occasion to read this work, I hope that Drs. Dume and Colwell will agree that I have not infringed the 'fair play rule' with respect to their dissertations.

The extracts from the works of W. B. Yeats are published by kind permission of Michael B. Yeats and Macmillan London Ltd., and in the U.S.A. by Anne Yeats and the Macmillan Publishing Company.

'No Second Troy', 'King and No King' are copyright 1912 by the Macmillan Publishing Co., renewed 1940 by Bertha Georgie Yeats.

'The Two Kings', 'Running to Paradise', 'The Hour Before Dawn', 'The Realists' are copyright 1916 by the Macmillan Publishing Co., renewed 1944 by Bertha Georgie Yeats.

'The Phases of the Moon' is copyright 1919 by the Macmillan Publishing Co., renewed 1947 by Bertha Georgie Yeats.

'The Circus Animals' Desertion', 'Under Ben Bulben' are copyright 1940 by Georgie Yeats, renewed 1968 by Bertha Georgie Yeats, Michael Butler Yeats and Anne Yeats.

'Autobiography and Journal' © M. B. Yeats and Anne Yeats 1972.

'The Danaan Quicken Tree' is © 1983 by Anne Yeats.

PART ONE:
NA TUATHA DÉ DANANN

1. BEFORE THE CELTS LEFT THE LAND OF SUMMER

'It was in a mist the Tuatha de Danaan, the people of the gods of Dana, or as some called them, the Men of Dea, came through the air and the high air to Ireland.' So begins Lady Gregory's *Gods and Fighting Men*.[1] But who are the Tuatha de Danaan, the mysterious and splendid race of Ancient Ireland, the ancestors of the fairies? The whole of Part One will be devoted to answering that question. We will consider their appearance, their powers, and their dwellings. We will consider them as gods, as ghosts, and as mortals. But in this chapter I will summarise their 'history' from their first appearance in Ireland until the Feast of Age, as that event is called when they withdrew from the world of men and became unmistakably supernatural. The Early Irish source on which I shall principally rely will be the *Lebor Gabála*, or *Book of Invasions*, with its related texts. The *Lebor Gabála* is not an ideal source. Though a repository of pagan mythology, it was written by monks, and this has given rise to various types of euhemerism. For instance, the *Lebor Gabála* links 'all the invaders of Ireland with Eastern Europe', and especially with Greece. This puzzling feature of Irish mythology is explained by the fact that it facilitates 'the invention of a Biblical ancestry' for those invaders.[2] The *Lebor Gabála* also treats the chief personages of the Tuatha Dé Danann as if they were a succession of mortal kings. It remains, however, the best source that we have. It will be necessary to begin summarising its contents from a point somewhat before the invasion of the Tuatha Dé Danann. I will begin, then, with the invasion of Nemed, and proceed from there.

I. The Invasion of Nemed[3]

Nemed, a Greek of Scythia, came to Ireland, with a fine disregard for geography, by rowing across the Caspian Sea until he reached the Northern Ocean. His voyage after that was not without misfortune. Many of his following were drowned at a golden tower in the ocean when the tide came in and covered it, and when, eventually, a year and a half later, he reached Ireland, his wife Macha died twelve days after landing. In order to take possession of Ireland, Nemed had also to overcome the Fomorians in three battles, at great cost to his own side.

II The Fomorians

Like the Tuatha Dé Danann, whom we have yet to meet, the Fomorians are a mysterious people, but, unlike them, they are far from splendid. According to the seventeenth century Gaelic historian Geoffrey Keating, who had access to texts now lost, they were 'navigators of the race of Cham, who fared from Africa'. Under the leadership of one Cíocal *cen chos*, or 'footless', 'they came fleeing to the islands of the west of Europe, and to make a settlement for themselves, and (also) fleeing the race of Sem, for fear that they might have advantage over them, in consequence of the curse which Noe had left on Cham from whom they came'.[4]

This, however, is obvious monkish refashioning. There is often a sort of ambiguity about the Fomorians, as to whether they are natural or supernatural entities. For instance, a regnal poem that may be as old as the sixth century A. D. contains this verse: 'A prince has entered the realms of the dead, the noble son of Sétnae; he ravaged the meadow-valleys of the Fomorians underneath the worlds of men.' This may seem an obvious allusion to the death of the said prince ('Mes Delmann of the Domnainn'), and it may be just that, but Francis John Byrne points out that 'the popular imagination readily invested the lands over the seas with the characteristics of the Otherworld'; consequently, the verse may commemorate a quite ordinary military expedition. The Fomorians, in fact, are 'often identified with human raiders from across the sea', and in this instance may be 'the piratical broch-dwellers of Scotland'.[5]

Despite this ambiguity, however, the supernatural connotations of the Fomorians always predominate. The very facts that they are associated with the oversea kingdoms and that those kingdoms are asociated with the Otherworld define the function of the Fomorians in Early Irish literature. They function like the monsters in *Beowulf*. In a famous passage, J. R. R. Tolkien said of that poem: 'we look down as if from a visionary height upon the house of man in the valley of the world. A light starts . . . and there is a sound of music; but the outer darkness and its hostile offspring lie ever in wait for the torches to fail and the voices to cease.'[6] Whatever their historical origin or reality, if any, the Fomorians in mythology exist beyond time. They are an eternal threat. Like Grendel, they haunt the edge of the world and seek always to exercise their baleful control over the centre.

We have still to account for the Fomorians' origin, though. If they are intrinsically monstrous, it will follow that their origin as well as their function ought to be sought in mythology, not in history. On the face of it, they are certainly monstrous. Cíocal's followers were half-men, with only one foot and one hand.[7] However, this is not necessarily typical of the Fomorians. After the Second Battle of Moytura (of which we shall shortly read), the Fomorian dead were found to include innumerable such half-men, but these were considered rabble.[8] There may also be a comparatively simple explanation of the deformity. J. F. Killeen has pointed to the magical significance, in Ancient Ireland and in other ancient cultures, of a single shoe, on or off the foot. Besides the deformity of the Fomorians, he calls attention to instances in Early Irish literature of dancing on one foot for magical purposes, and of physical amputation to create magicians. His conclusion is that in remote times shamans were actually mutilated; later, the mutilation was merely simulated; later still, the practice was dimly recalled when the Fomorians were thought of.[9]

A still simpler explanation is that the half-formed nature of the Fomorians is a mere misunderstanding. The Irish word used for the Fomorians found dead after the Second Battle of Moytura is *léth-dóine*. Literally, this means 'half-men'; but the word *léth* is also used idiomatically to denote one of a pair. Now, we sometimes hear of a practice in Ancient Irish warfare of binding soldiers in pairs to prevent them fleeing.[10] We are not specifically told that this was done in the Second Battle of Moytura, but we are at least free to infer as much from the word *léith-dóine*, rather than inferring that the Fomorians were deformed.[11]

Attractive as this explanation is, however, it must be remembered that the *léth* idiom is peculiar to Ireland, while unipeds in folklore and mythology are of far wider distribution. In view of the Viking occupation of Ireland, it is particularly worth noticing a Norse work, *Thorfinnssaga Karlsefnis*, in which Thorvald, a son of Eirik the Red, is killed in Vinland by an uniped (*einfaeting*).[12] This motif may be borrowed from the Eskimoes of Greenland, who also had a tradition of unipeds.[13]

Even if the Fomorians were not half-men, they seem certainly to have been giants. Cíocal and his mother are so described.[14] Outside the Mythological Cycle, the Fomorians are described as giants almost proverbially. In the *Táin*, for instance, the Ulster hero Cúchulainn, undergoing his warp-spasm or distortion by rage, is termed 'vast as a Fomorian giant or a man from the sea-kingdom.'[15] Henri d'Arbois de Jubainville points out that Giraldus Cambrensis renders the name *Fomorchaib* as *gigantibus*.[16]

In one way or another, then, it seems that the Fomorians are indeed monstrous. We have therefore to seek their mythological significance. Various theories have been put forward. Alwyn and Brinley Rees propose that the half-formed nature of the Fomorians symbolises 'the oneness which is split in the world of manifestation—and their hostility to the established order'.[17] If I understand it correctly, this makes the Fomorians distant cousins of the Serpent of Genesis: the symbol of the Fall. K. M. Briggs speculates that they represent a folk-memory of 'a primitive religion that entailed barbaric human and animal sacrifices.'[18] Both of these theories are plausible but unproven. The Rees brothers' theory probably cannot be proven. A. G. van Hamel stands on a firmer scientific ground when he writes: 'Cicul himself seems to be a dethroned god, it is impossible not to connect him with the Gaulish god Mars Cicolluis.'[19] As will be seen in chapter five, however, I do not find comparisons with Gaulish gods as helpful as they seem at first sight. It may be simply that the Fomorians were created to provide a national enemy older than the Vikings. The Irish have always perceived even their pre-history as a struggle to win or preserve national sovereignty. The repulsion of foreign invaders is a recurrent motif in the Fenian Cycle too.

Insofar as the word 'fairy' applies to the Tuatha Dé Danann, it would seem that it must also apply to the Fomorians. The two races cannot with much precision be said to represent good and evil, and in fact they may even enjoy temporary alliances, as we shall see. But even so, they are foils to one another, or two sides to the same coin. The Fomorians' fairy role, however, seems to have atrophied. When they feature in cycles other than the Mythological Cycle, they appear to be mortal, foes to the Milesians rather than to the Tuatha Dé Danann. They have not survived in folklore down to our own day, nor do they seem to have any descendants.

III. The Battle of Torinis and the Invasion of the Fir Bolg

We now return to the story of Nemed.[20] He himself, with three thousand others, eventually dies of plague. The remainder of his people, in spite of his victories, falls under the oppression of the Fomorians, who are led by Morc son of Dele and Conann son of Faebar. The Fomorians' head-quarters is a tower named Tor Conainn or Torinis Cetne on what is today called Tory Island. This tower is presumably a doublet of the golden tower where disaster befell the Nemedians while they were sailing to Ireland. The Fomorians make a sheep-land of

Ireland and levy a tribute of two thirds of the Nemedians' corn, milk, children, and so forth every Samhain, or Halloween (this may be a reminiscence of sacrifice). The Nemedians sail against Torinis but obtain one year's respite from battle on condition that they do not disperse. During this year, they appeal for help to Smol, king of Greece. He sends them warriors, druids and druidesses, wolves and venomous animals, and follows himself. The Nemedians challenge Conann to battle, and Conann begins without waiting for his co-leader Morc. The Nemedians gain the victory, kill Conann, and sack and burn Torinis with all its occupants. Their Greek allies depart.

Now, however, Morc arrives and renews the battle. While the fight goes on, the tide comes in, as previously at the golden tower, and all but thirty Nemedians and one shipload of Fomorians are drowned. The three surviving Nemedian chiefs divide Ireland between them, but soon abandon it for fear of the Fomorians, each other, and plague. One party goes to Greece and another to Britain.[21]

After this Ireland is deserted for two hundred years, until colonised by the Fir Bolg, the descendants of those Nemedians who emigrated to Greece. In Greece they fell into servitude and were forced to carry clay to make plains. They converted the leather bags used for this purpose into boats and fled in them, hence their name, Fir Bolg, or 'bag people'. That, at least, is the traditional explanation of the name, and it has been accepted, in one way or another, by several modern writers on the subject. Julius Pokorny agreed that the Fir Bolg were named after their hide boats, and proposed that they were Eskimoes! John Rhys thought that the Fir Bolg were originally identical with the Fomorians, who had 'bags or sacks for stealing the farmer's stores'.[22] There does appear to be some connection between the Fomorians and at least one sept of the Fir Bolg, called the Fir Domnann, but the evidence would seem to favour de Jubainville's theory that the Fomorians were the gods of the Fir Bolg. One of the chiefs of the Fomorians is called Indech son of Dea Domnann. *Dea Domnann* would seem to mean 'god of the Domnann'. In a poem by Flann Manistrech (d. 1056), Elloth of the Tuatha De Danann is said to have been slain *la dé nDomnand d'Fhomorchaib*, 'by a god of the Fir Domnann of the Fomorians'.[23] This evidence is strong, but there is not very much of it. If the Fomorians were ever gods of the Fir Bolg, it must have been at a very remote time, for the narrative evidence does not even hint at such a relationship.

The name 'Fir Bolg' was doubtless also responsible, as W. B. Yeats thought, for an item of modern folklore collected by Lady Gregory. One of her informants told her that there are two types of fairy, one called the Dundonians, and another that is 'more wicked and more spiteful'. On this second type, Lady Gregory's informant said: 'Very small they are and wide, and their belly sticks out in front, so that what they carry they don't carry it on the back, but in front, on the belly in a bag.' Yeats comments: 'The Dundonians are, of course, the Tuatha-de-Danaan, and those with the bag are the 'firbolg or bag-men;' we have now, it may be a true explanation of a name Pofessor [John] Rhys has interpreted with intricate mythology.'[24] What Yeats forgets is that the information provided by Lady Gregory's informant is only the ancient tradition itself, transmitted orally over many centuries and understandably corrupted in the process.

It is more probable that *bolg* in the context of *Fir Bolg* does not mean 'bag' at all. Van Hamel translated it as 'gaps' and explained that the Fir Bolg lived 'in the gaps of roads'. By these gaps, he means, I take it, crossroads, forks, and other points of indeterminancy. His theory is interesting, as these are traditionally the haunts of marginal beings in folklore. Timothy Lewis interpreted *bolg* as 'wall of defence', and so translated *Fir Bolg* as 'burghers'. These speculations are interesting but purely linguistic, not historical. As long ago as 1685, on the other hand, R. O'Flaherty remarked on the similarity of the name Fir Bolg to the name of the Belgae, a tribe of Continental Celts who were well known to Julius Caesar and who have given their name to Belgium. T. F. O'Rahilly has identified other cognate words. *Bolgios* occurs in Pausanias as the name of a Celtic chief. *Bolgos*, O'Rahilly says, was the name of a storm god, though since the word is unattested one would like to know his evidence. From here O'Rahilly works his way back to IE *bheleg-*, 'lightning'. The Fir Bolg and the Belgae are thus 'the men of the lightning'. This theory becomes still more convincing when the name of Cúchulainn's deadly spear, the *gaí bulga*, is taken into account. This spear represents the lightning itself, O'Rahilly concludes.[25] At least in comparison with all others that have so far been advanced, O'Rahilly's theory seems unassailable. Its most interesting feature, however, may be that already advanced by O'Flaherty, the identification of the Fir Bolg with the Belgae. If that is sound, the Fir Bolg are an historical people first, a mythological people only second.

The Fir Bolg are divided into three septs. Though the name is used generically of the whole race, only those who carried clay in Greece are the Fir Bolg proper. The other septs are the Fir Domnann, who dug the earth, and the Galeoin, whose name the *Lebor Gabála* derives from *gal-fhian*, or, roughly 'warriors of valour'. Like the Fir Bolg, the Fir Domnann and the Galeoin are also known historically. 'Domnainn,' says O'Rahilly, 'is a variant of *Dumnonii*, the name of the tribe who were in occupation of Cornwall and Devon at the time of the Roman conquest of Britain, and who afterwards, by emigration, gave their name to a district in Brittany.'[26] The Gaileoin, under that name, have left few traces, but they are apparently to be identified with the Laigin. The Laigin have given their name to Leinster. Beyond Leinster, place-names show the conquering movement of the Laigin sweeping 'across north Munster and the southern midlands to the Shannon and even beyond into Connacht and Clare'. Outside of Ireland, 'the Lleyn peninsula in Wales bears the name of the Laigin, and . . . the Irish are said to have been driven out of North Wales by Cunedda some time in the fifth century'.[27]

IV. The Invasion of the Tuatha Dé Danann and the First Battle of Moytura

The occupation of Ireland by the Fir Bolg passed off with no incident that need detain us. We leave them now in possession of the island and turn to the Tuatha Dé Danann themselves.[28] Like the Fir Bolg, the Tuatha Dé Danann are descended from Nemedians who emigrated to Greece. The Tuatha Dé Danann settled in a different part, in the northern islands. Far from falling into servitude, they there grew so wise that they considered their men of learning (but not the lower orders) gods. From this, says the *Lebor Gabála*, derives their name, *Tuatha Dé*, or 'peoples of the gods'. (*Dé* can also mean 'of the goddess'; the *Lebor Gabála* says nothing of *Danann*, which may well be the name of a goddess.) The cities of the Tuatha Dé Danann were Falias, Gorias, Findias, and Murias. From Falias came the *Lia Fáil*, or Stone of Destiny, which is supposed to have screamed under every king from Lugh, of the Tuatha Dé Danaan, until the birth of Christ, whereupon, like all oracles, it fell silent. It is now beneath the coronation throne in Westminster Abbey. From it Ireland gets her name of Inisfáil. From Gorias came the invincible spear of Lugh; from Findias the deadly sword of Nuada; and from Murias the inexhaustible cauldron of the Dagda. These are the Four Jewels of the Tuatha Dé Danann.

While still in Greece, the Tuatha Dé Danann form an alliance with the Athenians against the Philistines. Among their services, they magically reanimate the corpses of the Athenians. However, the druid of the Philistines advises his people to thrust pegs of hazel and quicken into the necks of their victims. These magic woods reduce the corpses to 'worms on the morrow'. Thus thwarted, the Tuatha Dé flee from the Philistines to Dobar and Iardobar in the north of Alba, or Scotland. They stay there under the leadership of their king Nuada for seven years, and then sail for Ireland, where they arrive on Beltaine (May 1) and burn their boats. In their mode of travel we have here parted company with the sentence from Lady Gregory with which we began this study. According to 'The Second Battle of Mag Tured', it was the smoke from the burning boats of the Tuatha Dé that gave rise to the legend that they arrived in a mist.[29] At any rate, it is under the cover of a magical darkness, or 'druid mist', that they now travel to the mountain of Conmaicne Rein in Connacht, where they demand battle or kingship from their cousins the Fir Bolg. Hence ensues the First Battle of Moytura, between the Fir Bolg, under their king Eochaid son of Erc, and the Tuatha Dé Danann under theirs, Nuada. The Tuatha Dé Danann win the day. Eochaid is slain, but Nuada also does not escape unscathed.: he loses one arm to Sreng, the champion of the Fir Bolg.[30] Diancecht the leech and Credne the brazier replace it with a silver arm (hence Nuada's epithet, *Airgetlám*), but Diancecht's son Miach lops this off and restores the original arm, for which Diancecht kills him, out of envy.[31]

As for the rest of the Fir Bolg, their fate is variously told. According to the text I am now following, they flee to the Fomorians in the outermost islands, which 'The Second Battle of Mag Tured' identifies as Arran, Islay, Mann, and Rathlin.[32] According to another text, however, the Tuatha Dé grant peace and Connacht to the last three hundred of the Fir Bolg, led by Sreng.[33] In fact, as befits a mythological people who are really an historical people — the Belgae or a branch thereof — the Fir Bolg become a race that will not go away, although they are often wished away. If we are to believe 'The Battle of Tailltin', for instance, the poets of Ireland 'put a bad name on the Firbolgs and the men of Domnann and the Gaileoin, for lies and big talk and injustice'. In this the Fir Bolg differ from the Gael, whom the poets consider brave and modest, and from the Tuatha Dé, who are musicians and wizards. In what looks like wishful thinking, the story then adds that 'the Druids drove them out of the country afterwards'.[34] A story from the Ulster Cycle claims that the Fir Domnann were destroyed in the Battle of Airtech, c. 33 A. D.[35] More than three centuries later, however, we hear of the High King Crimthann mac Fidaigh including in his royal tour, or Progress of Tara, the *Galianic* province of Leinster.[36] Mes Delmann of the Fir Domnann, alleged to have conquered the Fomorians, is an historical figure of the sixth century or later.[37] Indeed, even 'So late as the seventeenth century, the annalist Duald Mac Firbis discovered that many of the inhabitants of [Connacht] claimed to be the desendants of these same Fir Bolg'.[38]

In the Fenian tale of 'The Red Woman', on the other hand, the King of the Firbolgs appears as clearly a figure of folklore, like the kings of Sorcha and other mythical lands.[39] But that only proves the lateness of this story, for Eoin MacNeill, in an argument that relies on the evidence of Duald Mac Firbis, has shown that the Fenian Cycle itself 'originated among the Galeoin who dwelt in the neighbourhood of Almu', Co. Kildare.[40] Evidence of the Fir Bolg's survival, then, abounds, even to a comparatively recent epoch. If the Fir Bolg still existed in the seventeenth century, there seems no reason why they should not still exist in the twentieth century, albeit unrecognised. The importance of this is that, if the Fir Bolg were historical in the first place, and have never become extinct, they can have had little or nothing to do with the formation of the fairy faith. Lady Gregory's informant who spoke of fairies with bags on their bellies should not have called them fairies at all.

V. The Second Battle of Moytura[41]

After the First Battle of Moytura, Nuada forfeits the kingship of the Tuatha Dé Danann becase of the loss of his arm (which at this time has not been regrafted), the law being that the King of Tara must be free from blemish. The women of the Tuatha Dé insist on settling the kingship on a certain Bres, in order to cement an alliance with the Fomorians. Bres is the son of Elotha, the King of the Fomorians, and of Eri, a woman of the Tuatha Dé. The alliance proved unreliable, however, for the Fomorians lay tribute on Ireland and enslave her champions. One of these, Ogma, is forced to carry firewood, and another, the Dagda, to build raths, or fortresses, and to dig trenches around the rath belonging to Bres. Bres cooperates with the Fomorians in their oppression of Ireland and proves a most ungenerous king. The Tuatha Dé Danann eventually depose Bres, but grant him seven years' respite on condition that his generosity shall be enforced: he is to levy neither rent nor taxes, but is, on the contrary, to distribute all his wealth.

Parenthetically, let it be remarked that Bres cannot always have suffered such a poor reputation as he does in this story. Even here, it is curious that such a name for meanness and oppression should be put upon one described as so beautiful that 'every beautiful thing that is seen in Ireland, whether plain or fortress or ale or torch or woman or man or steed, will be judged in comparison with that boy, so that men say of it then 'it is a *bres*'. The *Cóir Anmann*, moreover, or *Fitness of Names*, has this entry: 'Bres *rí* 'king', that is, he was a king for royalty: i.e. royal was his action and his honour and his reign, and he routed the Fomorians in many battles, expelling them from Ireland.'[42]

To continue, Bres goes with his mother to the land of the Fomorians to raise help. His father, Elotha, is reluctant to provide it because of Bres's injustice, but sends him to Balor and Indech, two other Fomorian chiefs, who gather their troops and prepare to invade Ireland.

Nuada, whose arm has been regrafted, is now king again in Ireland. At this point Lugh enters the picture.[43] Lugh is the son begotten on Balor's daughter Ethlinn (elsewhere Ethne) by Cian of the Tuatha Dé Danann in revenge for Balor's theft of the magic cow Glas Gaibhnenn. It was foretold by a druid that Balor would die by his own grandson, and so he had Lugh thrown into the sea at birth, but he was rescued and fostered among the Tuatha Dé Danann.

The story now divides. I take it up first as it is told in 'The Second Battle of Mag Tured'. While Nuada is holding feast at Tara, Lugh, 'with a king's trappings', seeks admittance. To secure it, he lays claim to the mastery of numerous professions, but the Tuatha Dé already have a master of each. At last Lugh says that he alone is the master of all professions. Nuada requires him to prove his skill at chess. Lugh wins all the stakes and then makes his *cro*, or leap, over the ramparts and into the dun, or fort (a kenning, since, for the rightful king's taking his place).[44] Nuada admits him and he sits in the sage's seat. He then proves his strength and his skill at music. Nuada temporarily yields his throne to Lugh. A conference of war against the Fomorians ensues. The representatives of each profession boast to Nuada of what they will do, but the Dagda promises to duplicate all of it himself, hence his name, which means 'good hand', or perhaps 'good god'. (It should be noted that 'good' implies no moral quality — in fact, the Dagda's name appears to be a joke.) For seven years, the Tuatha Dé Danann prepare for battle.

A week before the Samhain of battle, the Dagda has a tryst with the Morrigu (one of the chief female personages of the Tuatha Dé Danann), whom he finds straddling the River Unius at Glenn Etin and washing herself in it with nine loosened tresses. She informs him that the Fomorians will land at Mag Scetne, and he assembles the Tuatha Dé Danann ready for combat.

This, now, is the story of the coming of Lugh as it is told in 'The Fate of the Children of Tuirenn'.[45] The Tuatha Dé Danann are gathered together to pay their tribute at Balor's Hill (later Usnech) when Lugh approaches with 'his army ... from the fairy-mounds, from the Land of Promise'. He and Nuada greet each other. The Fomorians' eighty-one tax-collectors arrive and Lugh kills all but nine of them, whom he sends back to their home in Lochlann (Norway or some other vaguely conceived Scandinavian country). There, Balor's wife Cathleann recognises Lugh by his description as the grandson of herself and Balor who will put the Fomorians out of Ireland.

Bres offers to kill Lugh for Balor, and subsequently lands with his men at Es Dara (Ballysodare, Co. Sligo). He plunders Connacht, whose king is Bodb Derg, son of the Dagda. Lugh goes to give battle, but Nuada will not help. Lugh meets his father Cian and his uncles Cú and Cethen and sends them to assemble the men of the fairy-mounds. The latter, after three days, catch up with Lugh, and so does Bodb Derg. They all give battle to Bres. The Tuatha Dé Danann are victorious, but Lugh spares Bres's life on condition that he will bring the Fomorians to the Battle of Moytura and, until then, keep peace.

I now return to 'The Second Battle of Mag Tured'. At Samhain Lugh sends the Dagda to spy on the Fomorians. In the Fomorian camp, Indech forces the Dagda to eat a huge porridge, which he does with pleasure before staggering off. Back in the camp of the Tuatha Dé, the representatives of the various professions repeat their boasts. Among them, the witches Be-culle and Diarann promise to enchant the trees and stones and sods to the appearance of warriors to frighten the Fomorians. The Dagda, as before, promises that he will both cast spells and make a great fight. On the other hand, the Tuatha Dé will not allow Lugh to endanger himself in the battle.

The battle begins. Diancecht with his children casts spells over the well of Slane and throws in the mortally wounded to be healed. The Fomorians send Ruadan, son of Bres and of the Dagda's daughter Brig (or Brigid), to spy and then to kill an artisan. He begs a spear and wounds the smith Goibniu, who kills him in return. Goibniu heals himself in the well. The Fomorians fill up the well with stones. Lugh escapes from his guardians and joins the battle. Balor kills Nuada. Now, Balor's chief feature is his evil eye, which was poisoned by the fumes of a concoction made by one of his father's druids. It takes four men to lift the eyelid with a polished handle passing through it. Balor orders it lifted now against Lugh, but Lugh drives the eye out through the back of Balor's head with a sling-shot. The Morrigu urges on the Tuatha Dé Danann. Ogma and Indech kill each other. Lugh captures Bres, who in return for his life offers to keep the cattle of Ireland in milk, but as he cannot control their age or offspring this is rejected. He offers four harvests a year, but the Tuatha Dé Danann prefer the seasonal pattern. Lugh offers to spare him if he will tell how to plough, sow, and reap. He says all three should be done on a Tuesday, and Lugh releases him. It is obvious that some sort of harvest or fertility myth is involved in this story. Máire Mac Neill interprets it thus: 'the secret of agricultural prosperity is wrested from a powerful and reluctant god by Lugh. Nuadu, Balor and Bres are three aspects of Lugh's opponent. Lugh displaces Nuadu, kills Balor and forces Bres to yield his knowledge.'[46] In this perspective the apparent triviality of Bres's information is unimportant. What matters is that he parts with it at all.

The Second Battle of Moytura ends with the Morrigu—here also called Badb—proclaiming the victory of the Tuatha Dé Danann and, oddly, prophesying evil.

According to Lady Gregory, four Fomorians survive the battle and go around spoiling food until driven out of Ireland one Samhain by the Morrigu and the Dagda's son Angus Óg.[47] Certainly the Second Battle of Moytura does not mark the end of the Fomorians in Irish mythology. At the time of the Ulster Cycle, the High King Conaire Mór has three Fomorian hostages.[48] At roughly the same time, King Conchobar of Ulster rides out with a war party wholly or partially composed of Fomorians.[49] In the Fenian Cycle, Laighne Mór, the only son of the king of the Fomorians, seeks battle with the Fianna in order to subjugate Ireland, but eventually makes peace when Finn reveals himself as a poet and a druid.[50] Also in the Fenian Cycle, Diarmuid Ó Duibhne kills a Fomorian named Ciach during his elopment with Grania.[51] 'The Coming of Laighne Mór' is simply a folk-tale, a *sceal:*[52] it does not ask to be taken seriously; but 'The Hidden House of Lugh' does, I think, mean to be taken seriously when it states that Conn of the Hundred Battles (High King of Tara c. A. D 200) used to mount the rampart of his fort each day 'lest the people of the fairy-mounds or the Fomorians should take Ireland unawares'.[53] It is possible, therefore, that the Fomorians were considered a real threat even in historical times. It is possible indeed, that the common people at first mistook the Vikings for Fomorians. But after the Second Battle of Moytura their power may fairly be described as broken.

VI. The Invasion of the Sons of Mil

We now come to the final mythical invasion of Ireland, the invasion of the Sons of Mil, or Milesians, who are simply the Gael.[54] After long wandering, these people have come to Spain, from a tower in which country Ith son of Bregan espies Ireland. He sails thither with his son Lugaid and others, arrives at Bentracht of Mag Itha, and learns that the land is Inis Elga and its kings Mac Cuill, Mac Cecht, and Mac Gréine (sons of the Hazel, the Plough, and the Sun, respectively). He offers to settle a quarrel between Mac Cuill and his brothers, merely exhorting to righteousness and praising Ireland, but his praise of Ireland is considered over-great and, lest he should have designs on the island, the nobles of the Tuatha Dé Danann decide to kill him. They wound him at Mag Itha and he dies at sea.

The Sons of Mil under Eber Donn[55] assemble their people at Brigantia and sail for Ireland to avenge Ith. On sighting Ireland Ir son of Mil outrows the rest, angering Eber Donn, but snaps his oar, so that he breaks his back against the thwart. His brothers, Eremon, Eber Finn, and Amergin, say that it would not be right for Eber Donn to enjoy the land that he has envied Ir. The Tuatha Dé Danann render Ireland invisible, so that the Sons of Mil circle it three times, finally landing at Inber Scéne on Beltaine. As the Milesians proceed inland, they meet three women (or goddesses) in succession, Banba, Fodla, and Ériu. Amergin, the poet, promises to each that he will name the land after her, as he does, but Ériu curses Eber Donn for a churlish word. At Tara the Milesians demand battle, kingship, or judgment from Mac Cuill, Mac Cecht, and Mac Gréine, who offer them nine days to depart, submit, or prepare for battle. The Sons of Mil, however, are unwilling to wait. The kings then offer them the judgment of their own poet, Amergin. Even though Donn is for battle at once, Amergin advises the Sons of Mil to withdraw for a distance of nine waves from Ireland and then to return for battle. Nine waves is considered a magical distance, proof against the infection of plague, for instance.[56] The Tuatha Dé Danann raise a druid wind against the Milesians' ships. Amergin, by singing a poem known as his Invocation, suppresses the wind, but it is revived against Donn, so that he is separated from the rest, and drowned, and buried at Tech Duinn in the Dumacha (now the Skellig Rocks; *Tech Duinn* means 'The House of Donn'). After coming ashore again, the Sons of Mil win victories at Sliabh Mis and Tailltiu, where Eremon slays Mac Cecht, Eber Finn slays Mac Cuill, Amergin slays Mac Gréine, Suirge slays Ériu, Caicer slays Banba, and Etan slays Fodla. The Milesians take the lordship of Ireland.

VIII. The Feast of Age

It is only now, however, in defeat, that the Tuatha Dé Danann put on their full magical identity, for Amergin gives the part of Ireland that is underground to them, and thus they 'went into the hills and fairy places, so that they spoke with the fairy folk underground'. They leave one of their number in each of the five provinces of Ireland, including Grici in Cruachan Aigle, now Croagh Patrick, and Gulban the Grey (probably the same as Goibniu) in the Ben of Gulban, now Ben Bulben, Co. Sligo, 'to excite war and conflict and valour and strife between the sons of Mil'.[57] Much later, St. Patrick also left immortal 'keepers' (*comētaidi*) in the very same places.[58] The Dagda, like the four Fomorians left after the Second Battle of Moytura, continues to destroy the corn and milk of the Milesians for a while until they make his friendship, after which he preserves their produce. He apportions the fairy mounds, but absent-mindedly leaves out his own son, Angus. The latter begs a day and a night in the Dagda's own *sídh*,[59] Síd in Broga, the Brugh of the Boyne at Newgrange, Co. Meath, but then explains that night and day are the whole world, so the Brugh of the

Boyne is his in perpetuity. 'Wonderful, moreover, (is) that land. Three trees with fruit are there always, and a pig eternally alive, and a roasted swine, and a vessel with marvellous liquor, and never do they all decrease.'[60] According to others, it was Manannan mac Lir who apportioned the *sídhe*, and 'put hidden walls about them,' and also made the Feast of Age, at which the Tuatha Dé Danann were served with the ever-renewed pigs of Manannan and with the ale of Goibniu, thereby aquiring eternal life and health.[61]

What I interpret this to mean is that Amergin, as a magician-poet, and the magicians of the Tuatha Dé split the world into two 'dimensions,' one for mortals and one for the Ever-living. These two dimensions, however, are by no means as far apart as heaven and earth. They are side by side and often, indeed, overlap. The Tuatha Dé, it seems, can pass between them at will. Mortals may suddenly find themselves caught up into fairyland by mere chance, or the more favoured among them may find the way made easy. The most favoured, the heroes, like Finn mac Cumhail, may pass almost as freely as the Tuatha Dé themselves. At Samhain, moreover, the spell is undone completely. At this time, as Proinsias Mac Cana says,

the normal order of the universe is suspended, the barriers between tha natural and the supernatural are temporarily removed, the *sídh* lies open and all divine beings, and the spirits of the dead move freely among men and interfere, sometimes violently, in their affairs. Conversely, this is the time when the *sídh* is most accessible and most vulnerable to those mortals daring enough to venture within its precinct.[62]

The mythological pre-history of Ireland bears an extraordinary resemblance, in one sense, to her early known history: both are characterised by succesive waves of invaders. For all that, mythology and history naturally remain very different things. Mythological events always involve at least some element of the supernatural, while historical events do not. Whatever else they may have been, the Vikings and Anglo-Normans were human and mortal. The Fomorians and Tuatha Dé Danann seem always more or less than human, and even the Fir Bolg and Nemedians, in mythological times, are akin to the Tuatha Dé Danann. The Invasion of the Sons of Mil forms a hazy borderline. It is an event partly historical and partly mythological. It certainly happened, but it certainly did not happen as it is told in the *Lebor Gabála*. At this time the natural and the supernatural begin to sort themselves out. The supernatural but already defeated Fomorians fade rapidly from the scene. The Fir Bolg, from now on, appear as a people no more supernatural than the Gael. But the Tuatha Dé Danann become wholly supernatural, the people of faery. They enter the magic land which continues to glimmer beneath the surface of Ireland.

2. THE EVER-LIVING

I. The Appearance of the Tuatha Dé Danann

A good description of one of the lords of the Tuatha Dé, Mider of Brí Leith, may be found in 'The Wooing of Etain':

> The tunic that the warrior wore was purple in colour, his hair was of golden yellow, and of such length that it reached to the edge of his shoulders. The eyes of the young warrior were lustrous and grey; in the one hand he held a five-pointed spear, in the other a shield with a white central boss, and with gems of gold upon it.[1]

This description may be taken as typical, and it requires little comment. The essential fact is that the Tuatha Dé look very much like mortals. Only the eyes appear to differ, and even there the 'lustrous and grey' of the original may as well mean 'greenish-grey' as 'silver'.

There is nothing to suggest that Mider is of anything less than average stature. This is almost always true of the Tuatha Dé Danann, and such few exceptions as there are all tend to prove the rule. The most obvious example is 'The king of the Lepracanes' journey to Emana, and how the death of Fergus mac Léide king of Ulidia was brought about', in which the fairies are very small indeed.[2] For instance, the 'prize feat' of 'the strong man of the region of the Lupra and Lupracan' is 'the hewing down of a thistle at a single stroke'; the Lepracanes' poet, Esirt, can stand on the hand of Aedh, the poet of Ulster, who himself can stand on a normal man's hand, and so on. This evidence is not of great value to begin with, as the story is evidently intended to be comic and may well have been intended for children. Its credibility is further undercut by the use of such names as Beg son of Beg, or 'Little son of Little'. Smallness is the whole point of the story, in fact, not incidental to it. But even if the evidence is acepted at face value, it is inherently exceptional. The Lupra and Lupracan and the Lepracanes of the title are, of course, the leprechauns of folklore. They are extremely rare in Early Irish literature and should probably not be thought of as belonging to the Tuatha Dé Danann at all. Leprechauns are unusual in having always been imagined as small.

Slightly taller are Finn mac Cumhail's fairy harper and his wife, Cnú Dheireoil ('sweet little nut') and Blathnait. Cnú Dheireoil is as tall as four of Finn's fists. The whole point about this couple, though is that they are unique (at least as far as the Fianna know), in stature as well as in musicianship. Cnú Dheireoil is the son of Lugh.[3] This cuts both ways: Lugh, of course, is of the Tuatha Dé Danann, but on the other hand there is some connection between Lugh and the leprechauns. Lady Gregory actually describes Cnú Dheireoil as four *feet* tall, but this may mean that either that Finn's fists are a foot wide, or , more probably, that Lady Gregory has mistranslated the same passage that O'Grady translates correctly.[4]

Finally, in 'The Pursuit of Diarmuid and Grainne', Finn's fairy nurse flies on a water-lily leaf to strike Diarmuid with darts, but this does not, I think, imply that she is always of that size: this is rather an instance of shape-shifting.[5]

As for dress, Mider's purple tunic is an example of the costume of a male member of the Tuatha Dé Danann. The same story, 'The Wooing of Etain,' provides a more elaborate description of the costume of Etain, a woman of the Tuatha Dé:

A cloak pure-purple, hanging in folds about her, and as for it, smooth and glossy. It was made of greenish silk beneath red embroidery of gold, and marvellous bow-pins of silver and gold upon her breasts in the tunic, so that the redness of the gold against the sun in the green silk was clearly visible to the men. Two tresses of golden hair upon her head, and a plaiting of four strands in each tress, and a ball of gold upon the end of each plait.[6]

The multiplicity of colours is particularly to be noticed. As a matter of fact, Etain is fressed rather modestly, for according to Keating, Tighernmas (dated A. M. 2186 = 1219 B. C.) 'first established it as a custom in Ireland that there should be one colour in the dress of a slave, two in that of a peasant, and so on to the nine colours in the dress of a king or queen',[7] and we should expect a noble lady of the Tuatha Dé to dress at least as well as her mortal counterparts. The particular colours worn by Etain are of no significance: she might have worn any she chose.

The question arises, then, how does one recognise the Tuatha Dé? And the answer is that one does not, necessarily. Unless they choose to reveal themselves in some way, they may be mistaken for mortals, though generally (not always) of great beauty.

II. The Domain of the Tuatha Dé Danann

The *sídhe* distributed at the Feast of Age remain the most typical dwellings of the Tuatha Dé Danann. They may be very literally imagined. After Mider of Brí Leith elopes with Etain to the *sídh* of

Femen, Eochaid, Etain's mortal husband, forces him to return her by the simple expedient of digging up the *sídh*.[8] They are not always imagined as part of the normal world in such a common sense, however, and the Tuatha Dé have other dwellings besides that are more remote from men.

For instance, they are frequently depicted as living in a land or archipelago out to sea. Although the various names for this fairyland are often used interchangeably, they are also used more specifically, for this country has a geography of its own. A few examples will be useful.

In 'The Sick-Bed of Cu Chulainn'[9] (on which Yeats's play *The Only Jealousy of Emer* is very loosely based), the mortal hero Cu Chulainn attempts to capture a pair of beautiful birds linked together with a golden chain. He misses them twice with his sling, but wounds one in the wing with his spear. They fly away beneath the waters of a lake. Cu Chulainn sleeps and dreams of two women who horsewhip him. He awakes from this dream very sick. Arthur A. Wachsler interprets this episode as an 'elaborate ruse' to lure Cu Chulainn to fairyland. The birds and the women are the same, of course. They must first trick Cu Chulainn into hurting them, so that they may then retaliate. When they have made him an invalid, they can then offer to cure him in their own country.[10] For this purpose, they send as their messenger Angus son of Aedh Abrat, who may be, as Yeats believed, Angus Óg, 'the master of love'.[11] The fairy women are Liban and Fann, the sisters of this Angus. Their motive is that Fann is in love with Cu Chulainn and has been abandoned by her husband, Manannan. Liban's husband, Labraid the Swift, will grant Frann to Cu Chulainn in return for one day's martial service against his enemies, 'The people of Manannan son of Lir'. Cu Chulainn and Labraid both keep their bargain, but eventually 'Manannan shook his cloak between Cu Chulainn and Fann, so that they might never meet again throughout eternity'.

In this story, then, we see a political division of fairyland between Labraid and Manannan. Of the two, Manannan seems the more dominant character. His role is complex; indeed, he seems to manipulate the whole action. Manannan's dominance of the marine fairyland is a standard motif. To cite, for the present, but one other example, in a story in 'The Colloquy with the Ancients', Ciabhan, son of Eochaid Red-Weapon, king of Ulster, is rescued from a storm at sea by an *óglaech* (warrior) riding horseback on the waves, who, again in return for service, brings him to Manannan's *cathair* (citadel) in Tír Tarrngaire (the Land of Promise).[12]

This type of story is called an *eachtra*, or Adventure. The *eachtra* that provides the most striking instance of the divisions within fairyland is *Laoi Oisín ar Thír na n-Óg*, or *The Lay of Oisín in the Land of Youth*, by the poet and antiquarian Micheál Coimín.[13] Although this poem dates only from about 1750, its genre, conventions and cast of characters place it in the tradition of Early Irish literature, rather than of eighteenth century folklore. Niamh Chinn-óir, the daughter of the king of Tír na nÓg, approaches the Fianna one day while they are hunting by Loch Léin. She says she has come for love of Oisín, and takes him with her to Tír na nÓg, where there is abundance, no decay, no failure, and no death. On their way, they see (as they will do again in Yeats's *Wanderings of Oisin*) cities and palaces and other marvels amid the waves of the sea. They come to a dun where a Fomorian giant holds captive the daughter of the king of Tír na mBeo (the Land of the Living), though under *geasa*[14] not to make her her wife until she has found a champion to fight him. Oisín beheads him. Next day the maiden leaves them for Tír na mBeo. A storm arises. When it clears, Oisín and Niamh sight Tír na nÓg. They are royally welcomed and promised eternal youth. After feasting for ten days, they are married. They have two sons and a daughter, for whom Niamh holds in regency 'Tír na n-Óg, na mBeo, 's na mBuadh' (the Land of the Young, of the Living, and of Virtues). The rest of this story need not detain us. Here, then, is a three-fold division within fairyland and a sort of border zone in which even Fomorians can be found. Since Niamh holds the joint regency, Tír na nÓg seems superior to Tír na mBeo and Tír na mBuadh.

Another *eachtra* is 'The Adventures of Connla the Fair.'[15] In this, a woman from the Lands of the Living summons Connla, the son of Conn of the Hundred Battles, to Mag Mell, the Plain of Delight, 'where there is neither death nor want nor sin . . . . A great fairy-mound (sid) it is, in which we live, wherefore we are called 'folk of the fairy-mound' (aes side)'. The king of Mag Mell, she says, is Boadach the Eternal. She gives Connla an apple, which is all he eats for a month, and it never diminishes. Then she comes again and tells Connla of another land, besides Boadach's where there are only women. Connla leaps into her crystal boat and they leave for ever.

The first similarity between this and the previous *eachtraí* is that fairyland is again divided. The Lands of the Living and the Plain of Delight appear to be two names for the same place, but the Land of Women is something else. The second similarity, though it is doubtful, is the role of Manannan. Cross and Slover's version of this tale states that Boadach is king of the Lands of the Living, but adds, in a verse that may originally have been separate, 'The Living, the immortal call to you;/They summon you to the people of Tethra . . .' Tethra actually features in the *Lebor Gabála* as a Fomorian, but some consider him the Fomorian equivalent of Manannan, and it may be that his name here is used as synonymous with Manannan's. Lady Gregory avoids all mention of Boadach but states, on her own authority, 'It is likely it was Manannan sent his messenger for Connla of the Red Hair . . . for it is to his country Connla was brought'.[16]

On the other hand, there are certain features about this *eachtra* that connect it with another type of story, the *imram*, or Voyage. The female messenger and the apple, for instance are reminiscent of an early *imram* called 'The Voyage of Bran'.[17] Of more significance are, first, the Land of Women, and, secondly, certain Christian elements, probably interpolations, in 'The Adventures of Connla the Fair'. The most obvious is that the fairy woman prophesies the coming of Patrick to 'annihilate the false law of the druids'.

The *imrama* extend the division of fairyland well beyond three parts. Fairyland becomes a whole string of islands, each exhibiting a single facet of humanity. The Land of Women is typical of these islands, but there are also Lands of Boys; lands of laughing and lands of weeping; and so forth. The problem lies in deciding to what extent these stories incorporate genuine traditions of fairyland. This problem is affected by historical, psychological, and religious considerations.

The historical considerations are narrow in scope, relating specifically to the Land of Women. Pomponius Mela mentions a community of wizard-priestesses called Gallizenae, capable, among other things, of shape-shifting, who inhabited an island called Sena, which is 'probably the modern Seine'. Posidonius likewise mentions an unnamed island of Namnite priestesses at the mouth of the Loire. Mela's priestesses lived 'in the holiness of perpetual virginity', but Posidonius' women 'sallied forth to seek temporary mates on the mainland'. For Alfred Nutt, this is the origin of the Land of Women.[18] The only problem with this theory is that it will not account for the other islands encountered in the *imrama*. The whole tradition can hardly stem from such a singular fact ('singular' in both senses of the word).

An alternative theory is that the succession of islands in the *imrama* represent a crude process of psycho-analysis. The hero of the *imram* 'enters a world where our world as we know it seems to resolve itself into its components', as the Rees brothers remark. This, to me, suggests a disintegrative process, in the Jungian sense. The Rees brothers, however, see it in rather different terms: 'In the 'Voyages', we submit, have been preserved the tattered remnants of an oral Celtic 'book' of the dead . . . . The Plain of Delight and the Land of the Women are but stages on the way.'[19]

This opinion of the Rees brothers sees the *imrama* as essentially pagan religious documents. Unfortunately, most of the *imrama* are explicitly Christian, and 'Some authorities', indeed, 'are inclined to place the ecclesiastical form' of the genre 'earlier than the secular'.[20] The Rees brothers, presumably, do not accept this view. Alfred Nutt's position is not easy to determine with any certainty. He dates the 'Earliest Irish eschatological (?) texts. Purely Christian' between A.D. 600 and 700 and the 'Irish non-Christian Elysium texts' between A.D. 700 and 800 The emphasis, I think, must be on 'texts,' as opposed to stories, for Nutt also says: 'the Voyage of Saint Brandan is but the latest and a definitely Christian example of a *genre* of story-telling which has already flourished for centuries in Ireland.'[21]

Now, if the *imrama* are pagan religious documents, it is obvious that their fairy traditions may be regarded as genuine. If they are, as it were, psychological documents, their fairy traditions will not necessarily therefore be invalidated, though a psychological explanation of the origin of the fairy faith itself will have to be sought. If they are Christian documents written for purely Christian purposes, their fairy traditions will be invalidated. It will by now be apparent that this is a complex and difficult problem, but I am inclined to agree with Eleanor Hull that the *imrama* are primarily mythico-religious documents with a certain psychological overlay, and that the progression from pagan *eachtra* to Christian *imram* is gradual and continuous. As Hull says: 'The Pagan Paradise or Land of Promise seems at first to retain its position in the stories independently of the Christian heaven, but inevitably it becomes in the later tales confused with it, and passes into it.' Early *imrama* like 'The Voyage of Bran' contain wonders which seem devoid of Christian significance. Later, the various islands visited are created for purely homiletic purposes. In literary terms, this is an unhealthy development. It generates at first a surplus of islands, and then, having spent its creative force, dispenses with islands altogether. The Voyage becomes a Vision and the Vision becomes a sermon.[22]

This means, on the other hand, that early *imrama* do embody genuine traditions about fairyland, and that this content fades away only gradually. The *imrama* should therefore be treated with caution but not ignored entirely. They do provide plausible evidence that fairyland was sometimes imagined as a veritable archipelago of countries, each possessing some peculiar characteristic of its own, and may provide other plausible data as well.

As well as being found *in* the sea, like the islands of the *imrama*, fairyland may be found *under* the sea, or even under fresh water. This is Tír Fó Thuinn, or the Land Under Wave. We have seen, in 'The Sick-Bed of Cu Chulainn', how the two birds who are in reality the fairy woman Liban and Fann fly away beneath a lake. In the Fenian tale of 'The Daughter of King Under-Wave', Diarmuid Ó Duibhne, seeking for his vanished fairy wife, catches a ship which takes him to land and then vanishes. A boat and boatman come and take him to a plain beneath

The Ever-Living

the sea, where he finds his wife.[23] Many other examples of this motif could be adduced.

Fairyland, then, is in the *sídh* or beyond the sea or beneath the water. In fact, it is often imagined as being in two or more of these places at once. In 'Ailne's Revenge', Finn mac Cumhail and Dáire of the Songs are carried to a *sídh* in the sea.[24] The wife of a king called Badurn acquired a magic vessel from two fairy women joined by a bronze chain (like Liban and Fann) whom she followed through a well into a *sídh*.[25] A particularly good example of this mixing of milieux occurs in 'Laeghaire mac Crimthann's visit to the fairy realm of Magh meall or 'the Plains of Pleasure', in which Laeghaire actually visits a *sídh*, which is in Magh Meall, which is beneath a lake.[26]

Stories like these fully justify T.F. O'Rahilly's statement that 'there was in Celtic belief but one Otherworld', although it was supposed to be located in innumerable different *sídhe*.[27] No one can imagine the Tuatha Dé Dannann living a life of spacious luxury *literally* within the *sídhe*, which anyone can see to be small, dark, dirty and grim. The *sídhe*, the hills, the lakes, the wells, and the sea are but doorways to Tír na nÓg, which is actually *elsewhere* — in another 'dimension'. Failure to note this fact had led certain scholars, particularly Myles Dillon, to construct elaborate and unnecessary hierarchies of Ancient Irish 'gods', classified by means of the places where they are supposed to live.[28]

The ability of Tír na nOg to be in two places at the same time gives rise to a quality of paradox which is clearly felt to be of the very nature of fairyland. For instance, Bran mac Febail is invited to 'the southern Plain of White Silver', where 'Coracle contends against chariot,'' as though it were firm and fluid at once.[29] This paradoxical quality is most apparent in relation to time, which seldom runs alike in this world and in the Otherworld. Finn may feast and sleep in fairyland and return after what the Fianna say has been only a short while.[30] Becfola, the wife of the High King Dermot mac Aedh Sláine, having missed an illicit tryst, wanders lost in Leinster with her handmaid, who gets eaten by wolves. She meets a young man named Flann who takes her to a fairy palace on an island. With his three brothers, he defeats his four nephews for possession of the island. He then restores Becfola's handmaid to life and returns them both to Dermot. During all this, not one moment has elapsed outside fairyland.[31] Likewise, no time elapses above ground while Nera, a retainer of Queen Medhbh's, spends three days in the Cave of Cruachan.[32]

In the *imrama*, the distortion of time tends to work in reverse. Cian's son Teigue spends a year in a certain island although he thinks it only a day.[33] Mernoke, a monk, spends six months in the Earthly Paradise, thinking it only half an hour.[34] Somtimes, it is true, even in the *imrama*, time does pass more slowly in fairyland than on earth. To Maeldune, on one island three months seem to be three years.[35] But it does seem as though an unnaturally rapid passage of time is the preferred motif in stories with a Christian colouring, for we sometimes find it in saints' lives, even without a visit to the Land of Promise. St. Mochae, for instance, stands enchanted by birdsong for 150 years, which to him are only an hour.[36] The Christian principle, presumably, is that time spent sweetly passes swiftly.

The seasons of Tír na nÓg may also be the reverse of the seasons of this world. Though it is winter in Ireland at the time, Cian's son Teigue comes across a beautiful land in summer.[37] Nera takes from the Cave of Cruachan garlic, primrose, and golden fern, all of them summer fruits, as proof that he has been in fairyland, for on earth it is Samhain.[38] This tradition has proved very persistent, and is often to be met with in modern folklore. One of Lady Gregory's informants told her of some men who went into a forth in Clare and heard 'the crying of young lambs, and it was November, for when we have winter, there is summer there'. Another informant repeated the information about the seasons and added that potatoes blighted on earth were sound in fairyland.[39] In an anecdote collected by Dermot MacManus, a little girl experiences difficulty in crossing a potato field at night, even though it is November. The field has, in fact, never been used for growing potatoes.[40]

Perhaps all these traditions regarding time in Tír na nÓg will account for the charm against the fairies of naming the day of the week: the day becomes an anchor in real time, as it were.

There is still one more respect in which fairyland may be said to be paradoxical. Although generally a land of delight, when invaded by force it becomes a land of horrors.[41] However, since every country presents an appealing face to its friends and a hostile face to its foes, this is perhaps not so surprising.

III. The Powers of the Tuatha Dé Danann

Though the Tuatha Dé Danann possess more power than mortals do, they fall some way short of omnipotence. Their main distinctions are immortality and the ability to shift their shape, but even their immortality is somewhat questionable. Several important members of the Tuatha Dé are killed in the course of the Mythological Cycle. Lugh, too, is supposed to have been killed at Uisnech by Mac Cuill, Mac Cécht, and Mac Gréine, who were killed themselves at Tailtiu.[42] Such killings go on even outside the Mythological Cycle. Caoilte, of the

Fianna, kills no less a person than Lir, the father of Manannan.[43] Lesser members of the Tuatha Dé Danann die with regularity in the Fenian Cycle. While still a boy, Finn kills Aillen son of Midhna, a hostile, fire-breathing fairy somewhat like Grendel,[44] and another fairy called Aed son of Fidga.[45] Elsewhere in the cycle, the Clann Morna kill nine women of the Tuatha Dé who are on their way to meet the Fianna.[46] Other fairies meet non-violent deaths. Etain of the Fair Hair, for instance, a grand-daughter of Angus Óg, dies of grief when her mortal husband Osgar is wounded at Beinn Edair.[47] Numerous other deaths from grief and shame can be found in 'The Colloquy with the Ancients'.

It may be argued of the Tuatha Dé slain before the Feast of Age that they had not yet put on immortality anyway. That, however is *too* logical. It seems highly probable that the tradition of the Tuatha Dé's immortality if older than the stories of the deaths of their principal personages. These stories were almost certainly the inventions of the monks who wrote the *Lebor Gabála*. Since they felt compelled to synchronise their traditions with European history and to trace genealogies to Adam, they were obliged to transform the Tuatha Dé from immortals to mortal kings. That they themselves were neither happy nor adept at this procedure is exposed by the fact that characters supposedly dead may be active again within a few pages. Lugh and Manannan continue to play a prominent role in mythology long after their reported deaths. The killing of Lir by Caoilte, which is exceptional, is perhaps inspired by the precedent of the *Lebor Gabála*. Lower-ranking members of the Tuatha Dé — the *Andé*, or 'non-gods' — being considered less divine, are perhaps considered also less immortal. Possibly they were even excluded from the Feast of Age. In any case, story-telling would be much the poorer if no fairy were ever to be killed.

As for shape-shifting, a few stories display this power in truly Protean versatility, especially 'The Quarrel of the Two Pig-Keepers, and How the Bulls Were Begotten', a *remscéal*, or 'before-tale', of the *Táin*. In this, the two eponymous pig-keepers, who belong to the Tuatha Dé, transform themselves to birds of prey and quarrel in that form for two years. They resume human form for long enough to prophesy war, but then turn to water-creatures and fight in that shape for two years. They then become two stags, two warriors, two phantoms, two dragons, and finally two maggots. Each of the maggots is swallowed by a different cow and eventually reborn as the two bulls of the Táin, the Finnbennach Aí and the Donn Cuailnge.[48] A fight in the Fenian Cycle is somewhat similar: the protagonists take the shapes successively of young boys, dogs, horses, and old men, before killing each other as birds.[49] In the story of 'The Leeching of Cian's Leg', a fairy first encountered as a hare turns to a young woman and then — three years later — to a brood mare, in order to break an unwelcome suitor's leg with a kick.[50]

It is apparent from such stories that the Tuatha Dé Danann may adopt any shape they please, but there are certain shapes that they seem to prefer. One of these is the swan. It is as two swans that Mider and Etain escape from Tara.[51] Angus Óg and his lover Caer also assume this shape.[52] Besides taking this form themselves, the Tuatha Dé may turn others, both mortal and immortal, to swans. By far the most famous instance of this is 'The Fate of the Children of Lir', one of the magnificent tales called the Three Sorrows of Story-Telling. Lir's three sons and one daughter are transformed to swans for nine hundred years by their jealous step-mother Aoife. At last, 'their skins fell off', revealing aged humans. St. Mochaomhog baptises them and they die and go to heaven.[53]

The falling off of the skin, of course, is the standard method of transformation in swan-maiden tales. The Irish sometimes use it of other beasts as well. In 'The Destruction of Da Derga's Hostel', some birds (not swans) drop their birdskins and draw spears and swords.[54] In the Fenian tale of 'The Cave of Cruachan', Caoilte cajoles three she-wolves into throwing off their skins so he can kill them.[55]

Another form favoured by the Tuatha Dé Danann is the deer. During the *Táin*, the fairy harpers of Es Ruaid come to charm the Connacht host, who take them for Ulster spies and chase them as deer to Liac Mór.[56] In a story in 'The Colloquy with the Ancients', a woman in the form of a fawn lures the Fianna to a secret brugh (or *sídh*) to give help to twenty-eight sons of Midhir Yellow-Mane against Bodhbh Dearg.[57] Such incidents are extremely common in the Fenian Cycle. An episode in the life of Patrick provides a Christian analogue. The High King Loegaire mac Néill has men lie in ambush for Patrick, but God spreads 'a cloak of darkness' over Patrick, his companion Benen, and eight clerics, so that the heathen see only deer. This is the origin of the famous hymn, 'Patrick's Breastplate', also known as 'The Deer's Cry'.[58]

Again, this form of shape-shifting may be turned against others. The fairy queen of Síth Aodha makes something of a specialty of this. Out of jealousy, she turns the hundred maidens of Donn of Dubhlinn from the Síth of Sliabh Mis to deer, though she protects them while Donn herds them. After Donn has ten times refused her a tryst, she turns him too to a stag, in which shape the Fianna kill him.[59] In a rather peculiar little story explaining the place-name 'Fafainn,' some Galeoin loose 'elves' at a girl called Aige, so that they turn her into a fawn. She is killed by the men of Meilge mac Cobthaigh, king of Ireland, and nothing remains of her but a bag of water, which Meilge throws into a river.[60]

Other shapes are less typical than the deer and the swan, but do occur. In 'Caoilte's Urn', for instance a man of the Tuatha Dé puts his own son in and out of a boar's shape, apparently with no hostile motive.[61] Some shapes are less mundane. 'The Red Woman', in the story of that name, turns herself to a great water-worm in order to attack Finn.[62]

The shape taken, furthermore, need not be animal, but can be that of another person. In 'Oisin's Children', Be-Mannair, 'woman-messenger of the Tuatha de Danaan', takes the form of Etain of the Fair Hair. This Be-Mannair, we learn, is renowned as a shape-shifter. 'And it is she that changes herself into all shapes; and she will take the shape of a fly, and of a true lover, and every one leaves their secret with her.'[63] Ailill Anglonnach, the lover of a different Etain, is likewise impersonated by Mider of Brí Leith.[64] This ability too can be applied to another. In 'The Pursuit of Diarmuid and Grainne', as Diarmuid's enemies one by one climb a tree to kill him, Angus Óg transforms them to Diarmuid's shape. Diarmuid kicks them out of the tree and their own comrades behead them, whereupon they resume their natural shape.[65]

Perhaps related to shape-shifting is the ability to appear in dreams. In 'The Sick-Bed of Cu Chulainn', Liban and Fann actually assault Cu Chulainn in a dream.[66] In 'The Wedding of Maine Morgor', an unidentified woman — the Morrigu? — first warns Conchobar in a dream that his enemy Maine Morgor is on his territory, and then warns Maine's mother, Maeve, in the same way, that Conchobar is attacking him.[67] This motif is not as common as it might be, but Yeats clearly remembered it when he had Aengus visit Aleel in a dream in the *Countess Cathleen*.[68]

Three lines before he recounts his dream in *The Countess Cathleen*, Aleel states, 'They who have sent me walk invisible'. This is also, perhaps, a form of shape-shifting: the shift to nothing. In 'The Pursuit of Diarmuid and Grainne,' as in *The Countess Cathleen*, it is Angus Óg who several times visits his foster-son Diarmuid invisibly.[69] In the *Táin*, Cúchulainn's supernatural father Lugh likewise comes to his assistance while invisible to the Connacht host.[70] If, as seems only logical, the ability to appear out of nowhere is the same power as invisibility, Mider's sudden appearances in 'The Wooing of Etain' are also relevant here. The description of him which opens this chapter follows upon his sudden appearance to Eochaid Airem. Towards the end of the story, Eochaid surrounds Tara with warriors to prevent Mider's approach, but he again appears suddenly in the midst of them.[71] Perhaps St. Patrick's hagiographer has this precedent in mind when Patrick too appears suddenly in the midst of the Feast of Tara.[72]

Yet again, invisibility can also be conferred on others. Whenever Angus Og comes invisibly to Diarmuid, he takes Grainne away with him under his cloak of invisibility. In the same story, Finn's fairy nurse makes the Fianna invisible.[73] In another sort of story (more a chronicle than a saint's life, however), St. Mothairén procures a mist to conceal and protect St. Molling, without the latter's knowledge of it.[74]

More than people can be made invisible. The greatest achievement of the Tuatha Dé in this respect is surely rendering the whole of Ireland invisible, to conceal it from the Sons of Mil. Their most lasting feat of invisibility, on the other hand, is the 'hidden walls' about the *sídhe*.

Several times we have seen a druid mist used as a synonym for invisibility. It has other uses too. For both Conn of the Hundred Battles and his grandson Cormac mac Airt it serves as a gateway to fairyland.[75]

One power that still remains to be described is the power of glamour, or power to create illusions. It seems likely that a genuine art of mass-hypnosis was known in ancient times not only to the Irish druids but also to their counterparts in other nations. There are accounts of it in Classical literature.[76] Nowadays it is only to be witnessed by those few travellers lucky enough to attend the Indian rope-trick. An illusion of this type, which may have a literary source though I cannot identify it, is described by Yeats in *The Resurrection*:

Once when I was a young lad I came upon a crowd of people at a street corner in Alexandria gathered round an Indian juggler. He had a table in front of him, and on the table a hen with a straw in its beak. I said: "What are you all staring at?" and a woman answered: "Cannot you see the hen with a great beam of wood in its beak?" Then I knew that the Indian juggler had enchanted them.[77]

In Ireland, the illusion most often created is one of armies. In 'The Second Battle of Mag Tured', the Dé Danann witches Be-culle and Diananncan enchant 'the trees and the stones and the sods of the earth' to the appearance of warriors.[78] In 'The Battle of the White Strand', three fairy women raise a phantom army from grass and watercress.[79] A detailed account of this form of magic is provided by 'The Death of Muircertach mac Erca'. Muircertach's evil fairy wife Sin, ostensibly just to prove she can do it, begins by creating two warring battalions. She also turns water to wine and fern to swine. In the morning, Muicertach's guards are all found to be in a decline, as if the illusion had somehow fed upon their vitality, as ghosts in Homer need fresh blood and ghosts in séances are said to need the medium's ectoplasm to manifest themselves. The story then seems to repeat itself, except that Sin raises four battalions of blue men and goat-headed men from stones, which Muircertach fights though they cannot be killed. Two battalions of blue men and headless men challenge Muircertach to battle. He falls exhausted but picks himself up and fights and Sin makes him king of them. He goes north to Cletech from Brugh na

Boinne and on the way Sin makes him fight two more battalions, but his friends find him still at Brugh na Boinne hacking stones and sods and stalks. He makes the sign of the cross on his face and comes to his senses. Later, while Muircertach is asleep, Sin raises a host of demons and tells him that they are the men of his enemy Tuathal Maelgarb. They fire the house. Muircertach seeks safety in a cask of wine and drowns.[80]

Occasionally such hosts are raised without any objective correlative, such as stones or sods. When Conaire Mór sees fighting and burning all around Tara it is a case of this kind,[81] and another occurs when Nera sees a fairy host burning Cruachan. These are cases of *pure* illusion, unlike Muircertach's demons, who do have the power to set a real fire. However, Nera is advised that his vision will come true unless he gives warning.[82]

In summary, then, the Tuatha Dé Danann inhabit a world of paradox. It may be in several places at once, and nothing that is true on earth is necessarily true in fairyland: time may run faster or slower, the seasons may be reversed, earth may be fluid and sea may be solid. For all that, it may be described in surprising detail. It has its several kingdoms, and its portals may be well known local landmarks on earth. Its inhabitants are equally paradoxical. We may gather a clear picture of their stature, complexion, and costume, but at any moment they may turn to swans or deer. The objects of our own world, moreover, are similarly unpredictable when under the power of the Tuatha Dé Danann.

3. DRAMATIS PERSONAE

By describing the Tuatha Dé Danann (individually now, rather than collectively), one might expect to define them, to arrive at a comparatively simple system of relationships. What happens is rather the reverse. At first glance, one seems to discern a niche for each one of the Tuatha Dé; at second glance, that niche turns out to be inadequate. However often the attempt is repeated, the result is the same. The Tuatha Dé Danann will not conform to an orderly system of classification in the same way that the gods of Greece and Rome do. This anticipates the question of whether the Tuatha Dé Danann are gods at all. A full consideration of that question must be postponed until chapter five. In this chapter it will not be possible consistently to avoid the words 'god' and 'goddess', but the reader is asked to treat them with caution. He is asked to remember that this chapter attempts no theory of the Tuatha Dé Danann in general. It seeks only to cultivate a closer acquaintance with a few of them.

I. Áine

No one could illustrate the difficulties of this chapter better than Áine. In a straightforward sense, it is not even clear who she is. Áine is one form of here name and Anu is another. Very probably she has more names then these, but that is where the first problem arises. She may be the same as Danu, or she may be the same as the Morrigu. She can hardly be both; she may be neither. If she is to be identified with the Morrigu, she may be a goddess of war. Alternatively, she may be a solar or a lunar goddess, a goddess of lunacy, a muse, or the patroness of prosperity, fertility, or health. All of these ideas have been suggested. We must consider each on its merits.

Danu herself is still more shadowy than Áine. If (as is no certainty) the meaning of *Tuatha Dé Danann* is 'The Peoples of the Goddess Danu', the unobtrusiveness of Danu is particularly strange, for the goddess whose name is so enshrined must surely be the greatest of the gods. Yet nowhere in Irish mythology, under the name of Danu, does she make a personal appearance. On the other hand, it would seem that she must have grown otiose, having once been far more conspicuous.

The evidence for this is the wide distribution of words and names which are cognate with her name. These include the River Danube, the Welsh goddess Dôn, and the Greek word χθων 'land'. 'Anu' may be another such name, having lost initial D through some accident.[1]

It seems probable that the name of Danu, rather than the nationality of the Vikings, is commemorated by the Dane Hills of Leicestershire. These hills, furthermore, are in contemporary folklore the home of a cat demon named Black Annis, or Cat Anna, who likewise seems related to Anu. As well as strengthening the connection betweem Danu and Anu, Black Annis might be expected to provide some clue to the character of this goddess, however named. Black Annis is very fearsome, and when she howls she can be heard five miles away. It may be on these grounds alone that Katharine Briggs characterises Danu as 'one of the goddesses of war'.[2] Such a description is most unusual, but there is some additional evidence to suggest that Áine, if not Danu, might be so characterised. 'According to living tradition', sacrifices used to be held on Cnoc Áine in Munster,[3] and there is so little spoken of sacrifice in connection with the Tuatha Dé in general that this in itself may impute a certain bloodthirstiness to Áine.

This evidence, however, is so tenuous that on its own it will scarcely justify the characterisation of Áine as a goddess of war. Such a theory would command more respect if Áine were a name, not of Danu, but of the Morrigu, who is undoubtedly a bloodthirsty goddess. This is Lady Gregory's speculation. She has nothing explicit to say about Áine's relation to Danu, but she does suggest that Áine may be a daughter of Manannan, and it is scarcely logical that the Mother of the Gods should be the daughter of one of them.[4] Lady Gregory's two suggestions are in conflict, however, for the Morrigu is the daughter of Ernmass.[5] It would seem that Lady Gregory has simply fastened upon the wrong Áine, for P. W. Joyce allows that 'Anann or Ana' is an alternative name for the Morrigu, while specifying that she is 'not the beneficent Ana'.[6] By 'the beneficent Ana', he means, without a doubt, the more celebrated figure here discussed.

If Áine is not the Morrigu, then, the chances are that indeed she is Danu. The weight of evidence, furthermore, will tend to justify Joyce's word 'beneficent' and certainly not support the theory that Áine is a goddess of war.

The theory that Áine is a solar goddess belongs to T. F. O'Rahilly. His reasoning is that 'the combination of meanings seen in *án, áine* (viz. brightness, heat, and speed) inevitably suggests the sun'.[7] Though linguistic evidence is often the most valuable, it must be admitted that this is rather flimsy. If Áine is to be sought in the heavens at all, folklore would suggest that she represents the moon. That is the conclusion of the Rev. J. F. Lynch, who cites as evidence the fact that on Cnoc Áine 'every St. John's Night the peasantry used to gather from all the immediate neighbourhood to view the moon'.[8]

The possibility that Áine has a lunar function is strengthened by her connection with the tides and with lunacy. The first, it is true, is not clearly evident, but I infer it from the fact that it was considered dangerous to bathe or to fish on Friday, Saturday, or Sunday, days when Áine's 'influence was particularly powerful'. By contrast, the connection with lunacy is emphatic. A stone called Cathair Áine (The Chair of Áine) near Dunany attracted lunatics and even rabid dogs from all over Ireland. Any sane man who sat upon it would become mad and any mad man would become incurable.[9] Gleann na nGealt (The Glen of the Lunatics) in Áine's own county of Kerry also attracts madmen. The King of France goes mad and flees there in 'The Battle of the White Strand'.[10] It is probably to be identified with the Glen Bolcain to which the mad king Suibhne Gealt repairs, 'a place of great delight for madmen'.[11]

If Áine's connection with lunatics were confined to making or keeping them mad, she could scarcely be called beneficent, but there is another aspect to Gleann na nGealt. There are two wells there with the common name of Tobernagalt, or the Well of the Lunatics, and the water of these wells, together with the watercress that grows around them, will restore a madman to sanity.[12] Here, then, Áine shows a kinder face.

Áine's cure for lunatics is compatible with Gregory's final description of her as a patroness of healing, poetry, and music (scarcely compatible with Gregory's earlier remarks about the Morrigu).[13] According to Wood-Martin, Áine's connection with healing was fully recognised until quite recently by practitioners of Irish folk-medicine, who regarded her 'as equivalent to what they designated the 'vital spark' . . . . Blood-letters would decline to operate on a day devoted to Aynia, for the efflux would carry away the 'vital spark' and the patient would die'.[14]

In her concomitant role as patroness of the arts, Áine is not unique. Any female fairy can function as a muse to a particular poet or musician, though Áine may befriend more poets than most. Such fairies are called *leannáin sídhe*, or fairy sweethearts, and their attentions are not wholly to be welcomed, for like the succubus they slowly drain the vitality from their mortal lovers. Accordingly, Áine tends to be pictured lamenting the deaths of poets or welcoming them (after death) to fairyland. Wood-Martin quotes two such verses in his own translation:

> The greater number of the inspiring geniuses
> of the learned,
> Shed tears in abundance through excessive
> grief;
> *Aeibhinn* and *Aine* were tearing their tresses;
>
> He accompanied Aine throughout the pleasant
> district of Fail,
> And visited all the full residences of the
> blooming *Bean-Sighe*,
> To quaff copious draughts of the supreme
> fountain of Druidism, from chaste,
> brightly-polished goblets,
> With the view of whetting his genius and
> firing his spirit.[15]

In either case, a poet is dead. In the first, Áine is among the 'inspiring geniuses of the learned,' or muses, lamenting; in the second, she is the *Bean-Sighe*, or 'fairy-woman', introducing the poet to her residences, the *sídhe*. In this function, Áine may be compared to the Queen of Elfland in 'The Ballad of True Thomas' (Child 37A), who for love of him admits the thirteenth century Scottish bard Thomas Rymour of Erceldoune to fairyland.[16] Oddly in the townland of Ballybriest, near Cnoc Áine, Co. Derry, Áine herself is supposed to have been a mortal woman taken by the fairies. There is also a similar tradition in West Mayo.[17]

One might expect a patroness of healing to preside over increase of life in a wider sense, and so it is with Áine. Indeed, the oldest text to assign a specific function to her describes her simply as a 'goddess of prosperity' (*bandía in tsónusa*).[18] The fertility of her own region around Cnoc Áine, Co. Kerry, naturally enough, is particularly ascribed to her. She is supposed to have transformed it from barren soil overnight, at the request of her mortal son, the magician-earl Gearóid Iarla.[19]

This final function of Áine's, as a goddess of fertility, may seem particularly appropriate if Áine is indeed another name for Danu. It is predictable that the Mother of the Gods should exercise a special care over the abundance of nature. But it cannot be said that either Áine or Danu is thus revealed in sharp focus. 'Goddess of prosperity' is a vague enough term. If there is any truth in the theory that Danu is also a goddess of war, she presides over functions that are barely compatible. Furthermore, at least some of Áine's functions are not peculiar to her. She is certainly not the only patroness of poets; it is unlikely that she is the only patroness of fertility. Thus, her example should demonstrate how hard it is to assign specific roles to the Tuatha Dé Danann.

11. The Dagda

If Danu, the Mother of the Gods, is shadowy, the Dagda, who is the father of a good many of them, is distinctly substantial. He is depicted as a gross buffoon of enormous strength and enormous capacity, clad in the short tunic which in Ireland is the normal costume of a churl. But although he is easily visualised, the Dagda's functions are not much more easily defined than Danu's. He is explicitly associated with earth and with fire. There is also good reason to associate him, like Danu, with abundance. In the final analysis, however, he seems to be an Odinic figure, a master of gnosis.

All of these functions are suggested by various names of the Dagda. Among his names, for instance, is Aedh.[20] This is simply the Irish equivalent of 'Hugh', but as a common noun it has the meaning of 'fire'. The *Cóir Anmann* offers an etymology of *Dagda* itself which seems to confirm this connection: 'Dagda, that is, *dag dé*, 'fire of god'. There is, however, a difference between 'fire of god' and 'god of fire'. Moreover, the *Cóir Anmann* immediately proceeds to contradict itself: 'He was a beautiful god of the heathens, for the Tuatha Dé Danann worshipped him: for he was an earth-god [*día talmhan*] to them because of the greatness of his (magical) power'.[21] As it addresses our concerns so directly, it is unfortunate that this passage is so unsatisfactory. Fire and earth are very different elements; it is unlikely that one god should preside over both. The Dagda's physical appearance is more suggestive of earth than of fire (being ponderous), but it is certainly not 'beautiful', as the *Cóir Anmann* would have it. Then, why should the Tuatha Dé Danann worship one of their own number? Where, in the Mythological Cycle or elsewhere, is the evidence that they did? And why should the greatness of the Dagda's magical power make him an earth-god? For the sake of the *Cóir Anmann's* general reliability, it is if anything a relief to find that this passage may not even belong to the authentic text: 'Cette définition se trouve à la page 582 du manuscrit H. 3. 18 du Collège de la Trinité de Dublin. Elle nous a été conservée par un glossaire. Son origine est inconnue; le manuscrit été écrit au seizièmle'siècle.'[22] The language, also, cannot be much older than the sixteenth century, though it may, of course, be adapted from an older original.

The Dagda has still another name, or title, that is of more significance than either Aedh or the Dagda: Ruad-Rofhessa. This, too, is the subject of a short explanation in a genuinely ancient text, the Dialogue of the Two Doctors in the *Book of Leinster*: 'on dit que le nom de celui-ci [the Dagda] était le seigneur à la Grande-Science [*in-Ruad-rofhessa*] . . . fils de tous les talents ou de tous les arts [*mac nan-ule n-dana*], c'est-à-dire le fils chez lequel sont tous les talents et tous les arts [*in dân uile*].'[23] This already suggests that we are dealing with more sophisticated concepts than fire and earth. It was, however, a brilliant modern scholar, Marie-Louise Sjoestedt, who first recognised the full implications of *Ruad-Rofhessa*. It will be remembered that in 'The Second Battle of Mag Tured' the Dagda twice boasts that he alone will perform all the feats which others have promised to perform separately. In a manner that invites comparison, Lugh gains admission to Tara by claiming the mastery of every profession. This earns him the title of *Samildánach*, or 'the one endowed with all arts'. This superficial similarity between the Dagda and Lugh, Sjoestedt argues, conceals a deeper difference:

> the Dagda is the *Ruad Ro-fhessa*, the 'Lord of Great Knowledge,' knowledge one and undifferentiated; the young Lug is the *Samildánach*, possessed of many skills, expert in the various specialities into which the unity of primitive culture is separated with the advance of technical ingenuity.[24]

The Dagda, then, is a figure like Odin. He is the fount of a gnosis that bestows power upon his own special followers, the *áes dána*, or 'men of art'. In the Irish sense, these include poets, druids, doctors, judges, and even smiths. This accords well with the fact that a harp is among his attributes.[25] He is not unique in this, but his own harp may be seen as emblematic of his knowledge. Irish poets were always harpers as well. It may be remembered that Odin aquired his knowledge by hanging for nine days over a pool while transfixed with a spear. He made of himself a sacrifice to himself. Thus his knowledge stems from a shadowland between life and death. This ambiguous position is likewise apparent in a second attribute of the Dagda's, an iron staff, with the rough end of which he kills nine men at a time, while with the smooth end he revives them.[26]

I am suggesting that the Dagda fulfils a function in Irish mythology parallel to that which Odin fulfils in Norse mythology, not that the two figures are actually to be identified. Odin has no attributes directly comparable to the Dagda's harp and staff. The latter, in fact, may be thought reminiscent of Thor's hammer. One god who resembles both the Dagda and Thor more closely than he resembles Odin is the Gaulish god Sucellos. He carries a mallet and his name has been translated as 'Good Striker'. Like the Dagda, he dresses in a short tunic, which in Gaul was the national costume, not the costume only of churls. He has a companion whose name is Nantosuelta. This name, says Sjoestedt, 'is obscure, but the first element is recognizable as meaning 'river' (cf. W. *nant* 'stream')'. The Dagda, likewise, is associated with the personification of the River Boyne. The most interesting

Yseult.[47] He is, however, as clearly associated with the sea itself as with the islands beyond it. He is characteristically to be met with riding in his chariot on the waves. Such a meeting occurs in 'The Voyage of Bran', when Manannan explains how the sea to him is a meadow.[48]

The changeable sea has its storms as well as its calms, and this may explain why Manannan, as a trickster, is not always benign. Though he obliges Deirdre and Naoise by fostering their children, he is also, in late *scéalta*, the cause of their tragedy. In one version of their story told by Lady Gregory, Manannan, even though he is here portrayed as Deirdre's father, precipitates the whole train of events by luring her unwelcome suitor Conchobar to her in the form of a hare. At the end of the story, at Conchobar's behest, he blinds Deirdre's husband and protector Naoise and so ensures her death.[49]

This is not very typical of Manannan, however. His tricks are generally more innocent and humorous. A story called 'The Kern in the Narrow Stripes' or 'O'Donnell's Kern', which must date from c. 1537, illustrates this well. A ragged churl, who by various signs is recognisable as a fairy, suddenly appears to a number of noblemen all over Ireland in turn, and equally suddenly disappears. While with each nobleman he performs tricks and practical jokes. For example, for five marks he offers to waggle only one of his ears. He does so by waggling it with his fingers. Another churl who offers to repeat the trick pulls his own ear off. Another stunt closely resembles the Indian rope-trick. The churl throws a thread from a bag into the clouds and from the same bag releases a hare to run up the thread, a beagle to chase it, a dogboy to chase that, and, from another bag, a young woman to protect the hare. After a while, he expresses a fear that the hound is eating the hare and the boy is fornicating with the woman. Pulling down the thread, he finds it so. He beheads the boy, to his host's displeasure. He replaces the head backwards, twists it into place, and vanishes. At the end of the story, one manuscript says quite suddenly that the churl is Manannan mac Lir.[50]

In stories such as this Manannan displays the playful and half-foolish side of his character. His major attribute, his crane-bag (*Corrbholg*), seems to display a different side. This bag, made from the skin of a woman turned to a crane, contains Manannan's shirt and knife, 'Goibhne's girdle' (*crios Goibhnionn*), 'a smith's hook from the fierce man', 'The King of Scotland's shears' . . . 'the King of Lochlainn's helmet', 'the bones of Asal's swine', and 'A girdle [*crios*] of the great whale's back'. All of these objects are visible at high tide, but at low tide the crane-bag appears empty.[51] This last detail, of course, reminds us of Manannan's association with the sea, and perhaps a little also of his trickiness. The crane-bag is like one of those simple conjuror's props with sliding panels, that appear to make their contents vanish and return. This much is clear enough. 'Asal's swine' can also be identified. They feature in the story of 'The Fate of the Children of Tuirenn': 'though they are killed every night they are found alive the next day; and every person that eats part of them shall not have disease or ill-health.'[52] What is not clear is what the rest of the contents of the crane-bag are, and why Manannan should use his bag to keep such a heterogeneous collection of objects. Robert Graves argues that the objects represent the letters of the ogham alphabet.[53] Readers of *The White Goddess* will recognise this theory as tendentious, but that is not to say it is wrong. Graves argues ingeniously and, as it is unchallenged by any other theory, his position seems strong. In that case, the crane-bag symbolises Manannan's role as a patron of learning. Could there be an implication that literacy itself is a sort of trick?

VIII. The Morrigu

Manannan's worst enemy is apparently the Morrigu (or Morrigan), for, if it be true that he was killed by Uillenn Faebarderg at Magh Cuilenn, the Morrigu delighted in his death.[54] Why she hates Manannan is unclear, but the Morrigu personifies war and hatred and violence in general. On the face of it, her name appears to mean 'great queen', and this etymology was accepted even in Old Irish times; in fact, however, *Mor-* is cognate with G. *mahr* 'nightmare' and OE. *mara* or *mera* 'demon'. 'Nightmare' and 'mare's nest' both derive from *mara*, and so, probably, does 'Mirryland', a mythical place sometimes mentioned in ballads and witch trials.[55] *Morrigu*, then, means 'queen of nightmares' or 'queen of demons'.

However, *Morrigu* is not this character's only name. Several members of the Tuatha Dé possess triadic form. Brigid is the clearest example as, although three persons are distinguished, they all share the same name. In her case the Christian formula of 'Three in One and One in Three' seems perfectly applicable. In other cases, it is not so clear whether a genuine Trinity is involved, or three separate but related persons, or one person with three names. The Morrigu is a case in point. As she can change suddenly from one person to another, though, and as two or more of her persons are only rarely seen together, it seems that for most purposes she is one person with several names. She is not, like Brigid, triadic, but four-fold at least. Besides being known as the Morrigu, she is also known as the Badb, as Macha, and as Nemain. Flood offers a fifth name, Fea,[56] and P. W. Joyce the name 'Anann or Ana'.[57] *Badb* means 'royston crow' or 'raven'. *Nemain* also has that meaning, as well as 'fury' or 'madness'. The Morrigu often appears in the form of a raven. It is possible, then, that Ériu herself is yet another manifestation of the Morrigu, for she also at moments looks like a crow.[58]

The Morrigu is involved in war from the Mythological Cycle onwards. We first encounter her shortly before the First Battle of Moytura. On this occasion, she appears in company with Macha and the Badb—the three of them, in other words, appear as separate persons. Their activity at this time is to put a dark mist on Teamhair (Tara) for the protection of the Tuatha Dé Danann.[59] The association with battle is typical, but the protective role is not. In the Second Battle of Moytura, the Morigu incites the Tuatha Dé to combat.[60] In the *Táin*, her troublesome role is pervasive. In a sense, she is the cause of the war between Ulster and Connacht. She steals a cow from the Cave of Cruachan for the Donn, or Brown Bull, of Cooley to mate with. When the calf of this union has fought unsuccessfully with Queen Medhbh's Whitehorned bull, it bellows that its father, the Donn, would not have been defeated. Hearing this, Medhbh swears that she will not rest until she has seen the two bulls fight. Thus the *Táin* is set in motion. During the course of the war, the Morrigu, Nemain, and the Badb on several occasions frighten large numbers of men to death, incite the Donn Cuailnge itself to violence, and generally stir things up by prophesying victory to both sides. The Morrigu reserves a special hatred during the war for Cúchulainn, whose death she unsuccessfully attempts to contrive during a fight at a ford by binding his ankles as an eel and attacking him as a wolf and a cow. The Badb has previously shown her enmity to Cúchulainn in 'The Sick-Bed of Cu Chulainn'. In 'The Great Gathering at Muirthemne', she somehow becomes confounded — by name — with one of the daughters of Calatin, three mortal witches who contrive Cúchulainn's death, at one point taunting him as a crow. At the eleventh hour, the Morrigu inconsistently tries to prevent Cúchulainn's death, but in the end sits with 'her sisters in the form of scald-crows' on his shoulders to let him enemies know that he is dead.[61]

Other heroes have felt the Morrigu's hostility well into historical times. As a crow, she confused Congal Claen at the Battle of Magh Rath; in the Battle of Dun Bolg, while Brigit supported Leinster, the Morrigu supported the rest of Ireland; as a crow again, she flew over Murchadh mac Brien at the Battle of Cluantarbh (1014).[62]

Although the Morrigu's connection with war is clear enough, the exact nature of that connection is not so clear. She furnishes here a good example of a problem that involves all the Tuatha Dé Danann to some extent. In short, the question is whether she can be accurately described as a goddess of war. One theory which suggests that she can was first advanced by C. Lottner in 1870, and subsequently revived by Charles Donahue in 1941. This theory equates the Morrigu, Nemain, the Badb, and the rest with valkyries. Some of Donahue's points are well worth remarking. For instance, he calls attention to a valkyrie called Herfjǫtur, who is mentioned in the *Grímnismál*. *Herfjǫtur* means literally 'army-fetter' or 'war-fetter'. and the word is used as a kenning to denote 'a terrifying weakness [which] comes over the warrior, hindering his ability and presaging his death'. Donahue is most impressed with this weakness, and not without reason, as Cúchulainn experiences such a weakness before his death. Equally, however, the term 'war-fetter' may remind us of the Morrigu's binding of Cúchulainn's ankles. On the other hand, Donahue's major points are less convincing. He asserts that the valkyries and the Irish 'war-goddesses' appear either 'alone or in groups of three', but lays great stress by an inscription which is neither Irish nor Scandinavian but Romano-British and refers to some obscure figures called *alaisiagae* who appear in pairs. We have seen, besides, that the Morrigu is at least four-fold, not three-fold. Donahue asserts that valkyries and Irish 'war-goddesses' favour single mortal 'companions,' but 'companion' does not well describe the relationship between the Morrigu and Cúchulainn. Donahue does not mention the Valkyrie's important role as psychopomp, which is definitely not shared by the Morrigu. He remarks, finally, that both Valkyries and the Badb appear as birds, but this is not surprising, since ravens do in reality frequent battle-fields. Most seriously, Donahue takes it for granted that valkyries were themselves deities. At best, this is surely unproven, which leaves the Morrigu's status still more unproven. The object of Donahue's argument seems unaccomplished.[63]

If the Morrigu was truly a goddess of war, it would seem desirable to show that she was the recipient of worship or sacrifice. Donahue does not attempt this, but Wood-Martin does. He points out that a gloss in the *Yellow Book of Lecan* defines Macha's 'fruit crop' as 'the heads of men that have been slaughtered'. This he connects with those heaps of skulls that archaeologists have unearthed in Ireland. Such heaps, he concludes, were sacrifices offered to Macha, or the Morrigu, presumably after battle.[64] However, the *Yellow Book of Lecan* says nothing specifically of sacrifice, while the Ulster Cycle offers considerable evidence that skulls were stored as trophies by warriors, in confirmation of their boasts.[65] The possibility of sacrifice cannot be excluded, but this evidence at leasts makes it less probable.

Whether the Morrigu can be described as a goddess of war will still depend on what, precisely, one means by the word 'goddess.' It does seem unlikely, however, that she patronises war in the same sense that Mars does. Perhaps she represents the spirit or mood of war. In one sense, this will render her more like Angus and Lugh, who may be best described as the patrons of ill-defined moods rather than of specific things.

Essentially, the Tuatha Dé Danann are heterogeneous and ill-defined. They are not grouped according to any reliable system. On the other hand, if one ceases to seek for correlatives in the outside world, one may find that the Tuatha Dé Danann begin to find places in the mind itself. Angus and Lugh, if it is true that they represent pure moods, then become the ideal members of the Tuatha Dé. The Morrigu will represent the mood of violence. Manannan will represent, not so much the tangible sea, as whatever mood the contemplation of the sea evokes. The system is still not perfect, for Ogma, as eloquence, will represent not a mood but a faculty of the mind. The Dagda, as wisdom, will represent, not a mood, but a quality. His buffoonish appearance and comical adventures suggest that, in quite another capacity, he may represent the mood of mirth. Áine — th' inconstant moon — must represent a wide range of moods and qualities, from madness to, possibly, comfort. What mood, quality, or faculty is associated with Midhir is still not easy to say. This is still not an orderly system, but it may be the best method of contemplating the Tuatha Dé. However, to describe them as personified moods (however imprecisely) accounts only for the response of the mythographers to these figures. It will not account for their origins, any more than one could deduce the story of the Crucifixion from the contemplation of a cross. The origin of the Tuatha Dé will be the subject of the rest of Part One.[66]

4. THE PEOPLE OF PEACE

There are essentially three theories to account for the origin of the belief in the Tuatha Dé Danann. One holds that they were first imagined as the spirits of the dead; one that they are the gods of Ancient Ireland; and one that they are a folk-memory of a race of mortals. All of these theories leave questions unanswered. The first, for instance, does not explain the subseqeunt evolution of the belief; the second has never settled the question of what sort of gods the Tuatha Dé Danann are. Although all of these theories display considerable ingenuity, none is as complex as the problem with which they deal. There is some evidence for each which is too strong to reject. The Tuatha Dé Danann must therefore be a combination of gods, ghosts, and mortals. Such a combination, however, has a name of its own: fairies. The Tuatha Dé Danann, at least as we know them, deserve to be considered as an independent creation. Their uniqueness is not always sufficiently appreciated. While it may be true to say that they are gods, ghosts, *and* mortals, it is equally true to say that they are neither gods, ghosts, *nor* mortals.

The aim of this and the following two chapters, therefore, is not to account for the fairies by giving them a different name, but to analyse the three original impulses that eventually combined in the concept of a fairy. In the process of combination, ghosts must have acquired the qualities of mortals and mortals the qualities of gods. That is not to say, though, that gods, ghosts, and mortals have all contributed to the concept of 'fairy' in equal measure. I propose that the Tuatha Dé Danann owe only a little of their nature to the spirits of the dead, more to the gods, but most to mortals. In this chapter I shall consider their debt to the dead.

The theory that the Tuatha Dé Danann are spirits of the dead found its most able advocate roughly a century ago in Henri d'Arbois de Jubainville. There were many both to agree and to disagree with him at the time, and so there are still. The theory is very simply stated: Early Irish mythology embodies a cult of the dead; the Tuatha Dé Danann are the dead, and where they dwell is the land of the dead. In de Jubainville's own view, Irish mythology is so closely identified with this cult that the Fomorians and certain Milesians should also be seen as spirits of the dead. Indeed, he seems to make little distinction between the various mythical races of Irish pre-history. This, I believe, is a weakness in his position. What may (or may not) be true of the Fomorians is not *ipso facto* true of the Tuatha Dé Danann. With regard to one particular Milesian, Donn, a connection with the dead seems highly probable, but this fact is exceptional, and will not contribute to de Jubainville's fundamental position. That position draws its greatest support from a very small number of stories. These stories seem sufficient to demonstrate that the Tuatha Dé Danann cannot be completely dissocated from the spirits of the dead, nor their land from the land of the dead. That this connection is more than vestigial is not well supported by other stories that have been adduced, nor yet by linguistic evidence. The very nature of the Tuatha Dé Danann, and of the belief in them, demonstrates, indeed, the unlikelihood of any far-reaching association with the dead.

I Narrative Evidence

The one story in which the connection of fairyland with the afterlife seems inescapable is the story of Baile and Ailinn, the Irish Romeo and Juliet, which Yeats has retold in one of his longer poems. Baile and Ailinn are two lovers whose planned meeting is forestalled by a mysterious person, probably Angus Óg, who tells each that the other is dead. On hearing this false news, both die of grief. The significant detail is that it was foretold by druids that Baile and Ailinn would meet and be happy for ever after their death, but not before.[1] That the land in which they will meet is Tír na nÓg is unstated but seems beyond reasonable doubt. This story is exceptional, but its evidence cannot be ignored.

Only slightly less important is an incident in 'The Destruction of Da Derga's Hostel'. On his way to the hostel where he is doomed to die, the High King Conaire Mór meets three fairies, coloured red all over, who sing the following cryptic verse: 'We ride the steeds of Donn Tetscorach from the fairy mounds. Though we are alive we are dead.' Later, the story explains that the Three Reds are under a curse to be destroyed three times by the King of Tara. Their third time is approaching.[2] Thus they are no ordinary dead men. That they can be killed and still live to be killed again argues, on the contrary, a form of immortality. Their curse also sets them aside from the rest of the fairies. Nevertheless, it cannot be denied that they are dead in one sense, though not in another. There is here a connection between the dead and the fairies, even though it s a very special case.

Oddly enough, Baile and Ailinn and 'The Destruction of Da Derga's

Hostel' are not stories by which de Jubainville and his followers lay great stress. The narrative evidence which they adduce is much weaker and tends only to emphasise the rarity of such stories as the above. De Jubainville finds particularly significant the story of the fight between the Nemedians and the Fomorians at Conann's Tower. He prefers to read this, not in the text of the *Lebor Gabála*, but in the text of Nennius. According to this, the Nemedians see on Conann's Tower 'something like unto men, *quasi homines*', from whom they can catch no sound. On this evidence de Jubainville argues that the figures on the tower are not men at all but the 'silent people', *silentes*, of Latin poetry. The 'silentes' are the dead, in Virgil and Ovid, Lucan, Valerius Flaccus, and Claudian.'[3] However, Nennius' details could be straightforwardly explained on the grounds that the Nemedians are out of earshot of the tower and too far away to make out the figures on it with any distinctness. The testimony of Ovid and other Latin poets is of no value as it rests only upon the unremarkable coincidence of silence. Most importantly, the figures on the tower do not profess to be of the Tuatha Dé Danann, but of the Fomorians.

A story which A. H. Krappe finds significant is 'The Pursuit of the Gilla Decair and his Horse'. In this, a deformed ruffian called the Gilla Decair, or 'Difficult Servant', captures thirteen of the Fianna and makes off with them by riding over the sea. Finn and the rest of the Fianna follow him to the Land of Promise where he frees his prisoners and makes amends. All of the Fianna then return to Ireland.[4] In Krappe's interpretation, the Gilla Decair is Manannan, Mannan is Death, and the Land of Promise is the land of the dead. Two persons called Feradach and Foltlebar, ostensibly sons of the King of Ind, who assist Finn in his pursuit, become 'les Dioscures celtiques, ceux-là même dont Diodore parle dans un passage souvent cité: "Τοὺς παρὰ τὸν Ὠκεανὸν κατοικουντας Κέλτας σεβομένους μάλιστα τῶν θεῶν τοὺς Διοσκουρούς."'[5] This evidence from Diodorus is only to the point if Krappe's identification of the Gilla Decair is also correct. The Gilla Decair is reminiscent of Manannan in riding on the sea. Also, in the late tale of 'The Kern in the Narrow Stripes', the trickster-protagonist, identified by the scribe as Manannan, calls himself at one point the Gilla Decair. As the two characters are somewhat similar, that is probably a conscious borrowing from this story. Here, on the other hand, the Gilla Decair identifies himself at first as a Fomorian, but is finally revealed to be Allchad's son Abertach of the Tuatha Dé Danann. Abertach is nowhere attested as a name of Manannan. Nor does Krappe advance any external evidence to associate Manannan with death. If the Gilla Decair is Death, why does he release his prisoners, and why do the Fianna return to Ireland? In short, Krappe's argument is tendentious. Only on the assumption that 'The Pursuit of the Gilla Decair' deals with death can any of its characters be identified as Dioscuri or as Death itself.

These last two stories are fair examples of the type which de Jubainville and his school find most favourable to their case. On the narrative evidence, then, though the relationship between the Tuatha Dé Danann and the dead must be confessed to exist, it is, in Eleanor Hull's words, 'only faintly shadowed in a few isolated and obscure passages in that part of the literature which seems to retain most of the pagan flavour and spirit.[6]

II. The *Lebor Gabála*

Individual tales aside, there is one recurrent feature of the *Lebor Gabála* which suggests that the scribes of that book did not consider the Tuatha Dé to be spirits of the dead. It is the insistence that the Tuatha Dé Danann originated in Greece. To be sure, this represents monkish interference with older traditions. The scribes of the *Lebor Gabála* favoured a limited euhemerism of the mythology they recorded. Had they wished to obliterate that mythology entirely, on the other hand, they would not have written the *Lebor Gabála*. Therefore, if they had had any inkling that the Tuatha Dé were considered spirits of the dead, they could not have assigned them an origin in Greece, as that would be nonsensical. A ghost originates in the place where it dwelt when alive.

It may be objected that a tradition connecting the Tuatha Dé with the dead did exist, but that the scribes were honestly unaware of it. The narrative evidence of Baile and Ailinn proves that there is a grain of truth in this. The tradition, however, cannot have been strong. In modern folklore there is indeed some confusion between ghosts and fairies. Had they been firmly identified in ancient times, we might expect a continuity of tradition linking that identification with the modern confusion. In that case, the scribes of the *Lebor Gabála* could not have been unaware of the tradition. The alternative is that the modern confusion owes nothing to the ancient identification, which must have been forgotten by the time *Lebor Gabála* was written. In that case, the identification can never have been strong, for one cannot forget that a ghost is a ghost. One can only conclude that the association of the Tuatha Dé Danann with the spirits of the dead has never been more than peripheral.

III. Kinship

Again, the Tuatha Dé Danann cannot be closely identified with the dead if they behave in a way quite impossible for the dead. One thing that the dead can never do is to interbreed with the living. To say otherwise is to deny that they are dead at all. And yet that is exactly what the Tuatha Dé Danann do. *Duanaire Finn*, for instance, contains two lays explaining in great detail the blood relationship between Finn, Lugh, and Cnú Dheireoil (Lugh is a son of Eithne and Finn is a grandson of hers; Cnú Dheireoil is a son of Lugh's). Finn, of course, is a mortal; Lugh is a lord of the Tuatha Dé Danann; and Cnú Dheireoil is a fairy of comparatively little importance.[7] Besides blood relationships, the Tuatha Dé often enter into relationships of fosterage with mortals. Dermot Ó Duibhne, for example, was fostered by both Angus Óg and Manannan.[8] The Fianna, indeed, are so closely related to the Tuatha Dé Danann by both blood and fosterage that Bodb Dearg is persuaded to bring the Tuatha Dé to the Fianna's assistance in 'The Battle of the White Strand' by being reminded that 'there is not a king's son or a prince or a leader of the Fianna of Ireland without having a wife or a mother or a foster-mother or a sweetheart of the Tuatha de Danann'.[9] One of the Fianna called Mac Lughach provides a case in point. His father is Dáire dearg of the Fianna, who is a grandson of Eithne, of the Tuatha Dé. His mother is Lughach of the White Hands, who is a daughter of Finn's but a foster-daughter of Eochaidh of the Smooth Joints (*ailtmhilla*), a member of the Tuatha Dé. Mac Lughach himself is raised by his mother until the age of seven, before joining the Fianna.[10] If he were not mortal, it would be hard to say to what race Mac Lughach belonged. This is nothing strange if the Tuatha Dé and the Fianna are both among the living; it would be very strange if the Tuatha Dé were among the dead.

IV. The Lord of the Dead

Another approach to this question is to consider who is the Lord of the Dead. If the Tuatha Dé Danann are closely identified with the spirits of the dead, the Lord of the Dead must surely be one of them. Krappe thinks Manannan is Lord of the Dead. Midhir has better claims. I prefer to side with those who favour the Milesian, Donn.[11] This is he, it will be remembered, who was drowned in the invasion of the Sons of Mil and buried offshore at Tech Duinn.

There is one story, 'The Wooing of Treblann', which will advance the claims both of Midhir and Donn to be Lord of the Dead. In this, Treblann, a daughter of Angus Óg and foster-daughter of Coirpre mac

Rosa Ruaid, elopes with a mortal named Froech. Compelled then to pursue some stolen property, Froech sends Treblann along with his own Stone of Equal Life to the House of Donn (who is surprisingly described as his foster-brother). Readers of *The Golden Bough*, ch. 66, will recognise in the Stone of Equal Life what Frazer calls 'The Motif of the External Soul'. Midir of Brí Leith now goes on behalf of Coirpre to Tech Duinn to demand Treblann as a bride for one Triath mac Faebuir, saying falsely that Froech has been slain in Lombardy. He also enchants Froech's Stone, so that it breaks. Oddly, this seems to do Froech no harm, but Treblann dies of grief. On hearing of her death, Froech besieges Brí Leith, demanding not only compensation for Treblann but also a promise that she will be restored to him. Midir is indeed eventually constrained to restore her, either, as Rudolf Thurneysen believes, revived, or else, as James Carney believes, as one of the dead, to bear Froech's body into Síd Froích after his own death in the *Táin*.[12] Thurneysen's position seems more natural. Froech surely need not resort to force of arms while still alive in order to secure his reunion with Treblann after death.

What we have here, then, is a clear relative of the Orpheus myth. What we do not have is a clear-cut Pluto: is it Dŏnn, or is it Midir? It is Midir who brings about Treblann's death, but he does so indirectly, and, one must suppose, accidentally. It is Froech's Stone that he breaks, and he has good reason to wish Froech dead; Treblann, on the contrary, he has good reason to wish alive. On the other hand, it is to Tech Duinn that Treblann is taken out of the world of mortals, and it is there that she actually dies. Midir restores her to life. It would be possible to argue, then that it is Donn who takes life and Midir who restores it. Alternatively, one might argue that Midir is the Lord of the Dead of the Tuatha Dé Danann while Donn is the Lord of the Dead of the Milesian race. In one way or another, the role of Pluto is shared between Donn and Midir. Midir's position remains unclear, but Donn does function as a Lord of the Dead.

Of course, the difficulty with this is that the Milesians are not normally considered, like the Tuatha Dé Danann, a supernatural race. As it happens, Donn's membership of the Milesians is not beyond all question. In an eighteenth century poem, Andrew Mac Curtin 'calls him brother or cousin of Aine and Aoife and 'of the great son of Lear [i.e. Manannán], who used to walk the smooth sea,' and relates him to Angus Óg, and Lugh the Long-Handed'.[13] The authority of this single late poem cannot be considered very great in comparison to the *Lebor Gabála*, but the authenticity of the *Lebor Gabála* on this point has itself been questioned. Kuno Meyer notes that in Nennius Donn is not numbered among the Sons of Mil and concludes that the scribes of the

Irish *Lebor Gabála* have introduced him into the narrative after first demoting him from a 'pagan god', presumably one of the Tuatha Dé Danann.[14] The use of Nennius to 'correct' the *Lebor Gabála* seems highly suspect. Nennius' work does not purport to be a full translation of the *Lebor Gabála* but an *Historia Brittonum*. Any omissions are easily accounted for by editorial abridgement on his part. The *Lebor Gabála* does state the Donn is indeed a Milesian.

His role as Lord of the Dead is attested in early Irish literature not only by 'The Wooing of Tréblann' but also by a verse already noted in 'The Destruction of Da Derga's Hostel': 'We ride the steeds of Donn Tetscorach from the fairy mounds. Though we are alive we are dead.'[15] In modern folklore, Donn's role is complex, but it certainly includes a Plutonic function. He is supposed to dwell at Cnoc Fírinne, Co. Limerick. There he presides over all those who die young or untimely deaths. A certain man who had pleased Donn and who entered Cnoc Fírinne alive was 'allowed to take back to the land of the living a brother and sister long supposed dead'.[16]

How, is it possible, then, that a Milesian functions as the Lord of the Dead? The answer may be inferred from Francis John Byrne's description of Donn as 'the ancestor god to whom all the Irish will journey after death'.[17] In the first two chapters of his book *The Destiny of a King*, Georges Dumézil analyses the function of several mythological figures who would also conform to Byrne's description, chiefly the Indian Yama and the Iranian Yima. These figures, he concludes, are not so much gods of the dead like, say, Osiris, as pioneers of the dead.[18] Donn has to be a Milesian, and therefore a mortal, for he is the first to die and to prepare a place in the beyond for those who will follow.

The importance of this conclusion is that it leaves the afterlife of the Milesians in their own hands. The Ancient Irish do not imagine themselves, when they die, as passing into the ranks or the keeping of the Tuatha Dé Danann. They remain Milesians under the leadership of a Milesian. If, then, the Tuatha Dé Danann are spirits of the dead at all they are spirits of the dead of a different race. For Milesians, like Baile and Ailinn, to join their number is wholly exceptional.

V. Linguistic Evidence

There remain certain Irish words which may seem to imply a connection between the Tuatha Dé Danann and the dead. For instance, the words *scath* and *scál* are sometimes applied to members of the Tuatha Dé, and may be translated 'spectre'. Both ancient and modern authorities agree, however, that the words may also be translated 'hero'. *Cormac's Glossary*, which dates from the late ninth or very early tenth century, explains the relationship of the two meanings thus: 'ASCAID [*Ascath B*] i.e. 'a hero,' unde *asgaete* [*ascata B*], i.e. heroic or championlike, from the terribleness of the hero, like a shade or like a phantom.' There is, therefore, no particular significance in the use of these terms.[19]

More important, and more difficult, is the word *sídh*. Besides this word, which means, of course 'fairy hill', there is another, *síth*, which means 'peace'. In Modern Irish the pronunciation of the two words is not identical, but in Old Irish it may have been very close. From this, some scholars have concluded that the two words are ultimately the same. We find this theory already roughly expounded in Robert Kirk's seventeenth century study of the Scottish fairy faith, *The Secret Commonwealth*. Kirk writes that 'our Highlanders [make] still a distinction betwixt *Sluagh Saoghalta* and *Sluagh Sith*, averring that the Souls goe to the Sith when dislodged'. He explains that 'our Busie and Silent Companions [are] called Siths [because they are] people at rest and quiet in respect of us'.[20] I believe it can be shown from Kirk's own words that this identification of *sídh* and *síth* is mistaken. His Gaelic, of course, is Modern, and in Modern Gaelic *síth* is the dative singular or a variant of the normal nominative singular, *síoth*. Following *Sluagh* ('host'), a genitive singular is required. The genitive singular of *síoth* is *síotha*, and so 'the host of peace' would be *Sluagh síotha*. In this context, then, *Sith* must be a variant spelling of *sídhe* (gen. sing.), i.e. 'of the hill'. This also agrees with the Modern pronunciation, which is roughly 'shee' for both *sídhe* and *síth*, but 'Sheeg' for *sídh*. In Kirk's context, 'peace' cannot be the meaning of *síth* anyway, as his reference to '*the* Sith' indicates. So the *sluagh sídhe* or *Sluagh Sith* (however spelt), remain the people of the hill, not those at rest.

It remains possible that, because of the similarity and covergence of *sídh* and *síth*, a sort of punning relationship may have arisen between the two words. At best, this could only prove that a confusion between the Tuatha Dé Danann and the dead followed upon a linguistic misunderstanding, not *vice versa*. But even this is unsound, as peace, after all, is not synonymous with death. Tomás Ó Cathasaigh argues for a quite different punning relationship: 'The state of peace secured by the kings of the mythical past, whose kingship was sanctioned by the Otherworld, is seen as a recreation in this world of the paradisal condition.' Elsewhere, Ó Cathasaigh adds: 'The Otherworld is the source of the king's cosmic Truth (*fír*) and peace is its symptom.'[21]

Alternatively, of course, there may be no relationship at all between *sídh* and *síth*. That was the opinion of Douglas Hyde, who thought *sídh* cognate with Skr. *Siddha* 'emancipated person'.[22] What matters here is that no matter how the relationship between *sídh* and *síth* is taken, it will not prove a connection between the Tuatha Dé Danann and the spirits of the dead. That connection, though it cannot be completely denied, depends almost entirely on the story of Baile and Ailinn. All the other evidence tends to de-emphasise such a connection. It will be recalled, however, that the case of Donn suggests a possbility that the Tuatha Dé Danann are the spirits of the dead of a different race from the Gael. This possibility may be the key to the whole problem. If it is true, there will be little difference between the Tuatha Dé as spirits of the dead and the Tuatha Dé as a folk-memory of another race. If that race is extinct in reality but alive in the imagination, there will hover about it, almost sceptically, a faint realisation that the Ever-Living are now only ghosts.

5. DEI TERRENI

If Henri d'Arbois de Jubainville is the strongest advocate of the theory that the Tuatha Dé Danann are spirits of the dead, the strongest advocate of the theory that they are gods may be T. F. O'Rahilly. However, this theory has always attracted so many adherents that it cannot very well be identified with any one scholar. Within this school of thought there are various competing sects. Some consider the Tuatha Dé Danann as simply the Gaulish pantheon transplanted. Others balk at the word 'pantheon' but consider the Tuatha Dé as gods of a more primitive, unsystematised phase of religion. To still others, they are gods whose godhead has been half-forgotten, in much the same way that a *scéal* may be described as a myth that has lost its meaning.

It is scarcely conceivable that so many scholars should regard the Tuatha Dé as gods if there were not good reasons for doing so. Such figures as Lugh and Manannan do indeed possess characteristics that can only be called divine, and there are strong arguments for extending that term to the Tuatha Dé in general. Terminology is the problem. What do we mean by 'god' and what do we mean by 'divine'? The question of the Tuatha Dé has been clouded by ethnocentricity. I propose that the primitive concept of a god did not develop in Ireland in the same direction as in other countries. The genuinely primitive gods of Ireland are unrelated to the Tuatha Dé Danann and their cult was abandoned at a very early date. Instead of producing further gods, the numinous impulse produced fairies. Fragments of divinity certainly cling to some or all of these fairies. Certain such fragments, including the very names of some of the Tuatha Dé, are borrowed from the gods of other nations. However, these are only incidental accretions. They do not reflect the essential nature of the Tuatha Dé Danann.

I. Linguistic Evidence

The first evidence for the divinity of the Tuatha Dé Danann is their collective name. *Dé* (with its related forms *día, dá*) is plainly cognate with L. *deus*, Gk. θεos, Zευs, and other words for 'god' spread all over

Dei Terreni

the Indo-European area. However, the name *Tuatha Dé Danann* does not expressly state that the Tuatha Dé themselves are gods. The immediate context of the word *Dé* may well suggest a different meaning. If it does not, the precise connotations of *Dé* must still be examined, and not taken for granted.

Tuatha Dé Danann, of course, is generally translated as 'the tribes of the goddess Danu'. It could alternatively mean 'the tribes of the gods of Danu'. Under either translation, the name is often taken to imply the divinity of the Tuatha Dé. In fact, as A. G. van Hamel points out, it is more likely to imply the reverse. If the Tuatha Dé are under the tutelage of the goddess Danu, it is unlikely that they are gods themselves. Van Hamel further adduces the evidence of a story in 'The Colloquy with the Ancients' which Lady Gregory entitles 'The Hound'. In this, three men and a dog from Norway (Iruath) give excellent service to Finn on condition that they be not spied upon after nightfall, when they are surrounded by a wall of fire. The dog vomits gold, silver, and ale as they are needed. After a year their privacy is violated. They slay the culprits and leave.[1] Van Hamel argues that the dog symbolises the gift of divine abundance, and that its loss is inevitably fated. This, he thinks, is a parable of the difference between the human and the fairy conditions. The fairies are the perpetual beneficiaries of a divine assistance which is perpetually denied to men. The name *Tuatha Dé Danann* thus implies that the difference between fairies and men is not that the former are gods but that they have gods.[2]

It must be admitted, however, that this is not how the *Lebor Gabála* explains the name *Tuatha Dé*. The *Lebor Gabála* expressly tells us that the people of Iobath son of Beothach son of Iarbanel son of Nemed settled in the northern islands of Greece and there grew so wise that they considered their men of learning gods. This, it tells us, is the origin of the name.[3] The story of 'Tuan, Son of Cairell' implies something similar when it says of the Tuatha Dé and their companions the An-Dé that 'where they came from the learned do not know, but it seems to them likely they came from heaven, because of their skill and the excellene of their knowledge'.[4]

Both of these passages, however, imply one important qualification. The *Lebor Gabála* says that the Tuatha Dé considered their men of learning gods, from which it follows that they considered the rest of their number not to be gods. These are the An-Dé explicitly named in 'Tuan, Son of Cairell'. *An-Dé* means simply 'non-gods'. This distinction is confirmed by the *Cóir Anmann*. 'Tuatha *Dé*, i.e. Danann, that is, *dée* were the poets and *an-dée* the husbandmen', it says (*Tuatha Dea* [.i. Donann] .i. *dée in t-áes dána] andée in t-áes trebhtha*). The *Cóir Anmann* illustrates this with an incident from the *Táin*, when Cúchulainn says to the Morrigu, 'The blessing of gods and non-gods be on thee, O damsel!' ('*Bennacht dée J anndée fort, a inghen,*' or *Cúculainn*). Again it explains: 'These were their gods, the magicians, and their non-gods the husbandmen' (*Batar é a ndée in t-aés cumhachta J a n-anndée in t-aes trebaire*).[5] From an Ancient Irish perspective, there is little difference between poets and magicians, but it is obvious that they will be outnumbered by the husbandmen. Thus the greater portion of the fairies are explicitly stated not to be gods.

However, we are still left with the poets and magicians. The Irish term, *áes dána* 'people of art', is actually of wider significance, covering everyone from druids to smiths. The status of the last class is confirmed by the presence among the Tuatha Dé of three smiths called Brian, Iuchar, and Iuchabar, and known collectively as *na trí dé danann*. This, it seems, if Irish orthography were more reliable, should be read with the first *a* in *danann* accented, and would thus mean 'the three gods of art', not 'the three gods of Danu.' That these three are singled out as *the* three gods of art may suggest a status for smiths even higher than that of poets. What requires explaining, though, is the word *dé*. Douglas Hyde would translate *danann* as always meaning 'of art', instead of 'of Danu'. He notes further that the Tuatha Dé considered *themselves* gods, on account of their learning. Under such circumstances, he thinks the word 'god' can only be metaphorical, and therefore he renders *Tuatha Dé Danann* as 'the men of science who were as it were gods'.[6]

Hyde quotes the *Cóir Anmann* in support of this, and it must be admitted that he plays fast and loose with the apparent meaning of that work. If the words *da, día, dé* can anywhere be shown to mean 'god', literally, Hyde's circumlocution can be no more than an attractive speculation. Van Hamel states that 'the word *dee* "gods"' is found only in *Tuatha Dé Danann*, in *na trí dé danann*, and in oaths.[7] Strictly speaking, this may be true, but the word or element *da* certainly occurs elsewhere, for instance in the names *Dagda, Nuada*. David Fitzgerald attempted to prove that this element should not be translated 'god' but 'hand', citing Michael O'Clery's gloss *dae .i. lámh*.[8] A rejoinder by Whitley Stokes (who thought himself personally slighted) is so violent in tone that its content might almost be overlooked, but Stokes does appear to have proved, on philological grounds, that *-da* in *Nuada* cannot mean 'hand', and probably cannot in *Dagda*.[9] It must be allowed that 'new hand' would be a most appropriate rendering of *Nuada*, but it is always possible that the myth conforms to the name, rather than *vice versa*. T. F. O'Rahilly adopts a position at an opposite extreme to Fitzgerald. There are a number of hostellers in Early Irish literature whose hostels seem always to be on the border of the Otherworld. These hostellers are called Dá Derga, Dá Coca, Mac Dá Réo, and Mac Dá Tho. Here, the word *Dá*, being accented is generally translated 'two'. O'Rahilly, however, argues that it should be read as 'a shortening, in pretonic position, of *dea, dia*, 'god, goddess''.[10] If this argument is admitted, Fitzgerald's position appears weaker still. At best, Fitzgerald's case must be considered unproven, and so, therefore, up to this point, must Douglas Hyde's.

However Fitzgerald, Stokes, and O'Rahilly are all concerned to seek a meaning for *da*, and not to seek a meaning for 'god'. It is at this point that the danger of ethnocentricity arises. If the Tuatha Dé Danann are gods, as the *Cóir Anmann* says, does that mean that they would be at home on Mount Olympus? Van Hamel thinks not. When 'gods' are invoked in oaths, he points out, 'the word *dee* is only used in the plural and there is no trace of personality in these 'gods''.[11] The Tuatha Dé Danann possess a great deal of personality, and therefore they are not gods of this description. They may be 'like them,' however — very powerful — and therefore Douglas Hyde's position could be justified on these grounds.

Probably, though, the truth is a little more complex than that. Ward Rutherford has pointed out the relevance of Dumézil's derivation of *dé* and cognate words in other languages from Proto-Indo-European *deiwos*, a word 'used to describe creatures in the likeness of humans, but possessing superhuman powers'.[12] In Ireland, it seems as though this concept, in one respect, has remained fossilised. In another respect, it has developed in an opposite direction to that taken in most languages. Instead of acquiring higher connotations, it has become almost devoid of connotation. The gods invoked in oaths are imagined as the sanction of the oath and nothing more. The Tuatha Dé Danann share the power of these faceless divinities, but they remain 'creatures in the likeness of humans'. In short, they are a human race endowed with abnormal powers. The Irish word *dé* is applied to them with perfect propriety, but this word will not bear the meaning 'god' in any sense normally sanctioned by the English language.

II. Evidence from Abroad

Besides sharing a generalised power with the gods of oaths, some of the Tuatha Dé Danann share names and attributes with specific gods from other countries. Ogma and Ogmios provide an obvious example. Nuadu has been identified with Nodens, a Romano-British god depicted as a fisherman in a fourth century temple at Lydney in Gloucestershire.[13] The names of the Morrigu and the Badb seem conflated in the name of an ancient Bohemian tribe, the Mara Bodbus, while many Continental towns, including Lyons, bear names related to that of Lugh.[14] Tribes and towns are not gods, of course, but we may suspect that they derive their names from the names of local deities. Going further afield, we find the Ethiopian earth god Medr sharing his name with Midhir of Brí Leith. Where names do not agree, attributes may, as in the case of the Dagda and Sucellos.

Naturally, similarities of name and attribute most often associate the Tuatha Dé Danann with gods of the Gauls, another Celtic people. Because of this, the Tuatha Dé Danann are 'usually regarded', in van Hamel's words, 'as a survival of an original Celtic pantheon'. In view of his position on the word *dee* it is not surprising that van Hamel finds this conclusion unjustified. It is supported by names alone, he remarks. 'It receives but little support from the Irish tradition.'[15] Names alone might seem very persuasive, but, as Eleanor Hull objects in the case of Nuada and Nodens, the coincidence of names may sometimes seem at odds with the other evidence: 'The attributes do not agree, and Nuada appears to belong to a later or different order of ideas.'[16]

I would suggest that such misleading coincidences derive from the peculiar development of the concept of *deiwos* in Ireland. Let it be granted that in remote times Nuadu and Nodens were identical. In Gaul (and Britain) this ür-Nuadu might have developed into a god while in Ireland developing into something quite different. This, indeed, is only to be expected. The Irish and Gaulish branches of the Celtic people, being physically separated by a considerable expanse of land and sea, are likely to have developed different cultures. Each culture is likely to have been influenced by the culture of the peoples whom the Celts displaced in Gaul and Ireland respectively. More importantly, Gaulish culture would have been influenced by the Roman example, and hence have developed gods in the Roman image.[17] This influence was not felt in Ireland. Therefore, to suppose on the evidence of names that the Tuatha Dé Danann are identical with the Gaulish pantheon is again ethnocentric.

It would not necessarily follow anyway that the Tuatha Dé Danann are gods in the sense to which we are accustomed. Instead of promoting the Tuatha Dé to the status of Roman gods, we have the option of demoting the Gaulish gods. While those of them who possess temples and demonstrable attributes, like Sucellos and Nodens, must also possess personality, there is evidence that other Gaulish gods have little more substance than those gods by whom the Irish swear. The form of oath most often found in the Ulster Cycle is 'I swear by the god that my tribe swears by' (*tongu do dia toinges mo thuath*). Cognate with *tuath* 'tribe' is the name of the Gaulish god Teutates. It seems likely, therefore, that *Teutates* is not strictly a name at all, but a form of shorthand for 'the god that my tribe swears by'.[18] The sphere of influence of such local oath-sanctioners would seem to have been very limited indeed. 'Of 374 names attested in the [Gaulish] inscriptions,' Marie-Louise Sjoestedt relates, '305 occur only once.' Sjoestedt also tells how on a stele at Malmaison the god called Tricephalus appears to trample Mercury and Rosmerta, while on a stele at Trier the same god appears to be trampled by figures referred to as 'the three *Matres* of the Treviri'.[19] There seems no purpose to these steles except to emblematise the superiority of one tribe over another. Gods reduced to such functions are surely better described as mascots.

Perhaps it is because of the poverty of Gaulish religion that a few scholars have taken the Norse pantheon instead as their model for the Tuatha Dé Danann. I have myself pointed out similarities between the Dagda and Odin, but I do not believe that many other such parallels can be drawn in respect of function. Jan de Vries, therefore, seeks to draw parallels in respect of martial technique. He compares Lugh, not the Dagda, to Odin, because he fights at a distance; he compares Nuada to Tyr, because he fights with a sword and loses a hand; and he compares Ogma to Thor, because he fights by main force.[20] These parallels are somewhat contrived. Ogma, for instance, does not fight with a hammer, like Thor. More importantly, parallels that rely solely on attributes are unlikely to prove fruitful unless there are other grounds for supposing a close affinity between Norse and Irish religion. Alfred Nutt, indeed, cautiously suggested that 'The belief . . . in the Tuatha De Danann . . . may be a product of that contact of the Irish folk-mind with the hardy and aggressive paganism of Scandinavian invaders of the ninth and tenth centuries.'[21] However, since the belief in the Tuatha Dé Danann easily precedes the Viking invasions, there seems no foundation for this theory.

In short, neither the Norse nor the Gaulish pantheon will shed very much light on the Tuatha Dé Danann. Despite incidental points of contact with foreign gods, they remain a feature of Irish belief and must be explained in Irish terms.

III. The Pantheon

When foreign pantheons have failed, some have sought to marshal the Tuatha Dé into a peculiarly Irish pantheon. Some, indeed, have thought it necessary to construct more than one Irish pantheon. Eleanor Hull is one of these. She discerns one pantheon consisting of 'hoary gods of the primeval time', who include Nemain, Ogma, and Brigit, and one consisting of 'a younger and more attractive race of deities', who include Angus, Manannán, and Lugh. The story of how Angus won Brugh na Boinne from the Dagda, in Hull's interpretation, 'seems to describe symbolically the transference of authority from the elder to the second race of deities'. In principle, this sounds quite plausible, but one would like to know Hull's criteria for distinguishing older from younger gods. Why is Midhir, for instance, included among the former? Like Angus, he is a son of the Dagda, and he is not unattractive.[22]

One's objection, however, is not so much to this pantheon or to that as to the whole notion of a pantheon in connection with the Tuatha Dé; to the notion, in other words, that we have in Ireland one god for the sun, one for the sea, and so forth. To compare the ways in which these functions have been distributed by various scholars is to see that they are just too slippery to hold.

For instance, Máire Mac Neill and Eleanor Hull (among others) consider Lugh to be the sun god, and Hull bases her opinion on Lugh's epithet, *Lámfada*, 'of the long hand, or arm'.[23] For Sjoestedt, however, *Lámfada* 'refers not to [Lugh's] solar nature, as has been supposed, although there is nothing in the mythology to confirm it, but to his manner of warfare' — that same ability to fight at a distance, with spear or with sling, which for de Vries relates Lugh to Odin.[24] Mac Cana considers that possible, but adds that *Lámfada* 'has also been compared with the similar epiphet of the Indian god Savitar, "of the wide hand," who stretches out his hand to control sun, moon and stars and to regulate the succession of day and night'.[25] This endows Lugh with a wider responsibility than would attach to a god who controlled only the sun.

Assuming, then, that Lugh is not the sun god, who is? Whitley Stokes awards the title to Manannan, despite the latter's associations with the sea. In forming this opinion, Stokes relies on a tradition recorded by John O'Donovan, according to which Manannan used to roll 'on three legs like a wheel through the mist'. Stokes compares this to 'the Vedic Vishnu with the three strides, i.e. the rising, the culmination and the setting of the sun'.[26] This, of course, is very like the reasoning which Mac Cana applies to Lugh. T. F. O'Rahilly selects neither Lugh nor Manannan but Áine, from the Tuatha Dé Danann, as a goddess of the sun, and Balor, from the Fomorians, as a god of the sun. He thinks that Balor's one eye symbolises the sun, which is plausible. However, he also thinks that Balor's solar nature is reflected in his name, which O'Rahilly derives (like that of the Fir Bolg) from IE *bhel- 'lightning'. Surely this is more likely to suggest a storm deity?[27]

The title of sun god, then has been liberally distributed. The wisest position, I think, is that of Proinsias Mac Cana. He observes that, to all intents and purposes, the only evidence that the Irish worshipped the sun at all is contained in a 'passage of St. Patrick's *Confession* in which he contrasts worship of the sun . . .with worship of the true Sun which is Christ'. As Mac Cana remarks, in all probability this is only 'one of the theological commonplaces acquired by Patrick through his religious reading and training'.[28] It follows that the attempt to identify any sun god is misguided.

In contrast, Manannan's claim to be a sea god seems comparatively well established. However, even here there are problems. David B. Spaan remarks that Manannan's invocation of a great mist and storm against the Milesians at the time of their invasion 'is the only instance I know of in which Manannan exercises direct control over the sea he is supposed to be god of, though the mist appears with him so much that it might almost be styled a *leitmotif*'.[29] Since Manannan may be met with on land as well as on sea, it is possible, then, that he is the personification of mist, and that his status as sea god is simply a misunderstanding.

Though that is pure speculation, the only one of the Tuatha Dé Danann whose name seems to associate him linguistically with the sea is not Manannan but Nechtan, another name for Nuadu. On the principle that Irish is a q-Celtic language, a substitution of *p* for *ch* will appear to relate Nechtan's name to Neptune's.[30] Krappe relates *Nechtan* also to Ir. *nigim* and Gk. νίζω 'wash' and to names of aquatic monsters in Old and Modern dialectal English and in German. Non-linguistic evidence, on the other hand, is so poor that Krappe is compelled to surmise that Nuadu's silver hand may symbolise water.[31] Besides this, there is only the fact that a well called Nechtan is the source of the River Boyne.[32]

Manannan and Nechtan are not the only candidates for the role of sea god. As though to underline the confusion, de Jubainville considers O'Rahilly's Fomorian sun god, Balor, analogous with Poseidon.[33]

The difficulty, of course, is not confined to sun gods and sea gods. Nuadu, in fact, illustrates very well the hopelessness of trying to attach any particular function to any particular member of the Tuatha Dé Danann. Though Byrne and Krappe think him a sea god, J. M. Flood thinks 'He was the great war-god of the Gael'.[34] To Arthur Bernard Cook, 'Nuada was a sky-god of some sort', and his sword 'may have symbolised the lightning'. For all that, Cook does not abandon the idea that Nuada was 'a river-god or sea-god.' Still not content, he argues that, although there is no evidence 'to show that Nuada was ever specialized as an earth-god', waters flow beneath the earth, and therefore 'he was *ipso facto* subterranean in character'.[35] Between them, Byrne, Krappe, Flood, and Cook have attributed to Nuadu nearly every function one can think of. What has not been considered, I think, is that the names Nuadu (plausibly related to Nodens) and Nechtan (related to Neptune) may be merely borrowed clothing. Irish mythological texts, indeed, may contain a good deal of foreign contamination, especially when they are of late date, like the *Lebor Gabála*. Such contamination must remain confined to detail, however. The myths themselves suggest that the Tuatha Dé Danann do not exercise specific functions. The only obvious exception is Manannan, and even he is in no way bound to the sea.

At least one attempt has been made to construct a pantheon in a way that does not require the distribution of narrowly defined functions. Jan de Vries groups the Tuatha Dé Danann in three broad categories. The first 'est celle de l'autorité suprême; elle a deux aspects, l'un sacerdotal et juridique, l'autre magique et royal; elle est représentée . . . par Nuadu et Lug'. The second function is military, and is represented by Ogma. In the third category we find 'par exemple Goībniu, le forgeron, et Dian Cecht, le médecin'. De Vries makes Nuadu, Lug, and Ogma superior to Goibniu and Dian Cecht because in his view they correspond to Tyr, Odin, and Thor. The rest of the Tuatha Dé Danann, it seems, tend to cluster in the third category, though where Manannan, for instance, is to take his place is left unclear. By this arrangement, the hypothetical parallel with Norse religion is forced into partnership with the mythological system of Georges Dumézil. However, De Vries's own system does not, in fact, agree very well with Dumézil's. The fact that the first function is represented by two gods, not one, is not entirely satisfactory. More serious is the condition of the third function. In Dumézil's system, this is supposed to be the agricultural function. In de Vries's system, it seems merely to embrace every activity not already covered by the first two. In the end, de Vries himself is compelled to admit: 'On dit souvent que les Tuatha Dé Danann sont des dieux de la fertilité . . . Or les arguments en faveur de cette thèse n'abondent pas.'[36] Without such arguments, de Vries's system has little theoretical support.

To sum up, then, if the Tuatha Dé Danann are gods, they are gods without a pantheon. In other words, their functions are not delimited. On the contrary, as Marie-Louise Sjoestedt says, 'General and complete efficiency is the character of all the Celtic gods'; 'we seek for a cosmos and find chaos'.[37]

IV. The Worship of Elves

That is evidently not the end of the matter, for Sjoestedt continues to speak of 'gods'. There is no reason, I suppose, why one should not

Dei Terreni

have gods with undifferentiated functions. It remains to be seen, then, whether the Tuatha Dé Danann are gods of that kind. There are two important items of evidence which suggest that they are. In 'Fiacc's Hymn' occurs the line, 'On Ireland's folk lay darkness: the tribes worshipped elves' (*Fortuáith hErend bai temel, tuatha adortais síde*). This is supported by the *Book of Armagh*, which refers to the sídhe as *dei terreni*.[38]

It should first be noted that in both these sources the word used is *síde*, not *Tuatha Dé Danann*. What renders this evidence suspect, however, is its authorship. Both 'Fiacc's Hymn' and the relevant passage in the *Book of Armagh* are inspired by Christianity of a fairly zealous and missionary kind. How far can they be trusted as evidence for the pre-Christian religion of Ireland? Nora Chadwick supposes that Christian scribes would censor any reference to the worship of the Tuatha Dé Danann. As for the sídhe at least, they clearly have not done so in these works. Surely Christian scribes would be equally likely to make gods of the Tuatha Dé Danann in order to make enemies of them. In spite of this, everywhere else in Early Irish literature, as Chadwick says, the Tuatha Dé 'do not emerge as gods in the usual meaning of the term. They are neither worshipped nor sacrificed to. They are supernatural beings with magical powers.'[39] This, I maintain, is not the result of censorship but the true picture. This can be proven not only in respect of worship and sacrifice, but also in respect of prayer and oaths.

Where there is worship, there will very probably be priests. If anyone exercised the function of priests in Ancient Ireland (which is by no means certain), it can only have been the druids. Now, druids exist among the Tuatha Dé Danann as well as among the Milesians. Already in 'The Second Battle of Mag Tured' we hear of Figol son of Mamos, a druid of the Tuatha Dé.[40] Fairy druids can also be found in 'Cliodna's Wave' and 'Oisin's Mother', among other stories.[41] The Tuatha Dé Danann can scarcely have priests of their own and still be gods. Presumably they do not worship themselves.

There remains the possibility that druids were not priests, and that the Ancient Irish made do without priests, but not without religion. Did they, then, offer sacrifices to the Tuatha Dé? We have already noticed a tradition that sacrifices used to be held on Cnoc Áine. However, this tradition may be inaccurate, for it is certain that other hills were used as places of execution, not of sacrifice. The name of Ardnaree, near Ballina, Co. Mayo definitely means 'hill of the executions.' Knocknarea, Co. Sligo, may have the same meaning, or it may mean 'hill of the kings'. The cairn on the summit is supposed to be that of Queen Maeve, and Eoghan Bel, the last pagan king of Connacht, was buried there after his death in the Battle of Sligo. There is no traditional or historical support for the translation 'hill of the sacrifices,' although that is sometimes offered.[42]

In two Early Irish stories, 'The Intoxication of the Ulstermen' and 'The Destruction of Dinn Rig', there are attempts to kill people by burning them to death in buildings call *bruidne*. Ward Rutherford translates *bruidne* as 'burning buildings in which people are destroyed', with the implication that that is the reason for the buildings' existence, and therefore concludes that these stories contain sacrifices. But there is no mystery about the word *bruiden* (plur. *bruidne*). It means 'hostel'. Arson is a common enough method of murder in any country, and both of these stories contain ample motive for murder without resorting to sacrifice. Rutherford also mentions a Connaught story which 'tells how a maiden had many wooers and how for each suitor a person was chosen from among his community and, at Samain, secretly killed.' The maiden, he concludes, is a goddess, and the persons slain are sacrificial victims. He does not name his story and I do not recognise it, but his summary does not seem to compel any such interpretation.[43]

G. F. Dalton holds ideas similar to Rutherford's, except that he seeks his sacrificial victims among Irish kings. He finds his chief evidence in the story of the death of the High King Eochaid Airemh, who is variously described as having been killed, at Samhain, by the tribe called the Feara Cúl, by the Tuatha Dé Danann, or by the Feara Cúl putting the blame on the Tuatha Dé Dannan. The confusion arises, he argues, because Eochaid was actually killed by the Feara Cúl disguised as the Tuatha Dé. The same theory accounts for the death of Muircertach mac Erca at the hands of 'headless men', 'blue men', and 'goat-headed men'. This is plausible enough, but Dalton runs into difficulty with the tale of 'The Adventures of Nera'. Nera sees Cruachan destroyed by fairies in an attack that turns out to be an illusion. Dalton argues that this is a mock attack. Such attacks would be ceremonially played out at Samhain, 'but might become real and dangerous if the country people had a sense of grievance'. This, too, is plausible, but killing for a grievance is quite different from killing for a sacrifice. All that Dalton has finally proved is that Irish kings were sometimes killed, which is no secret, and not that they were ritually killed.[44] We still have no compelling evidence of sacrifice in Ancient Ireland.

Next we may consider whether the Tuatha Dé Danann receive or answer prayers. One story in 'The Colloquy with the Ancients' may at first sight suggest that they do. Ruidhe, Fiacha, and Eochaid, the sons of the High King Lughaid Menn, on being refused a gift of land by their father, fast for it upon the Tuatha Dé at Brugh na Boinne. Bodhb Derg invites them into the *sídh* and many famous members of theTuatha Dé shower marvellous gifts upon the brothers. The latter live for 150 years and then return to the *sídh* for ever.[45]

Though it is true that in that story the Tuatha Dé grant the prayers of three mortals, there is another story in 'The Colloquy' which is almost the reverse. In this, Artrach, Aedh, and Angus, three sons of Bodhb Derg, seek and receive land from the High King Cormac mac Airt. They stay on it for thirty years, until the death of Cormac, and then return to the Tuatha Dé; so mortals can as well grant the prayers of the Tuatha Dé as the Tuatha Dé can grant theirs. In fact, a third story in 'The Colloquy' suggests that mortals are actually superior in this respect. A fairy kills a certain Dubh mac Treon out of jealousy, because the Tuatha Dé have none to match him for generosity.[46] There is nothing peculiarly divine about generosity and no reason to describe the Tuatha Dé as answering prayers. Like mortals, they merely grant favours.

As for oaths, we have already seen that the type most commonly used in the Ulster Cycle is an impersonal formula: 'I swear by the god that my tribe swears by.' Other oaths do not invoke the Tuatha Dé Danann but the sun and moon or the elements. The only exception that I know of is a poem in which Finn swears by *día tigernmas*, 'the god of lordly beauty'.[47] This god remains anonymous, if not strictly impersonal. It may possibly refer to Angus Óg, for instance, but it may equally refer to Christ. Finn is often depicted as a sort of Prophet of the Gentiles, with pre-Patrician knowledge of the Christian faith.

If, then, the Tuatha Dé Danann are not sworn by, answer no prayers except as mortals may, and receive no sacrifices, they surely are not gods. What is more, we have this virtually confirmed out of their own mouths. In the first place, they are friendly with the missionary saints of Ireland, and it is not often that rival gods establish friendship. While Patrick was fasting on Cruachan Aigli, now Croagh Patrick, he was visited by an innumerable flock of white, mighty birds. According to the seventh century *Breviarum of Tírechán*, these were the souls of all the saints of Ireland, past, present, and future, and according to the ninth century *Vita Tripartita* 'the souls which were to be saved' through Patrick, but according to the *Edinburgh Dinnshenchas* they were birds from the Land of Promise.[48] In 'The Colloquy with the Ancients', Donn mac Midir (presumably a conflation of Eber Donn and Midhir of Brí Leith) gives Patrick command over all the Tuatha Dé Danann.[49] We should also remember the fairy woman in 'The Adventures of Connla the Fair' who prophesies the coming of Patrick to 'annihilate the false law of the druids'.[50]

This friendship may seem rather grudgingly returned by St. Patrick, who admits his intention of banishing the Tuatha Dé Danann to the wild steeps of Ireland. However, he exempts his friend Cascorach, a fairy musician, from this punishment and even promises that he will be admitted to heaven. The strongest example of the lack of rivalry between saints and fairies occurs in the hagiographical tale of 'The Disappearance of Caenchomrac', in which the saint of that name pays frequent visits to a fairy monastery.[51]

Evidence of another sort that the Tuatha Dé are not gods is provided by the *Vita Tripartita*. While washing their hands at the well of Cliabach at Cruachan, Ethne the Fair and Fedelm the Ruddy, daughters of the High King Loegaire mac Néill, are amazed by Patrick's 'clerics in white garments', taking them for 'elves' (*fir síthe*), 'apparitions' (*fantaitsi*), or gods (dat.: *deib*). This clearly implies that elves and gods are not the same thing.[52] Of particular interest is an explicit declaration made by Aillenn, a daughter of Bodb Dearg, in another story of St. Patrick. 'I am not an everliving woman of the Sidhe,' she says, 'but I am of the Tuatha de Danann, having my own body about me.' Thus the Tuatha Dé Danann are not to be confounded with the Sidhe, and are not, apparently, divine. They are, however, more fortunate than humans: 'Everyone that drank at Goibniu's Feast . . . not sickness or wasting comes upon them.' St. Patrick, it seems, does not believe Aillenn, for he sends her 'back to your house among the Sidhe'.[53] Nonetheless, Aillenn's disavowal of divinity is repeated in yet stronger terms by Lugh himself in 'Baile in Scáil'. 'I am not a phantom and I am not a spectre,' he says, 'and I have come after death to be honoured by you, and I am of the race of Adam,' descended from Érimón son of Míl.[54] Lugh's words are echoed by Sin, the evil fairy wife of Muircertach mac Erca. She professes to believe in God and to belong to 'the race of Adam and Eve', although she adds that she can also work miracles.[55] In contrast to the evil Sin, a song in 'The Sick-Bed of Cu Chulainn' seems to imply that the Tuatha Dé are unfallen humanity. Loeg, Cu Chulainn's charioteer describes the fairy Fann as 'a mortal daughter of Adam without sin'.[56] It may well be objected to all of the foregoing passages that they betray an obvious Christian influence. The same cannot be said, however, of 'The Battle of the White Strand', a Fenian tale in which the Tuatha Dé Danann are described as 'another part of the men of Ireland that do not dare to be on the face of the earth, but that live in hidden houses under the earth'.[57]

V. Crom Cruach and Crom Dubh

One argument in favour of the Tuatha Dé's divinity remains to be refuted. It may be urged that men must worship something, and besides the Tuatha Dé there seems nothing else for them to worship in

Ancient Ireland. In fact, it is not true that men must worship something, and I propose that Patrick's mission succeeded so easily because the Irish at that time worshipped little or nothing. This had not always been the case, but the old religion had fallen into disuse. This old religion had nothing to do with the Tuatha Dé Danann.

The ancient Irish god of whom we have the strongest evidence is undoubtedly Crom, or Cenn, Cruach. According to the *Vita Tripartita*, he was the chief idol (*ardídal*) of Ireland, and was situated at Mag Slecht, in the company of twelve lesser idols. Patrick struck him a miraculous blow with his staff. The imprint of the staff remained in Crom Cruach, while the earth swallowed up the other twelve idols as far as their heads.[58] Although apparently dependent on the *Vita Tripartita*, the *Book of Leinster Dinnshenchas* adds that great human sacrifices were made to Crom Cruach.[59] Much later, in the seventeenth century, Geoffrey Keating states that the worship of Crom Cruach was initiated by Tighernmas 'about a hundred years after the arrival of the Gaels.' Also in the seventeenth century, *The Annals of the Four Masters* accord Crom Cruach a mention under the Year of the World 3656.[60]

We hear also of Crom Dubh, who may be a different god or may be the same as Crom Cruach. Some similarity seems apparent in a legend 'recorded in Iar-Chonnacht, the district between Cashla Bay and Galway town'. In this, Crom Dubh features as 'a tyrant, who demanded of his tenants that they should burn to ashes on his birthday the best beeves they owned; after his death the bonfire was transferred to St. John's Eve'. It is not much, but this Crom Dubh and Crom Cruach do have oppressive sacrifices in common. Crom Dubh is generally presented more favourably, however. In traditions of St. Patrick he is quite distinct from Crom Cruach. Normally he appears as a pagan first, and as Patrick's 'strong man' or champion after his conversion by the saint. In a legend recorded near Downpatrick Head, Co. Mayo, he nonetheless retains considerable power: 'the people thought it was he who regulated night and day and the change of the seasons.' This may well be true of Crom Cruach as well, if Douglas Hyde is correct in his surmise that the twelve lesser idols surrounding Crom Cruach were intended to represent the twelve months. However, Crom Dubh's special care was almost certainly the harvest. In the region of Lough Gur, Co. Limerick, it used to be said that 'Crom Dubh brought the first sheaf of wheat to Ireland on his shoulder; he stooped under the weight, hence the name 'Crom'. More significantly, the first Sunday in August, traditionally the beginning of harvest, was until quite recently widely known in Ireland as Crom Dubh Sunday. 'In the Ordnance Survey Name Books for the parish of Clahaan (Cloghane), dated 1841, there is the interesting statement that Croum Dhu was the god of the harvest whom the pagans worshipped until they were converted by Saint Brendan.' The unexpected mention of Brendan, rather than Patrick, here suggests that the distinction between Crom Cruach and Crom Dubh may have a regional or devotional origin. Possibly the old god was known as Crom Cruach in those areas converted to St. Patrick and as Crom Dubh in those areas converted by St. Brendan. Although both names now occur in connection with Patrick, Crom Cruach does not occur in connection with Brendan.[61]

Besides literary allusions and oral traditions, there is some further evidence for the worship of Crom Dubh and Crom Cruach. The idols on Mag Slecht have long disappeared, but it is possible that a wooden figure found in Relaghan Bog, Co. Cavan, and now in the National Museum of Ireland, is intended to represent Crom Dubh.[62] Less tenuously, there is a well sacred to Cruach in the townland of Ballon, Co. Carlow.[63]

Of other gods we do not hear very much. There was apparently 'a special idol-god, named *Kermand Kelstach*, that presided over Ulster. This stone-idol was still preserved in the porch of the cathedral of Clogher down to the time of the annalist Cathal Maguire (died 1498), as he himself tells us.'[64] The existence of a god Bél has also been proposed, but of this I am extremely sceptical. Keating imagined him to be not just any god but 'the arch-god, whom they adored', and found his name preserved in *Bealtaine*, the First of May. Cormac mac Cuillenáin, however, explains *Bealtaine* 'as if it were Bil-tene, "goodly fire," from the fires which the druids made on that day through which to drive the cattle'.[65] Proinsias Mac Cana, in our day, follows Cormac almost exactly, but proposes 'bright fire' instead of 'goodly fire', reading *bel* as an adjective meaning 'shining' or 'brilliant'.[66] David Fitzgerald, in the nineteenth century, read *bel* as a contraction of *bile* 'tree', and rendered *Lá Beltene* as if it were *Lá Bile-tenidh*, 'Day of the Fire-Tree'. The name, he suggested, 'came from the bonefire and May-tree usage'. Under the Year of the World 3503 the Four Masters record a Battle of Bile-Tineadh, which was 'perhaps nothing', thought Fitzgerald, 'but the fight at May between Summer and Winter which is represented by a mock battle on Celtic ground on May Day yet'.[67] In place-names, like Beltrá, *bel* may easily carry any of the meanings here suggested: 'goodly', 'bright', or 'tree'. Where the name Bél appears elsewhere, as apparently it does in 'the oldest version of 'The Wooing of Emer'',[68] if it is of any significance, it may well be a Christian interpolation, inspired chiefly by the biblical Baal.

Crom Cruach and Crom Dubh would thus seem to have been the pre-eminent gods of pre-Christian Ireland, or perhaps the only gods. However, all the evidence indicates that their cult was already

Dei Terreni

obsolesent, if not obsolete, at the time of Patrick's mission. It may be true, as the Christian propagandist tells us, that Crom Cruach was the recipient of sacrifices. His second name may mean 'bloody', which is suggestive of sacrifice.[69] But is is scarcely possible that human sacrifice on the scale indicated by the *Book of Leinster* took place in anything close to historical times. If it had, we should hear a great deal more about it. As P. W. Joyce points out, there is not a word about human sacrifice in St. Patrick's *Confession*, nor in Muirchu's nor Colgan's Lives of Patrick, nor in Tirecan's annotations, nor in the *Vita Tripartita*. All of these sources are older than the *Book of Leinster Dinnshenchas* and all would certainly have mentioned human sacrifice had they known of it. Neither do Keating, O'Flaherty, the Four Masters, or any other historian of the sixteenth or seventeenth century mention human sacrifice, which plainly suggests that they disbelieved the Book of Leinster.[70] So Crom Cruach had long gone without sacrifice.

It seems that he had also long gone without care and attention, for easily the most plausible translation of *Crom* is 'the stooped one'. This suggests that the idol was leaning away from the upright. In the alternative form of the name, Cenn Cruach, *Cenn* means 'head'. This may suggest that the idol had sunk in the earth as far as its head. We are told that the lesser idols sank that far when smitten by Patrick. If the idol were still revered, its upkeep could not be so neglected. Furthermore, the names indicative of the idols' neglect, Crom Cruach, Cenn Cruach, Crom Dubh, are the only names we have. They cannot have been the original names, but they have completely displaced them. This suggests that the idols' neglect was a thing of very long standing. This is further confirmed by the entire failure of early non-hagiographical literature to mention Crom Dubh or Crom Cruach.

One may conclude then that by Patrick's time the Irish had fallen into an interregnum of religion that made them ripe for any suggestion. What is of more importance is that neither Crom Cruach nor Crom Dubh, nor, for that matter, Kermand Kelstach nor Bél, have the faintest connection with the Tuatha Dé Danann. Whatever gods the Irish ever had, then, the Tuatha Dé Danann were not among them. They are not called gods, they cannot be defined as gods, they receive no worship, and their connections with foreign gods are essentially fortuitous. Such divine attributes and characteristics as they have are likewise essentially fortuitous. In short, they are not gods.

6. THE TRIBES OF THE GODDESS DANU

The third and final theory of fairy origins looks for the Tuatha Dé Danann neither on Olympus nor in Hades, but on earth in distant times. According to this theory, the Tuatha Dé represent a distorted and exaggerated folk-memory of an ancient and vanished race of mortal beings. Who these mortals were and where they came from is a question that has been very variously answered. Not surprisingly, those proposing answers include a considerable lunatic fringe. Theosophists believe the druids were Atlanteans, and no doubt believe something similar of the Tuatha Dé; Freemasons allegedly believe that the Tuatha Dé were of their own fraternity.[1] No doubt there are those today who believe they were extraterrestrials. Such theories, of course, cannot be conclusively disproven, and indeed they have as much — or rather, as little — evidence behind them as some that have gained more serious consideration. However, they are scarcely worth our time. More influential was David MacRitchie, who proposed in two books, *The Testimony of Tradition* (1890) and *Fians, Fairies and Picts* (1893), that the fairies were a pygmy race originating in the wilder regions of Northern Europe. However, MacRitchie too is now discredited, and the whole theory that the fairies are a folk-memory of a mortal race has rather fallen into desuetude. The minority that has continued to uphold it, like Julius Pokorny, has tended to perpetuate the eccentricity that has always marked this theory.

Nonetheless, I will myself propose a form of this theory. The error hitherto involved, I believe, has been an error of over-simplification. Even MacRitchie, though he distinguished several 'national' origins for the fairies, still perceived the fairies in Ireland (and Scotland) as essentially homogeneous. If, on the contrary, two races of fairies are distinguished, the problem becomes more amenable to solution. I believe it is possible to do this, and to trace to some extent the real, as opposed to the mythological, history of the fairies.

I. The Tuatha Dé Danann and the Sídhe

I have already cited a number of passages from Early Irish literature in which a distinction is made between the Tuatha Dé Danann and the

Sídhe. For example, when Lugh approaches the assembly of the Tuatha Dé Dannan on Balor's Hill, he brings with him an 'army . . . from the fairy-mounds'. It is with this army, and not with the army of Nuadu, the king of the Tuatha Dé, that Lugh assists Bodb Derg to repel the Fomorians. In the alternative version of the coming of Lugh, when he seeks admission to Tara on the grounds that he is a harper, he is refused because the harper 'Abcan son of Bicelmos whom the Tuatha De Dannan chose in the fairy-mounds' is already present. Thus there are already people in the fairy-mounds before the Feast of Age. After their defeat by the Milesians, the Tuatha Dé Danann go to join these people. As 'The Intoxication of the Ulstermen' says: 'The Tuatha De Dannan went into the hills and fairy places, so that they spoke with the fairy folk underground.'[2] Naturally, this is no new discovery. It was noticed by Eugene O'Curry, for instance.[3] Douglas Hyde adds two important points. He remarks that, because of their alliance, the Tuatha Dé Danann are 'confounded with the *Sidhe*'; and he remarks that, even after their withdrawal, the Tuatha Dé maintained some social intercourse with the Milesians, extending to occasional intermarriage.[4]

In short, omitting the Fir Bolg and the Fomorians, what the myths give us is the history of three races. One of these, the Milesians, defeated another, the Tuatha Dé Danann, who then took refuge with the third, the Sídhe. Behind this history pressures of population are discernible. P. W. Joyce has demonstrated that Ireland was very populous in early times. He quotes Caesar to the effect that, in the first century B.C., the inhabitants of Britain were 'countless and their buildings . . . exceedingly numerous'. Joyce adds that 'there seems no reason why Ireland should have been behindhand in this respect at that time and subsequently'.[5] When the numbers of the invading Milesians were added to those of the Tuatha Dé Danann, conflict over land would have been inevitable.

Given their defeat, it is probable that the Tuatha Dé Danann were less numerous than the Milesians. Since the Sídhe seem elusive even to the Tuatha Dé Danann, it is probable that they were less numerous still. If follows from this that the population of Ireland would not have been evenly distributed. Secure in their numbers until the Milesian invasion, the Tuatha Dé Danann would have congregated in the temperate and fertile valleys. Later, the Milesians would have done the same thing. The less numerous races, first the Sídhe and then the Tuatha Dé Danann, would have dwelt in more defensible places. The mountain-tops are the most obvious as well as forests and other wild places. There they could have remained secret, remote, and mysterious, while still able to visit the valleys and maintain some contact with the dominant race. Denied recourse to agriculture, they must have lived by hunting, fishing, and fowling. This last may explain the prominence of feathers, both as clothing and roofing material, in descriptions of Tír na nÓg.

It may be objected to this that we have seen the Tuatha Dé and the Sídhe described as living, not on mountain-tops, but underground. This is easily answered. They are not supposed to live very far under ground, but, as the texts say, in 'fairy-mounds', or else in souterrains. This raises a fresh objection, however. The fairy-mounds, or *sídhe*, are by no means confined to mountain-tops, but are common even in fertile plains and valleys. The answer to this is that the association of the fairies with these mounds is not so close as many suppose, and that 'fairy-*mound*', as opposed to 'fairy-*hill*', may not render the original meaning of *sídh*. For the sake of clarity, let us refer to the artificial mounds, for the time being, by their name of 'raths'. An informant of mine, an educated man originally from Inishmurray Island but now resident in Sligo,[6] tells me that the fairies are more associated with rath-*like* natural formations, such as Ben Bulben Head, than with artificial raths, and, what is more, that only these are properly to be called *sídhe*. Dermot MacManus states that 'in every trial of witches in which fairies were mentioned as living in the earth, it was invariably in a small natural hill that they dwelt and *not* in a barrow.'[7] As there were hardly any witch trials in Ireland, MacManus may be quietly introducing Scottish evidence, but it is significant nonetheless. Natural formations of this kind are likely to be found in mountainous country. Ben Bulben Head, for instance, though a small hill in itself, is perched on top of a large mountain by Irish standards.

The facts remain that raths are frequently called *sídhe* and associated with the fairies. To dismiss this as a confusion will be scarcely satisfactory, as, after all, raths do exist and their very existence calls for some explanation. A statement by one of Lady Gregory's informants (using yet another word for 'rath') may be helpful: 'There's a forth near our house, but it's not the good people that are in it, only the old inhabitants of Ireland shut up up there below.'[8] This informant clearly belongs to the minority who do not associate the raths with fairies. On the other hand, since I am arguing that the good people *are* the old inhabitants of Ireland, it may seem that we have not gained much ground. However, I take this informant to mean that the old inhabitants of Ireland are buried in the rath. Who built the raths and when is a puzzle that I must leave to the archaeologists, but it is probable at least that they were not intended as dwellings but as tombs. Human remains have been recovered from a good many of them. Souterrains, also, have other and more obvious uses than as dwelling places.[9] However, both raths and souterrains will give shelter, and raths in particular are eminently defensible in the short run. There are thus at least two ways in which the Sídhe might have used the raths. Bands of the Sídhe dwelling in dangerous areas might have used them as redoubts in times of emergency. Alternatively, bands or individuals of the Sídhe might have squatted, as it were, in the raths during times of peace.

The second alternative, which I am inclined to think more probable, suggests that the Sídhe were a highly primitive, almost feral race. By any civilised standards, raths and souterrains are not desirable dwellings. They are certainly not compatible with the luxury and splendour attributed to the Tuatha Dé Danann, and this race's connection with the raths must therefore be more tenuous than the Sídhe's. It is likely that they sought refuge there in the hour of their emergency, when they were received as refugees by the Sídhe, but that they remained in the raths for as little time as possible.

If the foregoing argument be correct, the Sídhe were a race of secretive lurkers in waste places and underground chambers who must always have seemed remote and mysterious to other inhabitants of Ireland. The Tuatha Dé Danann were a pre-Celtic race who withdrew from the Milesians into the mountains and wild places. At first they continued to intermarry with the Milesians, but as time went by, and their numbers grew fewer, they too must have come to seem increasingly remote and mysterious, and so their transformation to fairies was effected. What must still be determined is what relations were like between the Tuatha Dé and the Sídhe before the coming of the Gael, and why the Tuatha Dé are regarded as splendid.

II. The Charm of Iron

That the Tuatha Dé Danann preceded the Gael in Ireland is not, I think, in question. That the Sídhe preceded even the Tuatha Dé seems to me very likely. These would have been the truly aboriginal inhabitants of Ireland. First impressions of the Tuatha Dé, then, would have been formed by the Sídhe. If the Sídhe were as primitive as I suppose, it would not have taken much to impress them. They seem to have been most impressed by the Tuatha Dé's possession of iron. In the First Battle of Moytura, Bres, the champion of the Tuatha Dé, and Sreng, the champion of the Fir Bolg, each admire the other's spears. Sreng's are thick and heavy, with edges but no points; Bres's are thin and hard-pointed. Although this is not stated, it seems likely that Sreng's are tipped with stone, and Bres's with iron.[10] If that is true, what we have here is an encounter between an iron age and a stone age people. Now, although the stone age people are called the Fir Bolg, it seems unlikely, in view of their greater historicity, that the Fir Bolg were in Ireland before the Tuatha Dé, whatever the *Lebor Gabála* may say.[11] It may be, then, that the Fir Bolg are here confused with the Sídhe.

The strong impression made on these stone age people has been perpetuated in superstitions regarding iron down to the present day. A comparatively early example of these superstitions is provided by the story of 'The Enchanted Cave of Keshcorran'. In the prose version of this tale, Conaran mac Imidel, king of the Tuatha Dé Danann of the region of Keshcorran, is annoyed by the hunting of the Fianna, and sends his three daughters to take revenge on Finn. It is some confirmation of my argument regarding the Tuatha Dé's habitat that these hags do not live in a rath but in a mountain cave. At the entrance of this cave, 'Upon three crooked and wry sticks of holly they hung as many heathenish bewitched hasps of yarn, which they began to reel off left-handwise'. When Finn and Conan pass through the hasps, they lose their strength and are bound. Significantly, one of the hags is called Iaran, 'iron'.[12] In the verse version of the same tale, iron is the dominant motif. The hags do not hang up hasps of yarn. Instead, 'Rough grey iron of wizardy they had mounted on poles'. No other magical procedures, like the left-handwise (widdershins) motion of the prose version, are necessary.[13] Here, then, iron is clearly associated both with the Tuatha Dé Danann and with baleful properties.

The magical properties of iron are still recognised in many ways. Sick cattle, for instance, may be cured by a 'medicine' which consists of holy water in which various insoluble objects have been left. These objects always include 'elf-stones', or little round pebbles of quartz, and something made of iron, generally a nail. An iron horse-shoe nailed to the bottom of a churn will ensure that the butter comes, 'for an iron horse-shoe, or indeed an iron article of any kind, is looked upon as a potent charm to keep fairies away'.[14] Conversely, as an old gentleman from Co. Roscommon told me,[15] to lend iron while churning — that is, to send it away — prevents the butter coming. On Inishmurray, according to Dr. A, if a person was going on a dangerous journey — generally delivering illegal *poitín* to the mainland — the iron tongs would be thrown at his heels as he left the door to protect him from harm. Iron is used in many ways to prevent the fairies from taking changelings. For instance, the fairies cannot steal an infant with a needle in its clothes because they perceive the needle as 'a great beam of iron, too heavy to lift'.[16]

The difference between iron in the Fenian tale and iron in these items of folklore is that, in the former, it is the fairies who exercise the magic, while in the latter it is exercised against them. The explanation is, I believe, that the fairies who use iron are the Tuatha Dé Danann, who have always used it. The fairies who fear iron are the Sídhe, whom the Tuatha Dé Danann defeated with it.

III. Gold

Their possession of iron will explain why the Tuatha Dé Danann were considered awesome, but not why they were considered splendid. Iron is not a very lustrous metal. It may be that they also possessed gold. Lady Wilde, indeed, asserts positively that they did, and that their predecessors did not. She offers archaeological evidence for the latter assertion, but none for the former.[17] It may be that she relies simply on the Mythological Cycle, which does attribute gold to the Tuatha Dé, but was, of course, written by people who themselves possessed gold. A small point that may be of more significance is that in one of Lady Gregory's folk-tales gold, not iron, is the charm against the fairies.[18] If this tradition also originated among the Sídhe, then the Tuatha Dé Danann did possess gold.

IV. The Sídhe

Who, then, were the Tuatha Dé and the Sídhe? As for the latter, it is only fair to notice first a passage in 'The Second Battle of Mag Tured', according to which the Sídhe seem identical with the Fomorians. It speaks of Bres gathering against the Tuatha Dé, when they would depose him, 'the champions of the fairy mound, the Fomorians'. However, this passage flies in the face of all other evidence. Indeed, in 'The Fate of the Children of Tuirenn' the men of the fairy-mounds fight against Bres and the Fomorians, on the side of Lugh.[19]

MacRitchie's theories have less to do with mythology. They are something of a jumble, and fairly easily disproved. A point of entry is provided by Elizabeth Andrews, one of MacRitchie's chief disciples, who quotes a letter from her colleague Mann Harbison to the effect that 'the souterrains "were constructed by a diminutive race, probably allied to the modern Lapps, who seem to be the survivors of a widely distributed race"'. These souterrain-builders were presumably the Sídhe (in Harbison's view), and so the Sídhe were diminutive Lapps. This theory is supported, Andrews thinks, by the fact that in Donegal there is a tradition of a small, yellow race called Finns.[20] This is naive. 'Finn', as the name of a people, is an English word; in Irish, *finn* means only 'white', or 'fair', and presumably refers to these people's 'yellow' complexion, or else to their hair. Finns and Lapps are not the same anyway, but MacRitchie and his school seldom observe precise ethnic distinctions. They also number Picts in the same race as Finns and Lapps. Here the theory becomes untenable, for Picts survive as a separate people in Ireland and Scotland well into historical times. They are called *Pictae* in Latin and *Cruithin* in Irish. They were converted by St. Columba.[21] In 'The Destruction of Da Derga's Hostel', Picts and fairies appear side by side.[22] It is scarcely possible that a race could exist as a folk-memory at the same time as it existed as a living reality, and therefore the Picts cannot be the Sídhe.

MacRitchie's case is further undermined by his own assumption that the fairies were pygmies. With the exception of the leprechaun, Irish fairies never have been pygmies; neither, of course, have Finns, Lapps, or Picts. Evans Wentz, citing a certain Dr. Windle's introduction to Tyson's *Philological Essay concerning the Pygmies of the Ancients*, adds the following points: there is no evidence that any pygmy race ever inhabited the area; there are giants and dwarfs as well as fairies in folklore; and the Lapps of today have a fairy faith of their own, and so cannot be the fairies.[23]

Whoever the Sidhe may have been, there is good evidence to establish their relationship with later inhabitants of Ireland, including the Picts, The genealogies in the *Book of Leinster* mention an Ulster chieftain called Fiatach Finn, whose responsibility, they say, 'is . . . to warn the Fairy stations' (*Is leis arrobad for sídib*). Fiatach Finn was a Pict. Four of the 'Fairy stations' are named in the document, and John Rhys located three of them in mountainous situations which reminded him of aboriginal reservations. Thus, he suggested, the Sídhe attached themselves to Pictish chieftains in a vassal relationship. To this he added an invaluable analogy: 'Compare the Semang dwarfs living in the jungles of the Malay peninsula, who are usually invisible to strangers of importance, but can be readily summoned by their Malay lords or their herdsmen, as they are termed.'[24] Here is the tradition of the Sídhe's ability to render themselves invisible explained at a stroke. It further follows that their special relationship with certain Pictish chieftains would not diminish but enhance their reputation as fairies with the rest of the population.

We have already seen that Lugh summons the men of the fairy mounds in just the way that Fiatach Finn does. It seems, then, that the Tuatha Dé Danann exercised authority over the Sídhe before the Picts did. At a later date certain chieftains of the Gael seem to have exercised the same authority, for, according to *The Triumphs of Turlough*, as late as 1317, Donchad O'Brien, raising an army in Clare, summoned 'even the man in a souterrain (*uamh*) of a fort'. The fact that Donchad was reduced to summoning a single man shows the extent to which the Sídhe had declined in numbers. The same account may also provide evidence of the declining numbers of the Tuatha Dé Danann. On his way to battle with his army, Donchad encountered 'Bronach of Burren, of the Tuatha Dé Danann', who gave warning of death. It is possible that the man from the souterrain is historical, while Bronach is a folkloric embellishment of the story. This is the more possible because of Bronach's prophetic function.[25] But alternatively the Sídhe may have transferred their loyalty from the Tuatha Dé Danann to the O'Briens because the Tuatha Dé were no longer numerous enough to command an army. In this locale, the Picts may have played no part, as Clare, unlike Ulster, was never a Pictish colony.

Bronach of Burren, then, may well be one of the very last members of a race on the verge of extinction. The Sídhe may have proved more tenacious. Katharine Brigg's description of a brownie as a 'shaggy aboriginal hanging round the farm'[26] is so reminiscent of the Sídhe that it is hard to resist an identification. Brownies are reported in Scotland at least as late as the nineteenth century, so it is possible that in that country they cling unobtrusively to existence even now. In Ireland, brownies are unknown except among Ulstermen of Scottish extraction, but the cluricaun (in particular) does bear some resemblance to the brownie. The name of the Sídhe is not extinct; it is just possible that the people are not either.

V. The Tuatha Dé Danann

If the Sídhe are aboriginal, the Tuatha Dé Danann are not, so we are free to speculate as to their place of origin. The *Lebor Gabála*, or course, assigns them an origin in Greece, for reasons we have dealt with. It is possible that by sheer chance the scribes of the *Lebor Gabála* have hit upon the truth. On balance, however, I find it more likely that the Tuatha Dé Danann were Phoenicians.

In favour of the Greeks, there is the fact that the Celts were well acquainted with them in classical times, and enjoyed a close anti-Phoenician alliance with them from c. 500 to 300 B.C.[27] Though the Celts themselves were far from barbarian, they could not have failed to be impressed by Athenian civilisation. It is possible, then, that the Tuatha Dé Danann are a folk-memory of the Greeks. To my mind, the weakness of this hypothesis is that it supposes no physical connection between the Greeks and Ireland, whereas the Tuatha Dé Danann are intimately associated with Irish topography. Any Greek colony in Ireland would certainly have left historical and archaeological traces.

It is more plausible that the enemies of the Greeks and Celts, the Phoenicians, set foot in Ireland before the Celts did. It is well known that the Phoenicians traded with Cornwall for tin. They may have gone further afield to Ireland for gold. If the Sídhe were impressed by gold, it is not likely that they themselves possessed it. Thus, the Phoenicians would have had to mine it. Ancient mine-workings are still to be seen in Ireland, and there are still traces of gold in the Ox Mountains. We can imagine, then, a people already splendid by the standards of the Sídhe extracting from earth and smelting from rock a metal more splendid still. This process would be akin to magic to a stone age people, and the Sídhe would have looked on in awe. A mining camp of this sort, unlike a Greek colony, would not leave conspicuous archaeological remains. As we know so much less of the Phoenicians than of the Greeks, it is correspondingly more plausible that we should be ignorant of Phoenician penetration of Ireland. Though these mining camps would have been temporary in nature, it is possible that individuals became lost, or were deliberately marooned, or simply decided to stay. These individuals would be the first ancestors of the Tuatha Dé Danann.

VI. Fairy Speech

So far, this is pure speculation, but there is a little evidence to support it, which has to do with fairy speech. On this, there are three conflicting traditions. According to one, the fairies simply speak Irish. 'What language had they? Irish of course, what else would they talk?' said Mrs. Sheridan, a self-confessed ex-changeling, to Lady Gregory.[28] It is obvious that Mrs. Sheridan's imagination could not cope with the question. According to Kirk, the fairies 'speak but little, and that by way of whistling, clear, not rough.'[29] Kirk is borne out by another of Lady Gregory's informants, according to whom the fairies' speech 'was like the hissing of a geese, and there was one very big man, that seemed the master of them, and his talk was like you'll hear in a barrel when it's being rolled'.[30] This seems to be the tradition incorporated in the folk-tale of 'Teig O'Kane and the Corpse' as well: 'he heard them speaking amongst themselves, talking and crying out, and screaming like a flock of sea-gulls; and if he was to save his soul he never understood as much as one word of what they were saying.' Besides this, however, the fairies have another tongue that Teig can understand, presumably Irish.[31] The third tradition agrees that the fairies have a language of their own. It is extremely difficult to learn, and mortal captives who do learn it are 'expelled from the fairy realm, lest they should know any important secrets regarding the mysterious sprites.' According to this tradition, however, the language is quite unlike 'the hissing of geese'. A few words are known. The language of the British fairies includes the words *yyor*,[32] 'water', and *halgein*, 'salt'. Both of these words are cognate with Greek, but also with Welsh, so little is proved. In an Irish story occur the words *Tatther Rura*, apparently meaning 'Open, door!' These words are not obviously cognate with any language.[33] Other words recorded in Ireland, however, are more significant. The words *Hugga, hugga salach!* were spoken when 'dirty water was thrown out of doors . . . as a warning to the fairies not to get their clothes wet'.[34] *Salach* is simply the Irish for 'dirty', but *hugga* looks very much like Gk. υδορ, 'water,' again, with lenition of medial *d*, as would be normal in Irish. So in Ireland as well as in Wales one version of the fairy speech appears related to Greek.

Although this appears to tilt the weight of evidence back in favour of the Greeks, against the Phoenicians, it need not necessarily do so. Any Phoenician merchant would have spoken Greek, and might, like Romans of the Eastern Empire, have preferred to do so. Alternatively, those left behind in Ireland by the Phoenicians could have been runaway Greek slaves or marooned Greek captives.

The other language, consisting of whistles, hisses, and grunts, may have been the language of the Sídhe. Such non-vocal languages are not uncommon outside the Indo-European area, as witness, for instance, Zulu and Kiowa-Apache.

The Tuatha Dé Danann, then, were mortals, but it remains true that they do exhibit a few characteristics of gods and of the spirits of the dead. One might say that they are a combination of mortals, gods, and ghosts, but it is truer to say that they have transcended this combination. In the earliest surviving tradition, the Tuatha Dé Danann have already become an independent imaginative creation: not gods, nor ghosts, nor mortals. They are nothing but themselves. They are fairies.

PART TWO:
NA DAOINE SÍDHE

7. THE FAIRY FAITH IN TRANSITION

Although the Irish fairy faith has enjoyed an uninterrupted existence, it falls into two distinct periods. This is dictated by our sources of evidence. The ancient fairy faith is expressed by conscious artists, and we find it in the Early Irish manuscripts; the modern fairy faith is expressed by the folk, and we find it in orally collected folklore. With very few exceptions, however, oral folklore has been deliberately collected for only about 150 years. For centuries before that we have only the Gaelic poets to rely on, and the value of their evidence is much diminished by their reactionary attitude towards their art. Although they speak of fairies, they intentionally speak of them as their pre-Conquest forebears would have done, and not as their contemporaries would. While, therefore, the poets add to our knowledge of the ancient fairy faith, on the fairy faith of their own times their evidence is unreliable to the point of invalidity. Writers like Robert Kirk do fitfully illuminate the development of the fairy faith between the decline of Gaelic letters and the beginning of the systematic study of folklore. On the whole, however, this development can only be inferred. To resume a detailed study, then, we must pass on to the nineteenth and twentieth centuries.

In the nineteenth century, the fairy faith appears in some ways remarkably true to its ancient self, but in others much transformed. For the transformations that have occurred, two causes present themselves: the long oppression of the country, and the long-sustained influence of the Church. In ancient times, a knowledge of the fairies was part of a liberal education. The Church, in the long run, has naturally sought to impart another kind of education, while the British government was disinclined to encourage any sort of Irish education. Under such circumstances, the fairy faith has naturally grown confused. Among other things, the fairies are now divided into a multiplicity of types. On the other hand, even foreign oppression and clerical influence have their positive side. In some ways, both have contributed to the preservation of the fairy faith, even while casting it into a new form.

It may be thought, for instance, that the fairy faith continued to appeal to the peasantry partly because it constituted a body of knowledge not shared with the oppressor. Such knowledge was the key to a secret kingdom that still remained free. Thus, after the Flight of the Earls (1607), only the fairies remained to form a native, and therefore acceptable, ruling class in Ireland. Such a perception of the fairies is indicated by their Irish name *na daoine uasail* (literally 'the noble people') and their English name, 'the gentry'. Here, however, emerges one of those differences between poets and people. The fairies as perceived by the poets might constitute a ruling class in any country, for they are still the old nobility of the Tuatha Dé Danann: Angus Óg, Lugh, Manannan, and so forth. Among the people, on the contrary, nothing is more apparent than the decline of the Tuatha Dé Danann. That is the one name for the fairies hardly ever encountered in modern folklore. On the other hand, in Irish the name *na daoine sídhe* ('the people of the *sídh*') is probably more common than any. It is the uncouth aboriginals who have endured. If, then, the fairies remain a sort of nobility, they are strictly a peasant nobility. The splendour of the Tuatha Dé Danann is gone. The people, in other words, have not been the only victims of Ireland's oppression. As they have been reduced to a state of squalor, they have dragged their companions the fairies down with them.

The influence of the Church has been of another kind. Of course, even many Early Irish stories betray a Christian as well as a fairy colouring. From that alone, we may see thah the Church in Ireland has always been more powerful to build than to destroy. The Druidic system itself suffered none of that violent suppression which Christianity has perpetrated against its rivals in other lands. So far from fighting Druidism, the Church was much influenced by it. Charles Plummer points out that many of the Ancient Irish were converted *en masse*, and that 'conversion in masses involves, almost necessarily, the retention of a large measure of heathenism'.[1] The consequence is as Yeats describes it: 'Behind all Irish history hangs a great tapestry, even Christianity had to accept it and be itself pictured there. Nobody looking at its dim folds can say where Christianity begins and Druidism ends . . .'[2]

In the preservation of Druidism, the Church could be active, not just acquiescent. Keating mentions a quaint example: 'There was a priest in Tir Chonail in the time of Columcille who built or erected a church of precious stones, and he made an altar of glass therein, and he had images of the sun and moon set up in the church.'[3] It was, of course, by the sun and moon that the pagan Irish swore. In this case, the perpetuation of Druidism may be attributed to the ignorance of the priest; in general, however, the cause was quite the reverse. The old Druidic schools, which taught poetry, history, genealogy, and law, far from being suppressed by the Church, were, by the eighth century,

The Fairy Faith in Transition

incorporated into the monastic 'cities' side by side with the monastic schools.[4] Though the fairy faith was not taught as such at these schools, neither poetry, genealogy, nor history could have been understood without it.

This state of affairs was not to last. Whether the Church would have tolerated it indefinitely, we cannot tell. In the event, it was the Vikings who finished it. Ironically, the Druidic schools, or their descendants the bardic schools, outlived the monastic schools. The Church itself, of course, remained. It now found itself, not in conflict with the bardic schools, but not in harmony with them either. Certain aspects of the Christian religion would not conform to the general framework of the fairy faith, as still remembered in the bardic schools. The attempt to find room for these new beliefs within the old system threw the fairy faith into confusion. Particularly hard to assimilate were the belief in angels and the concern of the Church with the fate of the soul after death.

The consequences of this will be considered in chapter ten. What matters for now is simply that the chaos which in ancient times we found instead of a cosmos is now only further confounded. Folklorists have hitherto sought to impose some system of order, of classification, upon the fairies. I too shall seek to impose such order as I can, but the point to be proved is not merely that previous systems are inadequate to the facts, but that in the final analysis all systems are misguided. The fairies are capricious by nature, and mock all attempts to reduce them to order.

I. The Immortality of the Sídhe

Before proceeding to enumerate the various types of modern fairy, I will summarise such generalisations as can be made about them all. It is here that the similarities between the ancient and modern fairies are most evident. To begin with, the tradition of their immortality betrays the same contradications, or paradoxes, as it did in old times: the fairies are stated to be immortal, and yet they seem to die. On closer examination, however, this contradiction may be more apparent than real. Often, the fairies are said to possess, not immortality, but only great longevity. Kirk wrote in the seventeenth century that 'They live much longer than wee, yet die at last, or least, vanish from that State.'[5] The term of the fairies' longevity is frequently set at the Day of Judgment. It is not surprising if such longevity is confused with immortality. However, some accounts and stories would indicate that even in the meantime fairies can be killed. When they are killed, they often turn to slime or jelly.

The fact that the fairies are nonetheless supposed to be immortal, at least as the world turns, and yet are so rarely seen, may account for the tradition of their departure from Ireland. The most recent date given for this departure is apparently 5 January 1839, 'The Night of the Big Wind',[6] though the tradition is much older. On the other hand, the fairies have been sighted many times since 1839. They are truly a vanishing people, not a vanished one: always going, but never gone.

II. The Stature of the Sídhe

With the exception of the leprechaun, the fairies even today are seldom supposed to be very small, contrary to popular belief outside Ireland. Even when they are depicted as small, this is only by comparison with the average mortal adult. Thus, although they are described in one anecdote as 'little people', this is immediately qualified by the words, 'about the size of a child of ten years'.[7] Nor does smallness imply delicacy. The Ulster 'grogan', for instance, though 'low of stature', has 'broad shoulders' and is 'very strong'.[8] Even qualified smallness is unusual, however. Evans Wentz, in particular, was told again and again that the fairies were 'as big as any living people'.[9] They may, indeed, be bigger still.[10]

In a sense, this whole question is misleading. The fairies' stature is in the eye of the beholder. A fairy about four feet tall told a 'peasant seer' who was one of Evans Wentz's informants: 'I am bigger than I appear to you now. We can make the old young, the big small, the small big'.[11] This, of course, is an exercise of glamour, as Yeats recognised: 'the Sheogues . . . are usually of small size when first seen, though seeming of common human height when you are once glamoured.'[12] That the fairies 'are usually of small size when first seen,' however, is not borne out by the evidence. Yeats himself seems if anything to imply the reverse in a passage that hints at a semi-rational explanation:

Mary Battle, my uncle George Pollexfen's second-sighted servant, told me that 'it is something in our eyes makes them big or little.' People in trance often see objects reduced. Mrs. Piper [a medium] when half awakened will sometimes see the people about her very small.[13]

Mediumistic trances aside, 'lilliputian hallucinations' may also occur during the onset of either typhoid or cataracts.[14] This will account for the fact that those who see fairies often subsequently lose their sight[15] or even their lives.

In other aspects of their appearance than stature, the modern Sídhe, like the ancient Tuatha Dé Danann, do not differ pointedly from mortals. According to one of Yeats's informants, they have cloven hooves, but I have not heard of this elsewhere.[16] The fairies do seem to favour red hair. Elizabeth Andrews is particularly firm on this point, although she herself remarks that on Tory Island the fairies' hair may be red, white, or black.[17]

III. The Domain of the Sídhe

One passage in Kirk seems to suggest that the fairies' dwelling places may be virtually anywhere: 'Their bodies of congealed air, are some times carried aloft, other whiles grovell in different shapes, and enter in anie Cranie or cleft of the Earth (where air enters) to their ordinary dwellings.'[18] However, this may only refer to the fairies' mode of access to the Sídhe, for certainly those remain, in all other accounts, 'their ordinary dwellings'. The fairies' presence in some sídhe may be revealed to the ear by music and laughter. Sídheán an Gháire (The Little Sídh of the Laughter), three-quarters of a mile north-west of Ballymote, Co. Sligo, is notable in this respect.[19] To the eye, of course, the sídhe reveal fewer secrets. However, their normally invisible entrances can be found by walking nine times around the sídh at full moon.[20]

It is well known that it is dangerous to disturb a sídh. Digging is therefore out of the question. It is also forbidden to cut growing things on a sídh, especially lone bushes. Mr. D suggested to me that these taboos may originate in the fact that the sídhe were ancient-burial places, and so subject to the ordinary prohibition against disturbing graveyards. The idea of retribution protects them and trains the young to leave them alone. This theory is partially endorsed by Kirk, who writes that 'There Be manie places called Fayrie hills, which the mountain-people think impious and dangerous to peel or discover, by taking earth or wood from them; superstitiously believing the souls of their predecessors to dwell y^r'.[21]

There are paths between sídhe, and these paths are as magical as the sídhe themselves. In West Galway they are thought of as existing in the air, rather than on the ground, and as synonymous, in fact, with breezes. 'A soft hot blast indicates the presence of a good fairy; while a sudden shiver shows that a bad one is near.'[22] At night, particularly in November,[23] lights often travel along these paths and hover over the sídhe. They sometimes move in formation. They may be all white, or they may be of different colours — 'red, green, blue, yellow.'[24] A very old gentleman from Collraí, Co. Sligo (hereafter called Mr. C) tells me that the lights move rapidly, and I have myself seen white lights moving at high speed up the side of Ben Bulben, a mountain renowned for this phenomenon. These lights have been known in Ireland since antiquity. In 'The Colloquy with the Ancients,' Bodhb Derg refers to Brugh na Boinne as 'yonder *brugh* chequered with the many lights hard by you here.'[25] Such lights are not confined to marshy ground and so cannot be will o' the wisps. They are genuine phenomena, but no scientific explanation has been found for them.

By mortals, fairy paths are best treated with respect. In a story remembered by an Irish-American immigrant, a man found himself unable to cross a fairy path at night and had to walk three miles around it.[26] This was only a mild inconvenience compared to the punishments that may be inflicted on those who obstruct such a path. A man at Aughavanagh extended his fenced cabbage garden across a path. In retaliation, 'about fifty horses' and numerous goats would whinny and bleat at his windows by night, while at midday fairies would carry a coffin to his house. Finally, after the man's two sons had died, he let out the land and the haunting ceased.[27] Houses built across a path are liable to be thrown down, though the punishment is not always so great. Mr. B and his son (henceforth Mr. F) told me how their old home in Roscommon had been haunted by noises which Mr. B described as 'hammering something in the kitchen' and Mr. F as breaking sods. According to Mr. F, it was as though fairies were walking through the house or trying to knock it down. On the other hand, he agreed with me that such noises might be caused by an underground stream. It should be added that the fairies are often associated in one way or another with running water, so it would not be surprising if one of their paths were to follow the course of an underground stream.

Such troubles with the fairies can be avoided by the simple expedient of consulting them. If one is in doubt whether a projected house will obstruct a fairy path, 'the usual practice . . . is to turn one sod on the site in the evening and leave it overnight. If in the morning it is found turned back again, then the fairies disapprove and some other site must be found'.[28] If, on the other hand, one rashly wishes to retaliate, two straws laid across a path will cause the fairies to stumble.[29]

Besides the *sidhe*, the fairies still retain their larger kingdom of Tír na nÓg, though its stated location is sometimes rather peculiar. According to a schoolchild from the barony of Kiltartan, Co. Galway, Tír na nÓg is located in or behind the Caves of Cill Corney in the mountains of Burren, Co. Clare.[30] More often, however, Tír na nÓg is still located overseas. This land, formerly Emain Abhlach, is now sometimes called Brasil, or Hy-Brasil. (The country of Brazil is named after it.) Hy-Brasil is supposed to be a spectral island only rarely visible to mortal eyes,

The Fairy Faith in Transition

which may be all to the good, as a sighting is said to portend national trouble. Wood-Martin suggests, nonetheless, that Hy-Brasil may not be entirely unreal. It is marked on a map in *La Navigation de l'Inde Orientale* (Amsterdam, 1609), along with another unknown island, Brandion, which is closer to Ireland. Wood-Martin theorises that Rockall is all that now remains of Brandion, and the Porcupine Bank all that remains of Brasil. Even so, a Captain Nesbett is alleged to have landed on Hy-Brasil on 2 March 1674.[31] Inishbofin, which is now a stable and inhabited island, is also supposed to have been spectral at one time. It was disenchanted by a burning coal.[32]

8. A FIRST CENSUS OF FAIRYLAND

As indicated earlier, the modern fairy world is more specialised by types than the old. This chapter examines those types individually.

I. The Leprechaun

The essential facts on the leprechaun can be found in one of Roinn Bhéaloideas Éireann's manuscripts. This is the one type of fairy which is remarkable for its smallness. According to this manuscript, the leprechaun's height is eighteen inches. He is said here to dress in green, with a red cap and black, pointed shoes. He mends the fairies' footwear and thereby earns money, which he hides in a black pot under a tree.[1] Other sources attribute a different origin to his wealth. According to Lady Wilde, the leprechaun can discover gold 'by the power of a certain herb'.[2] Besides his crock of gold, he possesses also *sporrán na scilinge*, 'the purse that was never without a shilling', and an *adhastar buidhe*, or 'golden bridle, which, whenever shaken, was found with [a] yellow steed attached to it'.[3]

Naturally enough, the leprechaun's wealth is much coveted by mortals. Lady Wilde says that 'no one has ever yet obtained from the tricksy little sprite the name of the herb or the words of the charm which reveal the hidden treasure',[4] but this is an unusually pessimistic view. RBÉ SMS 158 states that if the leprechaun is captured and thrice fails to escape he will surrender his gold (p. 51). Mr. D, who must think the leprechaun smaller than eighteen inches, believes that he should also be mildly tortured by being squeezed in the fist. This should be done without taking your eyes off him, or even blinking, lest he should vanish.

Others believe that the leprechaun will yield his gold to favoured mortals without constraint, though not without conditions. He may stipulate that the treasure-hunter 'must seek the treasure at a particular time, not utter a word during the search, and keep the secret of its discovery for seven years after'.[5] The conditions naturally grow harder in proportion to the leprechaun's reluctance. A 'wee red man' approached some labourers digging for a pot of gold in Ulster — how they had found it is not told — and, although permitting them to proceed, informed them that they would not find the gold unless they sacrificed a life. 'The labourers thereupon sent for permission to kill a dog belonging to the gentleman owning the farm, but he refused and stopped the exploration', as we may suspect the leprechaun intended. 'This episode is supposed to have happened about the year 1840, and is firmly believed to be true'.[6] Often a terrible guardian is assigned to the treasure. In one instance, it is said to be a dragon.[7] Even if the treasure is obtained, it may simply be snatched away again. This happened to a Mr. Stephenson, who had learnt of the treasure's location in a dream. Had he waited until he had dreamt three times of the treasure, he might have kept it.[8]

It may be as well that fairy gold is so hard to win, for it often brings evil. It appears from one folk-tale that gold and silver given to a woman taken to attend a fairy lying-in will, within six days, set fire to every house it enters. In the same story, a shawl given by the fairies splits a tree when wound around it.[9] More often still, however, fairy gold turns out to be only the product of glamour anyway, and will revert to dead leaves or ashes in the morning. The converse is also true: if gold is glamoured ashes, ashes are glamoured gold. In particular, fragments of bone and charcoal found in ancient funeral urns are thought to become gold by night, and it is fondly believed that, 'with proper precautions and ceremonies', they will remain gold by day. This belief has cost archaeologists dearly, for, when the 'proper precautions and ceremonies' fail to work, the urn is generally smashed in a rage. Wood-Martin points out that 'The proverb, ἄνθρακες ὁ θησαυρὸς πέθηνεν, i.e. 'our treasure turned out to be charcoal,' appears to demonstrate that the deceitfulness of 'fairy gold' was a current delusion among the ancient Greeks', and goes on to cite other analogues among the Arabs and Fellaheen.[10]

The leprechaun's gold is often hidden under a lone bush. This is also where he lives, which accounts for the prohibition against cutting a lone bush.[11] Jeanne Cooper Foster implies that such lone bushes are always whitethorns.[12] This may be true in Ulster, but it does not seem to be true elsewhere, although Mr. C called whitethorn 'the fairies' bush' and he and his brother-in-law (hereafter Mr. E) agreed that it was unlucky to bring it into the house. Mr. D suggested to me the theory that lone bushes might originally have marked the sites of isolated graves,[13] and that monastic treasures might subsequently have been buried beneath them to escape plunder by the Vikings.[14] This would have made their disturbance doubly taboo and at the same time given rise to the tradition of the crock of gold. Plausible as this is, it makes no allowance for the one exception to the rule against cutting lone bushes.

Lone bushes, especially those growing on *sídhe*, may be cut and even preferred for use as May trees.[15] Of course, the may-pole ceremony is a fertility ceremony, and the fairies might give with their blessing anything needed for such a purpose.

A number of theories have been proposed for the origin of the leprechaun himself. Among the least convincing is that of David Fitzgerald, to whom leprechauns 'seem to have been originally fire- and mine-dwarfs'. His evidence basically boils down to three points: leprechauns guard treasure; they generally have red hair or red clothing; and they made a tapping noise as they work at their shoes, as do mine-spirits in other countries.[16] The guarding of treasure is the only one of these points that is really significant. Other types of fairy wear red, and the leprechaun's cobbling is sufficient in itself to account for the tapping noise.

Fitzgerald adduces no linguistic evidence, but this evidence is crucial. Four derivations of *leipreachán* have been proposed: from *lucharmunn*;[17] *leath-*, or *leith-*, *bhrógán*;[18] *lugh-chorpán*;[19] or *luchorpán*.[20] The first of these is the weakest. It may be translated as 'small gentleman', but only in Scottish Gaelic. In Irish it has no meaning, nor does it much resemble *leipreachán*.

Leath-bhrógán, which would mean 'little one shoe,' is attractive. It would obviously refer to the one shoe on which the leprechaun may be seen working. The leprechaun's association with shoes and shoe-making is of considerable antiquity. It may derive, as P. W. Joyce thinks, from the ransom of a pair of magic shoes paid by the leprechauns to the King of Ulster in 'The King of the Lepracanes' Journey to Emania', but I suspect that it is older still.[21] It is probably not accidental, as single shoes seem to have possessed a magical significance.[22]

However, the connection with shoes makes a derivation from *lugh-chorpán* even more attractive. This word is obviously very similar to *luchorpán*, but whereas *luchorpán* means only (and redundantly) 'little, littler body', *lugh-chorpán* means 'little Lugh-body'. In the story of 'Math the Son of Mathonwy', Lugh's Welsh namesake Llew Llaw Gyffes poses as a shoemaker for a while.[23] Thus Lugh and cobbling are already related. There exists, furthermore, an inscription to the Lugoves (pl.) set up by the guild of cobblers at Osma in Spain.[24] *Lugoves*, like *lugh-chorpán*, would appear to be a diminutive of *Lugh*, and, in view of their votaries, these would appear to be the Spanish leprechauns. Further evidence connecting the leprechauns with Lugh is provided by Winberry, who sees in the leprechauns' vulnerability to a fixed stare a reminiscence of Lugh's combat against Balor's evil eye.[25]

The leprechauns' antiquity is already sufficiently attested by 'The

A First Census of Fairyland

King of the Lepracanes' Journey to Emania' and by the 'Life of Brendan of Clonfert'. In the latter, St. Brendan comes upon an island 'filled with demons in the shapes of dwarfs and leprechauns opposing them, whose faces were black as coal'.[26] The connection with Lugh now carries the leprechauns back to the remotest surviving stratum of mythology. A middle term between Lugh and the leprechauns may be visible in an Early Irish tale from South Munster called 'Cath Cinn Abrad', in which a king of the Mairtíne named Lugcorp mac Temais is mentioned.[27] Whether this Lugcorp was a purely legendary character or a 'man from the souterrain' is uncertain. In view of his regal status, the former would seem more probable. We have, at all events, a process of degeneration from Lugh, who is something like a god, through Lugcorp mac Temais, who is a king, to the leprechaun, who lives in a hole beneath a bush. Furthermore, while Lugh is the master of all arts, the leprechaun is master only of the humble art of shoe-making. The concept is ultimately the same, but it is now better suited to an unskilled peasantry. Finally, the unity of Lugh and even of Lugcorp is now fragmented. There are many leprechauns. The leprechaun, then, provides a good example of the decline of the Tuatha Dé Danann.

II. The Cluricaun

Closely related to the leprechaun is the cluricaun. In South Munster, indeed, 'cluricaun' is simply the local name for the leprechaun,[28] and in Thomas Keightley's story of 'The Little Shoe' the cluricaun appears as a shoe-maker.[29] It does seem probable that the leprechaun and the cluricaun were originally one and the same. The names can both be derived from *lugh-chorpán*, the intermediate form in the case of 'cluricaun' being *lucharban* and/or *luracán*.[30] Also, even when he is not otherwise connected with shoe-making, the cluricaun may wear 'a short leather apron',[31] which is functionally quite redundant unless an original identity with the leprechaun is assumed. Like the leprechaun, the cluricaun may also have treasure. He hides his, however, under 'a plant of ragwort — a boliaun', not a lone bush.[32]

Normally, though, the cluricaun is more like a brownie, or even a poltergeist, for he will 'haunt' a particular family, and, even though he may 'protect that household against various dangers, he can also disturb its order; and many folk accounts portray him as a mischievous prankster.' His only useful activity, from other fairies' point of view, is to play his pipes at their dances. His preferred pastime is drinking and smoking in other people's wine cellars, and this preference is betrayed by the 'shiny red nose' in the middle of his 'withered face'.[33] He also enjoys 'riding sheep and shepherds' dogs for a livelong night, until the morning finds them panting and mud-covered'.[34] Larger fairies may ride horses and cattle in the same way.

III. The Mermaid

Mer-people of both sexes are known to Irish folklore. The Irish word is *murdhuacha*, roughly transliterated 'merrow', but English-speakers regularly use the English terms 'mermaid' and 'merman'. A connection may exist between leprechauns and mermaids, for one informant states that they intermarry. The same informant also states that mermaids cannot talk, but make signs with their hands.[35] However, all folk-tales in which they occur contradict this assertion. Merrows are scarcely beautiful. They have, of course, fishes' tails, though they may have legs as well. In any case, the lower part of the body, legs included, is scaly.[36] (The children of mortal-merrow unions are also 'sometimes said to be covered with scales.')[37] In addition, merrows have 'short arms like fins', 'a small web between the fingers', 'green hair, long green teeth, a red nose, and pig's eyes'.[38] On land, they may take the form of 'little hornless cattle'. One little-known fact is that they are often said to be of enormouse size. A mermaid recorded in *The Annals of the Four Masters*

was 160 feet in length, her hair eighteen feet (comparatively short), her fingers were seven feet in length, and so was her nose. These exact measurements were possible because she was cast up by the sea. This was said to have happened in about A.D. 887.[39]

St. Brendan of Clonfert revived and baptised a giant mermaid dead from a spear-thrust.[40] A mermaid in the Scottish folk-tale of 'Columcille and his Brother Dobhran' also seems to be huge.[41] It may be, however, that a mermaid's growth, like a fish's, is determined by its habitat, for they can swim upstream and settle in fresh water lakes.[42] A 'monster' killed by St. Colman Ela in Lough Ela would appear to be of this type. It is described as 'a *small* pointed gaping apparition in the shape of a woman' (emphasis mine).[43]

It may seem strange that a mermaid should dress at all, but she is described as wearing green,[44] with the exception of her small, red, feathered cap, or 'cocked hat', the *cohuleen driuth* (in Croker's spelling), which enables her to survive in the water. Stealing this cap is one way to win a mermaid for a wife.[45] Others say that it is her 'sloak', or tail, that must be stolen. Although RBÉ SMS 157 speaks of 'cutting off' this tail, that would surely be disabling at the very least.[46] Presumably, then, the tail is detachable, like a lizard's. Normally, if the mermaid recovers her cap or tail she will depart.

In cases of marriage, it seems obvious, the mermaid cannot very well be huge or hideous.

Dr. A told me that on Inishmurray the mermaid, like the Lorelei, was always combing her hair. A mermaid in the folk-tale of 'The Great Worm of the Shannon' has a pair of scissors as well as a comb, and her comb is described as venomous. Despite this, she is friendly to men.[47] Not all mermaids are friendly, however. In some cases, the harm that they do may be only psychological: 'They say if you once heard her sing you'd never do a day's good after, thinking long on it.'[48] Although reminiscent of Homer's sirens, this is a property attributed to the music of the Sídhe in general. In other cases, the mermaid's dangers are more physical. The proverb, 'Save a stranger from the sea,/And he'll turn your enemy,' and 'the wide-spread reluctance amongst primitive seaside folk to rescue a drowning man' certainly express a belief that water spirits must have victims,[49] and mermaids are plainly water spirits. There is a rule governing the danger of mermaids: 'there was a boy saw a mermaid down by Spiddal not long ago, but he saw her before she saw him, so she did him no harm. But if she'd seen him first, she'd have brought him away and drowned him.'[50] This is sometimes said of other types of fairy too, and the motif even arises in contexts where the fairies are not involved at all. For instance, a druid called Reon boasted that the earth would swallow St. Patrick when he saw him. Patrick, hearing of it, said that he would see Reon first. So he did, and the earth swallowed Reon.[51]

The mermaid is occasionally said to have been originally a mortal woman 'who was saved from drowning by the fairies and she got the power of living in the water from them'.[52] This tradition does not account for the fact that there is more than one mermaid. A well known, more rational theory holds that the mermaid of the high seas is actually the dugong, an aquatic mammal with humanoid breasts, but there are no dugong anywhere close to Ireland. On the other hand, there are, of course, seals. Yeats tells us that seal-people are distinct from merrows, but in at least one story, 'The Conneelys and the Seals', there seems to be no real distinction made. There are some slight differences, however. Seal-people are generally supposed to be the most harmless of fairies (but again Yeats tells us that 'A whistling seal sank a ship the other day'). Seals have cloaks, by which presumably their skins are meant, which they put off to take human form. To win a seal-woman, it is this cloak, not a cap or tail, that must be stolen. At least one such woman, after recovering her cloak, did not leave for ever, but returned every day for five years to see her children. Several numerous families, ranging 'from O'Shea in Kerry to Flaherty and Conneely and others in the West of Ieland, and to MacCodrum . . . in Scotland', are supposed to be descended from the union of an ancestor with a seal. 'In some versions, the descendants of the seal-women were said to have webbed hands and feet.'[53] This may be the origin of the whole tradition of the seal-people, and perhaps of the merrows as well. Webbed hands and feet as an hereditary deformity are not very rare, and descent from some sort of aquatic person might be invented to account for it.

The tradition of the seal-people sufficiently accounts for the taboo against killing seals. On Inishmurray, however, as Dr. A tells me, the taboo was explained on the grounds that seals were human souls in Purgatory.

IV. The Banshee

Intermarriage again provides a link between the mermaid and the banshee, as the latter is occasionally said to be 'the daughter of a mermaid and a human man'. There are other connections, too. Like the mermaid, the banshee 'has long hair and . . . continually combs it'.[54] The banshee's name (Ir. *bean sídhe*) means simply 'fairy woman', but, as is well known, her function is to give warning of death. The mermaid also may fulfil this role. She is said to appear in the water 'When there is going to be a drowning.'[55]

The banshee's main method of warning is keening. The keen is a long, ululating kind of wail also uttered by mortal women at funerals. Until quite recently, certain women were specially engaged for this purpose. The details of the banshee's wail may be significant. They may, for instance, indicate the number that will die. On one occasion in this century, the banshee was heard to wail precisely twice (as well as to scrape her feet on the shore) just before a young man was drowned. A second man, who swam around for half an hour hoping to rescue the first, died about five weeks later.[56] In theory, the banshee keens only for members of the old Gaelic nobility, but at least one Norman family, the Desmonds, possess a banshee,[57] and in practice she may keen even for persons who have no connections with nobility of any kind. It is said that when she does keen for a family traditionally possessed of a banshee, persons not of that family may be present and still not hear her.[58] It is often hard to locate the source of the banshee's wail. One schoolchild writes, for instance, 'No sooner was the banshee in the house than she was ten miles from it'.[59] Finally, when 'someone very great or holy' is to die, several banshees may keen him at once.[60] It should be said that all of these rules have many exceptions.

Traditions regarding the origin of the banshee are quite varied. Some make her a ghost, rather than a fairy. She may be the ghost of a damned woman or of an unbaptised infant; or, if she is 'a hateful or vengeful banshee,' she may be the ghost of 'a woman . . . murdered by a member of the family she now cries'.

If the banshee is considered benign, she may be either the ghost of an 'ancestor . . . who retains a special interest' in the family or the ghost of a professional keening woman. If such a woman was retained exclusively by a certain family in life, she might remain in death exclusively that family's banshee, 'until either the family name became extinct or until a certain generation had died'. Other keening women who might become banshees were 'those who died before they could fulfil their obligations of keening [and] those who neglected to perform their duty.'[61]

However, in view of the banshee's name, any tradition which makes her out to be a ghost rather than a fairy must be regarded as a comparatively late contrivance. Sometimes she is said to be a woman 'abducted by the Fairy Host';[62] but it seems her connection with the fairies is both older and deeper than this. The names of hereditary banshees are very often the names of known members of the Tuathe Dé Danann who preside over the districts where the affected families dwell. Here, for instance, is a list compiled by John O'Donovan:

Aeibhinn (now Aoibhell) of Craigliath, near Killaloe, the banshee of the Dal-gCais of North Munster; Cliodhna of Tonn Cliodhna, at Glandore, the banshee of the Mac Carthys and other families of South Munster; Aine of Knockany in the county Limerick;[63] Una of Cnoc Sidhe-Una, the banshee of the O'Carrolls; Cailleach Beirre of Dun Caillighe Beirre, the banshee of some of the Leinster and Meath families; Grian of Cnoc Greine in Munster; Aine of Lissan in Tyrone, so attached to the family of O'Corra; Eibhlinn of Sliabh-Fuaid, &c., &c.[64]

All of these women are members of the Tuatha Dé Danann, with the possible exception of Cailleach Beirre, the Old Woman of Beare. Aine and Aeibhinn lament the deaths of poets, and Aine is probably related to Black Annis, whose howl, like the banshee's wail, can be heard five miles away.[65] According to *The War of the Gael with the Gaill*, by Brian Boru's arch-poet Mac Liag, Aoibheall of Craig Liath appeared to Brian on the eve of the Battle of Clontarf to warn him of impending death.[66]

However, just as behind the multiplicity of leprechauns there stands the single figure of Lugh, so behind all these banshees there stands the single figure of the Morrigu. Strangely, this is either overlooked or denied by many eminent Celticists, but the evidence is inescapable. There is, to begin with, the evidence of names. It will be recalled that the Morrigu often took the form of a crow, and was consequently known as *An Badhb*. In at least two parts of Ireland, Co. Waterford and South Tipperary, the banshee is known by that name today. Another name for her in South Tipperary is *bo chaointe*, which name is also current in Kilkenny, while in Wexford and Wicklow she is known as the *bow*.[67] I think it far more probable that *bo* and *bow* represent the local pronunciation of *badhb*, rather than *bó* 'cow' (*chaointe* means 'keening'). In fact, the scald-crow functions rather like a banshee. Its call is very unlucky, even in dreams. If it flies round a person, that person risks, at the very least, some great calamity. If it perches on a dwelling place, even if that place be only a cattle byre, one or more of the occupants face death or serious illness.[68]

Badhb is not the only one of the Morrigu's names still carried by the banshee. In a list of Ulster banshees, Jeanne Cooper Foster includes 'Nein Roe, the banshee of the O'Neills of Shane's Castle . . . in Co. Antrim'.[69] 'Nein' is surely the Ulster pronunciation of 'Nemain'. The name 'Morrigu' itself seems to have survived in the Anglo-Scots word 'worrie-cow', quite often used by Sir Walter Scott. The change of *m* to *w* is easily accounted for by lenition, which is grammatically required in the nominative and accusative singular after the definite article. Scott himself glosses this word: 'a bugbear, a scarecrow, a ghost or goblin.'[70] 'However, in every context where the word occurs in Scott's works, 'banshee' would make perfectly good sense. The etymology offered by both the OED and *The Scottish National Dictionary* seems to belong to a bygone age of philology:'? From *worry* in the Eng. sense of harrass, pester + Cow, n[4], 'says the latter, to which the OED adds 'as if "a goblin apt to worry"'. I submit that 'worrie-cow' derives from *Morrigu* and originally meant 'banshee'.

The Morrigu and the banshee are also connected by their behaviour. The banshee is to be seen at fords washing 'the grave-clothes of those about to die'. In this capacity, she is sometimes called 'the Bean-Nighe or Little-Washer-By-The-Ford'.[71] This behaviour is also associated with the Morrigu. She is straddling the River Unius and washing herself in it when the Dagda meets her before the Second Battle of Moytura.[72] Cormac Conloingeas, on his way to take the throne of Ulster (but actually on his way to death) meets her 'washing her chariot and her harness' at a ford. (On this occasion she has a second woman with her who urges Cormac to turn back, almost as though the Morrigu and the banshee stood side by side.) When Cúchulainn meets her on his last ride, she is actually called a *bean sídhe* and is washing bloody clothes in a ford. The druid Cathbad tells Cúchulainn that the clothes are his own.[73]

She is also called a *bean sídhe* when Osgar of the Fianna meets her under precisely the same circumstances. Later, he hears a keening-song on a harp.[74]

Two fairies that bear a passing resemblance to the banshee are the *leannán sídhe* and the *geancánach*. The *leannán sídhe*, or 'fairy sweetheart', is a succuba. She makes love to mortal men and drains their vitality in the process. The *geancánach* is apparently her male equivalent, the incubus. Yeats adopted the name (though not the spelling) for the *nom de plume* under which he published *John Sherman* (1891), believing that it meant 'love-talker.' The Irish language certainly provides grounds for this interpretation (though one would prefer the second *a* to be unaccented), but the most up-to-date Irish dictionary renders the word as 'Fairy cobbler'. Also, *píopa geancánaigh*, 'acorn-bowl', is synonymous with *píopa clutharacháin*.[75] On this evidence, then, the *geancánach* would seem to be simply the leprechaun or cluricaun.

9. A SECOND CENSUS OF FAIRYLAND

There is only a blurred line between the fairy kingdom and the animal kingdom. The fairies are still proficient shape-shifters, and any animal may be a fairy in disguise. Some fairies, indeed, exist only in animal form. But hardly any animal, even if it is not a fairy, is altogether 'right'. All animals are mysterious, and know secrets that humans do not. Consequently, in Irish tradition, there is almost no distinction between the natural and the supernatural world. Though we are seldom visibly surrounded by fairies, we are never far from animals, who have as much in common with the fairies as they do with us. The extent of Irish lore regarding animals is far too broad to cover in this chapter, but I shall examine those traditions which have most to do with the fairies.

I. Omens

An immediate difficulty is that of distinguishing genuine fairy phenomena from omens. The point is best illustrated by portents of death in which animals are involved. As a first example, before the line of Lords Preston became extinct, great numbers of foxes would congregate around the house of the incumbent Lord on the night before his death.[1] As another example, on Inishmurray, as Dr. A tells me, the cuckoo, which is not normally found there, would portend a drowning. Elsewhere, pigeons and water-wagtails may both give warning of death.[2] Mr. F tells me that a frog coming into the house portends death. (A frog at the door, on the other hand, portends marriage.)[3] The question is this: should we regard all these traditions as auguries, in which the animal is only the unconscious agent of fate? Or should we regard the foxes, cuckoos, pigeons, water-wagtails, and frogs as forms of the banshee, and therefore as fairies? I do not believe there can be a firm answer to this question. What we are really asking is whether the animals are 'right' or not, and, as to that, one simply cannot tell. It is cases like these that demonstrate just how blurred the distinction is between fairies and animals.

II. Swans and Hares

One cannot tell whether an animal is 'right' because the fairies can take any form they please. For instance, they have even been known to take the form of flies.[4] However, there are certain forms that they prefer. At least one of these is a survival of ancient tradition: the swan. It is strictly forbidden to kill a swan, and Dr. A believes that this is because, even now, a swan may be one of the Children of Lir, or someone else in the same predicament.

Even more than the swan, however, the fairies prefer the shape of the hare. On the other hand, this tradition is not straightforward, as a hare may not be right and still not be a fairy. This point emerged while I was interviewing Mr. C and his brother-in-law, Mr. E. Mr. C told me that the hare is often 'supposed to be acting the fairy', although 'you can't tell if it's a right hare or not'. He then told me how he had once pulled the trigger of his shot-gun three times at a hare sitting stock still about seventy yards away, but the gun would not fire. Then the hare tossed its head and went away. Mr. C pointed his gun in the air and pulled the trigger again, whereupon it did fire. At this point, Mr. E interrupted to say that it is wrong to shoot a hare. Mr. C first denied ever having heard of such a taboo, but then explained it on the grounds that you might be shooting, not at a fairy, but at a human being.

One may ask what sort of human being could take the form of a hare. The answer is a witch. Mr. C proceeded to tell me a tale well known to folklorists. A man could not get his butter to come. He saw a hare sitting outside his creamery and guessed that it had 'taken the butter out of his churning'. He set his dog after it. The hare ran for a house and jumped in the window, but the dog gave it a bite as it did so. Inside, the man found a woman in bed, whom he discovered to be wounded where the dog had bitten the hare; 'and she was the magic, you see'.[5] Witches often turn themselves to hares for the express purpose of stealing milk from the neighbours' cows.[6] Even as ghosts, they may continue to shift shape in this way.[7] Such shape-shifting may not always be voluntary: 'There was a common belief, though it is not much heard of now, that priests could turn people into hares.'[8] The origins of this tradition appear to be of great antiquity: 'In Celtic Britain, as Caesar recounted in his *Gallic Wars* (V, xii), the hare was a sacred animal; consequently in Christian times it was associated with the exorcised paganism, witchcraft.'[9]

It may seem odd that one should refrain from killing a hare for fear that it may be a witch — all the more reason to kill it, one might think. In fact, hares used to be killed on May Day for just that reason.[10] It seems that the taboo is more against eating the hare after killing it than against killing it in the first place. This is reasonable: it is simply the taboo against cannibalism. Furthermore, if a hare is a witch, 'a great shriek' may be heard when it is killed or cut up, which must serve as something of a deterrent.[11] Pregnant women, especially, 'must never eat the flesh of the hare',[12] perhaps because their offspring might turn out to be witches (or perhaps they would simply be hare-lipped). At any rate, it makes more sense to refrain from eating a hare lest it be a witch than to refrain lest it be the reincarnation of one's grandmother, as folk in Kerry used to believe.[13] If this tradition is accurately reported, it held that grandmothers, but not mothers and great-grandmothers, became hares. Few traditions are as illogical as this.

To decide whether a hare is a witch or a fairy is made no easier by the fact that witches and fairies have considerable traffic with each other. They dance together at Samhain, for instance. Both ride other people's horses to exhaustion and steal the milk from cows. Witches may even 'steal babies out of their cradles and sell them to the fairies'. Also, the 'superhuman hags' of Early Irish literature, whose original status is unclear, are now sometimes said to be witches.[14]

A final point about hares: one may see into fairyland by looking through a hole in the shin-bone or collar-bone of a hare.[15] Many other types of ring may serve the same purpose, however, including a ring made by one's thumb and index finger. The technique is sometimes said to leave the eye blind.

III. Cats

With hares there always remains the possibility that the animal is merely natural. According to one of Lady Gregory's informants, no such possibility exists with cats. All cats, without exception, are 'not right . . . And there's some have heard them together at night talking Irish'; 'For cats is faeries.'[16] In Early Irish literature, fairy cats occur in the tale of 'Bricriu's Feast.'[17]

IV. Weasels

The same informant went on to say that 'Weasels are not *right*, no more than cats; and I'm not sure about foxes'. His opinion seems to be based mainly on observation. He says that weasels 'are enchanted and understand all things'. Weasels are indeed very shrewd and intelligent. He also says,'If you treat them well they will treat you well', and again it is true that weasels seldom trouble humans, although they can be singularly vicious when provoked.[18] The folklore of the weasel is based on tradition as well as on observation, however. In many respects, it resembles the folklore of the hare. An unusually complex tangle of transformation motifs occurs in the folk-tale of 'Paudyeen O'Kelly and the Weasel'. A witch takes the form of a weasel, while her son, a cluricaun, takes the form of a black dog.[19] Like the hare, the weasel is supposed to steal milk from cows.

Despite its normal respect for humans, there is one time when the weasel is not to be trusted. If you meet one in the early morning, you should spit at it, 'for if it spits at you first, a great misfortune will befall you'. This is obviously a variant of that motif according to which it is dangerous to be seen first by a fairy. The weasel can also spit fire.[20] Despite its potential savagery, the weasel is another animal that ought not to be killed, chiefly, it seems, for fear of retribution.[21]

V. Frogs and Fishes

The frog is yet another animal that should not be killed. It is 'considered holy in a sense'.[22] This is an odd choice of word, but may refer to the fact that frogs, like so many other animals, tend to be fairies in disguise.[23] So, too, do fishes. This, in fact, is a particularly common shape, for there are more fairies in the sea than on land. A fish that seems eager to leap into a boat is most likely to be a fairy.[24]

VI. Psychic Powers of Animals

Even when they are not fairies themselves, animals are believed to possess a higher awareness of fairyland than men do. 'The peculiar whistle of the starling', for instance, 'is regarded with especial trepidation by the peasantry as they are supposed to be communicating with the fairies'. Domesticated animals, on the other hand, though they possess this power to an even greater degree than their wild counterparts, may be trusted to use it to the advantage of their owners. A cock, for example, especially one from a March clutch, will give warning if 'there is something outside it would be bad to meet'.[25] Beliefs of this sort are no doubt a mixture of observation and sentimentality. The apparent ability of many animals to perceive things invisible to humans is well known; but the intelligence attributed to them is often an anthropomorphic illusion.

VII. Pigs

The animals we have dealt with so far, if they are not 'right,' are forms of glamour. An enchanted hare, for instance, is not really a hare at all, but a fairy pretending to be a hare. Things are not always this simple. Pigs provide an example of the difficulty. This is another form which the fairies may assume, and in this form they are extremely dangerous,[26] but there seem to be some pigs that are fairies in their own right, while others are only disguises. The Manx Arkan Sonney, or 'Lucky Piggy', can be clearly recognised as a fairy because it is white with red ears, the traditional colouring of fairy creatures,[27] but a pig need not possess this colouring to be a fairy. Also, is Arkan Sonney a single pig or a type of pig? The Black Pig is equally problematical. I shall defer a close study of it until Part Three, but one cannot decide whether it is an omen, a fairy, an apparition, or a symbol. The Black Pig is a unique case, but the Black Dog presents even greater difficulties of classification.

VIII. The Black Dog

To begin with, the name 'Black Dog' is a misnomer, for by no means all the supernatural dogs of Irish tradition are black. We find them in all colours and in combinations of colour, just like any other dog. K. M. Briggs consequently attempts to discriminate between two types of supernatural dog. Genuine fairy dogs, she thinks, are white with red ears, like Arkan Sonney. Black dogs are not fairies but 'ghosts or demons, and generally masterless.' Of dogs which are neither black nor white with red ears she says nothing, but they are presumably to be classed with black dogs. Unfortunately, this system has little to support it. White dogs with red ears are familiar chiefly from *The Wanderings of Oisin* and its Fenian source. They are not very common in folklore. Briggs herself has to concede that 'Lady Wilde records black dogs that belonged to the Cave fairies'.[28] Steven Ruan, a piper of Galway, 'saw a dog with a white ring around his neck . . . and the oldest men round Galway have seen him, too, for he has been here for one hundred years or more. He is a dog of the *good people*, and only appears at certain hours of the night.'[29] This dog's colouring is quite unremarkable. It is his age that sets him apart as a fairy dog. The implication is, then, that a supernatural dog's colouring is not significant, and no distinction between different types of supernatural dog can be based upon it.

This leaves us with a creature that may be either a fairy, a ghost, or a demon. All are attested. One Black Dog's role is truly

Mephistophelean, for his purpose is to prevent a repentant wizard from disposing of his *grimoire*.[30] A natural black dog is also supposed to provide protection against demons,[31] which may be explained as fighting fire with fire. Another Black Dog in a folk-tale is unequivocally a man's ghost.[32] Already, then, the Black Dog may be any one of three different things. These three things may be strangely combined. A Black Dog encountered on the road from Galway to Kinvara, though lone and malevolent and much like a demon, is explicitly termed a *sídheóg*. It cannot cross running water, and 'it is said that no fairy can cross water'. The horse and man that encountered the Dog died soon afterwards: 'it is said that the fairies took them.'[33] More strangely still, one Black Dog in a folk-tale turns out to be the form assumed by a changeling when disturbed in its grave.[34] Still other elements than fairy, ghost, and demon may be involved. 'Near Ballycroy on Blacksod Bay', though the Black Dog is apparently a ghost, it is also an omen of death.[35]

Confused as this tradition appears, it may perhaps be simplified by seeking a lowest common denominator. Dogs actually seen in company with the fairies may be set to one side. Other 'Black Dogs' may in fact be of any colour, but are nearly always frightening. Hence, frightening dogs are to be met with on the roads. To this mundane observation may be added the fact that in every account of the Black Dog that purports to record a personal experience the Dog's supernatural quality is purely a subjective impression. It seems likely, then, that the Black Dog is nothing remarkable at all. Men have been frightened by dogs and have endowed those dogs with a supernatural existence in order to excuse their own fear.

IX. Water-Horses

One tradition of the Dog of the Tumulus on Inis Saor, Aran Islands, remains to be noticed. This dog changes from a small size to something 'much longer than any cow or bullock on the Island'. At the same time, its footprints change from those of paws to those of hooves.[36] In other words, it changes from a dog to a great horse. This introduces us to the two types of fairy horse. Both types have in common the peculiarity that water is their natural element, although they can also live on the land. However, there is a distinction between the water-horse proper and the pooka. The true water-horse is a fairy in its own right, not a form of glamour. It is always equine. This is not clearly the case with the pooka. Also, the water-horse is a noble beast, while the pooka is generally mischievous.

Another difference is that a true water-horse can be trained and domesticated. According to one tradition, Cúchulainn's horses were water-horses.[37] Saints, too, sometimes acquire water-horses miraculously. God sent one to St. Finan to replace a horse that had broken its foot.[38] St. Féchín of Fore likewise summoned a water-horse to replace a dead chariot-horse. Although this water-horse is described as 'tamer and gentler than any other horse', St. Féchín evidently did not approve of it, for in releasing it he said, 'Do thou meet no one, and let no one meet thee hence for ever'.[39] One need not be a saint or hero or rely upon miracles to tame a water-horse. This can be accomplished simply by keeping a foal in a dark cellar for a year. Once tamed, however, a water-horse should not be made to work after noon on Saturdays, or else it will return to the water.[40]

A great source of water-horses used to be the sometimes flooded Caves of Corney in the Burren, Co. Clare, behind which Tír na nÓg is supposed to lie. According to some, many horses issued from these caves, while according to others all the horses of Co. Clare are descended from a single 'white stallion that emerged from a cavern in the Burren'. Lady Wilde thought the breed extinct, but a schoolchild of Kiltartan affirmed in 1937–39 that it was still to be found, adding the convincing detail that it can be recognised by a whisker on the upper lip.[41]

X. The Pooka

A vellum manuscript at Trinity College, Dublin, confirms that the pooka is not the same as the true water-horse, but adds a rather peculiar statement relating them to each other. John O'Donovan translates thus into Latin:

Damh-Dile (Bos diluvii) Bestia de Letter-Dallain caput humanum habuit; forma follis fabrilis in reliquâ parte fuit. Equus aquatilis, qui erat in lacu juxta ecclesiam copulavit cum filiâ sacerdotis (ecclesiae) ita ut generavit hanc Bestiam ex eâ.[42]

Admittedly, it is possible that *Damh-Dile* should not be rendered 'pooka' at all, but this creature seems to fit the general requirements, which are vague enough. Besides horse and pony, the following forms have been ascribed to the pooka: eagle, bat, ass, bull, and goat. MacManus adds 'dog', but I think he confuses the pooka with the Black Dog, especially as he states that 'Whatever form it is in, it must be jet black and with blazing fiery eyes'. MacManus firmly denies that the pooka's form is ever human,[43] but T. J. Westropp states quite to the

A First Census of Fairyland

contrary that on the coast of Connacht the pooka is always 'of human shape,' never 'ponylike or goatlike'.[44] The humanoid pooka resembles a brownie, for, like that fairy, it can be laid by a gift of clothing. Indeed, in 'The Phooka of Kildare', this fate even befalls a pooka in the shape of an ass. To complicate matters further, this last pooka describes itself as 'the ghost of an idle kitchen boy'.[45] The pooka of the Dun of Clochanpooka, Kilkenny, assumes the strangest shape of all, that of 'an enormous fleece of wool, [which] issuing from [its] cavern rolls over the ground with astonishing speed, uttering a mysterious buzzing sound which inspires terror in all who hear it'. Wood-Martin, who records this last tradition, sensibly sums up thus: 'Indistinctness, like that of an imperfectly remembered dream, seems to constitute the chief characteristic of the Pooka.' But behind all this welter of confusion it remains true that the pooka is most often, and typically, equine.[46] Even the humanoid pooka retains a connection with horses. Patrick Waters, of the Co. Sligo (and so within Westropp's ambit), told Evans Wentz that 'Pookas are black-featured fellows mounted on good horses; and are horse-dealers. They visit racecourses, but usually are invisible'.[47]

In its true equine form, the pooka's favourite trick is to crouch by night in a marsh until someone steps over it, whereupon it springs to its feet and rushes away with its victim until cock-crow, when it hurls him into a pond. Other fairies ride horses to exhaustion; the pooka is a horse that rides men to exhaustion. It is more mischievous than malevolent, however, and will sometimes give a more welcome ride to a footsore traveller. A peculiar and unrelated tradition about the pooka is that it spoils the blackberries on Michaelmas Day.[48]

Though one could go on to speak of hens and cows and other creatures, the foregoing should provide a fair survey of fairy traditions regarding animals. Most of these traditions differ from those recorded in chapter eight in that they do not derive from antiquity. There is also, as is only natural, less communication between men and fairies in animal form than between men and fairies in human form. Most of these traditions spring from the observation of nature. As nature is not predictable, these traditions are not systematic. They add up to a picture of a quirky, unreliable world in which anything may happen and things are seldom what they seem. This world is a suitable setting for the activities of the humanoid fairies.

10. THE QUICK AND THE DEAD

I come now to consider the two ways in which the fairy faith has been influenced by Christianity. In the first place, the fairies have had to find a niche for themselves within a hierarchy of souls that makes no provision for them. This has led to an entirely new conception of what the fairies actually are. Further, although the saints and priests have been surprisingly tolerant of the fairy faith, they could not entirely approve of a creed unrelated to their own. This, too, is reflected in the new concept of the fairies. The Sídhe are not altogether trusted. It is not certain that they wish well to mankind. For all that, men do not exactly hate the fairies; but they suspect that God may do so.

The second aspect of Christian influence concerns the fate of the soul after death, which the Church has taught men to ponder. The Church cannot justly complain if parishioners have not always arrived at the same conclusions as their priests. The soul, in orthodox teaching, is a spiritual substance; the fairies seem made of much the same substance. This invites the thought that there must be some connection between the two. Are fairies, then, the souls of the dead? In modern times, as in ancient times, the answer remains ultimately 'No', but in modern times that answer requires a good deal more qualification.

I. Angels

In the Christian hierarchy of souls, the one concept that most disrupted the pagan Irish system of belief was the concept of angels. In the pagan system, there was a place for the Tuatha Dé Danann, a place for the Sídhe, a place for men, and even a place for the Fomorians. There was no great difficulty in finding a place for God at the head of this 'chain of being'; but where were the angels to be placed? Conversely, in the Christian system, where were the fairies to be placed? The two questions answer each other. The fairies had somehow to be assimilated with the angels. They could not simply be identified with them, however, for no-one could fail to see that Angus Óg and Gabriel had very little in common. In many countries, they would have been identified with devils, but that was not the case in Ireland. The

Irish already had devils, in the form of Fomorians, and Lugh and Satan (say) had no more in common than Angus Óg and Gabriel. Some middle ground had to be found, then: the fairies are neither angels nor fallen angels; they are half-fallen angels.

Even in the earliest Irish semi-Christian (and therefore semi-pagan) stories, this idea is beginning to take hold. In 'Altrom Tige Dá Medar' ('The Nurture of the Houses of the two Milk-Vessels'), Manannán gives Angus Óg a spell to dispossess Elcmar of Brugh na Boinne. It is the same spell 'which drove the rebellious angels from heaven and the Fir Bolg from Ireland and which the Men of Ireland used against Manannán's people in their turn'. In the same story, Angus refuses baptism from St. Patrick.[1] Elsewhere, one of the islands discovered by St. Brendan is a Paradise of Birds. These birds were once angels, but played a minor part in Lucifer's revolt and so are mildly punished by this metamorphosis. They turn white each Sunday.[2] White birds may be blessed souls, but may also be the birds of fairyland.

In modern folklore, the tradition runs that so many angels chose to leave heaven with Lucifer that God was in danger of being left alone. He therefore ordered the gates of heaven and hell to be shut simultaneously. Those who had already fallen as far as hell became devils; those who had not fallen at all remained angels; while those who were caught in-between became fairies.[3] The fairies, in fact, are occasionally known as 'little angels'.[4] Patrick Waters, of the Co. Sligo, professed a somewhat different and rather idiosyncratic belief. He made an unusual distinction between the 'gentry' and the 'good people'. The former, according to him, 'are a big race who came from the planets,' while the latter 'were next to Heaven at the Fall, but did not fall; they are a people expecting salvation'.[5]

II. Eschatology

On Patrick's last point, opinion is far from unanimous. Kirk carefully straddles the fence. From his strongest pronouncement on the subject, one would gather that he thinks the fairies irretrievably damned:

They are said to have ... no discernible Religion, Love or Devotione towards God the Blessed Maker of All. They disappear whenever they hear his name invoked, or the name of Jesus ... nor can they act ought at that time, after hearing of that Sacred Name.

On the other hand, Kirk believes, if I follow him, that the fairies have at least had their chance of salvation, for by the Harrowing of Hell he understands Christ's ministry to the fairies. He consequently attributes to them doubts which he seems to share himself: 'Som say their continuall sadness is because of their pendulous state . . . as uncertain what at the last Revolution will becom of them, when they are lockt up into an unchangable condition.'[6]

Even the saints cannot agree on this question. The fairies persuaded Crom Dubh (here, of course, St. Patrick's servant, not the pagan god) to ask Patrick, 'What time will the Slánagh Sídhe go to Paradise?' Patrick's answer, though not gladly received, at least admits the possibility that the fairies will eventually be saved: 'Not till the Day of Judgment, for certain.' However, when no less a person than Manannan mac Lir put the same question to Colum Cille, that severer saint replied unequivocally, 'There is no forgiveness to be got'. Manannan very reasonably retorted: 'Woe is me! for years I've helped the Catholics of Ireland, but I'll do it no more, till they're weak as water.'[7]

Modern authorities are no less divided. Lady Wilde, who asserts surprisingly that the people regard the fairies 'as inferior beings to themselves', adds that 'they know well that all the fairy spite against them is caused by envy and jealousy because man has been created immortal, while the Sidhe race is doomed to extinction at the last day'.[8] Lady Wilde's own husband, Sir William Wilde, takes quite the opposite view: 'They believe that God will admit the fairies into his palace on the day of judgment, and were it not for this that they would strike or enchant men and cattle much more frequently.'[9] Sir William is on good authority, for a fairy himself told one of Evans Wentz's informants that 'We could cut off half the human race, but would not . . . for we are expecting salvation'.[10] Yeats is on the pessimistic side. According to him, the fairies and even their human captives are 'happy, the story has it, but doomed to melt at the Last Judgment like bright vapour, for the soul cannot live without sorrow'.[11] This is Yeats's early prose at its most beautiful, but the words 'the story has it' cannot disguise the fact that Yeats's image owes as much to his own imagination as it does to folklore. The happiness ascribed to the fairies here does not agree with Kirk, with the usual tradition, nor even with Yeats's own early poem, 'The Priest and the Fairy' (1889). This poem is specifically based on 'The Belated Priest', in Patrick Kennedy's *Legendary Fictions of the Irish Celts* (1866),[12] but concerns the same sort of question as those put to Patrick and Colum Cille. A fairy asks a priest, 'Man of wisdom, dost thou know/Where the souls of fairies go?' In reply, "They are lost, they are lost, each one," cried he'. Consequently, '. . . all the *sad* fay chivalry/Upraised their voices bitterly' (emphasis added).[13] It is strange that Yeats's pose, alike in this poem and *The Celtic Twilight*, is so consistently pessimistic, for one of his own informants told him that the fairies 'are getting scarce now, because their time's over, ye see, and they're going back' to paradise.[14] Privately, Yeats did not believe the fairies to be angels at all.[15]

Those who believe the fairies to be damned sometimes add an escape clause, though without much faith in it. According to a beggarwoman of Derry, 'They say if there's wan drap o' blood in them at the Judgment Day they'll be pardoned, but I don't believe they have wan drap o' blood in them'.[16] The Church, on the other hand, used to encourage intermarriage between mortals and fairies, on the grounds that 'The consummation of such a marriage conferred a soul upon the soul-less fairy or elemental, and the children of such a marriage were, by virtue of having one christian parent, possessed of christian souls'. Margaret Dean-Smith thought this confirmed somewhere in the works of Paracelsus and St. Thomas Aquinas, though she could not remember where.[17]

There is obviously no sense in attempting to adjudicate on this question, but it may not be irrelevant, as Professor Francis John Byrne has pointed out to me in conversation, that the early Irish Church was somewhat influenced by Pelagius, who held that even Satan will be saved in the end. Traces of this heresy can be found in 'The Voyage of Brendan' and Adomnan's *Life of Columba*.

III. Ghosts

The relationship of fairies with ghosts is much more complex than their relationship with angels. Kirk, at least, did not think that fairies were ghosts, but was aware of a second opinion:

But other Men of the second sight being illiterate and unwary in their observations [aver] those subterranean people to be departed souls attending a whil in this inferior state, and cloth'd with bodies procured through their Alms-deeds in this Lyfe called *cuirp dhaondachbach* viz. fluid, active aethereal vehicles to hold them, that they may not scatter, nor wander and be lost in the Totum, or their first nothing.[18]

Something like these *cuirp dhaondachbach* can be seen in 'The Voyage of Brendan', in which Brendan and his party find the ghost of Judas Iscariot sitting on a rock in the ocean while temporarily released from Hell. He has a cloth on his head which he gave to a leper on earth, but because he bought it with the Twelve's money it beats in his eyes. He has also two ox-tongues which he gave to the priests on earth. The fish gnaw these ox-tongues and so do not gnaw him. His rock is one that he placed in a boggy path on earth.[19]

In times more recent than Kirk's, whether fairies be ghosts or not seems to depend as much on the folklore collector as on the informant. Evans Wentz was nearly always told that they were, though one of his informants did say that 'Besides the *gentry*, who are a distinct class, there are bad spirits and ghosts, which are nothing like them'.[20] Rare traditions do emphatically support the identificiation. For instance, 'In Ireland the Fairy Fair is called 'The Fair of the Dead', and is held on November Eve, but these dead are sometimes called the Fairies, and their King, Finvarra, is called the Fairy King'.[21] On the other hand, I was always told that the fairies were not ghosts. It behooves the collector to examine his evidence carefully, for fairy tales and ghost tales can resemble each other closely while still remaining quite distinct. A pertinent example is Lady Wilde's 'Kathleen', in which a girl is given a 'ring of herbs' by 'a beautiful lady'. By burning a leaf of it, she can see her dead lover, 'very pale but crowned with gold, and dancing in a noble company'. When her mother makes the sign of the cross, the girl dies, exclaiming: 'Mother! Mother! the dead are coming after me! They are here!' Both Lady Wilde herself and K. M. Briggs think this demonstrates a connection between ghosts and fairies, but the fact is that fairies are never mentioned in the story. Briggs is on much surer ground when she says that the story is an example of 'folk tales which show the danger of longing too much after the dead'.[22] Terminology is also important. MacManus points out that a Donegal name for the fairies, '*Sluagh Beatha*, the hosts of life', strongly suggests 'that they were considered to be not those dead and buried in barrows but vital and eternally living people'.[23]

What one has most carefully to consider in weighing the evidence is whether a given tale or tradition reflects on the fairies themselves or on their human captives. It is these last who can very reasonably be taken for ghosts. If they are mistaken for true fairies, they naturally cause confusion. Mr. C, for instance, emphatically denied that ghosts were fairies, but, when I pressed him on the matter, he conceded that dead children were believed to become fairies. In illustration, he told me this story, supposed to have happened locally. A girl died. A little later, her mother was cutting grass on the side of a hill when suddenly the dead child appeared before her, demanding the sickle. The mother was too terrified to respond. There came a sound of fairy music, and the child said, 'Ah, it's too late now, I'm done for', and vanished.

According to Mr. C, it is only dead children who may become fairies. Other traditions specify other types of ghost. On Tory Island, according to Elizabeth Andrews, 'and in some other parts of Donegal it is believed that those who are drowned become fairies. In Tory Island I also heard that those who exceeded in whisky met the same fate.'[24] Yeats likewise says that 'There is something mysterious about the ghosts of the drowned that I do not well know. They seem to have a more intense life in them than other ghosts, or to be under the power of the fairies, or in some other way distinguished among the commonality of ghosts.' This extends to drowned cattle as well as to drowned men.[25] A fourth type of ghost was specified by John Graham, an old man who lived near Tara. According to him, 'People killed and murdered in war stay on earth till their time is up, and they are among the *good people*'.[26]

Now, running over these examples again, we see that the child in Mr. C's story, if she is a fairy, is not glad to be. She has her chance to escape, but loses it when other fairies approach, as indicated by their music. Yeats suggests, not that the ghosts of the drowned are fairies, but that they are *'under the power of* the fairies'. It is likewise reasonable to suppose that the ghosts of drunkards are being punished, not rewarded. Again, John Graham says, not that the ghosts of war-victims are fairies, but that they are *among* the fairies, and stay with them only until 'their time is up'. In other words, these traditions do not assert that any type of ghost becomes a fairy. What they do indicate is summarised by Reidar Christiansen: '. . . when so many visitors to the subterranean world have there met people known to have died long ago . . . the reason is not that the Little People are identical with the dead but that they are their guardians.'[27]

IV. The *Cóiste Bodhar*

There is more than one set of circumstances under which the dead may consort with the fairies. One involves the *cóiste bodhar*. The name means literally 'deaf coach', but in Louth and Meath the *cóiste bodhar* is more appropriately known as the 'Dead Coach'. It is an omen of death, and also the vehicle of the dead. It may, indeed, combine these functions. When there is to be a death in a certain Limerick family, the *cóiste bodhar* 'drives up to the hall door, and on arrival there every seat save one is seen to be occupied by the ghost of an ancestor'.[28] Elsewhere, it may be the driver, rather than the passengers, who is a ghost.[29] More often, however, the driver will not be recognisable anyway, as, like the horses, he will be headless.[30] Alternatively, the whole contraption may be invisible, and known only by its sound. In this way, it may 'pass even through a crowded town'.[31] Occasionally, the Devil is said to hunt the soul of a sinner in the *cóiste bodhar*.[32] This seems a forced adaptation of the motif to a different tradition.

One suspects that originally the *cóiste bodhar* was a purely ghostly phenomenon, as there seems no need to involve the fairies with it at all. The fairies are, however, frequently involved with it. It is not very surprising that the banshee sometimes rides in it, but more so that in 'Paudyeen O'Kelly and the Weasel' a local king and queen of the fairies enjoy that convenience.[33] A very strange motif in one story is that a man saw two fairies churning inside the *cóiste bodhar*.[34] It is also surprising that the *cóiste bodhar* is not always regarded with horror. One of Evans Wentz's informants described it as accompanied by the 'most beautiful singing, just like fairy music, but she could not understand the words'.[35] When one of Lady Gregory's informants saw it, 'it was full of ladies, letting the window up and down and laughing out at her. They had golden hair, or it looked so with the lights. They were dressed in white, and there were bunches of flowers about the horses' heads.'[36]

V. Burials

When the *cóiste bodhar* is seen carrying the dead, one cannot help thinking that it is as much a hearse as a coach, even if the dead are alive within it. Sometimes they are not alive, and it really is a hearse. 'About two months ago', wrote a child from Kiltartan in 1938, a guard saw a hearse surrounded by 'people dressed in white' deliver 'something' to a graveyard, where the people buried it. 'The freshly dug grave can be seen there now and people are afraid to open it.'[37] Supposing there is no rational explanation for this incident, several possibilities suggest themselves which again mingle fairies with the human dead. This burial may have been a reflection, a sort of mirage, of a funeral in the natural world. The fairies are said to participate in human funerals. 'So are they seen to carry the Bier or coffin with the Corps, among the middle-earth men to the grave,' says Kirk;[38] and Lady Gregory: 'There was never a funeral they were not at, walking after the other people.'[39] Of course, 'midle-earth men' were not present, at least as participants, at the burial in Kiltartan, but the two phenomena seem similar at any rate.

A second possibility is that the 'something' buried in Kiltartan was itself a fairy. This goes against the tradition of the fairies' immortality, but that is nothing unusual. There are many stories in which a man is compelled by the fairies to carry a coffin from graveyard to graveyard until at last he is allowed to bury it, and in these stories the occupant of the coffin is presumably a fairy.[40]

A final possibility is that the fairies were not burying anything, but

The Quick and the Dead

digging it up. In Jeremiah Curtin's 'Mor's Sons and the Herder From Under the Sea', the fairies carry a coffin that contains a mortal who, from their point of view, is alive, although her relatives believe her to be dead and buried.[41] This mortal is, of course, a changeling. This brings us to the tradition in which ghosts and fairies are most closely associated.

VI. Changelings

A changeling is either a mortal stolen by the fairies or someone or something left by the fairies in place of that mortal. The belief in changelings is very old. Baile and Aillinn, for instance, may be considered changelings, but clearer examples can be found in 'The Colloquy with the Ancients' and three Lives of St. Coemgen. In 'The Colloquy', Aedh, the son of Eochaid Lethderg king of Leinster, is captured with fifty other youths by Slad and Mumain, daughters of Bodhb Derg, during a hurling match. The captives are imprisoned in the *sídh* of Liamhain Soft-smock, but escape after three years and take refuge with St. Patrick, who eventually restores them to Eochaid Lethderg. Eochaid begs, 'let not the *tuatha dé danann*'s power any more prevail against the lad' (Aedh), and Patrick replies, 'that death which the king of Heaven and of Earth hath ordained is the one that he will have'.[42] In the Lives of Coemgen, we are told that Colman son of Coirpre, the king of Úi Muiredach, gave his last-born son Faelan to Coemgen to foster because fairies had stolen all his other children. In all three Lives, the language is very specific and worth quoting. The first says: 'Sprites used to carry off his children by druidism' (*ó mbeirdís siabhra a cland uadha tre draidheacht*). Solomon's Verse Life of Coemgen says:

> The fairy folk carried off the children
>   Of the king . . .
> (But) this child to be baptized to Coemgen
>   Through fear of the fairies he sent.
>
> (*An táos sithe rucc a clanna*
>   *An righ sin* . . .
> *An ghein da bhaisttedh go Caoimhghin*
>   *Tre ceist an tsiodha docuir*).

Finally, Solomon's Prose Life says: 'And the reason why [Colman] sent [Faelan] to [Coemgen] was because every son that had been previously born to him had been destroyed by the bright people or fairy courts' (*I* as uime dochuir chuige é, do brigh go millthighe leisan aois áin, no leisna siodh-bhruighibh, gach mac dá mbeirrthi roimhesin dó).[43] In modern times, to cite one example, the child in Mr. C's story above (p. 134) is evidently a changeling.

Anyone at all may be taken for a changeling. Old people are safest, because they are of least use, but at least one sexagenarian was taken at Coole. Biddy Early, a famous wisewoman, explained: 'Wouldn't he be of use to them to drive out their cattle?'[44] Even the cattle themselves may be taken for changelings, especially if they appear to have drowned.[45] Bulls and bullocks, however, are said to 'possess immunity from fairy assaults'.[46] One alleged reason why the fairies need changelings is that, 'once in seven years', they have 'to pay a tribute to Hell' (called the teind, or 'tithe,' in Scotland), and they prefer 'to sacrifice mortals rather than their own kind'.[47] However, although this belief exists in Ireland, I suspect it is more native to Scotland; it is certainly a minority opinion. Normally, changelings are taken for playmates, at best, or for slaves, at worst. Precisely why they are taken depends on what sort of person they are. Children may be most at risk. Quite often the fairies are said to need mortal children because they have none of their own. By the same token, mortal women may be taken in order to bear children. One of Lady Gregory's informants, however, denies this tradition, saying, 'don't believe those that say they have no children'. On the other hand, this informant states that 'A boy among them . . . must be matched with a woman from earth. And the same way with their women, they must get a husband here. And they never can give the breast to a child, but must get a nurse from here.'[48] This last point is seldom disputed, although Briggs apparently doubts that it is a case of fairies being *unable* to suckle; in her view, 'Human milk is much esteemed by the fairies; there seemed to be a notion that it might give fairy babies the chance of a human soul.'[49] Besides wet-nurses, the fairies also require mortal midwives. Midwives are not true changelings, as their visits to fairyland are of short duration and nothing is left in their place; the same is generally true of wet-nurses. However, mortal women who bear children in fairyland are changelings. A less plausible reason for the fairies' taking women is that 'they make queens' of them 'for as long as they live or that they are satisfied with them'.[50] The fairies may not be able to provide their own children, but surely they can provide their own queens?

It is young men and women who are most likely to be taken for playmates. Of one young man it was said, 'It's always the like of him that's taken, that are good for singing or dancing or any good thing at all'.[51] Yeats refers often to one young woman who 'After seven years . . . was brought home again . . . but she had no toes left. She had danced them off'.[52] Besides such amusements, young people may also be taken to assist the fairies 'in their fights and in their work'.[53] In ancient times, Cu Chulainn was taken to assist in the wars of the Tuatha Dé Danann,[54] but such fighting is now uncommon. More symbolic combat like hurley is normal. This, too, dates from ancient times: there is, for instance, an account of the Tuatha Dé Danann at hurley in 'The Pursuit of Diarmuid and Grainne'.[55] Like midwives, men taken to assist at this sport are only temporary captives. Though normally capable of giving good blows of their own, the fairies seem to need from a mortal hurley-player some more earthy strength than theirs, just as they need the more substantial milk of a mortal wet-nurse.

Though it may seem odd to a dualistic mind, it must be understood that the fairies take their captives body and soul. This is even considered true when the body of the victim appears to be present, recognisable, and frequently conscious. When the sufferer is not dead or seriously ill, we would say that he had lost his wits. But the Irish explanation is that this only seems to be the victim's body; in reality, it is a changeling made to resemble him through glamour. If the victim is human and conscious, the changeling is probably a fairy, 'either a fairy boy who did not thrive, an old fellow of whom they felt themselves well rid, or even at times a family man who wanted a rest from the responsibilities of his position'. In some cases, the fairies may be injuring one of their own as well as the human family afflicted. This is obviously true of the 'old fellow', but even in the case of a child the fairy mother may be 'as anxious as the mortal to undo the exchange'. If the victim is unconscious, and especially if she is female, the changeling is probably a 'stock', or mere piece of wood. This may be of roughly human shape to begin with, but glamoured as well. A 'stock' is also left when cattle are stolen. In this case, it may actually move about, though only for a short time.[56]

For some reason, fairies substituted for infants are often pipers. When they play upon their tiny bagpipes, anyone listening will be forced to dance until he drops exhausted.[57] This may amuse the changeling, but it also gives him away. Alternatively, he may be tricked into adult speech, and so exposed.

There are two main ways to get rid of a changeling. One is to treat him with great kindness, whereupon the fairies, in gratitude, will not only undo the exchange but also bestow prosperity on the gentle parents. The other way, which is unfortunately more often practised, is to torment the changeling, usually by burning. This may drive him away, or compel the other fairies to fetch him, but it will also invite punishment. A third way to get rid of a changeling occurs in Crofton

Croker's 'The Young Piper': the changeling takes himself off when he would otherwise be compelled to cross running water.[58] However, all methods besides kindness are accompanied by danger, quite apart from earning the enmity of the fairies. One changeling, about to be drowned, drowned his tormentor; another, about to be burnt, 'gave three great puffs and blew the fire all over the room, and set the house on fire', again killing his tormentors while escaping himself.[59]

An adult victim often invites his own fate by talking about himself too freely to a stranger who turns out to be a fairy. It may be sufficient for the fairies to know a man's name to gain power over him.[60] The next stage will be the 'touch' or 'stroke', actually a violent blow delivered by a fairy hand, whether visible or not. This is the origin of the word 'stroke', meaning 'apoplexy', in medical parlance. The victim, to all appearances, then either quickly dies or remains alive but useless. Actually, he is with the fairies. The worst strokes are those of a fairy queen, which cannot be cured, and of a fairy fool (*amadhán*), which can be cured only by the touch of the queen. This last is not given gratis. In return for healing one victim, the queen will generally demand another, 'sometimes a good looking young man to be her husband'. The fool is 'ugly and deformed', and his stroke, if it does not kill, always produces 'some deformity of body or mind'.[61]

People taken for changelings may in due course return. (In plain English, they recover their health or their wits.) Their period of captivity may be only an hour or two, but if it is longer it is generally seven years or a multiple thereof: fourteen or twenty-one. A person who has been 'away' will normally not remember anything of fairyland. There are exceptions to this rule, however, and in fact such persons are often suspected, not only of remembering fairyland, but also of enjoying a preternatural knowledge of this world. For instance, they may know the location of lost objects. The suspicion can seldom be confirmed, for such persons are either unwilling or unable to communicate their knowledge.[62] Unless the fairies grant them immortality, all who are taken do return at last, if only to die. When a mortal changeling's days are numbered, 'she'll be put in the place of some other one that's taken, and so she'll get absolution'. What is extraordinary is that even those believed to be dead and buried may return. An example recorded by Lady Gregory can only be set down without comment:

Mike Folan was here the other day telling us newses, and he told the strangest thing ever I heard — that happened to his own first cousin. She died and was buried, and a year after, her husband was sitting by the fire, and she came back and walked in. He gave a start, but she said, 'Have no fear of me, I was never in the coffin and never buried, but I was kept away for the year.' So he took her again and they reared four children after that.[63]

The exchange of fairies and mortals, though for obvious reasons not appreciated by the latter, does have its advantages. For instance, the healing powers of 'fairy doctors' have to be brought from the Otherworld somehow. Biddy Early, the famous wisewoman of Feakle, Co. Clare, is an outstanding example. She possessed not only healing powers and a knowledge of herbs but also a mysterious bottle which she used like a crystal ball to diagnose diseases. There are several variant legends as to how she obtained her powers, her knowledge, and her bottle, but all involve the changeling tradition. In one version, she made friends with a fairy changeling, who gave them to her. Others say that she received them from a relative, either her brother or her son, on his return from fairyland. Still others say that she was 'away' herself for seven years. She, apparently, boasted that she went voluntarily with the fairies every night, while others report that she used to confer with them in her stable. It is said that when necessary she was even able to send her patients home with the fairies.[64] Although Biddy Early was blessed by the fairies, the coin does have another side, for those taken by the fairies who fail to live up to their expectations may be cursed. Men whose assistance in battle proves inadequate may be sent home with a crooked neck or a lame leg.[65]

Various precautions should be used to prevent the fairies taking changelings. For instance, someone should always say, 'God bless us!' when a bride sneezes, for if she sneezes three times without this precaution she will be in danger.[66] A child that never sneezes, on the other hand, is regarded as already enchanted.[67] Conversely, a stricken child may be cured (with elaborate ceremony) by making it sneeze three times. 'A new-married couple should retire to rest at the same time, for if the bride was left alone, the fairies would come and steal her away for the sake of her fine clothes.'[68] One tradition holds that 'If a man leaves the house after his wife's confinement, some of his clothes should be spread over the mother and infant, or the fairies will carry them both off' (the mother for a wet-nurse).[69] This has an obvious bearing on the much-debated question of whether the Ancient Irish practised the *couvade*.

Besides such precautions, there are numerous protective charms that may be used against the fairies. These charms prevent changelings, but are of wider application too. Probably the most powerful is rowan wood, also known as 'quicken' and 'mountain ash'. In Ulster it is called the 'Gentle Bush' ('fairy bush', in other words).[70] In *Duanaire Finn* there is a song in praise of a Wry Rowan (*Cáortsthann Cas*) in Gleann Da

Ghealt, which suggests that it may have been sacred to Danu in ancient times.[71] A cross or branch of rowan wood is effective if hung over the churn, the door, or the cradle. Cows may be protected by tying a withe of the wood round the horns.[72] Presumably only fallen wood should be used, as Mr. C tells me that it is unlucky even to touch rowan, and unluckier still to cut or burn it. Fallen withes, however, cannot be easy to find.

In ancient times, yew was still more potent than rowan. In modern times, however, I have come across only one mention of its use in place of rowan.[73] Primrose is a more common alternative on May Eve (a dangerous time), and Mr. B and Mr. F tell me that the urban working class may substitute furze. Primroses are scattered over the threshold as well as hung over the door. Louis C. Jones, however, thinks this is the reverse of a charm against the fairies; he thinks it is to welcome 'them back from the hills after the winter'.[74]

Other charms to prevent the fairies from taking changelings include: a small bag tied round the neck, 'with three rounds of red ribbon or thread, containing a nail from the shoe of an ass and some hair of a black cat'; the blood of a crowing hen; a black-handled knife; iron in general; the Bible; bread; salt; charcoal; and flax. Flax is potent not only in its green state, but even in the form of finished linen.[75] Since linen underwear always has been worn even by the poorest classes in Ireland,[76] one cannot help thinking that there is some absurdity here.

Prevention is better than cure, but cures can be effected as well. Since a fairy changeling resembles the mortal he has replaced, one must first ascertain whether one's patient is already a changeling. A certain concoction of herbs can be used for this purpose. If it stays green when boiled, the patient is still 'right'; if it turns yellow, he is a changeling. In either case, he should then be given the mixture to drink. Alternatively, digitalis may be administered. Either potion will heal the patient if he is 'right'; otherwise, he will refuse it, or die.[77] Other cures involve oat-meal and hen's dung, but require the healer to have himself been 'away'.[78]

Medical means are not the only means for recovering a person in the fairies' power, however. There is always the resort to force, especially when the victim is female. In this case, the changeling body is ignored. One has to find the victim herself among her fairy captors. These, of course, are normally invisible, but if by some device the victim can be observed on the road with them, dust or milk may be thrown at the fairies, or the prisoner may be stroked with a branch of rowan, or with ground-ivy (*athair-luss*).[79] Any of these actions will liberate her.

If the captive cannot be found on the roads, then one must go to the *sidh* itself. The entrance can be found by walking nine times around the hill at full moon. One may enter and leave with impunity provided that he carries a stick of green rowan and, once inside, refrains from eating or drinking, or from kissing a fairy. He can then grab the prisoner and run away with her. A knife left across the entrance of the *sídh* will prevent pursuit.[80] What vengeance the fairies may take later is a different question.

Its failure to distinguish between body and soul marks the changeling tradition as very primitive, and two of the more ingenious theories put forward to explain it suppose it to be a folk-memory of primitive rites. The Rees brothers suppose the rite to have been 'analogous to baptism'. In this rite, the human child would have been 'ritually "expelled" or "exposed" so as to separate it from the supernatural and save it from being possessed by its mysterious 'other' self'.[81] One weakness here is that the child would always be restored to normality, or, if the exposure was severe, perhaps die. It does not explain how modern changelings may continue to live. Also, it does not account for adult or bovine changelings. Alfred Nutt's theory could be applied to adult changelings, though he himself confines it to children. He proposes that the changeling tradition is a folk-memory of human sacrifice. If children were anciently sacrificed to the fairies, in Christian times the fairies would be remembered as stealing the children. Furthermore, sacrificial victims would have to be in acceptable physical condition, and this would explain the belief that the fairies 'carried off the healthy and left in exchange the sickly'.[82] The essential objection here is just that there is no reason to believe that humans ever were sacrificed to the fairies. A further weakness with both these theories is that the changeling tradition does not express itself as a memory but as a belief in something that is happening now.

That objection does not apply to the appealing medical theory of a certain von Sydow, who 'has pointed out that the onset of rickets may transform, sometimes quite suddenly, a healthy child into a deformed cripple, and that this may have been responsible for the idea of the fairy changeling'.[83] This, again, will account only for infant changelings, but apoplexy will account as well for adult changelings. No such explanation is required for cattle, as stolen cattle always die. These medical phenomena must have reinforced the changeling belief, but whether they will wholly account for it may be doubted on the grounds that they clearly will not account for other traditions associating ghosts with fairies, such as the *cóiste bodhar*.

Primitive as the changeling tradition is, the earliest texts which clearly incorporate it — 'The Colloquy' and the Lives of Coemgen – are still late enough to be explicitly Christian, and the tradition may be the unintended result of Christian influence. The first Christian missionaries preached to the Irish that the soul after death goes to the Otherworld. That was easily understood, but the Irish were unlikely to appreciate that the Christian Otherworld (Heaven or Hell) was not the same as their own (Tír na nÓg). Hence, the soul after deaths joins the fairies. This shares with the orthodox Christian belief the great appeal of denying that the dead have ceased to exist. It was no great step to extend this belief from those who are dead and buried to those who are only 'dead to the world'. From this belief may stem all other beliefs associating the dead with fairies.

And yet the fact remains that mortals in fairyland are not the same as fairies. They are not there of their own accord and they would generally be glad to leave. They presumably do not share all of the fairies' powers (otherwise, they could leave); certainly the fairies do not share all of theirs. For instance, the fairies require human milk and strength at hurley. If they did not, they would not take captives. Fairies and mortals are differently affected by charms: whereas rowan impedes the fairies, it liberates their captives. Finally, and most importantly, mortals do not remain in fairyland for ever. In the end, they die indeed. As the fairies themselves are between men and angels, fairyland is between earth and heaven. It is a sojourning place for the soul, not a final destination. As Christiansen says, the fairies are not among the dead, but the guardians of the dead. In the final analysis, then, it may be flatly stated that the fairies are not ghosts.

11. THE HOST OF THE AIR

I now turn to the alleged distinction between the trooping fairies and the solitary fairies. This distinction is based on three tenets: first, obviously, the trooping fairies are social while the solitary fairies are not; second, the trooping fairies are supposed to 'wear green coats and red caps while the solitary fairies . . . wear red';[1] third, one class is hostile to men, and the other friendly. However, the fact is that none of these distinctions will conform with the evidence. There is little or no difference between the solitary and the trooping fairies, except in the minds of folklorists.

I. The Costume of the Solitary Fairies

As the leprechaun is a typically solitary fairy in his habits, as normally portrayed, it is significant that in an RBÉ manuscript account he wears the very colours attributed above to the trooping fairies: green, with a red cap and black, pointed shoes.[2] An old lady from Ulster, who claimed to have seen a leprechaun, differed only in giving him a black hat instead of a red cap.[3] Lady Wilde has him dressed in green even to his cap.[4]

The mermaid's magic cap is always red. A rare description of the rest of her costume makes it green. She too, in other words, wears the costume normally ascribed to the trooping fairies.[5]

The banshee, on the other hand, is sometimes described as wearing red. Mr. C told me that two young men at Glencar, Co., Sligo, saw and heard the banshee around 1940, and on that occasion she wore red, 'with something over it'. She wears a red coat in an RBÉ manuscript, too.[6] The banshee of Shane's Castle, however, while she wears a 'scarlet mantle', also wears 'a green kirtle'.[7] Briggs describes the banshee (generically) as wearing 'a grey cloak over a green dress', but quotes an account in which the banshee wears white.[8] White is also what she wears in 'a remote region of the Decies without Drum, County Waterford'.[9] This tradition may be spurious, however, as Patricia Lysaght points out that a 'faulty etymology often translates *bean sí* as if it were *bán sí*, meaning "white fairy"'.[10] According to

Wood-Martin, the banshee wears white if she is young, but black if she is old.[11] One thing that is nearly always red about the banshee is her hair,[12] although Lysaught states that 'Most often it is . . . grey or white — the hair of a very old woman'.[13]

II. The Costume of the Trooping Fairies

It seems, then, that there is nothing typical about red as the costume of the solitary fairies. Nor does green, as the costume of the trooping fairies, seem much more authentic. Evans Wentz was told of 'a whole tribe of little red men living in Glen Odder, between Ringlestown and Tara', and, on the other side of the country, in Co. Sligo, of 'a great company of *gentry*, like soldiers, in red'.[14] Somewhat further south, Lady Gregory heard of 'red men riding through the country and going over ditches;[15] while up in Ulster one man saw a 'company of wee people in scarlet' at a holy well.[16]

Red, of course, is the colour that the trooping fairies are particularly supposed *not* to wear. It would appear, however, that red and green do not distinguish trooping fairies from solitary fairies but one faction of trooping fairies from another, for a man in Co. Antrim 'met . . . two regiments of *them* . . . coming along the road towards Glenavy. One regiment was dressed in red and one in blue or green uniform'.[17] Another man 'saw a battle between the green jacket fairies and the red'.[18] The possibility that the Antrim fairies' uniforms were blue, not green, is a real one, as a group of fairies 'dressed in bright blue' has been seen in Co. Limerick[19] and in Co. Sligo a blue-clad fairy who 'seemed to be like a soldier of the *gentry* on guard'. This still by no means exhausts the colours that trooping fairies have been seen in. Patrick Waters said that 'The *gentry* . . . usually appear white',[20] and companies of fairies in white have been seen in Kiltartan at least twice.[21] On Tory Island, on the other hand, the fairies dress in black.[22] On Innisbofin, Co. Galway, 'a number of fairy girls, dressed in brown,' were once seen.[23] In addition to these colours, the fairies' clothes need not be of a single colour at all. According to Kirk, the Irish fairies wore 'Suanochs', or tartan clothes,[24] and Mrs Sheridan, an ex-changeling, told Lady Gregory that 'the others' wore striped or 'bracket' (literally, 'speckled or variegated') clothing, which, as Yeats comments, seem to be 'a description of the plaids and stripes of medieval Ireland'.[25]

It seems, then, that , in modern as in ancient Ireland, all fairies wear simply what it pleases them to wear. As one old man said to W. B. Yeats, 'they have dresses of all kinds of colours'.[26] Possessing the power of glamour, they can in any case change colour at will.[27] It follows that the colour of the fairies' clothing cannot be predicted and so cannot be used as a criterion to distinguish solitary from trooping fairies.

III. The Disposition of the Solitary Fairies

A distinction between fairies on the basis of their disposition towards men is not promising to begin with. Those who propose it cannot agree with each other as to whether it is the solitary fairies or the trooping fairies who are malevolent. Indeed, they have difficulty in maintaining their own consistency. Yeats states in his *Irish Fairy Tales* (1892) that the solitary fairies are the malevolent ones, but strongly implies in his note to 'The Host of the Air' (1899) that the trooping fairies are.[28] Katharine Briggs, in her *Dictionary*, attributes particular malevolence to the solitary fairies. However, in quoting with approval from William Allingham's 'The Fairies', 'Wee folk, good folk,/Trooping all together, she fails to notice that 'good' is euphemistic, since 'We daren't go a-hunting/For fear of little men'.[29] In my view, both the solitary fairies and the trooping fairies are malevolent at some times and benign at others, and so no distinction can be made.

Detailed evidence for the disposition of the solitary fairies is available in chapter eight. In summary, the leprechaun may present you with treasure, but if possible will trick you out of it. The cluricaun is light-fingered and unkind to animals. In general, though, both the leprechaun and the cluricaun are fairly harmless, but will not go out of their way to do favours for mortals. Some mermaids are friendly to men and some are killers. The banshee is a truly ambiguous figure. Is it a service or a disservice to give warning of death? The fact that the banshee bewails the death seems to prove that she is at least sympathetic. Of the banshee of Shane's Castle we are told, 'There is no harm or fear of evil in her mere presence, unless she is seen in the act of crying.' This particular banshee, apparently, is often seen simply taking her ease.[30] On the other hand, one banshee, Cleena, used to lure to destruction the very men whose deaths she lamented.[31] In general, then, there is no telling whether a solitary fairy will prove dangerous or not.

IV. The Disposition of the Trooping Fairies

It is equally true of the trooping fairies that their conduct towards men covers the whole spectrum from sheer helpfulness to sheer harmfulness, with a sort of rough justice in-between. A story told by Mr. C amusingly exemplifies the helpful end of the spectrum. A man going home one very wet, dark night had a 'wee river' to cross that was too broad to jump, and, although he knew that there were stepping-stones, he could not find them. All of a sudden he heard a yell and lights shone out. On the hill behind him, he saw 'thousands of people, waltzing and a-dancing, and the lights shining down over him and across the river'. He looked up and said, 'Thank you, gentlemen', and crossed the river. On the other side he turned round and said again, 'Thank you now and God bless you!' The crowd responded, 'James is safe now, we'll go back; we'll go back now, James is safe.'

By 'rough justice' I mean punishment inflicted by the fairies on those who interfere with them in some way. Those who help them may by the same principle be rewarded. Crofton Croker's 'Legend of Knockgrafton' is an obviously fictitious but pleasant example. A hunchback who hears the fairies singing *'Da Luan, Da Mort, Da Luan, Da Mort'* (i.e. *Dé Luain, Dé Máirt*, 'Monday, Tuesday') improves their song by adding *'augus Da Cadine'* (i.e. *agus Dé Céadaoin*, 'and Wednesday') and is rewarded by the removal of his hump. Another hunchback seeks to emulate him but only spoils the song by adding *'augus Da Hena'* (i.e. *agus Dé hAoine*, 'and Friday'). The fairies inflict on him a second hump, from which he soon dies.[32] Such even-handed justice is comparatively rare, however. More typical is the case of a man punished with a hump and a beating and a speedy death for throwing stones at the fairies.[33] The most common offence, of course, is meddling with raths and lone bushes. One man was punished with a twisted face for cutting a lone bush; another got a pain in his knee and died in two days.[34] A girl near Finntown who washed clothes in a stream frequented by the fairies had 'Her eyes turned to the back of her head'.[35] Blinding is a fairly standard punishment. In many stories, it is inflicted on a midwife who steals some ointment bestowing the second sight while assisting at a fairy birth.[36] Spying merits the same punishment, which is why the simple technique of kneeling on the right knee with the left eye closed in order to see the fairies is not more frequently employed.[37] However, the fairies often content themselves with blinding only the eye that spies. A different sort of prying was committed by a woman who met the *cóiste bodhar* and got inside. She was beaten with pieces of iron.[38] Changelings forcibly recovered from the fairies may be stricken deaf and dumb, perhaps so they cannot tell what they have seen.[39]

In all the above cases, even the last, there is some offence against the fairies, but it is hard to see why those who come across them accidentally should be punished. Nonetheless, a boy who did so at Buncrana, Co. Donegal, was struck dumb. Still more unfair was the case of a child whom the fairies surrounded of their own volition while he was asleep. He was left deaf and, although after ten years he did recover his hearing, he died when seventeen.[40] There seems little excuse, either, for the fairies' practice of afflicting hens and cows. Some say they only strike the cows accidentally, but they severely punish 'conjurers' who heal them again.[41]

V. The Stray Sod

Two special expressions of fairy malice deserve paragraphs to themselves. One is the Stray Sod, also known as the *Foidín Seachrain*, or 'Lone Sod'.[42] What happens is that one suddenly becomes lost, or 'takes a stray', in the Irish expression. This can happen even in a place that one knows very well, or in a place where it ought not to be possible. For instance, the gate of a field may disappear. Fairy paths are places where one is particularly likely to take a stray.[43] Other, unpredictable places have a bad reputation for being dangerous at certain hours of the day.[44] Any number of people can be affected. In the 'Life of Brendan of Clonfert', the entire army of Munster takes a stray.[45] A counter-measure is to turn one's coat inside out (the cap and waistcoat are sometimes added), but it is acknowledged that this often does no good. On 'mountain or moorland' 'a sprig of furze or gorse' is said to be more effective. Some accounts do not associate the stray sod with the fairies. It is said to occur where an unbaptised child is buried,[46] or where the water used to wash a corpse has been thrown away or the cloth used to dry it has been buried. This last type of stray sod wears off after a year.[47] Throwing any water out immediately after a person has left the house will cause him to go astray.[48] Normally, however, the stray sod is considered a fairy phenomenon. It is provoked by any misdeed of the victim's and, though it may sound like a comparatively harmless practical joke, the humour is invariably lost on the person who has taken a stray. The experience of one girl in particular suggests that it is much more sinister than a practical joke. Having taken a stray in woodland, she was twice forcibly turned round to walk in the wrong direction by a jolt inside her, and then prevented from leaving the area by an invisible wall. She herself was invisible and inaudible to a search party which she could clearly see and hear as little as twenty or thirty yards away. The whole experience was accompanied by a strong sensation of malevolence emanating from a point on the edge of a nearby *sídh* (Lis Ard, Co. Mayo).[49]

VI. The *Féar Gortach*

Similar in many ways to the stray sod is the *féar gortach*, or 'hungry grass'. What happens in this case is that one suddenly becomes famished to the point of collapse, and cannot rise again until he has something to eat, no matter how little. For this reason, one should always carry at least a single grain of oats wherever one goes.[50] The *féar gortach* is less often associated with the fairies than the stray sod. According to MacManus, it 'Occurs only where an uncoffined corpse has been laid on its way to a burial',[51] while, according to Mr. F, it marks a famine grave. Sir William Wilde, however, does say that the *féar gortach* is *'fairy-enchanted* grass' (emphasis his).[52] Again, the attack is unprovoked and so serious that an unprepared victim may starve to death where he falls.

VII. The Homogeneity of the Fairies

So, then, the trooping fairies are as likely to help a man find his way in the dark as they are to starve him to death without cause. Likewise, the solitary fairies may be the best of neighbours or the worst of enemies. Both are creatures of whim and cannot be counted on for evil or for good. They can no more be distinguished from each other by their conduct than they can by their clothing.

There remains only the obvious distinction that the solitary fairies appear on their own and the trooping fairies in groups. But in fact not even this will stand up to examination. In 'The King of the Lepracanes' journey to to Emania' the leprechauns have a society equal to that of Ulster, and in the 'Life of Brendan of Clonfert' they appear in a host.[53] In modern times, Thomas Keightley has a story called 'The Three Leprechauns', which he thinks is 'the only instance of more than one Leprechaun being seen at a time'.[54] It is not, however, for two of RBÉ's informants state that the leprechaun 'lives in a fort with the fairies'.[55] As for the cluricaun, 'A nineteenth-century Waterford account' describes 'a company of cluricauns' in terms unmistakably reminiscent of the trooping fairies: they are 'often heard and seen hunting, with sound of horns, cry of dogs, tramp of horses, cracking of whips, and 'tally-ho!' of huntsment'.[56] Banshees may congregate in groups to foretell 'the death of someone very great or holy'.[57] It appears, then, that there is no distinction whatsoever between the trooping and the solitary fairies. They are one and the same thing.

VIII. The *Sluagh Gaoithe*

How did this false distinction ever arise? Folklorists have sought in the world of faery a division which they would not expect to find in the world of men. Any person may be on his own at one moment and in company the next. So it is with the fairies. Today's solitary fairy is tomorrow's trooping fairy. But folklorists have been encouraged in this misunderstanding, I think, by the existence of the *Sluagh Gaoithe*, 'the host of the air'.

The *Sluagh Gaoithe* is named in a prayer from the Aran Islands which W. B. Yeats quotes at the end of his story 'The Adoration of the Magi':

> Seven paters seven times,
> Send Mary by her Son,
> Send Bridget by her mantle,
> Send God by His strength,
> Between us and the faery host,
> Between us and the demons of the air
>
> (*Seacht b-páidreacha fó seacht*
> *Chuir Muire faoi n-a Mac,*
> *Chuir Brighid faoi n-a brat,*
> *Chuir Dia faoi n-a neart,*
> *Eidir sinn 'san Sluagh Sidhe,*
> *Eidir sinn 'san Sluagh Gaoith.*)[58]

Yeats and other folklorists have read the terms *Sluagh Sidhe* and *Sluagh Gaoith* in this prayer as appositional. They are not. They are two different things.[59] All that I have denied in the case of the *Sluagh Sídhe* is true of the *Sluagh Gaoithe*: it exists only in the form of a troop (which is a black wind to mortal senses), and it is relentlessly malicious. Lady Gregory describes a typical experience. An old man

> was out in a small field, and was after binding up the grass, and the sky got very black over him and very dark. And he was thrown down on the ground, and got a great beating, but he could see nothing at all. He had done nothing to vex them, just minding his business in the field.[60]

Now this, of course, is an Irish account. That the *Sluagh Gaoithe* was known in Ireland in ancient times can be inferred from the 'Life of Brendan of Clonfert'; that it is known in Ireland today is evident from Yeats's statements and from his sources, the Aran prayer and P. W. Joyce's story of 'Fergus O'Mara and the Air-Demons'; from Lady Gregory's report; and from Douglas Hyde's folk-tale of 'The Old Hag of Dingle'. However, the *Sluagh Gaoithe* is primarily a Scottish phenomenon. In Scotland there exists a clear distinction between the Seelie Court (or good fairies) and the Unseelie Court (or bad fairies), and the *Sluagh Gaoithe* may be classed (as Briggs classes it) with the Unseelie Court. This fact, together with the confusion between the *Sluagh Gaoithe* and the *Sluagh Sídhe*, has, I believe, led folklorists to invent an Irish Unseelie Court and to call it 'the trooping fairies'. However, even the *Sluagh Gaoithe*'s inclusion in the Scottish Unseelie Court seems problematical, for, as Briggs herself remarks, it is not a host of fairies, but of damned souls.[61]

This appears clearly in the 'Life of Brendan'. Through the power of prayer, Brendan delivers the soul of a bad monk named Colman from torment in a black cloud to bliss in a white one.[62] Likewise, in 'The Old Hag of Dingle', the face of a woman damned for killing three unbaptised children is seen in a shower at sea.[63] The story told by P. W. Joyce on which Yeats partly relies is called 'Fergus O'Mara and the Air-*Demons*', not the air-fairies. Yeats himself hints at the likelihood of a connection between the names of the *Sluagh Gaoithe* and the Prince of the Powers of the Air.[64]

There is, as it happens, a very simple and appealing physiological explanation for the *Sluagh Gaoithe*. All the details in accounts like Lady Gregory's are compatible with the symptoms of epilepsy.[65] But that at present is not of the first importance. What matters for now is that the *Sluagh Gaoithe* is a primarily Scottish cloud of damned souls upon which has been built (in the minds of folklorists) a false tradition of an Irish troop of wicked fairies — all too literally, a castle in the air.

The Irish fairies are distinguished from one another by the roles they play *at any given moment*. Thus, a woman giving warning of death is at that moment a banshee. Tomorrow she may ride with the host and be a trooping fairy among others. There is nothing significant about what dress she happens to be wearing. Like all who are fallen from heaven, she is a mixture of good and evil. Though she is descended from the Morrigu, she retains only the Morrigu's habits, and not her steadfastness of character, for she is become a participant of the world of the Irish peasant, which is inconsistent by nature. The banshee differs from the mermaid and the women of the host, as the leprechaun differs from the cluricaun and the men of the host, only in the accidents of circumstance. All fairies are fundamentally alike, and their likeness consists in their capriciousness; for they have the power of glamour, and so may be great or small, red or green, as they choose. Unlike the mortals whom they steal and detain between heaven and earth, they are not sure that Christ has died for them, and are untrammelled by the webs of good and evil. They may choose at will to strike or refrain from striking. They are unpredictable. That is what it means to be a fairy.

PART THREE:
THE UNAPPEASABLE HOST

12. *THE COUNTESS CATHLEEN*: 'LONGING FOR A DEEPER PEACE'[1]

I. Yeats and the Fairies

The first transmutation of the fairy faith, from the mythology of Ancient Ireland to the superstition of modern Ireland, was very gradual and organic: the product of the slow influence of Christianity (and of sheer forgetfulness) upon an old pagan system, as over the centuries dripping water will transform a stone. The second transmutation was very different. It took place, not over centuries, but (as William Blake would say) in 'the pulse of an artery'; not for its own sake, but for the sake of art. This transformation occurred, not in the racial consciousness, but in the consciousness of a limited number of writers. One might mention Sir Samuel Ferguson, Aubrey de Vere, William Allingham, Standish James O'Grady, James Stephens, and others, but I am here concerned only with the work of W. B. Yeats as no-one better combined erudition, commitment, and expression than he.

It should not be thought, however, that we are dealing now with a mere literary plaything. Yeats does, of course, use the fairies symbolically, but they are not just symbols to him. A comparison with William Blake makes the point quite obvious: Blake could believe in almost anything, but no-one has suggested that he believed in the literal existence of Urthona. Yeats did believe in the fairies. His letters prove that beyond a doubt. His theories of fairy nature could be relatively sophisticated, as when he disclosed, as one theosophist to others, that 'The fairies are the lesser spiritual moods of that universal mind, wherein every mood is a soul and every thought a body'.[2] At the same time, however, he could believe in the fairies simply as little men. Nothing in his early work was more important to him. He 'realised', indeed, 'that Old Irish Mythology with modern Irish folk-lore was the mine from which he would draw all his material'.[3] As this implies, Yeats was equally attracted by the ancient myths of the Tuatha Dé Danann and the modern traditions of the Sídhe. On the other hand, the atmosphere in which his fairies move is always reminiscent of ancient times. The splendour of the Tuatha Dé Danann is fully restored in Yeats's poetry. In one respect, this was a nationalist gesture: it redeemed 'the matter of Ireland' from the curse of the stage Irishman. In another respect, it was a personal gesture: it acknowledged the powerful hold which the fairies exerted on Yeats's own imagination.

In determining what the fairies were and what they meant Yeats did not proceed in the dark. He was familiar not only with the myths and traditions of the fairies but also with the scholarship concerning them. He was, of course, to number Lady Gregory and Douglas Hyde among his closest friends. He was probably introduced to Henri d'Arbois de Jubainville by Maud Gonne in Paris in 1896. Certainly he read de Jubainville's works and referred to them favourably in several places. He was also familiar with Alfred Nutt's essays in Kuno Meyer's *The Voyage of Bran*, the second volume of which he reviewed for *The Bookman* in September 1898.[4] More than once, he cites in his works the *Hibbert Lectures* of Sir John Rhys. It is therefore something of a half-truth to say, as Ernest Boyd does, that 'With a singular imaginative power [Yeats] was able to obtain the freedom of a region of Celtic legend and romance which more painstaking scholars had surveyed without ever apprehending its true atmosphere.'[5]

It is true that Yeats himself was no scholar. His observations on folklore in his prose are often valuable, but in his poetry at least his presentation of the fairy faith does not proceed by intellectual analysis but by imaginative response vacillating between the attraction and repulsion of fairyland.

An early but naive view of Yeats's response to 'Gaelic Mythology' was formed by Patty Gurd: 'Here the poet found his own thoughts expressed by a people who had lived centuries before him, a people as mystic and as subtle-minded as he is himself.' What are those thoughts? There is certainly more to them than a 'pagan love of beauty . . . and . . . a note of melancholy mourning at the passing away of beautiful things'.[6] Early as Gurd's work on Yeats is (1916) a reviewer using the initials A. M. had penetrated Yeats's mind more deeply twenty-one years before: 'The consciousness of two worlds is ever present in his dreams, not this and that of a dim future, but one co-existing with and invading the other, each disputing the other's claims.'[7] To A. M., then, Yeats's poetry has an immediacy where Gurd detects only nostalgia; and there is about the proximity of fairyland something forceful, and even menacing.

These two positions have become touchstones for much later criticism. Dorothy M. Hoare, for instance, does not agree with Gurd that Yeats shares a common attitude with the ancient mythographers, as she considers that the latter exhibited a 'fidelity to fact, the comprehensiveness of a complete response to life.' Yeats's attitude, on the other hand, demonstrates 'the escape, sentiment, trance, of an

The Countess Cathleen: 'Longing for a Deeper Peace'

incomplete response'.[8] With respect to Yeats, then, Gurd and Hoare are objectively of one mind. Both see him as a sentimentalist and escapist, scarcely to be distinguished from J. M. Barrie. Gurd approves of this, while Hoare finds it despicable. Neither takes cognisance of A. M.'s position.

While A. M. emphasises the nearness of fairyland in Yeats's poetry, Harold H. Watts thinks that Yeats differs from the mythographers in the distance that he puts between himself and the fairies. For Yeats, the fairy faith can no longer 'speak plainly and flatly — as it did for the framers of myth — of the inseparable texture created by the eternal mingling of the sensory and the Other, and the This and the That'.[9] In other words, the Tuatha Dé Danann will not rub shoulders with Yeats, as they did with the Fianna. Although they are apparently contradictory, the opinions of A. M. and Watts can be reconciled. Thomas L. Byrd observes that 'A science-fiction story might treat Yeats's view of the universe in the form of a fourth dimension, but for Yeats the barrier that exists for us is a purely artificial one created by modern culture'.[10] The rift between the worlds, then, is equivalent to the Fall of Man, as understood by William Blake. We have lost the whole vision of the Giant Albion, which was also shared by the Fianna of old, and consequently, although the Tuatha Dé Danann still do walk among us, they 'walk invisible' (*The Countess Cathleen*, VPl 83). Thus, in the introductory poem to *The Shadowy Waters*, Yeats asks the 'immortal, mild, proud shadows':

> . . . do you gather about us when pale light
> Shining on water and fallen among leaves,
> And winds blowing from flowers, and whirr of feathers
> And the green quiet, have uplifted the heart?

The question is not entirely rhetorical, but on the whole expects the anwer, 'Yes'. What we must do, then, like Blake, is 'beat upon the wall/Till Truth [obey our] call' ('An Acre of Grass', VP 576). That is not likely to be easy. A good deal of the tension of Yeats's poetry arises from this difficulty, and a good deal more from the fact that, even if we succeed, we are not necessarily the happier for it. In this respect, the image of the Fall is ultimately misleading.

Fairyland, like Eden, does represent perfection. In his later work, of course, Yeats was to place the Sídhe under Phase Fifteen of the Moon. But whereas, in the traditional conception of Eden, perfection is of all things most greatly to be desired, Yeats is undecided whether it can be born. One thing that is certain is that visitors to fairyland remain changelings: one must purchase that life at the cost of this. The achievement of fairyland, of vision, or of perfection entails the destruction of this world. Sometimes the destruction of this world seems equivalent to its transfiguration; at other times, however, it seems that to enter the Otherworld we must literally die — and perhaps the world will die with us. Hence arises the vacillation that characterises Yeats's response to fairyland. Never, indeed, does he simply reject it. When that point comes, he ceases to write about it. But there are times when Yeats strives towards vision only to find at last that the sight of the gods cannot be endured, and other times when he would embrace perfection come what may. As G. S. Fraser says: 'Often he hated life for not being perfection. Sometimes, also, he feared perfection for not being life.'[11]

The period of Yeats's career which is relevant to this analysis begins with *The Countess Cathleen* and ends no later than *Responsibilities*. The fairies of Yeats's earlier work are 'trumpery little English fairies, degenerate descendants of Oberon and Titania,' in the words of Louis MacNeice,[12] not Irish fairies, while those of his later work are so shaped by *A Vision* as to fall outside the scope of this study.

II. *The Countess Cathleen*

The Countess Cathleen is the starting point for Yeats's exploration of his relationship with fairyland, and partly because of this it differs from other works in several respects. At least on a superficial level, we are not faced with a dichotomy between earth and fairyland, but with a three-sided contest involving fairyland, heaven, and hell. On another level, however, this trichotomy does resolve itself into a dichotomy. For Yeats, Christian imagery, when it is not the vehicle of Rosicrucian philosophy, is seldom the vehicle of his own sincere and passionate belief, but merely 'a convenient symbol of conventional and prudent belief'.[13] Furthermore, after her renunciation of the 'clouds on clouds of saints', (VPl 127) the Countess is not, like Faust, motivated by a desire for personal fulfilment, but by a desire to end the earthly suffering and subsequent damnation of her tenants. Thus her final commitment is neither to heaven nor to hell but to earth. In making this commitment, the blandishments that she has to resist are those of fairyland. On this level, then, the Countess's choice of worlds is that which Yeats will continue to face in subsequent works.

This play is again unusual in that it is the Countess, biographically representing Maud Gonne, who has to face the choice, while Yeats's surrogate Aleel is already committed to the fairies. In real life, we know that Yeats did agonise over this choice while Maud Gonne did not. The

The Countess Cathleen: *'Longing for a Deeper Peace'*

biographical element in the play, then, is unfortunate, though its importance has been overrated. It misdirects the development of the theme, and hence thwarts its resolution. The passage generally quoted in explanation of the biographical element is a stanza from 'The Circus Animals' Desertion':

> And then a counter-truth filled out its play,
> *The Countess Cathleen* was the name I gave it;
> She, pity-crazed, had given her soul away,
> But masterful Heaven had intervened to save it.
> I thought my dear must her own soul destroy,
> So did fanaticism and hate enslave it,
> And this brought forth a dream and soon enough
> This dream itself had all my thought and love.
>
> (VP 629–30)

Since the publication of Yeats's *Memoirs*, we know that this was no faulty recollection of old age:

I told [Maud Gonne] after meeting her in London I had come to understand the tale of a woman selling her soul to buy food for a starving people as a symbol of all souls who lose their peace, or their fineness, or any beauty of the spirit in political service, but chiefly of her soul that had seemed so incapable of rest.[14]

That was written in 1915 or somewhat later. There are certainly lines in the play to give substance to this allegory, for example:

> A learned theologian has laid down
> That starving men may take what's necessary,
> And yet be sinless.
>
> (VPl 67–69)

Padraic Colum has remarked that 'That was what Maud Gonne told the villages during a near-famine when she was encouraging the country people to resist seizures of their possession for rents'.[15] However, the most significant words in 'The Circus Animals' Desertion' are 'soon enough/This dream itself had all my thought and love'. The allegory will not stand. It may be tactful to Maud Gonne, but it is not reasonable to represent a fanatical, hate-enslaved woman by a pity-crazed one. It is also poor advice. The Countess Cathleen is saved *because* she gives her soul away, but 'masterful Heaven' would not intervene to save Maud Gonne. Because of this confusion at the heart of the action, the dilemma of the play is finally unresolved. The question of fairyland, which Yeats tries again and again to answer in his subsequent works, in *The Countess Cathleen* is only asked.

The first priority is to determine what that question is. This entails, first, putting the play in the context of Early Irish mythology, and, second, explicating the symbolism present in the scenery of the play.

III. The Context

Leonard E. Nathan has complained that *The Countess Cathleen* 'suffers from wrong emphasis'. The Countess' dilemma, he believes, is between 'her own salvation and the salvation of the peasantry', and so he thinks it a mistake that the demons receive as much attention as the Countess. However, he then says: 'The vague fairy folk and the sowlths and tavishes [sic] (lost souls of men) are even more on the fringes of the action than the demons and angels.' Thus, he first objects that the demons appear too much and then that they appear too little. Beyond this, he objects first that not enough time is devoted to Cathleen, and then that the demons, angels, *and* fairies are all on the fringes of the action. Who else is left? The point is that *The Countess Cathleen* is not a simple tussle between good and evil, but a three-way struggle, with the third side represented by the fairies. More or less equal time is devoted to all three sides. Nathan considers Kevin (in later versions Aleel) an irrelevant character, and cannot see why the demons fear him. The reason is that Kevin is the champion of the fairies, and so as fearsome to the demons as an angel would be.[16]

At the beginning of the play, the only denizens of Cathleen's estate are mortal and Catholic. 'The scene should have the effect of missal painting' (VPl 5). On Ellmann's interpretation, then, this is the world 'of conventional and prudent belief' — the ordinary world. The scenery, being like a missal painting, is itself a kind of charm to keep the supernatural world, both faery and diabolical, at bay. 'This country's full o' them [the fairies],' an Ulsterman told Wood-Martin, 'only there's so much scripture spread abroad that they canna get making themselves visible.'[17] One by one, the protective spells are broken by the rash and impious words of mortals. This is most obvious in the earliest version of the play. First Shemus says:

> ... I'll chew the lean dog-wolf
> With no less mirth if, chaired beside the hearth,
> Rubbing its hands before the bogwood flame,
> Be Pooka, Sowlth, or demon of the pit.

A step is heard outside and Mary expostulates, 'Who knows what evil you have brought to us' (VPl 20). Then the demons enter. One is reminded of Mephostophilis' words to Faustus:

> For when we hear one rack the name of God,
> Abjure the scriptures and his saviour Christ,
> We fly in hope to get his glorious soul.[18]

Shemus's invocation of the demons is closely paralleled by the invocation of the fairies, which is the work of Kathleen herself:

> Would that like Adene my first forebear's daughter,
> Who followed once a twilight piercing tune,
> I could go down and dwell among the shee
> In their old ever-busy honeyed land.

This time it is Oona who protests: 'You should not say such things — they bring ill-luck (VPl 60–62). It is appropriate that Kathleen breaks the spell with an appeal to the example of Adene, her 'first forebear's daughter,' for her relationship to Adene is closer than she realises, and because of it her story is predestined.

The relationship is confirmed by Kathleen's own surname. This does not appear in the play, but in order to find it we have only to turn to the sources. The most prominent of these is Léo Lespès's *Les Matinées de Timothé Trimm*, which Yeats quotes in his note to the play. This names the Countess as either O'Connor or O'Donnor. The latter version is that of the note in early texts; O'Connor first occurs in 1912. However, Yeats first read the story of the Countess Cathleen, not in *Les Matinées de Timothé Trimm*, but 'in what professed to be a collection of Irish folklore in an Irish newspaper' (VPl 170). The version that he read there he rewrote for his edition of *Fairy and Folk Tales of the Irish Peasantry*, under the title of 'The Countess Kathleen O'Shea.'[19] The O'Sheas, with the O'Connells and the O'Falveys, are among the chief families of the Ernaan tribes of the Western Isles. They are descended from the High King Conaire Mór. His grandmother was Etain Echraidhe.[20] 'Adene', of course, is simply an anglicised spelling of 'Etain'.

The story of Etain is as follows. She is first successfully wooed by Angus Óg on behalf of Midhir of Brí Leith. After that, however, Midhir's first wife, Faumhnach, turns her into a great purple fly and banishes her out to sea. She is rescued by Angus but banished again, until at last she is accidentally swallowed by the wife of Edar, an Ulster hero, and consequently born again, 1,012 years after her first birth, with the same name but with no memory of her previous incarnation. In due course she is married to the High King Eochaid Airemh, but then approached again by Midhir. She refuses to return to him, unless it be with the consent of Eochaid. Midhir beats Eochaid at chess and demands as his prize 'My arms around Etain and a kiss from her.' When he gets it, the pair of them fly away to Tír na nÓg in the form of swans. Later, Eochaid, seeking the return of Etain, is duped with her daughter. He eventually recovers Etain by threatening to dig up Brí Laith. Later still, Midhir, through his grandson, takes Etain for a third time, and even after that the fairies punish Conaire Mór, the grandson of Eochaid and Etain, in revenge for the damage done to Brí Leith. Máire Mac Neill, who interprets this as a Persephone myth, comments that 'The re-play between daughters, grand-daughters and grand-sons is but a reflection of the continually recurring mythical drama'.[21] In other words, reincarnation is a mainstay of this myth. In *The Countess Cathleen*, the cycle of incarnations is continued. Cathleen, the descendant of Etain, is yet another incarnation of Etain. It will be noticed that it is Aengus, the protector of Etain, who appears to Aleel to bid him summon the Countess to 'go down and dwell among the shee' like Etain before her (VPl 62, 83).

However, the story of Etain does not simply keep repeating itself. Etain's first father — Cathleen's 'first forebear' — is named Ailill. In her second incarnation, Ailill Anglonnach, or Ailill of the One Stain, is the name of her hopeless lover, who is also her brother-in-law. In *The Countess Cathleen*, Aleel is again a hopeless lover, though not a relative. Revolving relationships of this type may have suggested to Yeats the theory that later appears in *A Vision*:

We all to some extent meet again and again the same people and certainly in some cases form a kind of family of two of three or more persons who come together life after life until all passionate relations are exhausted, the child of one life the husband, wife, brother or sister of the next.[22]

The passionate form of Aleel's relationship with Cathleen has changed, but not its inner nature, for, like her, he retains close touch with Tír na nÓg. Etain-Cathleen's role also changes through her various incarnations. In her first, she was rejected by Tír na nÓg; in her second, she was accepted; it is now her turn to reject it.

There is one other respect in which Cathleen differs from Etain. She has a Christian soul. This naturally affects her relationship with heaven and hell, but also with fairyland. I make no quarrel with the usual identification of Yeats's fairyland with the realm of the imagination, but that identification does not completely elucidate this play. Imagination is a human quality, but the Countess's option of retiring to fairyland is not open to all men. She belongs by virtue of her previous incarnations, to a privileged élite.[23] For mankind in general, it seems,

The Countess Cathleen: 'Longing for a Deeper Peace'

the fairies can do nothing to alleviate the famine; nor is there much to indicate that they would if they could. They are a selfish people. Here, the precise quality of imagination, as symbolised by fairyland, demands close scrutiny. It is seen as neutralising the common man's dilemma, the dilemma of good and evil. A weariness with this dilemma is a recurrent theme of the Nineties and of the later Irish Renaissance alike. 'Good and evil are two peas in one pod,' says James Stephens' First Philosopher;[24] 'Come clear of the nets of wrong and right,' says Yeats, in 'Into the Twilight' (VP 747). In *The Countess Cathleen*, the fairies are not 'risen in arms with evil or with good' (VPl 84). This amorality cannot appeal to the devout Cathleen as it appealed to Etain. The fairies have 'but breath in their kind bodies' (VPl 163). They have no souls. Cathleen does, however. This soul stands between her an Tír na nÓg.

IV. The Imagery

Before we can proceed with this line of reasoning, we must examine the emblematic attributes of the three domains, heaven, hell, and fairyland. The blessed are associated with trees, but fairies and demons with more animate imagery. The emblematic animal of fairyland would appear to be the swan: 'He bids me go/Where none of mortal creatures but the swan/Dabbles' (VPl 85). The swan is, of course, one of the fairies' preferred shapes. In the present context, it is particularly relevant that Midhir and Etain escaped from Tara in the form of swans. However, Yeats may have had reasons over and above tradition for choosing this emblem. As a creature of land, water, and air, the swan seems sufficiently ambiguous to pass between the worlds;[25] in its typical pose, serenely contemplating its own beauty reflected in the water, it anticipates the white heron of *Calvary* and exemplifies the quality that Yeats later associated with Full of Moon, the fairies' phase; finally, William Blake depicted the creative imagination as a swan-headed creature in Plate 11 of *Jerusalem*.[26]

Damnation is associated with wolves by the rumour that the demons have wolves' heads (VPl 115) and by the wolf which Shemus brings in for food, perhaps precipitating the whole affair. It is also associated with bats (VPl 7). But the dominant image here is that of the bird of prey. The demons themselves take the form of man-headed owls. There also occur the lines, 'A scented flame flickering above that peace / The bird of prey knows well in his deep heart' (VPl 30), 'Their eyes burn like the eyes of birds of prey' (VPl 72), and 'Is that peace/Known to the birds of prey so dread a thing? (VPl 132–34).[27] In Early Irish literature, birds of prey are most obviously associated with the

Morrigu. Man-headed birds, also employed by Yeats in *The Shadowy Waters*, date back as far as Ancient Egypt, where they were used to represent the souls of the dead. In Ireland, one of Lady Gregory's informants — not, unfortunately, one of her most reliable — 'Saw one time a big grey bird about the cowhouse, and I went to a comrade-boy and asked him to come and help me to catch it, but when we came back it was gone. It was very strange-looking and I thought that it had a head like a man.'[28] It is true that neither this bird nor the souls of the dead are necessarily evil, but in Ulster the banshee is sometimes said to have 'the body of a bird and the face of a person who died soon after'.[29]

Also of ill omen in *The Countess Cathleen* are the deformed humans who haunt the land:

> ... at Tubber-vanach
> A woman met a man with ears spread out,
> And they moved up and down like a bat's wing.
> ....
> Two nights ago, at Carrick-orus churchyard,
> A herdsman met a man who had no mouth,
> Nor eyes, nor ears; his face a wall of flesh;
> He saw him plainly by the light of the moon.
>
> (VPl 5-7)

Such monsters are traditional portents of prodigious events in Ireland. During the Black and Tan War, a man with two thumbs on his right hand was supposed to wander the roads of Co. Leitrim.[30] Flat-faced men (*cláireinigh*) are surprisingly common in Early Irish literature. Most appear to be either leprous or syphilitic, not supernatural or evil, and four are even saints,[31] but in the 'Life of St. Magnenn of Kilmainham' the Antichrist himself is described as having 'his entire face ... but one flat surface'.[32]

V. The Scenery

We have seen now that *The Countess Cathleen* takes place against a background of mythology and folklore. In a more literal sense, of course, the play's background is its scenery. These three elements are interwoven, and all contribute powerfully to the play's theme.

The scenery functions symbolically to emphasise the conflict between natural and supernatural in the play. However, Yeats's symbols are never allegorical; they can never, in other words, be reduced to singularity. Rather, as Richard Ellmann says: 'Each symbol is a kind of

The Countess Cathleen: 'Longing for a Deeper Peace'

revolving disc . . . Not only are the symbols double-natured in different poems; they usually take on shifting implications within the same poem, as if they were being slowly revolved.'[33] Of necessity, then, Yeats's symbols are ambiguous; they may even seem to reverse their meaning at times; nevertheless, if carefully followed, they will prove constantly illuminating.

With regard to the symbolism of Yeats's scenery, however, I do not mean to suggest that every text of *The Countess Cathleen* is equally effective. Through the successive productions and revisions of the play, Yeats and his collaborator Gordon Craig sought to minimise the visual impact of the scenery, so that it 'would be forgotten the moment a good actor had said, 'The dew is falling', or 'I can hear the wind among the leaves'.'[34] Such a practice is theatrically commendable, no doubt, but more appropriate when the scenery is less important. As it is, scenic effects in early texts that should be highly successful are often discarded in later texts, and opportunities for the symbolic enrichment of the play through its scenery and costume often go unseized. Peter Ure, for instance, has remarked that the contrast between the 'real rags' of the Ruas and the 'gorgeous livery' of Cathleen's musicians foreshadows 'what is later to be the Countess's choice: retreat into the artifice of fable or acknowledgement of a land where people die of hunger, their mouths 'green with dock and dandelion'.'[35] Yeats later toned down the costumes along with the scenery, so that contrast was lost. That is typical. The major focus for 'the artifice of fable' is the 'tapestry representing the wars and loves and huntings of the Fenian and Red-branch warriors' in the great hall of the Countess (VPl 42), but all detail on that tapestry is lost after 1912. Moreover, trees are dimly visible through the arches in Cathleen's hall after 1895. Trees are also visible from the Ruas' cottage, so a contrast between the two sets is lost by this innovation.

What that contrast might have signified is apparent in the text of 1912. In that text, the background to the Ruas' cottage is described as 'the trees of a wood, and these trees should be painted in flat colour upon a gold or diapered sky. . . . The scene should have the effect of missal painting' (VPl 5). This effect is maintained in Scene II: 'A wood with perhaps distant view of turreted house at one side, but all in flat colour, without light and shade and against a diapered or gold background' (VPl 51). These scenes from a missal book contrast with the tapestry. The latter represents the Otherworld, while the former represent this world. The missal is, of course, a church book, but it is also 'the book in the priest's hand' (VPl 33) and the 'book of the world' (VPl 111). The demons who 'walk upon its leaves' (VPl 111) and 'ride/ Even upon the book in the priest's hand' do so in the sight of the audience.[36] The effect of missal painting, however, was added to the stage directions in 1912, the same year in which the details of the tapestry were lost, and so the inherent contrast between the two was never developed.

In early texts, the place of the missal painting is taken by a 'little catholic shrine', accompanied from 1907 to 1908 by 'a little shrine of the Virgin Mother' (VPl 5–6). It was the trampling of this shrine that most outraged Yeats's pious enemies, and so he got rid of it, because 'In using what I considered traditional symbols I forgot that in Ireland they are not symbols but realities' (A 279). In fact, this was a great improvement. When the shrine is trampled, its symbolic power is obvious, but while hanging it is not likely to be conspicuous. Besides, it can carry only the strictly religious connotations of the missal. To move the centre of symbolism from a detail of the scene to the whole expanse of the scene was a stroke of genius, but it does not compensate for the unachieved contrast with the tapestry.

However, even if the two sets of the play present no great contrast with each other, each is powerfully symbolic in its own right. The great hall of the Countess Cathleen is dominated by two contrasting symbols, the tapestry and the oratory. The threads of the tapestry extend well beyond its borders. In the texts of 1895 to 1908 there is an explicit congruence between the tapestry and the mind of Aleel:

> Alone in the hushed passion of romance,
> His mind ran all on sidheógues, and on tales
> Of Fenian labours and the Red Branch kings,
> And he cared nothing for the life of man.
>
> (VPl 141)

In other words, Aleel is obsessively preoccupied with the very things depicted in the tapestry. Since Fergus was among 'the Red Branch kings',[37] Oona's song is also related to the tapestry:

> Who will go drive with Fergus now,
> And pierce the deep wood's woven shade,
> And dance upon the level shore?
> Young man, lift up your russet brow,
> And lift your tender eyelids, maid,
> And brood on hopes and fears no more.
>
> And no more turn aside and brood
> Upon Love's bitter mystery;
> For Fergus rules the brazen cars,
> And rules the shadows of the wood,
> And the white breast of the dim sea
> And all dishevelled wandering stars.
>
> (VPl 52–56)

The tapestry itself, Aleel, and Oona's song all confront Cathleen with her dilemma. Oona's is not a rhetorical question. It is addressed specifically to Cathleen. Fergus, once an earthly king, has receded into the fairyland depicted on the tapestry. Will Cathleen now follow him? Aleel, of course, is the most direct of the Countess's tempters. It is he who brings the message from Aengus, inviting the Countess to flee to fairyland. While the tapestry symbolises the allure of fairyland, or imaginative salvation, the oratory symbolises the Countess's Christian duty.[38] As the tapestry loses its details, the oratory comes into greater prominence, and Cathleen is less sympathetic to the fairies. In the texts of 1895 to 1908, Aleel has only to say, 'One walked in the fire with birds about his head', for Cathleen to respond at once, 'Ay, Aengus of the birds', as if, like Etain, she knew him (VPl 83). After that date, Cathleen replies less confidently to Aleel's remark, 'I have heard that one of the old gods walked so', and Aleel's response, 'It may be that he is angelical', allows her twice to distinguish between the old gods and angels and to side with the latter:

> No, not angelical, but of the old gods,
> Who wander about the world to waken the heart —
> The passionate, proud heart — that all the angels,
> Leaving nine heavens empty, would rock to sleep.
>
> (VPl 83–87)

Between 1895 and 1908, however, Cathleen lives in her tapestry almost as much as the Ruas live in their missal book. It may be thought unreasonable that in Scene I the Countess must ask some peasants the way to her own home. The reason is that she and those with her have taken a stray, or fallen into the fairies' power. Cathleen's previous incarnations as Etain have predisposed her towards fairyland, which renders the struggle in her breast between heaven and fairyland all the harder. This is further intimated by the dichotomy in the play between heart and soul. In the passage above, the heart is clearly not the same as the soul, or the angels would not wish to rock it asleep. The heart is claimed by the old gods, or fairies. It is true that at one point the demons also appear to claim the heart, when they speak of 'A scented flame flickering above that peace / The bird of prey knows well in his deep heart' (VPl 30). At this point, however, they are deliberately deceiving Shemus and Teig with fairy-talk, for they also speak of their wine 'that can hush asleep the petty war / Of good and evil.' This implies that they are neutral in this war, but they are, of course, on the side of evil. They state themselves that it is the fairies who are neutral, 'neither one with angels or with us, / Nor risen in arms with evil or with good' (VPl 84). They are, then, trying to lull the misgivings of Shemus and Teig by posing as fairies, not as demons. Essentially, the demons' speech confirms, then, that the heart belongs to the fairies. It is the business of demons and angels to contend for the soul. Cathleen's dilemma is that she has a great heart as well as a great soul. Her heart is strong enough, as it were, to take heaven by force instead of grace:

> This heart shall never waken on earth. I have sworn,
> By her whose heart the seven sorrows have pierced,
> To pray before this altar until my heart
> Has grown to Heaven like a tree, and there
> Rustled its leaves, till Heaven has saved my people.
>
> (VPl 87)

Her soul is strong enough to command the great price the demons pay for it. Aleel, by contrast, has an 'impetuous heart' (VPl 129), but a soul that he would give away without a price.[39] Here is another factor, then, that deepens the Countess's dilemma. She is savagely torn between heaven and fairyland. That is why it is so shocking that in the end she must choose hell.

The symbolic importance of the oratory becomes more evident if Cathleen's inner struggle is considered in a different light. 'Yeats is trying to show, in Cathleen and Aleel, what he was later to call Artist and Saint confronting each other upon the stage,' says Peter Ure, and the tension between them 'has to do with the war between dreams and responsibility, between the land of pagan images of Fergus and Adene, Usheen, young Neave and the Fenians on one side and the 'burden of the world's wrongs,' the famine, and the starving peasantry on the other'.[40] In a brilliant essay, James Lovic Allen has shown that these two types, Artist and Saint, represent two forms of mystical experience. The Saint 'aspires to and struggles toward' union with God, while on the Artist 'the divine precipitantly strikes from above to enrich or momentarily illuminate [his] experience'. Each of these types is associated with certain typical symbols. The Saint's symbols are 'ascent motifs — stairways and ladders, upward-pointing towers, birds in flight, arrows shot into the heavens, sacred mountains and so forth'. The Artist's symbols, all 'descent motifs', include lightning, 'the downward flight of a divine bird', meteors, and 'dazzling beams of light from the sun or moon'. In addition, the Artist tends to wander aimlessly 'in semiconscious or unconscious anticipation' of the moment of illumination.[41] Since Aleel is a poet, Ure is obviously correct in considering him an Artist. When Cathleen first encounters him, he is drifting without direction:

The Countess Cathleen: 'Longing for a Deeper Peace'

> And this young man, that should have known the woods —
> Because we met him on their border but now,
> Wandering and singing like a wave of the sea —
> Is so wrapped up in dreams of terrors to come
> That he can give no help.
>
> (VPl 17–19)

Like Cathleen, he has taken a stray. It is not the spirit of God but the spirit of fairyland that has touched him, and when his moment of illumination comes, it comes from Aengus:

> I was asleep in my bed, and while I slept
> My dream became a fire; and in the fire
> One walked and he had birds about his head.
>
> (VPl 83)[42]

Aengus has chosen an Artist for his messenger but a Saint for the recipient of his message.

The oratory confirms Cathleen's Sainthood. It is her ascent motif, the more so as it is raised above the level of the stage, 'with steps leading up to it' (VPl 81). In early texts, the confrontation between Artist and Saint is silently enacted by this oratory and the tapestry. Cathleen is called from the oratory to meet Aleel by a servant. After 1912, however, the focus of symbolism shifts from the scenery to the situation. Cathleen is actually 'kneeling in front of the altar in the oratory' when Aleel enters, saying:

> I have come to bid you leave this castle and fly
> Out of these woods . . .
> They who have sent me walk invisible.
>
> (VPl 81–83)

Cathleen is thus clearly characterised as the Saint, and Aleel as the Artist, the representative of fairyland. When, at the end of this scene, Cathleen does not flee to Tír na nÓg but returns to her oratory, Aleel is defeated. Although the Countess cries out, 'Mary, Queen of angels, / And all you clouds on clouds of saints, farewell!' (VPl 125–27), she chooses renunciation, not escape. She wins heaven by choosing hell.[43] As though to emphasise this point, Yeats rewrote the ending of the play after 1892 so that the final set should be dominated by the visionary 'sacred mountain'. This effect, extremely difficult to achieve on the stage, contradicts Yeats's professed desire for simplicity, but allows the play to close with an 'ascent motif,' signifying the Countess's triumph.

The background to the Ruas' cottage is dominated by trees. Nathan considers these trees gratuitously symbolic but dramatically irrelevant: 'like other elements in the play, [they] secure only minor effects, for all their portentous suggestiveness.' However, he points out himself that 'the hazel in Yeats's own words is regarded as the 'Tree of Life . . . under its common Irish form'; the berries of the quicken (or rowan) tree 'are said to be the food of the gods'.'[44] This is surely of more than minor significance. Although, when Yeats speaks of the 'Tree of Life', he is not thinking in exclusively Christian terms, his expression may nonetheless confer a Christian sanction upon hazel wood. Quicken, being sacred to the Tuatha Dé Danann, is not blessed by Christianity, but is not cursed by it either. The pious Maire says: 'Shemus! Shemus! What, would you burn the blessed quicken wood?' (VPl 18–20).

Hazel, then, offers Christian protection while quicken offers pagan protection. Both are symbols of a benign providence. It is true that in texts of 1895–1904 and 1908 Maire describes the woods, and especially, it seems, the hazels, as 'malevolent' (VPl 21). However, this is anomalous, and that is perhaps why the line was deleted. The fact that the woods are otherwise benevolent is confirmed by the fact that all 'the sentient grass and leaves / Bow towards' the fairies, 'and the tall, drouth-jaded oaks / Fondle the murmur of their flying feet', because 'The green things loved unknotted hearts and minds' (VPl 84). From the sowlths and tevishes, on the other hand, true creatures of evil, 'the grass and leaves / Shiver and shrink away and sway about' (VPl 94).

The Christian connotations of the trees, furthermore, agree with Allen's explication of Yeats's symbolism. The tree is the pre-eminent symbol of 'the union with godhead achieved and sustained'.[45] This is confirmed by the verbal imagery, when Cathleen says that her heart will grow 'to Heaven like a tree' (VPl 87). There is nothing mystical about the Ruas' set. The rapturous, mystical experience, whether with God or with the fairies, is pursued in Cathleen's great hall. The trees around the Ruas' cottage, painted as in a missal painting, symbolise the world as perenially cradled by divine providence. It is this bond between earth and heaven that is dissolved by Shemus' invocation of the demons, and can only be restored by Cathleen's sacrifice. There is, however, a flaw in this picture. The famine precedes the entry of the demons. Why does divine providence allow this? Here, of course, we have the fundamental problem of evil. It is here that *The Countess Cathleen* is weakest. Yeats challenges the complacent certainties of 'the world of conventional and prudent belief' by raising the problem of evil, but resolves it only by blurring the issues.

VI. Conclusions

The essential fact is that the Countess, forced to choose between heaven, hell, and fairyland, is completing the experience of Etain. Fairies, of course, are neither angels nor demons, but half-fallen angels. Christianity proposes certain moral values and responsibilities. The demons invert these, but the fairies neglect them. They are neutral in the war between good and evil. This presents a new challenge to Cathleen, who hitherto, as Etain, has only been concerned with fairyland, not heaven. For her, fairyland is no escape: it is her home already. Her escape is *from* fairyland: an escape into responsibility. It is thus that she succeeds in reversing the choice of fairyland that she made as Etain.

As Peter Ure points out, this is a reversal for Yeats as well. In *The Wanderings of Oisin*, says Ure, 'Oisin finally chooses the Fenians and rejects St. Patrick; in the play the Countess reverses this choice'.[46] Yeats was quite conscious of this 'counter-truth'. In the 1892 text of *The Countess Cathleen*, the tapestry in the great hall actually depicts a scene from *The Wanderings of Oisin*, to make the point explicit (VPl 44). Yeats implies that Pre-Raphaelite dreaming is insufficient. As he was to say twenty-two years later, 'In dreams begins responsibility' (VP 269).

This point is supported by the door imagery which, as Michael Goldman has observed, is very pervasive in *The Countess Cathleen*. Both Goldman and Frank Hughes Murphy (the latter without reference to this play) interpret the door in the same way: 'an 'occult or spiritual' world that 'lures' man away from his material condition'; 'a necessary passageway on the path to another, timeless existence.' One door image that Goldman has surprisingly overlooked is that in Aleel's song:

> He who could bend all things to His will
> Has covered the door of the infinite fold
> With the pale stars and the wandering moon.
>
> (VPl 129)

The fact that the door here is hidden perhaps adumbrates Cathleen's rejection of fairyland. Towards the end of the play, however, the connotations of the door shift, in the manner typical of Yeats's symbols: 'the verbal figure reappears,' says Goldman, 'first as the open door of hell, next as the 'half-closed gates of Hell,' and finally, as the open 'gates of pearl' through which Cathleen will pass.'[47] As the Countess says herself, 'Old man, old man, He never closed a door / Unless one opened' (VPl 123). As the door to fairyland closes, the door to heaven opens.

Notwithstanding Yeats's intentions, though, Cathleen's salvation is a close call for us all. An obvious objection to the play is that, in order fully to unravel its complexities, one needs a good deal of esoteric knowledge (the Countess's surname, the genealogy of the O'Sheas). A more serious objection is that, in a play where the distinctions between heaven, hell, and fairyland are so important, they are dangerously blurred. Since Aleel tempts Cathleen toward fairyland, he is her spiritual enemy. From a Blakean perspective, it is entirely appropriate that he is also her lover, but dramatically one fact is likely to obscure the other. In addition, the sacred mountain at the end, though supposed to afford a glimpse of the Christian heaven, seems, with its armed angels and distant horns, 'remote from Christian imagery', but close to 'that of Wagner's *Götterdämmerung*'.[48] In isolation, the symbol is all the more archetypal and effective because of this, but it blurs the line between the Christian and the pagan, between heaven and fairyland.

The line between fairyland and hell is still more blurred. Yeats is faced with something like Milton's difficulty. That fairyland is attractive is entirely proper, for otherwise there would be no virtue in resisting its attractions; the problem is that hell seems rather attractive too. Aengus invites Cathleen to fairyland, where she may

>   ... live in the hills,
> Among the sound of music and the light
> Of waters, till the evil days are done.
>
>   (VPl 83)

A. G. Stock asks whether there is 'any difference except in the degree of refinement between this ... and Shemus's preference for being drunk and merry?'[49] If anything, Stock understates the problem. 'That peace known to the birds of prey' and the 'eternal revelry' (VPl 143, 155) are more likely to command enthusiasm than the vegetative imagery associated with the blessed. Further, the stars of heaven are twice called pale: once in Aleel's song and once at VPl 165. 'She was more beautiful than the pale stars'. Images of brightness, on the other hand, are all the demons': their gold, and the flame in the heart of the bird of prey. Consequently, one might almost think that Cathleen renounces heaven for the sake of hedonism. Her own utterances do little to disarm suspicion. Her cry, 'But there's a world to come' (VPl 73), because of its conventional diction carries little conviction, while 'Old man, old man, He never closed a door / Unless one opened' is, without benefit of hindsight, pretty cold comfort. Cathleen explains why 'demon hordes are born' (VPl 125), but not why there is famine. (The demons claim responsibility for the famine only in texts of 1895–1908, VPl 139. It is a poor bargaining counter for them.)

The Countess Cathleen: 'Longing for a Deeper Peace'

Furthermore, the door which God opens is the sale of Cathleen's soul, as she believes, which seems a sadistic doctrine of Grace.

The problem of evil, then, is really not resolved at all in *The Countess Cathleen*. By the same token, neither is the problem of good, nor the problem of the fairies' neutrality. Shemus Rua's line, 'God and God's mother nod and sleep' (VPl 16), seems to dominate the play, and there seems no answer to it. From such a world, in the end, one would sooner see Aleel and the Countess winging away like white swans. And so, one suspects, would Yeats. And yet he chooses to have his Countess reject fairyland, and appears to commend her for it. This can hardly be said to constitute a response to fairyland at all. It is more like a refusal to respond. *The Countess Cathleen*, in other words, is the expression of a state of indecision.

13. THE ROSE AND HER SERVANTS[1]

If, in *The Countess Cathleen*, Yeats poses a question but provides no answers, it might almost be said that in those of his works that are dominated by the symbol of the Rose he provides too many answers. The Rose itself is notorious in this respect. What does it signify? No-one could be blamed for replying, 'Everything and nothing'. One might justly complain that the Rose is a cliché of Aesthetic imagery presented by Yeats as if it were a new discovery. To George Brandon Saul, it is 'tiresome because overworked, diffusely vague in intimation (and therefore suspect on the score of sentimentality), and somehow suggestive of the hothouse'.[2] The same objections might be raised to the fairies. Yeats's works of 1892–97 are quite densely populated by fairies, but some might wonder why. Saul would no doubt consider them sentimental as well — provided merely for the sake of tone, to convey an atmosphere of cheap wonder, of quaintness, or even of whimsicality. Yeats's response to the fairies is all the harder to define because it is so much a part of his response to the Rose. The ambiguities of the Rose only obscure, not illuminate, the role of the fairies. Yeats's attitude to nature is subject to the same vicissitudes. Indeed, every element of the symbolism is part of the same nexus.

That being the case, however, we do at least have unity of theme, if not of response. Yeats's failure to respond consistently to the symbol that inspires him and the concerns that drive him is sufficient to mark *The Rose* as inferior to *The Wind Among the Reeds*, but not to damn it entirely. Even if the Rose is a poetic cliché, and even if Yeats does not succeed in rejuvenating the cliché for his readers, for him it is much more than a cliché.

For Yeats, the Rose and the fairies are sufficiently important not to merit a quick and easy response. He knows that his symbols move him; he does not know precisely how they move him. Before he can provide an answer, he must first work it out. The Rose-dominated works record Yeats's search for an answer. It is a struggle, one may even say a courageous struggle, to 'hammer his thoughts into unity'. For a clearer response to fairyland, we must wait for *The Wind Among the Reeds*, but the solution is worth nothing without the equation.

This struggle for truth is a struggle in the Dionysian mood, and it is because the Dionysian urge, the urge to escape from form, is a frightening, almost suicidal urge that Yeats hesitates and vacillates. The Rose inspires, dominates, and eventually symbolises this urge. She is, in effect, a savage goddess. The fairies are perceived sometimes as savage gods, simply an alternative expression of the Rose. They may, however, be creatures subordinate to the Rose, as angels are subordinate to God; or, contrariwise, they may be companions to man in the struggle for truth, just as the Rose symbolises not only what is sought but also the search itself. At still other times, they are portrayed as having either gained or abandoned the quest, and as having found peace by doing so. Their peace is a peace beyond morality, because they are creatures of whim. As the fairies are so variously portrayed, it is not odd that Yeats is ambivalent towards them. Nature is almost equivalent to fairyland, and so subject to a like ambivalence.

Occasionally, Yeats adopts a straightforward and optimistic attitude. Truth is knowable, and ought to be known. Fairyland is both desirable and accessible. More often, however, fairyland remains a suggestion that our fallen vision can never quite apprehend. If, indeed, we could for an instant apprehend Truth, the awesomeness of that knowledge would at once confound our vision anew. Thus, the scheme of *The Rose* and *The Secret Rose* is to present a variety of paths towards Truth and a variety of travellers on those paths. These paths are genuine; they do lead to the Rose; but, before journey's end can be attained, the approaching splendour of the Rose becomes too great to be borne, and the seeker recoils in a kind of horror. Though failure is inevitable, it is better to seek and fail than not to seek. One can always seek avoidance of the quest in love, which may seem to restore a purpose of its own to existence, but this purpose is somewhat suspect. If love does bestow contentment, the contentment is cheap; if it does not, one is driven forth to seek again. The way of the seeker, though eternally unsatisfied, is the nobler way. However, the price of failure is high. To him who has had even a glimpse of the Rose, the world becomes well nigh intolerable, and death itself may seem the only solution.

I. The Rose

Any detailed explication of these works must naturally begin with the symbol of the Rose. Frank Hughes Murphy has conveniently listed seventeen meanings attributed by Yeats himself or his critics to the Rose:

spiritual love; eternal beauty; woman's beauty; a compound of beauty and peace; a compound of beauty and wisdom; Shelley's Intellectual Beauty, altered to sympathize with human suffering; physical love; Ireland; religion; Maud Gonne; the sun; the divine nature; the flower of the Virgin; Apuleius's flower (*The C⁻¹len Ass*); the female impulse toward life (as opposed to the male impulse toward death [symbolised by the lily]); the female generative organs; a key Rosicrucian symbol.³

These meanings need not be mutually exclusive, and they are undoubtedly stronger in combination than in isolation; but they are not of equal value, and none, indeed, is tremendously illuminating. To say that the Rose symbolises 'the female generative organs' is surely to betray the limitations of Freudian criticism. Yeats himself identifies the Rose with 'the flower of the Virgin' and 'Apuleius's flower', *inter alia* (VP 811), but this in no way explains the symbol. The Rose in combination with the lily and the Rose in combination with the Cross ('a key Rosicrucian symbol') are special cases. The Rose as 'woman's beauty' and the Rose as Maud Gonne are obviously connected, and need further consideration.

That the Rose may at times represent Maud Gonne is clear enough from 'The Rose of the World':

> Bow down, archangels, in your dim abode:
> Before you were, or any hearts to beat,
> Weary and kind one lingered by His seat;
> He made the world to be a grassy road
> Before her wandering feet.
>
> (VP 112)

The title tells us that 'one' is the Rose. She is here 'suffering with man and not . . . pursued and seen from afar' (VP 842). 'One' is also Maud Gonne. Yeats added this stanza to the poem when Maud came home exhausted but warmly disposed from a walk in the Dublin mountains. 'The White Birds' has a similar genesis. Seeing a pair of seagulls on the cliffs at Howth, Maud had told Yeats that she would like to be reincarnated as a gull.⁴ Facts like these are not uninteresting, but they underline the triviality of the biographical approach to Yeats's poetry. Like many others, these two poems are clearly 'about' Maud Gonne in a sense, but they are about much more than her. The Rose, if it is Maud Gonne, is not only Maud Gonne.

For one thing, Maud is not the only possessor of 'woman's beauty' in these poems. She enters 'The Rose of the World' as an afterthought in the final stanza. She has to share her role with Helen and Deirdre:

> For these red lips, with all their mournful pride,
> Mournful that no new wonder may betide,
> Troy passed away in one high funeral gleam,
> And Usna's children died.
>
> (VP 111)

The similes in the second stanza of 'The Sorrow of Love' ('Doomed like Odysseus . . . proud as Priam . . .') again suggest Helen, though in 'A girl arose' Lester Conner sees suggestions of Botticelli's Venus.[5] That Venus, as described by Walter Pater, seems to be more obviously present in 'The Rose of Battle'.[6] A. G. Stock has shown that the Rose in 'To Ireland in the Coming Times' is related to 'that Lady Beauty' of Dante Gabriel Rossetti's 'Sibylla Palmifera'.[7] I think it probable that Yeats also has Danu in mind when he writes of the Rose. As the mother-goddess of the Tuatha Dé Danann, she holds the keys to fairyland. In a certain sense, the pursuit of the Rose is always the pursuit of fairyland. As a woman, then, the Rose is very much a *donna mobile*. Maud Gonne's contribution to her is slight and incidental.

The Rose is also an ideal woman. In this sense, Maud's relation to her is that of a medieval troubador's lady to the Virgin Mary: a sort of Neo-Platonic hook, a visible form of beauty that induces the mind to the contemplation of ideal beauty, or of Shelley's Intellectual Beauty. The fact that Yeats imagines the Rose as 'suffering with man' in no way diminishes her ideal stature, though it is somewhat disingenuous to claim that he does not imagine her 'as something pursued and seen from afar'. She is the ideal which man pursues and also the ideal form of that pursuit. She is Truth as being, and also Truth as Becoming. In all transcendent experience, or would-be experience, she is subject as well as object. The emphasis must be on 'transcendent'. Even though the Rose may suffer with man, she has nothing to do with the material world. The 'knight of Palestine' in 'Out of the Rose', the founder of a mystical order analogous to the Rosicrucians as well as to the Grail Knights, 'had seen a great Rose of Fire, and a Voice out of the Rose had told him how men would turn from the light of their own hearts, and bow down before outer order and outer fixity' (M 162). Thus, the rose dwells within the heart, beyond the outer world which she opposes.

As a goddess, then, the Rose is related to Dionysus, not Apollo. The Dionysian, as one would expect, is conceived in traditionally Romantic terms: none shall escape the curse in 'Out of the Rose' 'except the foolish good man who could not think, and the passionate wicked man who would not' (M 163). This is the rebuke of the imagination to the reason. It is in this sense that the Rose is a religious symbol. In this respect, the 'great Rose of Fire' derives from the multifoliate rose of

Dante's *Paradiso*. Still in 'Out of the Rose', we read that 'the Kingdom of God . . . is in the Heart of the Rose' (M 163). The old knight in the story (not the knight of Palestine) aspires to this heaven when he cries, 'O Divine Rose of Intellectual Flame, let the gates of thy peace be opened to me at last!' (M 157). But this is not Dante's heaven, for all that. The figures involved in the prefatory poem to *The Secret Rose* are not the saints of Christendom but the heroes of the imagination. Yeats's quest, therefore, is a poetic one. He seeks the truths of the imagination. The failure of the quest may be said to represent the limitations of art — the impossibility of conceiving or communicating a perfect image of the transcendent.

The facts that the Rose means many things, that it symbolises at once the reward of suffering and the pain of suffering, the quest and the object of the quest, are the reasons why Yeats's attitude towards it is so inconstant. His vacillation is best seen in 'To the Rose upon the Rood of Time'. As has often been pointed out, Yeats spends the first stanza bidding the Rose 'Come near'. He begins the second stanza in the same way, but abruptly changes his mind: 'Come near, come near, come near — Ah, leave me still/A little space for the rose-breath to fill!' At the end of the poem, he then changes his mind again: 'Come near' (VP 101). This is the pattern of *The Rose* as a whole condensed into a single poem. It is Yeats's courage that falters. He has always the option of writing the poetry of Young Ireland, 'one /With Davis, Mangan, Ferguson' ('To Ireland in the Coming Times', VP 138), and of winning greater popularity as a result. Should he, after all, devote his life to the Rose? He hesitates, he vacillates — but in the end, of course, he decides he should.

II. The Fairies

The fairies are part of the same problem. Should Yeats devote his life to them? Fairyland continues, as in *The Countess Cathleen*, to represent the realm of art and imagination. In 'The Man Who Dreamed of Faeryland,' Tír na nOg is described as 'a *woven* world-forgotten isle' (VP 126; emphasis added) — a peculiar choice of adjective until one remembers the tapestry in *The Countess Cathleen*. Fairyland is again a tapestry or artistic creation. Since the Rose is also an imaginative power, there is an obvious temptation to identify fairyland with the Rose. This is, in fact, the case in 'The Man Who Dreamed of Faeryland'. The effects of dreaming of faeryland, in this poem, are the same as those of pursuing the Rose in others.

In subtler poems, however, the fairies and the Rose may both stand for the imagination without standing for precisely the same thing. The Rose may be the source of imagination — and ultimately unbearable — while the fairies are manifestations of imaginative power, messengers from the source to the mind of man, messengers who can be entertained without injury. In his essay on 'The Philosophy of Shelley's Poetry' (1900), Yeats wrote: 'Intellectual Beauty has not only the happy dead to do her will, but ministering spirits who correspond to the Devas of the East, and the Elemental Spirits of mediaeval Europe, and the Sidhe of ancient Ireland' (E &I 74). This passage has close analogues in the poetry. The 'happy dead' appear in 'To the Rose upon the Rood of Time': 'But seek alone to hear the strange things said/By God to the bright hearts of those long dead' (VP 101). The 'Elemental Spirits' appear in 'To Ireland in the Coming Times': 'For the elemental creatures go/About my table to and fro' (VP 138). As the Rose's messengers, the fairies function in men's eyes as lures or decoys. In pursuing fairies, who are at least imaginable, men actually pursue the Rose, which is ineffable.

Alternatively, the fairies may be seen as participating with man in the pursuit of the Rose. This is most evident in 'To Ireland in the Coming Times': 'Man ever journeys on with them/After the red-rose-bordered hem' (VP 139).

Unlike men, however, the fairies are often depicted as having found their peace. Since they stand closer to the Rose than men, it may be that they can endure the knowledge of the Rose, and so find their peace by fulfilling the quest. More often, though, they seem to have found a separate peace without the Rose, as if they were not driven to the quest. This is emblematically suggested in 'The Heart of the Spring':

> Beyond the lilies and the roses the ferns were so deep that a child walking among them would be hidden from sight, even though he stood upon his toes; and beyond the fern rose many hazels and small oak-trees.
> 'Master,' said the boy, 'this long fasting, and the labour of beckoning after nightfall to the beings who dwell in the waters and among the hazels and oak-trees, is too much for your strength.'
>
> (M 171)

The fairies dwell beyond the roses, or without the Rose, in apparent content; but to emulate them is too much for mortal strength, like the knowledge of the Rose itself. The monks in 'The Crucifixion of the Outcast' have their own way of shunning the Rose through the false knowledge of their degenerate religion, but theirs is a despicable expedient. Their false knowledge is a warped reflection of what may be called the fairies' true ignorance, which is not despicable but joyful. The monks, being obsessed by morality, have arrived at an inverted morality that excludes the Rose through fear that she will liberate them from the moral law. The fairies, on the contrary, have no need of the Rose because they are untroubled by moral scruples in the first place: 'their blossoming dreams have never bent/Under the fruit of evil and of good' ('To Some I have Talked with by the Fire', VP 136–37). The fairies have no morality because, like the fairies of folklore, they are creatures entirely of whim. The fairy child in *The Land of Heart's Desire* says so explicitly: 'For we are but obedient to the thoughts/That drift into the mind at a wink of an eye' (VPl 206).

Yeats, therefore, has reasons for ambivalence on the fairies over and above his reasons for ambivalence on the Rose. At one moment the fairies may offer the same daunting challenge as the Rose, while at another they may offer the no less daunting challenge of escape from the Rose to their own unimaginable and unattainable peace. 'The nets of wrong and right' cannot be escaped by mortals, except by those rare fools and 'passionate wicked' men who, like the fairies, do not think but respond to thoughts that 'drift into the mind' from elsewhere, perhaps from the Rose itself. As the Rose's messengers, the fairies may even be malicious, luring men onto the quest which none can achieve. Yeats knows that the fairies' attractions, like the sirens', may conceal a deeper peril.

III. Nature (i)

The same ambivalence colours Yeats's attitude towards nature. Because of his poor eyesight, Yeats never had any minute knowledge of nature. To him, it was almost an abstract thing, something he was free to transform as he would. Characteristically, he transformed it into another version of fairyland. Yeats's Innisfree bears little resemblance to the actual island in Lough Gill. On the other hand, Thomas MacDonagh referred to it in 1916 as 'a vivid conception of the land of heart's desire' — an expression he would hardly have used had he not had Yeats's play about fairyland in mind.[8] This is not a trivial prettification of nature. Thomas L. Byrd has noticed that islands like Innisfree are, for Yeats, closer to the Rose than the mainland is ' — perhaps a place of preparation and meditation in which one loses the false reality of the world of materialism and finds the true reality of Being'.[9] This does not mean that Yeats is redeemed by nature in the way that Wordsworth is. Yeats's view of nature is Blakean, not Wordsworthian, so 'materialism' is to be read as synonymous with (Blake's word) 'Corporeal' nature. So Yeats comments upon Blake:

'Imagination may be described as that which is sent bringing spirit to nature, and seemingly losing its spirit, that nature being revealed as symbol may lose the power to delude.'[10] Thus nature is in itself a snare and delusion. It is only valuable as a symbol, as an indication that something else is present. That 'something else' Yeats calls 'Imagination', but he represents it by the fairies. The outstanding example is the fairy child's identification of herself with the process of nature in *The Land of Heart's Desire* (VPl 203):

> When winter sleep is abroad my hair grows thin,
> My feet unsteady. When the leaves awaken
> My mother carries me in her golden arms.
> I'll soon put on my womanhood and marry
> The spirits of wood and water, but who can tell
> When I was born for the first time? I think
> I am much older than the eagle-cock
> (That blinks and blinks on Ballygawley Hill,)
> And he is the oldest thing under the moon.

Similarly, the 'elemental creatures' in 'To Ireland in the Coming Times' are, as Ellmann reminds us, literally the spirits of the elements.[11] The earliest text specifically enumerates 'flood and fire and clay and wind' (VP 138). If, then, nature is simply fairyland in disguise, it follows that all the ambivalence which Yeats feels towards fairyland must pertain to nature also. That is why nature need not always be the paradise of Innisfree but a threatening environment.

IV. *The Land of Heart's Desire*

'Innisfree', however, is a good example of a mood which Yeats indulges only rarely. In this mood he seems to believe that the fairies — and perhaps even the Rose — though hidden, can be painlessly found out. Again, the best example is *The Land of Heart's Desire*.

In biographical terms, this is not a happy play. Yeats tells us that he 'put into it [his] own despair' over Maud Gonne's rejection of him.[12] Henry Goodman considers that this unhappiness shades the play's internal theme: '*The Land of Heart's Desire* combines Yeats's concern for the imagination with the fear of the unconscious'.[13] It would be only natural if that were true, but I cannot interpret the play in that fashion. To my mind, its message is that full knowledge of fairyland is both possible and desirable. The point is proved by a detailed comparison of the play with *The Countess Cathleen*. The structural machinery of the two plays is identical, but the judgments of the earlier play are reversed.

Mary's invocation of the fairies in *The Land of Heart's Desire* parallels Cathleen's in the earlier play, but is still more reminiscent of Shemus' invocation of the demons:

> Come, faeries, take me out of this dull house!
> Let me have all the freedom I have lost;
> Work when I will and idle when I will!
> Faeries, come take me out of this dull world,
> For I would ride with you upon the wind,
> (Run on the top of the dishevelled tide,)
> And dance upon the mountains like a flame.
>
> (VPl 192)

Bridget's reproach is actually spoken before this, but parallels the reproaches of Oona and Maire Rua nonetheless:

> You know well
> How calling the Good People by that name,
> Or talking of them over-much at all,
> May bring all kinds of evil on the house.
>
> (VPl 191–92)

After Mary's invocation, there is a pregnant pause before the Child enters, as there is before the demons enter in *The Countess Cathleen*.[14]

In addition, both plays employ the protective charm of a 'branch of blessed quicken wood' (VPl 185). The demons persuade Shemus to burn his, while the Child snatches away the quicken bough in *The Land of Heart's Desire*. Some texts of the latter play substitute primroses for quicken. These are actually preferable, as it is debatable whether they are a charm against the fairies or a charm to please the fairies. The play exploits that doubt. They are flung down 'to bring good luck into the house', but Maurteen observes that the fairies 'can work all their will with primroses'. The Child bears him out by scattering the primroses and using them as a charm against the priest and the family (VPl 186–87, 204). As well as burning his quicken bough in *The Countess Cathleen*, Shemus destroys his Christian protection by trampling his shrine. This is paralleled in *The Land of Heart's Desire* by the hiding of the crucifix.

Both Mary and the Countess Cathleen daydream about Edain. Mary's speech contains one line, 'Deep in the dewy shadow of a wood' (VPl 184), that invites comparison with a line from Oona's song, 'And rules the shadows of the wood' (VPl 56). At Maurteen's urging, Father Hart mildly rebukes Mary:

The Rose and Her Servants

> Put it away, my colleen;
> (God spreads the heavens about us like great wings
> And gives a little round of deeds and days,
> And then come the wrecked angels and set snares,
> And bait them with light hopes and heavy dreams,
> Until the heart is puffed with pride and goes
> Half shuddering and half joyous from God's peace;)
> For it was some wrecked angel, blind with tears,
> Who flattered Edain's heart with merry words.
>
> (VPl 184–85)

This echoes Cathleen's rebuke to Aleel, and the wrecked angel is a close analogue of Aengus. Mary disputes Father Hart's opinion of the fairies, asking, 'are not they, likewise, children of God?' (VPl 187). This is the old argument as to whether the fairies will be saved, but it also parallels Aleel's suggestion that Aengus is angelical.

One further parallel illustrates the way in which the judgments of *The Countess Cathleen* are reversed in *The Land of Heart's Desire*. In the latter, as in the former play, gold is used as a bribe:

> Come, sit beside me, colleen,
> And put away your dreams of discontent,
> For I would have you light up my last days,
> Like the good glow of the turf; and when I die
> You'll be the wealthiest hereabout, for, colleen,
> I have a stocking full of yellow guineas
> Hidden away where nobody can find it.
>
> (VPl 189)

In *The Countess Cathleen*, however, gold is used to entice souls into another world (hell, as it happens); here, it is used in a vain attempt to keep Mary on earth. The pro-Christian leaning of *The Countess Cathleen* is also reversed in *The Land of Heart's Desire*. When Father Hart says, 'By the dear Name of the One crucified,/I bid you, Mary Bruin, come to me,' the Child retorts, 'I keep you in the name of your own heart' (VPl 206). There can be little doubt which way our sympathies will run, particularly as the Child's reaction to the crucifix has already reinforced its unappealing connotations. In addition, Balachandra Rajan has called attention to this passage:

> ... by love alone
> God binds us to Himself and to the hearth,
> That shuts us from the waste beyond His peace,
> From maddening freedom and bewildering light.
>
> (VPl 193)

'The very use of the words "freedom" and "light",' he says, 'however qualified, undermines not simply the security but the validity of life within the house. On the other hand the world of faery is seen in terms of fulfilment.' He quotes in support of this VPl 205, 'Where beauty has no ebb, decay no flood,/But joy is wisdom, time an endless song,' but then goes on to retract much of his position on three grounds. These are that 'the lonely of heart is withered away' imports 'change into the changeless', and so vitiates the perfection of fairyland; that the play develops the same 'disquieting' ambivalence as 'The Stolen Child' in *Crossways*; and that 'the price of fulfilment is death'.[15] This retraction is unnecessary. 'The lonely of heart' are excluded from fairyland and therefore wither away in this world:

> The wind blows out of the gates of the day,
> The wind blows over the lonely of heart,
> And the lonely of heart is withered away;
> (While the faeries dance in a place apart . . .)
>
> (VPl 210)

'The Stolen Child' is loaded with images of domestic bliss:

> He'll hear no more the lowing
> Of the calves on the warm hillside
> Or the kettle on the hob
> Sing peace into his breast,
> Or see the brown mice bob
> Round and round the oatmeal-chest.
>
> (VP 88)

Thus the child has much to lose by going with the fairies. In *The Land of Heart's Desire*, on the other hand, the images of domestic life are images of hardship and squalor:

> Stay and come with me, newly-married bride,
> For if you hear him you grow like the rest;
> Bear children, cook, and bend above the churn,
> And wrangle over butter, fowl, and eggs,
> Until at last, grown old and bitter of tongue,
> You're crouching there and shivering at the grave.
>
> (VPl 205–06)

Thus, Mary has nothing to lose. She does not even lose her life, for although Shawn cries, 'She is dead!' Bridget immediately contradicts him:

> Come from that image; body and soul are gone.
> You have thrown your arms about a drift of leaves,
> Or bole of an ash-tree changed into her image.
>
> (VPl 209–10)

This is a 'stock'. Mary is not dead but taken for a changeling, as she desired.

Thus this play has a happy ending. Merely by asking for it, Mary has achieved complete union with the fairies. She has exchanged this life for a better one.

V. Optimistic Poems

The optimistic conclusion of *The Land of Heart's Desire* can also be found in a few poems. 'To Ireland in the Coming Times' is the best example; 'To Some I have talked with by the Fire' is another. 'To Ireland' stands as a sort of manifesto to *The Rose*, and so may have been one of the first poems written in that collection. That might explain its optimism: Yeats might not yet have realised the difficulties of his material. In this poem the fairies are fellow seekers with man 'After the red-rose-bordered hem.' Moreover, 'he who treads in measured ways/May surely barter gaze for gaze' with the fairies (VP 138–39). At the same time as they seek the Rose, the fairies serve her, for 'Gazing', as Denis Donoghue has pointed out, is used as a 'technical term' by Yeats for a meditative technique inducing self-transcendence.[16] And to transcend oneself, of course, is to know or at least to approach, the Rose. In an important sense, then, 'To Ireland in the Coming Times' is still more optimistic than *The Land of Heart's Desire*. Yeats suggests that we can gain knowledge of the fairies *and* the Rose.

There is, however, a sting in the tail, if not a crippling one. 'To Ireland in the Coming Times' and 'To Some I have Talked with by the Fire' both end with 'a glimpse of angelic hosts disappearing into the dawn of eternity, the flashing feet of a multitudinous ascension. . . . From this it seems that all things supernatural as well as natural have their day, and are merged at last in God.'[17] This merger is simply a white-out: 'the white hush'; 'For God goes by with white footfall' (VP 137, 139). In this state, creativity and all other human faculties are stunned:

> And we, our singing and our love,
> What measurer Time has lit above,
> And all benighted things that go

> About my table to and fro,
> Are passing on to where may be,
> In truth's consuming ecstasy,
> No place for love and dream at all.
>
> (VP 139)

The triumph of the imagination, then, is simultaneously its failure. To experience truth is to lose the power to express it. Even in these poems, there is a sort of despair.

VI. Fallen Vision

Normally, even such transcendence is impossible, because of our fallen vision. It is possible to see every story in *The Secret Rose*, especially when arranged in historical order, as marking one stage in the deterioration of our vision. Two stories are particularly significant in this respect: 'The Crucifixion of the Outcast' and 'Out of the Rose'. In the former, there are several sunken allusions to the Fianna. When about to be crucified, the gleeman Cumhal offers a tithe of his food to the poorest of the beggars. 'And thereupon was a great clamour, for the beggars began the history of their sorrows and their poverty, and their yellow faces swayed like Gabhra Lough when the floods have filled it with water from the bogs' (M 155). James McGarry assumes that Gabhra Lough is to be identified with Lough Gabhair, but points out that, while the story is set in Co. Sligo, Lough Gabhair is in Co. Meath. He suggests that Yeats is confusing Lough Gabhair with Lough Gara, which extends from Co. Sligo to Co. Roscommon.[18] But Yeats grew up virtually on the banks of Lough Gara, so it is most unlikely that he would mistake its name. Gabhra Lough is, I believe, a deliberate allusion to the Battle of Gabhra, the last stand of the Fianna. The beggars are the degenerate descendants of the Fianna. Only the gleeman himself is an undegenerate descendant. 'I ask no more delays, for I have drawn the sword, and told the truth, and lived my dream, and am content,' he says (M 154). In 'The Colloquy of the Ancients', Patrick asks, 'Who or what was it that maintained you so in your life?' and Cailte replies, 'Truth that was in our hearts, and strength in our arms, and fulfilment in our tongues'. Cumhal berates the monks for lacking just these qualities which he shares with the Fianna: 'O race that does not draw the sword and tell the truth!' (M 149). The other quality in which the monks are pre-eminently deficient is generosity, and this again is the quality in which Finn excelled. As Cailte says: 'Were but the brown leaf which the wood sheds from it gold — were but the white billows silver — Finn would have given it all away.'[19] the fact that Cumhal's name is the name of Finn's father makes it unlikely that these allusions are the product of coincidence.

The degeneracy of the monks (especially) extends to their imaginative vision. A recurrent theme in the 'Colloquy' is the misgiving of Patrick and his clerics as to whether they should listen to the pagan reminiscences of the old Fenians. An angel intervenes to tell them that they should not only listen but take notes. At the time of the Colloquy's composition this may have constituted a reproach to contemporary clerics who had been rejecting secular tales.[20] The clerics in 'The Crucifixion of the Outcast' certainly reject such stories:

'Gleeman,' said the lay brother, as they led him back to the guest-house, 'why do you ever use the wit which God has given you to make blasphemous and immoral tales and verses? For such is the way of your craft. I have, indeed, many such tales and verses wellnigh by rote, and so I know that I speak true! And why do you praise with rhyme those demons, Finvaragh, Red Aodh, Cliona, Aoibheal and Donn? I, too, am a man of great wit and learning, but I ever glorify our gracious abbot, and Benignus our Patron, and the princes of the province.
(M 152-53)

The lay brother is not only a hypocrite but, more importantly, a Phillistine. When the gleeman is crucified, the old vision of the Fianna is finally lost.

A further deterioration is marked in 'Out of the Rose'. Once again, the most relevant passage is this:

He had seen a great Rose of Fire, and a Voice out of the Rose had told him how men would turn from the light of their own hearts, and bow down before outer order and outer fixity, and that then the light would cease, and none escape the curse except the foolish good man who could not think, and the passionate wicked man who would not.
(M 162-63)

Even as it stands, this is a prophecy of the lapse of vision; but the old knight is telling this to the village idiot, surely an example of 'the foolish good man who could not think'. To him are entrusted the remains of unfallen vision. However, his imagination turns out to be as weak as his reason. The best response that he can muster is this: 'He has told me a good tale . . . for there was fighting in it, but I did not understand much of it, and it is hard to remember so long a story' (M 164). He then begins to dig the knight's grave, but leaves even that task unfinished when he hears a cock crow, for his only amusement is cock-fighting and he wants to steal the cock. This is surely 'the cock/That crowed when Peter dared deny his Master' (*The Countess Cathleen*, VPl 151). The lad has betrayed such vestiges of vision as still remained, and now there is no escape from imaginative blindness.

It is that blindness which is now fallen upon us that makes the quest for the Rose impossible. With regard to *The Secret Rose* in particular, a good deal of criticism stops short of this crucial point. Augustine Martin believes that in every story 'The human situation builds itself to a point of intensity that can be answered only by a final, upward thrust into the numinous', to be rewarded by 'a transnatural insight'.[21] In a way, that is quite true, but what is the effect of this transnatural insight? Robert O'Driscoll concludes that 'All of the characters who achieve spiritual triumph in *The Secret Rose* . . . having seen the truth turn from the 'corrupted' material world'.[22] Forrest Reid, on the other hand, long ago perceived in *The Secret Rose* 'a darker atmosphere, through which flame wild unearthly lights that lure the soul to its destruction'.[23] There is some truth in both these views. In many stories (though not all), the protagonist does turn from the material world, but he does not do so in a pleasant fashion. We have only to think of the crucifixion of Cumhal, the ignominious death of the old knight in 'Out of the Rose', the self-imposed exile of the protagonist in 'The Wisdom of the King', or the massacre of Sir Frederick Hamilton's men in 'The Curse of the Fires and of the Shadows'. In the ambiguous ending of 'The Heart of the Spring', the fate of the old man, if it is not death, is an ironic transformation to a thrush. What is told by parable in *The Secret Rose* and somewhat more explicitly in *The Rose* is that fallen vision cannot endure the sight of Truth. If indeed the seeker finally gains a glimpse of the Rose, that glimpse is binding and searing. It bestows no peace. In the moment of vision, vision is thwarted, and life and contentment are blasted.

VII. The Eternal Gospel

Those who seek the vision nonetheless have their choice of many roads. The three royal roads are the subject of a trilogy of poems, 'The Rose of the World', 'The Rose of Peace', and 'The Rose of Battle'. These three poems follow the system of *The Eternal Gospel* of Joachim del Fiore. Joachim's doctrine, one may recall, is celebrated in 'The Tables of the Law'. 'The Rose of the World' is the Son; 'The Rose of Peace' is the Holy Ghost; and 'The Rose of Battle' is the Father. The Son is emotion; the Holy Ghost is spirit; and the Father is thought ('Battle' is therefore 'mental strife,' as in Blake).[24] This triadic structure is replicated within 'The Rose of Battle'. A. G. Stock has commented on the lines 'Beauty grown sad with its eternity/Made you of us, and of the dim grey sea'

(VP 115) that the Rose 'belongs to eternity and was before men and angels, yet in another sense she is an emanation of earthly sorrow'.[25] The Rose in eternity represents the Father, while the Rose self-generated from 'earthly sorrow' represents the Son, or incarnate 'man of sorrows'. There remains 'the dim grey sea', which surely suggests the Holy Ghost, or 'Spirit of God [that] moved upon the face of the waters'.

Now it is not hard to see how these poems embody the quest for the Rose and its failure. In 'The Rose of the World' the Rose passes through the world by virtue of incarnation, like the Son, although, unlike the Son's, her incarnations are recurrent: she is Helen, she is Deirdre, she is many others whose identities are not disclosed. Her passing arouses men's emotions, which leave behind them monuments of art (the *Iliad*, 'The Exile of the Sons of Usnach'), but the direct emotional vision of the Rose destroys the beholder: 'Troy passed away in one high funeral gleam,/And Usna's children died' (VP 111). As Giorgio Melchiori says: 'Through the figure of Helen [Yeats] absorbed the decadent idea of the fusion of love and death, of beauty and destruction, of (in the words of Ary Renan) "le carnage et la volupté." '[26]

The significance of 'The Rose of Peace', as John Unterecker has pointed out, is contained in the one word 'If':

> *If* Michael, leader of God's host
> When Heaven and Hell are met,
> Looked down on you from Heaven's door-post,
>
>   (VP 112; emphasis added)

the universe might be perfected; but Michael will not. Joachim's Age of the Holy Ghost is the age that is yet to come. Thus 'The Rose of Peace' is 'illusion only. Reality, "The Rose of Battle," is in conflict.'[27]

'The Rose of Battle' is the most opaque of these three poems. Unterecker finds it a fundamentally optimistic poem. According to him, the followers of this road — 'unhappy lovers, "The sad, the lonely, the insatiable," poets and occultists' — 'will, waging God's battles, penetrate the mystery of Old Night. Mortal, they will necessarily go down to defeat; but they will have experienced revelation.'[28] This position apparently equates 'Old Night' with the Rose, but the allusion is surely to Milton: '*Chaos* and Old Night'. The phrase also has connotations of death. This is no Rose that we know. The fragility of Unterecker's conclusion can be seen by reversing its terms: 'They will have experienced revelation; but they will necessarily go down to defeat.'

Frank Hughes Murphy also disagrees with Unterecker: 'The poem ends, not in the triumph of revelation before death, as Unterecker says, but rather in a failure to achieve revelation.' Unfortunately, Murphy's argument is open to several objections. He bases much of it on what he considers the suspicious 'stasis' of the ships, failing to notice that they are merely waiting to be boarded. This stasis he oddly identifies with 'physical action', concluding that 'physical action is not the path to vision'. The sails of the ships, he thinks, 'represent mere thought, as opposed to imagination, and are therefore inadequate' for the quest. However, the loosing of the sails represents 'The substitution of imagination for thought', but this too 'is not enough for this exalted quest'.[29] By successively rejecting action, thought, *and* imagination, Murphy only obscures the issue; but what he says about 'The tall thought-woven sails' (VP 113) remains valid. Knowledge of the Rose is an imaginative revelation, and so thought is naturally unable to encompass it. It is the imagination that constantly troubles the thinkers who are the subject of this poem. It is not revelation or vision that offers them comfort in the end; it is simply surcease from that 'little cry'. The Rose visits 'the wharves of sorrow' like a siren or like Cliodhna of the Wave,[30] to beckon these men to their death. As in 'The Rose of the World', then, she is a savage goddess. These three poems are a trilogy of failure.

VIII. The Seekers

Besides defining various roads to the Rose, Yeats's method is to distinguish various types of seeker after the Rose. In *The Rose* itself, such figures are Fergus, Cuchulain, The Countess Cathleen, 'The Man Who Dreamed of Faeryland', and one known simply as 'I', presumably thought of by Yeats as closest to himself. David Daiches rightly understands these figures as symbolising Platonic ideals.[31] It remains to ask what these ideals are. The answer is in a letter by Yeats published in the Dublin *Daily Express* on 27 February 1895: 'The creations of a great writer are little more than the moods and passions of his own heart, given surnames and Christian names, and sent to walk the earth.'[32] Yeats's poem called 'The Moods', though collected in *The Wind Among the Reeds*, was first published in August 1893. Already in *The Rose*, Yeats uses his characters to symbolise the moods.

IX. Fergus

One such character is Fergus. In 'Who Goes With Fergus?' there is a single word that illuminates the way in which these characters

The Rose and Her Servants

function. That word is 'rules':

> For Fergus rules the brazen cars,
> And rules the shadows of the wood,
> And the white breast of the dim sea
> And all dishevelled wandering stars.
>
> (VP 126)

The meaning of 'rules' is not in doubt, but the word can have many nuances. The precise nuance here, I suggest, is astrological, as in 'Saturn rules the artistic temperament'. In an astrological sense, Fergus is the 'governor' of a certain mood symbolised or evoked by 'the shadows of the wood', 'the white breast of the dim sea', and 'all dishevelled wandering stars'.

What is that mood? The quality with which Fergus is normally associated by the critics is wisdom. Up to a point, this is obviously correct. In 'Fergus and the Druid', for instance, Yeats writes:

> What would you, Fergus?
> Be no more a king,
> But learn the dreaming wisdom that is yours.
>
> (VP 103)

For this reason (among others), 'The Wisdom of the King' is a story that may be said to be 'ruled' by Fergus. However, the following passage from that story bears particular comparison with 'Fergus and the Druid': '. . . wisdom the gods have made, and no man shall live by its light, for it and the hail and the rain and the thunder follow a way that is deadly to mortal things' (M 170). This clearly shows the limitations of wisdom. If the word has any meaning, wisdom must exist somewhere, and presumably, therefore, with the Rose, in the absolute. But 'no man shall live by its light'. It is unattainable; or, if it can be attained, it is unbearable. That is why Harold Bloom's characteristation of Fergus as 'a poet-king of wish-fulfillment' is misleading. Insofar as Fergus obtains his 'little bag of dreams,' his wish is fulfilled; but insofar as he hopes to obtain happiness thereby, his wish is not fulfilled. For this reason, Bloom himself feels compelled to limit his observation to 'Who Goes with Fergus?', saying, 'This is not the defeated Fergus of *Fergus and the Druid*',[33] but Yeats has a higher sense of consistency than this implies.

There is only one Fergus. The negative, and more dominant, side of his rule is dissatisfaction. M. L. Rosenthal finds the initially escapist imagery of 'Who Goes with Fergus?' growing 'increasingly disturbed.

"White breast of the dim sea" and "disheveled wandering stars" suggest no diminution of desire or of its frustrations, but only their endless continuance.'[34] 'Who Goes with Fergus?' is only ostensibly an invitation; in reality, it is a warning. The poem is also, of course, Oona's song in *The Countess Kathleen*. There, the Countess responds: 'My heart is longing for a deeper peace/Than Fergus found amid his brazen cars' (VPl 60).

In 'Fergus and the Druid', Fergus's dissatisfaction is plain to be seen:

> A king and proud! and that is my despair.
> I feast amid my people on the hill,
> And pace the woods, and drive my chariot-wheels
> In the white border of the murmuring sea;
> And still I feel the crown upon my head.
>
> (VP 103)

The imagery of this passage is carried over bodily to 'Who Goes with Fergus?', thus adding substance to Rosenthal's criticism ('chariot-wheels,' cf. 'brazen cars'; 'the white border of the murmuring sea', cf. 'the white breast of the dim sea'). Fergus is dissatisfied because he feels his life to be aimless: 'A king is but a foolish labourer/Who wastes his blood to be another's dream.' This is spoken before he has taken the little bag of dreams. We may say, then, that dissatisfaction with his aimless existence is what goads Fergus to seek the Rose in the first place, and wisdom is the means by which he hopes to find her. Having gained wisdom, however, he finds himself as aimless as ever: 'I see my life go drifting like a river/From change to change.' The Druid, of course, has achieved only the same baleful wisdom. That is why he too has 'changed and flowed from shape to shape.'

When these characteristics are borne in mind, other poems and stories align with the Fergus poems, besides 'The Wisdom of the King'. Cumhal, the gleeman of 'The Crucifixion of the Outcast', partakes of Fergus' aimlessness. 'For learn, there is no steadfastness of purpose upon the roads, but only under roofs and between four walls,' says the abbot (M 151), and two pages later Cumhal himself says, 'my soul is indeed like the wind, and it blows blows me to and fro, and up and down, and puts many things into my mind and out of my mind, and therefore am I called the Swift Wild Horse.' It may be significant that Fergus' own patronymic, mac Róigh, means 'Son of the Great Horse'. Cumhal is certainly happier in his aimlessness than Fergus, but in the end he is crucified. The Dionysian aimlessness of his wandering must feel the Apollonian constraint of the world. Even 'The Rose of the World' is, to a limited extent, a Fergus poem:

The Rose and Her Servants

> Amid men's souls, that waver and give place
> Like the pale waters in their wintry race,
> Under the passing stars, foam of the sky,
> Lives on this lonely face.
>
> (VP 112)

Men's aimlessness is apparent in the first two lines, and, as in 'The Crucifixion of the Outcast', this is crucified upon the fixity of the 'lonely face', with the catastrophic result of the destruction of Troy and the sons of Usna. Thus, in all the Fergus poems and stories, aimlessness, dissatisfaction, and wisdom combine to wreck the protagonist.

X. Cuchulain and 'Out of the Rose'

If Fergus is the wise man, Cuchulain is already the 'violent man' of 'Crazy Jane on the Mountain' (VP 628). Though no pugilist himself, Yeats was never squeamish about violence: 'Money is good and a girl might be better,/But good strong blows are delights to the mind' ('Three Songs to the Same Tune', VP 544). Indeed, Yeats's attitude towards violence was remarkably consistent. How it can be a path to the Rose is best seen in one of his very last poems, 'Under Ben Bulben':

> You that Mitchel's prayer have heard,
> 'Send war in our time, O Lord!'
> Know that when all words are said
> And a man is fighting mad,
> Something drops from eyes long blind,
> He completes his partial mind,
> For an instant stands at ease,
> Laughs aloud, his heart at peace.
>
> (VP 638)

That is the mood which Cuchulain represents. He is a much less complex figure than Fergus.

The old knight in 'Out of the Rose' combines elements of Fergus and Cuchulain. He is obviously a violent man, and yet he believes that he follows wisdom. He follows the Rose explicitly. He even wears on his helmet 'a small rose made of rubies' (M 157). His resemblance to Fergus is particularly apparent in 'his face, which was the face of one of those who have come but seldom into the world, and always for its trouble, the dreamers who must do what they dream, the doers who must dream what they do' (M 157). The fusion of Fergus and Cuchulain turns out to be Don Quixote. He dies in knightly combat for a pair of pigs. His wisdom turns out to be foolishness. Although he thinks that he has 'found the thing [he] sought' (M 164), he has been so often wrong that he may be wrong again. Patty Gurd remarks that in dying 'after a wasted life' this knight is only a slightly less extreme form of the knight in the early poem 'The Seeker' (1885), who also follows blindly all his life a private call, only to discover that it is the call of Infamy.[35]

XI. The Countess Cathleen, 'The Man Who Dreamed of Faeryland,' and the First-Person Persona

The Countess Cathleen (represented in *The Rose* by 'The Countess Cathleen in Paradise') stands for piety. She does ultimately attain the Rose, though in the form of a Christian, not fairy, salvation, but she does so only in death. 'The Man Who Dreamed of Faeryland' is her match for piety, if so we may call it, but after the fairy fashion. His distinguishing characteristic is the obsessiveness of his inner life. He does not even find 'comfort in the grave' (VP 128).

The final persona of *The Rose* is the first-person speaker of 'To Some I have talked with by the Fire' and 'To Ireland in the Coming Times'. As the other characters represent Yeats in the grip of various moods, this unified 'I' presumably represents a combination of all the others. Appropriately, then, these are survey poems. In 'To Some I have Talked with by the Fire', Yeats moves from 'the dark folk who live in souls/Of passionate men' (VP 136), who may be associated with that passionate man Cuchulain, to the fairies dreamed of by a certain man, to the angels associated with the Countess Cathleen. In 'To Ireland in the Coming Times'. Yeats presents himself first as a warrior-bard:

> True brother of a company
> That sang, to sweeten Ireland's wrong,
> Ballad and story, rann and song;
> ....
> ... one
> With Davis, Mangan, Ferguson.
>
> (VP 137–38)

This passage has obvious associations with Cuchulain, while the ellipsis includes a passing reference to 'the angelic clan'. Yeats next presents himself as a poet of wisdom, like Fergus. This is best seen in the original text:

> Because to him who ponders well
> My rhymes more than their rhyming tell
> Of the dim wisdoms old and deep,
> That God gives unto man in sleep.
>
> (VP 138)

The reference to dreaming in the last line dovetails with ten lines about the fairies to give another picture of 'The Man Who Dreamed of Faeryland'. The poem then concludes, like 'To Some I have Talked with by the Fire', in the white blur of unity, or 'truth's consuming ecstasy'.

XII. The Sin Against the Rose

These, then, are the personae of *The Rose*: the wise man, the violent man, the pious man (or woman), the obsessive man, and the man who possesses all these moods. Of all these figures it may be said, in the words of the original title of 'The Rose of Battle', that 'They went forth to the Battle, but they always fell'. In the quest for the Rose, they are all failures.

However, even if it is impossible to find the Rose, it is more shameful not to seek her than to seek her and fail. Compared to this quest, even love is of secondary importance. Requited love may satisfy the heart that can otherwise be satisfied only by the unattainable Rose, but Yeats suggests that this satisfaction is too cheaply bought. This is explicit, or nearly so, in 'The Rose of Battle':

> *Turn if you may from battles never done,*
> *I call, as they go by me one by one,*
> *Danger no refuge holds, and war no peace,*
> *For him who hears love and sing and never cease,*
> *Beside her clean-swept hearth, her quiet shade:*
> *But gather all for whom no love hath made*
> *A woven silence, or but came to cast*
> *A song into the air, and singing passed*
> *To smile on the pale dawn; and gather you*
> *Who have sought more than is in rain or dew*
> *Or in the sun and moon, or on the earth,*
> *Or sighs amid the wandering, starry mirth,*
> *Or comes in laughter from the sea's sad lips,*
> *And wage God's battles in the long grey ships.*
>
> (VP 114)

There can be little doubt that of the two types presented here the love-lorn seeker is nobler than the contented homebody. Frank Hughes

Murphy observes that those of the latter type 'are somehow smothered by love . . . so that their spiritual selves are extinguished, and their finer thirsts can never be satisfied'.[36] Under such circumstances, the Rose, for all its pains, is actually 'a refuge from earthly love'.[37] Unrequited love, on the other hand, may actually stimulate the seeker of the Rose. This is suggested by the departure of the king to fulfil 'his ideal destiny' in 'The Wisdom of the King'.

The quest for the Rose is not an exercise of love, but of the imagination. Quite a number of poems and stories contain hints of reproach or threats of punishment to those who deny, or oppose, or will not exercise the imagination. Thus, in 'The Curse of the Fires and of the Shadows', as the troopers of Sir Frederick Hamilton burn the Abbey of the White Friars at Sligo, 'Behind them shone the Abbey windows filled with saints and martyrs, awakened, as from a sacred trance, into an angry and animated life. The eyes of the troopers were dazzled, and for a while could see nothing but the flaming faces of saints and martyrs' (M 178). These figures in the stained glass bear an extraordinary resemblance to the 'sages standing in God's holy fire/As in the gold mosaic of a wall' of 'Sailing to Byzantium,' a poem written twenty-nine years later (VP 408). Like them, they may be taken as miracles of artifice, saints of the imagination. Those who have so disturbed them have committed sacrilege against the Divine Imagination, and are duly punished by the fairies, functioning here as servants of the Rose.

'The Old Men of the Twilight' introduces a judgment of the imagination of wider scope. This story concerns some old men cursed by St. Patrick to live as herons for centuries, until some accidental chance should kill them. Their specific offence was that they 'disputed concerning prosody and the relative importance of rhyme and assonance, syllable and accent' (M 193), while Patrick 'preached the commandments of God', and the clicking of their 'knives writing [their] thoughts in Ogham alone disturbed the silence' (M 194). However, their sin was not so much against 'the commandments of God' as against the commandments of the imagination in general, for they were as inattentive to the Druids as to Patrick. They were obsessed with poetic form as opposed to imaginative content (a flaw which Yeats was beginning to suspect in his own verse), and for this they were punished as Sir Frederick Hamilton's troopers were punished.[38] After the lapse of many centuries, one of the herons is shot by an old 'voteen' (a man given over to superstitious piety). This voteen repeats, and even exacerbates, the old men's sin. He is as devoted to Patrick's words as the old men were to their own, but Patrick's words in their turn have become a mere empty babble in his superstitious mind. He seals his sin by refusing to allow the dying heron-man whom he has shot (and who

The Rose and Her Servants

is now restored to human form) to touch his rosary. The voteen clearly belongs to the same class as the monks in 'The Crucifixion of the Outcast', where there is 'not only a depiction of the poet as Christ, but an obvious parable of the situation of the artist in Ireland, with the priests representing the Church and the beggars the mass of men'.[39] Similar representatives of the rabble who sin with their fallen vision against the Divine Imagination are the peasants in 'Out of the Rose', the lovers in 'The Wisdom of the King', and the boy in 'The Heart of the Spring'. The fall of human vision and the offence of the reason against the imagination are dealt with schematically in 'The Two Trees', a rather overrated poem that is too dependent on esoteric Kabbalism. By gazing too much in the 'bitter glass' of 'unresting thought' (VP 135–36), 'By insisting on the priority of human reason to imagination and the boundless life of the impersonal world, men had lost contact with the eternal, multiplied individuality and had torn human life away from the divine.'[40]

'The Old Men of the Twilight' and Sir Frederick Hamilton's troopers are sinners against the imagination, but fallen vision is the state of sin in which they are bound. Though these sinners are punished, and not forgiven, Yeats is a good enough Blakean to know that it is the state of sin which must be abolished. This implies that fallen vision will be renewed. More than one critic has seen this prophecy as part of a cyclical structure in *The Secret Rose*. Thus Ellmann says: 'The conception of history as cyclical, and of a divine incarnation at the beginning of each round, is implicit in many of [Yeats's] early stories in *The Secret Rose* . . .'[41] Augustine Martin points out that the decadence of the old voteen's religion in 'The Old Men of the Twilight' 'suggests that Patrick's era may be coming to an end', and that 'the image of the heron man coasting the skies for almost twenty centuries throws our mind back over the book's time-span — "twenty centuries of stony sleep" — now that it is approaching its momentous conclusion' in the alchemical stories.[42] The end of one cycle, of course, is the beginning of another, when the door of perception will be cleansed. But the new cycle too must undergo its own decline. Our vision will fall and fall again, but for a moment perhaps it will be capable of facing the Rose. Only such a hope will justify Yeats's insistence that the Rose must be sought and his contempt for those who will not seek her.

XIII. The Price of Failure

This justification is sorely needed, for the price of failure in the quest for the Rose is high, although inevitable. Failure can induce all manner of neurosis. It can, for instance, induce *angst*, as in 'The Pity of Love'; or solipsism, as in 'The Sorrow of Love'; but above all, it can induce alienation. We see this, for instance, in a passage from 'The Wisdom of the King' that is reminiscent of T. S. Eliot's 'Journey of the Magi':

> While they listened to him his words seemed to make all darkness light and filled their hearts like music; but when they returned to their own lands his words seemed far off, and what they could remember too strange and subtle to help him in their lives. A number indeed did live differently afterwards, but their new life was less excellent than the old: some among them had long served a good cause, but when they heard him praise it, they returned to their own lands to find what they had loved less lovable, for he had taught them how little divides the false and true; others, again, who had served no cause, but had sought in peace the welfare of their own households, found their bones softer and less ready for toil, for he had shown them greater purposes; and numbers of the young, when they had heard him upon all these things, remembered certain strange words that made ordinary joys nothing, and sought impossible joys and grew unhappy.
>
> (M 168–69)

This is the effect of only a glimpse of the Rose at second-hand; from this we can imagine how much greater is the king's own despair. In 'The Heart of the Spring', also, we hear of 'the doom of loneliness which always falls upon the wise' (M 172). This is reminiscent of 'Fergus and the Druid', but the poem that best conveys the doom of alienation is 'The Man Who Dreamed of Faeryland'.

For Harold Bloom, this poem is 'a demythologised version of Blake's beautiful epyllion *The Book of Thel*'. In his opinion, the worldly concerns with which each stanza commences are the course of wisdom, while the dream of faeryland is folly.[43] But surely what is both humdrum and unrewarding, like 'money cares and fears', cannot be wise; nor does Yeats call it wise, but 'prudent', a very different thing. Edmund Wilson's summary of the poem is more accurate:

> to the mortal who has lived among the fairies, who has lost the sense of human laws in their world, the consequences may be terrible — for he has preferred something else to reality — he has escaped the responsibilities of human life and he must fail of its satisfactions.[44]

It is true that the man in the poem has not lived among the fairies. He has only dreamed of them, but the consequences are the same. He has failed to achieve the supreme happiness of fairyland, but his very imagination of that land is sufficient to alienate him from this. He falls between two stools, and his unhappiness is as great as would his happiness have been in the impossible event of success.

XIV. Nature (ii)

This necessitates a reconsideration of nature, for if nature to Yeats is but one aspect of fairyland, the man who dreams of Innisfree must face the same alienated frustration as 'The Man Who Dreamed of Faeryland'. One of the major problems in the poem of that name is why the man is reminded of fairyland by such humble prompters: a pile of dead or dying fish, a lug-worm, a stalk of knot-grass, and his own grave-worms. David Daiches' opinion is perhaps the most convincing: 'A man involved in ordinary human emotions and ordinary human affairs is made aware, on suddenly confronting objects from the natural world, of the strange otherness of that world, and after that he can know no peace.'[45] Nature, then, is still the symbol of something other than itself. It is still the disguise of fairyland. The more ordinary the details of nature, the more awesome is that disguise. But, being one with fairyland and partaking of the Rose, nature, like them, must reject and alienate its suitors.

Even in 'The Lake Isle of Innisfree', superficially Yeats's most accessible and conventional lyric, we may watch this feeling of rejection setting in. The more deeply one examines the symbolism — for the imagery is symbolic — the more sombre does it appear. For example, Ellmann explains that in Yeats's system of symbolism water, such as 'lake water lapping with low sounds by the shore', 'suggests tears and sorrow, therefore loss and therefore death'. Even the 'small cabin . . . of clay and wattles made' is suspicious. Clay often stands for earth in Yeats's system, and 'the darkness of earth suggests a connection with night and sleep such as Yeats made in his Esoteric Section journal, and, because of the connotations of blackness, is often regarded as malevolent.'[46]

These are the ugly secrets of Innisfree, but of course that particular poem remains primarily a light pastoral idyll. The darker side of Yeats's attitude to nature emerges less mistakably in the companion poem to 'The Lake Isle', called 'The Danaan Quicken Tree.' This was published only once in Yeats's lifetime, in *The Bookman* of May, 1893. As the poem is not well known, it will be as well to quote it in full:

> Beloved, hear my bitter tale!—
> Now making busy with the oar,
> Now flinging loose the slanting sail,
> I hurried from the woody shore,
> And plucked small fruits on Innisfree.
> (Ah, mournful Danaan quicken tree!)

> A murmuring faery multitude,
> When flying to the heart of light
> From playing hurley in the wood
> With creatures of our heavy night,
> A berry threw for me — or thee.
> (Ah, mournful Danaan quicken tree!)
>
> And thereon grew a tender root,
> And thereon grew a tender stem,
> And thereon grew the ruddy fruit
> That are a poison to all men
> And meat to the Aslauga Shee.
> (Ah, mournful Danaan quicken tree!)
>
> If when the battle is half won,
> I fling away my sword, blood dim,
> Or leave some service all undone,
> Beloved, blame the Danaan whim,
> And blame the snare they set for me.
> (Ah, mournful Danaan quicken tree!)
>
> Cast out all hope, cast out all fear,
> And taste with me the faeries' meat,
> For while I blamed them I could hear
> Dark Joan call the berries sweet,
> Where Niam heads the revelry.
> (Ah, mournful Danaan quicken tree!)
>
> (VP 742–43)

'Dark Joan,' Yeats explains in a note, 'is a famous faery who often goes about the roads disguised as a clutch of chickens.' Niam, of course, is the bride of Oisín, whom Yeats imagines, here as in 'The Hosting of the Sidhe', as leading the fairy host. The poem itself is on the same theme as Christina Rosetti's 'Goblin Market', but the imagery of alienation is especially prominent. The last stanza is particularly reminiscent of the Biblical Fall, with the difference that Adam is tempting Eve. However, this is a second Fall. Adam found himself alienated from Paradise. The speaker of this poem finds himself alienated even from the fallen world, while unable, like 'The Man Who Dreamed of Faeryland', to join Niam and her revelry. He must expect the world to reject him too, for the fourth stanza shows that he is apt, like Suibhne Gealt, to run mad and apparently turn coward in the midst of battle (to neglect his responsibilities, in other words). This can only win him, like 'The Seeker', infamy.

Both aspects of Yeats's attitude toward nature, the rather facile celebration of 'Innisfree' and the darker alienation of 'The Danaan

Quicken Tree', derive from Blake. Visible nature, the 'whole bulk of outer things', is what Blake calls the 'Covering Cherub', and what Yeats calls 'the self-devouring serpent, Nature — at once the garment of God and his negation'. Yeats follows Blake in pouring out upon it 'his most vehement hatred and his most tender love'. Furthermore, 'In "Jerusalem" the [Covering] cherub is said to be the body of Christ which He puts off upon the Cross,' and this is the same cross which features in 'To the Rose upon the Rood of Time'.[47] Yeats thus begins *The Rose* with a poem in which he disavows nature. Nature is as dangerous as fairyland, and for the same reason.

XV. The Meaningless Universe

The sense of alienation induced by failure to attain the Rose may expand to cosmic proportions, to a perception of the universe as meaningless. For instance, this is implied by the allusion to 'Chaos and Old Night' in 'The Rose of Battle'. This perception is one to which Fergus is particularly prone. It is part and parcel of his aimless dissatisfaction. Thomas Byrd considers that the image of Fergus 'driving his chariot in "the white border of the murmuring sea" ' (in 'Fergus and the Druid') evokes 'a mood of being on the edge of true existence'.[48] After he takes the 'little bag of dreams', his perception is expanded from the single life in which he has felt himself imprisoned to the whole cycle of his lives, but with no diminution of his sense of aimlessness:

> I see my life go drifting like a river
> From change to change; I have been many things —
> A green drop in the surge, a gleam of light
> Upon a sword, a fir-tree on a hill,
> An old slave grinding at a heavy quern,
> A king sitting upon a chair of gold—
> And all these things were wonderful and great;
> But now I have grown nothing, knowing all.
>
> (VP 104)

It is not enough that all these things were 'wonderful and great'. If the universe is to have meaning, it must have a system of priorities: some things must be more 'wonderful and great' than others. Fergus' shattering realisation is that this is not the case.

This illustrates one of the respects in which the fairies differ from men. As we know, they are neutral angels. They are not on the side of evil or of good. They have no priorities. This is the source of their happiness, and of their peace. Because they make no demands of the universe, they have no need of the Rose. However, it is an illusion to suppose that a like amorality will bestow a like happiness on men. 'The Old Men of the Twilight' are men who attempt it. They will listen neither to those druids who welcome Patrick nor to those who oppose him; they live 'where the feet of the angels cannot touch your heads, nor the hair of the demons sweep your feet-soles'; but because of this they are punished with the same curse as Fergus, not to 'be certain about anything for ever and ever' (M 193–95).

Cuchulain, the violent man, is also forced to recognise a meaningless universe. The moral of 'Cuchulain's Fight with the Sea' is that the violent man cannot hope to attain the Rose because violence is self-defeating. This in itself implies a measure of meaninglessness, which the detail of the poem aggravates. Cuchulain's son knows whom he has to kill.[49] The elder Cuchulain does not have this advantage. Thus he is compelled by a pointless vow — not to reveal his name except under duress — to fight an unknown man against whom he bears no grudge, and then to discover that he was fighting against his own interests. While Cuchulain broods on the meaninglessness of this event, Conchubar fears that he will respond with a still more meaningless deed, the slaughter of his friends. At Conchubar's behest, the druids therefore provoke Cuchulain to the most meaningless action of all: a futile struggle against the sea, itself symbolic of invincible chaos.[50] The Druids must symbolise the acme of human wisdom, but the extent of their wisdom is to 'Chaunt in his ear delusions magical' (VP 111). Indeed, the wisest response to a meaningless universe *is* only delusion.

Yeats's response, therefore, to the Rose, to fairyland, to nature, and to the universe itself is profoundly pessimistic. This response demands a fresh response. How is one to cope with such pessimism? One response is simply to stop agonising, to seek repose in oblivion. 'A Faery Song' is a poem of this type:

> We who are old, old and gay,
> O so old!
> Thousands of years, thousands of years,
> If all were told:
>
> Give to these children, new from the world,
> Silence and love;
> And the long dew-dropping hours of the night,
> And the stars above:
>
> Give to these children, new from the world,
> Rest far from men.
> Is anything better, anything better?
> Tell us it then:

> Us who are old, old and gay,
> O so old!
> Thousands of years, thousands of years,
> If all were told.
>
> (VP 116)

Here the fairies are friendly to man and unattached to the Rose. They cannot share their own contentment with Diarmuid and Grania ('these children'). They do not offer to make them 'gay', like themselves. But they offer the next best thing: oblivion. Nothing, indeed, is better — for mortals.

XVI. 'The White Birds' and 'The Heart of the Spring'

This longing for oblivion is of course very close to a death-wish. However, the death-wish is explicitly rebuked in 'Out of the Rose': 'this . . . was evil, for we . . . took out of the hands of God the choice of the time and manner of our death, and by so doing made his power the less' (M 163). It is true that to apply this out of context is to beg the question, as a meaningless universe is Godless, but the passage does demonstrate a desire to transcend meaninglessness rather than to succumb to it. If the material universe (nature) is meaningless, there remains the hidden universe of fairyland. If this land is the realm of the imagination, Yeats is free to supply his own meaning. Art, in other words, is meaningful. This is the implication of 'The White Birds'. We are in fairyland. Yeats is explicit about that: 'The birds of fairyland are said to be white as snow. The Danaan Islands are the islands of the fairies' (VP 121). But the nature of this fairyland is implicit in the lines: 'Soon far from the rose and the lily and fret of the flames would we be,/Were we only white birds, my beloved, buoyed out on the foam of the sea! (VP 122). As usual, the rose symbolises the female impulse towards life, while the lily symbolises the male impulse towards death. This fairyland, then, is neither life nor death, but a state beyond both, as it is also beyond sex. This is the eternal realm of art, which reappears much later in 'Byzantium'.

However, 'The White Birds' still remains the expression of an unfulfilled wish. In 'The Heart of the Spring', this wish is fulfilled for the protagonist. The old man may not become a white bird, but he does become a bird, a thrush. His singing is his art. It is appropriate, however, that there is an element of irony in this story. If the old man has found a kind of eternal youth, it is not the kind that he sought. He dreamt of eternal youth as a man, in 'a palace of white marble amid orange-trees' (M 174). To some extent, then, 'The Heart of the Spring' is an exercise in self-mockery on Yeats's part. He can always make his art, but how can he be his art, as 'The White Birds' demands?

Thus the final question raised by the Rose meets no positive answer. If the universe is meaningless, neither death nor art seem to provide acceptable remedies for that situation. What can one do, then, but sally forth anew to seek the Rose, in the hope that she can provide meaning. But she, if found, will prove unendurable. One recoils from her presence, alienated again in a universe once again meaningless. It is a treadmill that man treads, an endless vicious cycle. The fairies lurk on the outside grinning, generally none too kindly. Whether they serve the Rose or ignore her, they rarely lighten man's burden. Their estate can be envied but not emulated. Yeats has thus written himself into a straitjacket. Eventually, in *The Wind Among the Reeds*, he will burst free by a violent gesture. In the meantime, the *Stories of Red Hanrahan*, by a deft change of perspective, suggest for the first time the possibility of an escape.

14. 'THE CAULDRON, THE STONE, THE SWORD, THE SPEAR': STORIES OF RED HANRAHAN

The *Stories of Red Hanrahan*, which constitute a separate section of *The Secret Rose*, are interconnected and add up to make a short novel. More accurately, they add up to make two short novels; for when Yeats revised them, with Lady Gregory's help, in 1904, he rejected entirely the original first story, 'The Book of the Great Dhoul and Hanrahan the Red', and substituted the completely different 'Red Hanrahan'. He also made significant alterations in 'The Death of Hanrahan'. Although the intervening stories remain much the same except in style, these changes alter the meaning of the entire sequence.

Many poets of the nineteenth and twentieth centuries, Yeats included, have attempted to adapt the form of the folk-ballad to a more complex significance than it might traditionally carry. The *Stories of Red Hanrahan* apply the same technique to the folk-tale. At least in 'Red Hanrahan', the experiment is highly successful. Yeats takes the story of one man's relations with the fairies, a story which in nearly every detail might have been heard around any peasant fireside, and with those details speaks simultaneously of mythology, of romance, of the occult, of the nation, and of imaginative creativity, without ever ceasing to speak of fairyland, of its nature, and of its effect upon us. Every theme flows into and reinforces the others. Red Hanrahan, a man who has fallen into the fairies' power, suffers accordingly, as the personae of *The Rose* must suffer, but eventually comes to terms with his fate. He provides Yeats with a rare and happy ending, and remains vital in the memory when figures like Fergus have begun to cloy. The *Stories* of 1897 are narrower in scope and less successful than the *Stories* of 1904, it is true, but they cannot be entirely ignored and will be considered first.

I. 1897

The *Stories* of 1897 have but one theme, the theme of nationalism versus art. This theme is inherently less interesting to modern readers than it was to Yeats, or even to his contemporaries. It is all the less interesting for being often repeated. And it is less interesting still when it is imperfectly worked out, as it is in the 1897 *Stories of Red Hanrahan*. Here, Yeats rejects nationalism in favour of art. That did not prevent him from writing *Cathleen Ni Houlihan* five years later. In 'To Ireland in the Coming Times' Yeats had already advanced the proposition that his art and his nationalism were identical. He was to do so again in 'The Grey Rock', but that subtlety had temporarily escaped him in 1897.

These stories are made symmetrical by the correspondence of the bat in the first story with the eagle in the last. In 'The Book of the Great Dhoul and Hanrahan the Red', Cleena (of the Tuatha Dé Danann) sends Hanrahan a bat so that he may use its blood to invoke her by magic. He does so, but rejects her. The end of his long punishment for this comes in the last story when he falls while climbing a tree for a fish that an eagle has dropped there.

It is explicit in the text that the eagle represents air, the fish water, and the tree earth.[1] The fourth element, fire, has already destroyed Hanrahan's house. The elements remain the 'elemental creatures', or fairies; put together, they add up to nature, and nature remains a symbol of the Rose. The entrance of the Rose into these stories is again quite explicit. Thus does Cleena put her curse on Hanrahan:

> Owen Hanrahan the Red, you have looked so often upon the dust that when the Rose has blossomed there you think it but a pinch of coloured dust; but now I lay upon you a curse, and you shall see the Rose everywhere . . . and seek to come to it in vain. . . . A sorrow of all sorrows is upon you.

Cara Ackerman comments that the Rose is still participating in man's pursuit of her, and that Cleena herself is the Rose. She wears a robe with a 'red-rose-bordered hem'.[2]

Hanrahan apparently understands that the elements symbolise the Rose, but he mistakes the Rose for Kathleen the Daughter of Hoolihan, or Ireland. In this text, his *aisling*, or vision of Ireland, reads as follows:

> O tufted reeds, bend low and low in pools on the Green Land,
> Under the bitter Black Winds blowing out of the left hand!
> Like tufted reeds our courage droops in a Black Wind and dies:
> But we have hidden in our hearts the flame out of the eyes
> Of Kathleen the Daughter of Hoolihan.
>
> O tattered clouds of the world, call from the high Cairn of Maive,
> And shake down thunder on the stones because the Red Winds rave!
> Like tattered clouds of the world, passions call and our hearts beat:
> But we have all bent low and low, and kissed the quiet feet
> Of Kathleen the Daughter of Hoolihan.

> O heavy swollen waters, brim the Fall of the Oak trees,
> For the Grey Winds are blowing up, out of the clinging seas!
> Like heavy swollen waters are our bodies and our blood:
> But purer than a tall candle before the Blessed Rood
> Is Kathleen the Daughter of Hoolihan.
>
> (VP 206–08)

Ellmann comments on 'Red Hanrahan's Song about Ireland' as it stands alone in *In The Seven Woods* that Yeats 'employs fire as the immortal element with which he can connect Kathleen-Ny-Hoolihan . . . and makes the other elements the mortal ones which contrast with it.'[3] In the context of the 1897 *Stories*, however, Hanrahan finds that all the elements are against him, including fire, because he has sinned against the Rose. He hopes by his hymn to placate her, but he only compounds his offence. In the first place, by erecting an altar before her, he wishes Cleena to remain still the 'Far-off, most secret, and inviolate Rose', as in 'The Book of the Great Dhoul', when she has offered him her intimate companionship.[4] In the second place, he mistakes the Rose for a patriotic idol, and so finds that Cathleen ni Houlihan's way is indeed a thorny way.

Hanrahan's offence is actually two-fold: he rejects Cleena in the flesh because she is only flesh and not an ideal; but the ideal which his imagination creates is tawdry by comparison with the Rose. His imagination lacks human sympathy and also penetration. It remains superficial until the end of his life. In 'The Death of Hanrahan', he recoils from the touch of Whinny Byrne. He can see only her madness and her decrepitude. It is nothing to him that she, like him, was once renowned for her wisdom and her singing, nor that she now proclaims herself immortal. He fails to recognise his own qualities in her; he fails to realise that it was for those qualities that Cleena sought his love in the first place; he fails to recognise that those qualities are Cleena's own. He forgets that even Cathleen ni Houlihan, the idol of his own invention, is a Poor Old Woman as well as a young woman with the walk of a queen. 'Not until Cleena can be seen' in her own form 'does he understand that the Rose has once again blossomed in the dust.'[5] The moral is that the image of Ireland is an inadequate and ignoble idol for the true artist; he must turn inward to worship at the shrine of the Divine Imagination.

The 1897 text of the *Stories of Red Hanrahan* does have one advantage over its later counterpart. It better sustains the tragic quality of Hanrahan's life. In the 1904 text, we see Hanrahan in various tragic incidents. Even in some of these — 'Red Hanrahan's Curse,' especially — the vitality of the character and the gusto of the narration are apt to induce an inappropriate sense of comedy. Between tragic incidents, there is nothing to prevent us from imagining a life full of good times for Hanrahan. In the 1897 text, on the other hand, we can see that Hanrahan's whole condition is tragic. This is particularly apparent in 'The Twisting of the Rope'. Hanrahan is a man between two worlds. His contact with this world is incomplete, because he belongs more to the milieu of old romance than to events of the present. Thus, he spends 'a night in the cave where Grania found a little peace, before the boar slew Dermot', and he flatters his girl by likening her to Deirdre.[6] Even with such praises, Hanrahan fails. Though he can still charm mortal women, he can no longer succeed with them since his encounter with Cleena. It is as though there is no world ready to accommodate him.

In a sense, however, the tragic quality of the 1897 text is responsible for one of its greatest weaknesses, the incongruity of its comic ending. Hanrahan fails and fails and fails — and then suddenly succeeds, for no good reason. His actions are all mistakes. In the 1904 text, the ending is much better prepared. Hanrahan's actions are not all mistakes. He creates his own destiny as much as it is created for him. In fact, he deserves to succeed.

II. The Symbol

The 1905 text begins with 'Red Hanrahan', a story excellently adapted from folklore. Like all good stories of the supernatural, it takes place on the Eve of Samhain. Hanrahan finds himself in company dominated by a strange old man with a pack of cards. This man is clearly a fairy. Even his possession of the cards is an indication of this. Many *scéalta* begin with a fairy's tricking a man into a *geis* by gambling with him at cards. This old man's amazing card trick is to transform his cards into a hare and a pack of hounds. Yeats had heard of this trick from 'An old woman from the borders of Sligo and Mayo', who remembered 'a wild old man in flannel who came from Erris' and used to perform the trick, as the woman's father told her.[7] Daniel Hoffman thinks the hare is the soul of Mary Lavelle, and it is for Hanrahan to rescue her from the hounds, or 'reclaim her spirit from the Happy Otherworld'.[8] Unfortunately, this ingenious theory is unsupported by the text. Mary Lavelle is not dead, nor is she the same as Echtge. Hanrahan has no thought of her when he pursues the hounds. It is only because he has forgotten her that he has lingered long enough to be ensnared.

In fact, the hare and hounds are simply glamoured cards, and their function is simply to lure Hanrahan onto Slieve Echtge. It is the cards in their unglamoured form that are more interesting. They are, in an obvious sense, the cause of the whole story. They are also at the centre of the story. In a way, they *are* the story. Yeats uses them as a grand symbol, uniting several different streams of tradition, mystical and otherwise. He was able to do this because he realised that the conventional pack of cards, as used by the old man, is a debased form of the Tarot pack.[9] In its turn, the symbolism of the Tarot is of wider application. A. E. Waite proclaimed with an air of discovery in 1929 that the suits of the Tarot are 'The Canonical Hallows of the Grail Legend . . . the Cup, the Lance, the Dish, and the Sword'.[10] It is certain, however, that Yeats was aware of this correlation, and of a further correlation between the Grail Hallows and the Four Jewels of the Tuatha Dé Danann, well before 1929.[11] Indeed, Gwladys V. Downes speculates that Waite may have learnt his allegedly ancient and Celtic method of divining by the Tarot from Yeats;[12] if so, he may have learnt of the relationship between the Tarot and the Grail Hallows from Yeats as well, though one suspects that the relationship has always been more widely recognised than Waite insinuates. Yeats explained the complete system to Maud Gonne in connection with his fantasy of a sort of patriotic Irish magical order. This order was to have its headquarters on an island in Lough Key, and this 'Castle of the Heroes' was to be

> decorated only with the Four Jewels of the Tuatha de Danaan, with perhaps a statue of Ireland, if any artist could be found great enough to make one, which we doubted.
>
> The Four Jewels, as Willie explained, are universal symbols appearing in debased form on the Tarot, the divining cards of the Egyptians and even on our own playing cards, and foreshadowed the Christian symbolism of the Saint Grail, whose legends Willie loved to trace to Ireland.
>
> The Lia Fail, the Stone of Destiny, he said, corresponded with the Altar, which, as Catholics know, even when made of wood should have a stone embedded in it;
>
> The Cauldron of the Dagda, the Good God, called also the Cauldron of Recompense, the Chalice, the Grail Cup;
>
> The Gold Spear of Victory of Lugh the Sun God, the Lance which pierced the side of Christ for the salvation of mankind;
>
> The Sword of Light, the Cross-handled sword of the Crusaders, or the Knights of the Grail.[13]

The symbolism of the old man's cards, then, branches out through the Tarot to include magic, through the Four Jewels of the Tuatha Dé Danann to include Ireland and the fairies, and through the Hallows to include the Grail Quest. Red Hanrahan's story is reflected in each of these mirrors. Unlike 'The Man Who Dreamed of Faeryland', the 1904 *Stories of Red Hanrahan* really will stand comparison with 'The Book of Thel'. In literal terms, Hanrahan is offered admission to fairyland. That plane of existence is, in Nietzschean terms, Dionysian, and, in Blakean terms, Innocent. Before he can accept the offer, however, Hanrahan must pass an initiation test; but he fails it. He must spend the rest of his life training for his second attempt. Like Thel, he must prepare for Innocence by passing through Experience; for the Dionysian by passing through the Apollonian. At the second attempt, Hanrahan passes. In the *Stories of Red Hanrahan*, Yeats reverses the perspective of *The Rose*. Hanrahan is a man who has not only dreamed of faeryland, but been there. His fate is what others fear when they recoil from the Rose. His alienation is no neurosis of the mind, but a genuine estrangement of the spirit. Hanrahan may never come to terms with this world, but in the end he does come to terms with the fairies and enters their kingdom.

III. The Tarot

In magical terms, there may be no better way to follow Hanrahan's development than by reading the stories with the Tarot spread out on the table. The major characters of the stories are actually pictured in the Tarot. The old man is the Magician, or Juggler, the first of the Greater Trumps. Aleister Crowley identifies the Juggler with Mercury, and, although Yeats does not normally agree with Crowley, it is true that the old man is the messenger of Echtge. Before him on the Tarot card are the emblems of all the suits. These represent, according to Waite, 'the elements of natural life, which lie like counters before the adept, and he adapts them as he wills'.[14] Although we never see the old man again after he has first summoned Hanrahan to Echtge, he continues to manipulate Hanrahan's life so as to bring him back to Echtge in the end. One may even identify the old man with Yeats himself.

Hanrahan is the Fool of the Tarot, or the Joker of the conventional pack. The Fool is the only Tarot card which has no number. Likewise, 'The neophyte of the Order of the Golden Dawn was assigned the number O = O'. The initiation of a magical neophyte may be seen as symbolically encapsulating his whole life. It may also be seen as his rebirth. The ambiguity applies to Hanrahan. His exit from the house in 'Red Hanrahan' is on one level symbolic of his literal birth: 'If . . . Hanrahan is . . . the soul who leaves eternity for the journey of time, the door that shut after him as he went might seem to signify the irrevocability of birth into this world.'[15] On another level, however, the same incident symbolises his rebirth or magical initiation. This is virtually the undoing of his original birth: 'As the central characteristic of this refining of the soul is immersion in chaos, the collapse of both the phenomenal and noumenal aspects of one's world, that night Hanrahan goes "stumbling out the door like a man in a dream" '. By this reading, Hanrahan's loss of Mary Lavelle becomes 'a necessary preliminary, a first sacrifice of the flesh to the spirit'.[16] His stumbling flight becomes symbolic of the rest of his life. Though he fails to win Echtge at the first encounter, he is in one sense already initiated. He carries away the memory of Echtge as a souvenir and a reminder of what he is striving for, as the Fool in the Tarot carries — significantly — a white rose.[17] He does not yearn for fairyland as for a place from which he is forever excluded, like 'The Man Who Dreamed of Faeryland'. Hanrahan is alienated in a Gnostic sense: 'He is a prince of the other world on his travels through this one . . . . His wallet is inscribed with dim signs, to show that many sub-conscious memories are stored up in his soul.' That is why the Fool is pictured as a dreamer.[18] It is because he is a dreamer that Hanrahan's pace is stumbling. He is also capable, however, of withdrawing sudden memories from his 'wallet.' Thus he does not compose his 'Song about Ireland' but sings it spontaneously. It has been in his sub-conscious since his night on Slieve Echtge. In the 1907 text, Cathleen ni Houlihan is not a false but a true image of Echtge.

Echtge herself is the Priestess of the Tarot, who is always veiled. Winny Byrne is her veil. Winny bears a close inner resemblance to Hanrahan. They are both singers who have fallen first into the hands of the Sídhe and next into the hands of old age. Winny represents Hanrahan's 'unfinished soul, and . . . Echtge the radiant soul of the initiate'.[19] As Hanrahan's spiritual double, however, Winny also represents his fetch. She, his unfinished soul, summons Hanrahan to his death; but at the same time she drops her veil and so completes his soul. Winny reveals herself as Echtge; Hanrahan is enlightened, initiated, and admitted to fairyland.

IV The Grail Quest

That Hanrahan's story parallels the Grail Quest is a point that will not need labouring. When he first encounters Echtge, she is in an enchanted sleep, with 'the tired look of one that had been long waiting' (M 220). She is named as 'Echtge, daughter of the Silver Hand' (M 221), a clear reference to Nuadu, who lost his arm in the First Battle of Moytura, and afterwards was fitted with a silver one. Echtge's torpor and her connection with mutilation make her a surrogate for the maimed king of the Grail Quest.[20] Before her, old women display the Hallows, but Hanrahan, struck dumb by Echtge's beauty, is unable to respond and redeem her from sleep, and so win fairyland for himself. The Hallows symbolise Courage and Power, Knowledge and Pleasure. Thus they comprise the ideal essence of every cardinal human faculty. If apprehended and united, they would bestow an ideal life on Hanrahan: a life beyond change, and so beyond mortality. However, since he fails his initiation, Hanrahan must learn to be worthy of immortality by first experiencing the full process of mortality.[21] When he has learnt that lesson, he once again beholds the Hallows, though this time, like Echtge herself, they are veiled with the forms of their common, sublunar counterparts. At the same time, Hanrahan finds himself confronting sparks of light which take form as sword-points 'turned towards his heart' (M 259). These swords are thus Swords of Light, like the Sword of Nuadu, but they also recall the Masonic initiation ceremony, in which entrance is denied at sword-point until the initiate speaks the pass-word. It is as though the Hallows are challenging Hanrahan to discover them. This time he understands the riddle and responds with the classic questions of the Grail Quest: 'The Cauldron, the Stone, the Sword, the Spear. What are they? Who do they belong to? And I have asked the question this time' (M 259–60). At once the veil falls away from Echtge, the veil of mortality falls from Hanrahan, and he enters fairyland.

V. The Nation

The Grail theme is closely interconnected with the theme of nationality, as Winny Byrne and Echtge represent not only the imperfect and perfect states of Hanrahan's soul but also the two faces of Cathleen ni Houlihan, the Poor Old Woman and the young girl with the walk of a queen. In addition, Echtge, like the maimed king of the Grail Quest, inhabits a wasteland, which in this case is Ireland. 'Red Hanrahan's Song about Ireland' provides a description of this wasteland, whose devastation can be understood either 'literally (as under the English oppression) or spiritually'.[22] The poem combines metaphoric physical ruin ('The old brown thorn-trees break in two high over Cummen Strand') with political disaster ('Angers that are like noisy clouds have set our hearts abeat,' surely a reference to the Parnell controversy) and spiritual debility ('Our courage breaks like an old tree in a black wind and dies'). Hanrahan's rejection of Echtge, then, is not only a personal failure but also a betrayal of his country, inasmuch as he denies 'the return to Ireland of a benevolent and fruitful goddess'. Richard J.

Finneran divides Hanrahan's career into four stages, of which that is the first, his sin. It is followed by his suffering, his repentance and his redemption. Finneran finds the suffering, presumably, in 'The Twisting of the Rope', the repentance in 'Hanrahan and Cathleen, the Daughter of Houlihan', and the redemption in 'Hanrahan's Vision', as there Hanrahan meets and shuns the arch-betrayers of Ireland, Diarmuid and Dervorgilla.[23] This reading makes 'The Death of Hanrahan' redundant, but that story is admittedly more important in the Grail and Tarot themes.

VI. The Fairies

All of the foregoing readings, though valid and self-sufficient, are properly only commentaries on the story itself, which is simply the story of how Hanrahan adjusts to fairyland. Robert O'Driscoll considers that this theme is embodied in Hanrahan's relations with women, beginning with 'an immortal queen' but continuing with a string of lovers each one fouler than the last. This argument works fairly well for the first three stories, but thereafter would have been better abandoned. For instance, Nora in 'Red Hanrahan's Curse' is neither Hanrahan's lover nor fouler than Margaret Rooney. What remains valuable in O'Driscoll's argument is his reason for concentrating on Hanrahan's relations with women in the first place. They illustrate, he thinks, 'The dichotomy between spiritual longing and material decay, and the impossibility of ever reconciling the two'.[24] This is certainly the crux of Hanrahan's difficulty. His alienation stems from the fact that he is mortal and Echtge is not. He floats uncomfortably with no world to set foot on until he learns to reject his own mortality, whereupon he gravitates again towards fairyland. From the start, however, there is a natural affinity between Hanrahan and the fairies because he, like them, is a creature of whim. It is through this weakness that the fairies influence his life. For instance, his decision to stay and play cards in 'Red Hanrahan' is just such a whim. However, this whim, once taken, has the strength of a resolve. Once the old man has played his card trick, on the other hand, even Hanrahan's whims are unstable. Thus, in 'The Twisting of the Rope', he says that he will not dance, then at once decides to dance with Oona, and then at once decides not to. This is symptomatic of the bewilderment that has been put upon him on Slieve Echtge.

Still more symptomatic is Hanrahan's wooing of Oona. This he does mainly by singing 'The Happy Townland' to her, although the whole of the poem is not printed until 'Hanrahan's Vision'. Although Hanrahan sings as though he would entice Oona away to fairyland, he cannot, of course, arrange even his own *entrée* to that land. In fact, his song exposes his uncomfortable suspension between this world and the other. The first sign of trouble is his inability to keep out of his poem the Four Jewels of the Tuatha Dé Danann that have so disturbed him on Slieve Echtge. They appear only subliminally, but that fact alone testifies to their obsessiveness. They are referred to under their Tarot forms. Swords are mentioned explicitly. Cups appear in a simile ('Their hearts would be like a cup / That somebody had drunk dry') and also in Gabriel's drinking horn. The 'spade' that 'the strong farmers' would let lie is an agricultural implement, but it naturally suggests the suit of spades, which in its turn is related to the Tarot suit of Spears. Dishes are suggested by 'When the supper has been spread'.

In the poem, Hanrahan imagines himself as riding back to the Happy Townland of which these symbols remind him. But, again, he cannot keep out of his poem the sun and moon, which, as Ronald Schleifer points out, 'are enough to impede the journey'. They represent time, that ally of mortality, which constantly intervenes to thwart Hanrahan's desires. Even 'the comic apocalypse of food and drink in the last stanza' is 'put off into the future'. Sheila O'Sullivan states that '*The Happy Townland* was intended for inclusion in a play to be called *The Country of the Young*. The poem was to be a riding song, in which a poor child, riding on a kitchen 'form',' imagines himself riding to fairyland. Like that child, Hanrahan can ride to fairyland only in his imagination. 'The act of imagining, like the journey itself, is situated in the world', says Schleifer; that is why 'The fact that such a place is imagined is the bane of the world', instead of a cause for joy.[25]

On the other hand, there is no need to ride to the Happy Townland at all. Hanrahan knows that he is already half in it: 'It is very near us that country is, it is on every side; it may be on the bare hill behind it is, or it may be in the heart of the wood' (M 230). But for all that, like a Platonic essence of this world, it avoids realisation. Hanrahan can imagine the Happy Townland because he is constantly reminded of it, but he cannot go there since he was shown the Platonic Ideals — the Four Jewels — on Slieve Echtge and failed to respond to them.

Hanrahan's quandary is not simply a question of how to get to the Happy Townland. Although he is inviting Oona to accompany him there, he is not certain that he wants to go himself. A significant passage is this:

> Gabriel will come from the water
> With a fish-tail, and talk
> Of wonders that have happened
> On wet roads where men walk.
>
> (M 247)

Kathleen Raine points out that Yeats follows Porphyry in associating wet souls with generation. The Happy Townland, fairyland, is beyond this life, of course, but it is of wonders in this life that Gabriel is speaking. A dry soul is one like Mary Bruin in *The Land of Heart's Desire*, who opts firmly for fairyland, but Raine remarks that these 'lines suggest that Yeats already doubted the greater wisdom of the dry souls, for generated life provides all the good stories told at the feast of eternity'.[26] Here on the 'wet roads', however, Hanrahan still sings of the Happy Townland. After all, then, it has not lost its charm for him; but what he has learnt from Gabriel is the necessity of treading those 'wet roads where men walk' if he is ever to qualify for admission to the Happy Townland. This is the book's theme in a nutshell.

When Hanrahan has finished singing 'The Happy Townland', the plight which he has been expressing is suddenly made very real for him by the ruse of Oona's mother. Andrew Parkin equates the rope which Hanrahan twists as he backs out of the door with the rope which Aibric cuts in *The Shadowy Waters* while Dectora says, "as if Eve suddenly had turned and defeated the serpent: 'O ancient worm / Dragon that loved the world and held us to it, / You are broken, you are broken'."[27] This rope, of course, is life, and the house from which Hanrahan is expelled symbolises the world. Hanrahan does not cut the rope by his own choice, but it is thrown out after him and the door slammed against him.

And he felt the strands of the rope in his hand yet, and went on twisting it, but it seemed to him as he twisted it that it had all the sorrows of the world in it. And then it seemed to him as if the rope had changed in his dream into a great water-worm that came out of the sea, and that twisted itself about him, and held him closer and closer. And then he got free of it, and went on, shaking and unsteady, along the edge of the strand, and the grey shapes were flying here and there around him. And this is what they were saying: 'It is a pity for him that refuses the call of the daughters of the Sidhe, for he will find no comfort in the love of the women of the earth to the end of life and time, and the cold of the grave is in his heart for ever. It is death he has chosen; let him die, let him die, let him die,'

(M 232–33)

This ending is ironic, for it is not so bleak as it seems. Hanrahan is crushed by life. Death will be an escape for him, not because it will destroy him, but because it will admit him to the immortality of the fairies. 'Let him die, let him die, let him die' is thus an enticing invitation rather than a threat. The irony is that neither Hanrahan nor the reader will know this until 'The Death of Hanrahan'.

'The Twisting of the Rope' nonetheless marks the low point in

Hanrahan's trial by endurance. The turning point comes in 'Red Hanrahan's Curse'. The crucial passage is this:

.'My grief!' he said. 'I have set Old Age and Time and Weariness and Sickness against me, and I must go wandering again. And, O Blessed Queen of Heaven,' he said, 'protect me from the Eagle of Ballygawley, the Yew Tree of the Steep Place of the Strangers, the Pike of Castle Dargan Lake, and from the lighted wisps of their kindred, the Old Men!'

(M 245)

Mary Helen Thuente considers Hanrahan's curse an aggravation of his original offence, and many will agree with her.[28] Hanrahan himself knows only that he 'must go wandering again', that he is doomed to further suffering. However, Hanrahan's suffering is only earthly. His curse, I believe, is not an aggravation but an expiation of his offence. He has made the best enemies that he could. In defying Old Age and Time and Weariness and Sickness, he has defied his own mortality. From now on, like one of Swedenborg's angels, he begins to grow back towards the fountainhead of his youth and so to be worthy of Echtge.

First, however, Hanrahan must still enhance his visionary power. He must learn to perceive the Four Jewels behind the implements of Winny's kitchen, and Echtge behind Winny herself. This, after all, is the initiation that he failed before and now must pass. Thuente remarks that in 'Hanrahan's Vision' his powers of vision 'obviously represent a deterioration when they are compared to those of ancient Ireland where the gods had continually interacted with mortals'.[29] On the other hand, though, 'Hanrahan's Vision' represents an improvement when compared to anything since 'Red Hanrahan'. At the beginning of 'The Death of Hanrahan', the improvement is maintained: 'As the days went by it seemed as if he was beginning to belong to some world out of sight and misty, that has for its mearing the colours that are beyond all other colours and the silences that are beyond all silences of this world' (M 253). 'Out of sight and misty' is how this new world appears to fallen vision; to Hanrahan, it is more and more marked by 'the colours that are beyond all other colours'. As Hanrahan's vision begins to penetrate the veil between earth and fairyland, so naturally he himself begins to belong more to fairyland. The description is also, of course, that of a dying man. This is all the more to the point, for Hanrahan's death is literally his marriage with Echtge and with eternity: 'He saw then that the house was crowded with pale shadowy hands, and that every hand was holding what was sometimes like a wisp lighted for a marriage, and sometimes like a tall white candle for the dead' (M 260). This marriage comes amid a music like 'the continual clashing of swords' (M 259). Osgar, of the Fianna, when asked what music he liked best, replied, 'The best music is the striking of swords in a battle'.[30] At his death, then, Hanrahan has regained the full vision of ancient Ireland.

After Echtge has revealed herself, Winny Byrne, like Hanrahan, appears to die: 'She did not come back that night or any night to the cabin' (M 261). Her last recorded words are the same as her first:

I am young: look upon me, mountains; look upon me, perishing woods, for my body will be shining like the white waters when you have been hurried away. You and the whole race of men, and the race of the beasts, and the race of the fish, and the winged race, are dropping like a candle that is nearly burned out. But I laugh aloud, because I am in my youth.

(M.261)

It is now apparent that she is telling the truth. Her youth is Echtge. The rest of her is dispensable. Similarly, Hanrahan's youth is the bridegroom of Echtge. 'In the west of Ireland the country people say that after death every man grows upward or downward to the likeness of thirty years . . . and stays always in that likeness.'[31]

Written as they were in 1897 and rewritten in 1904, the *Stories of Red Hanrahan* form at the same time a bridge between *The Rose* and *The Wind Among the Reeds* and a sequel to *The Wind Among the Reeds*. They deliver Yeats from the impasse of *The Rose* and prepare him for the reckless plunge into fairyland of *The Wind Among the Reeds*. However, the personae of *The Wind Among the Reeds* (a rather different Red Hanrahan among them) enter fairyland out of desperation and with a feeling that they are as likely to be going to their doom as to their reward. By contrast, the Hanrahan of the stories enters fairyland rather as a good Christian is supposed to meet his Maker. Indeed, he even mistakes fairyland for heaven at first: ' "I am after my death, he said, 'and in the very heart of the music of Heaven. O Cherubim and Seraphim, receive my soul!"' (M 259). In the end, after all his tribulations, he enters fairyland with confidence and there is little doubt that he will find there comfort and repose. It is not only Hanrahan who has found this peace, of course, but Yeats himself, and he could not have found it had he not at last worked out his desperation in *The Wind Among the Reeds*.

15. 'THE FLAMING DOOR': *THE WIND AMONG THE REEDS* AS PSYCHIC NARRATIVE

The 1899 text of *The Wind Among the Reeds* continues *The Rose*'s use of personae, but introduces a new cast of them. Instead of Fergus, Cuchulain, and so forth, we now have Aedh, Hanrahan (in earlier texts O'Sullivan Rua or O'Sullivan the Red), Michael Robartes, and Mongan. The first three, of course, are characters from *The Secret Rose*; Mongan is a figure from mythology.[1] The employment of these personae is not outstandingly successful. As Ellmann says, 'The distinction between the characters is not perfect; they are ... "Principles of the mind" rather than "actual personages," and even as principles of the mind are not perfectly separated.'[2] For instance, the poem that began life in 1896 as 'O'Sullivan Rua to Mary Lavell' in 1899 became 'Michael Robartes remembers Forgotten Beauty'. Yeats himself was evidently not best satisfied with his personae, for in the end he dropped them altogether. That different 'principles of the mind' are involved in *The Wind Among the Reeds* remains true but it is seldom very helpful to give names to those principles. Furthermore, at no time did Yeats allow his personae to determine the scheme of *The Wind Among the Reeds*.

Instead, he simply arranged his poems so as to form a continuous narrative. At the risk of oversimplifying, one may say that these poems have two themes, fairyland and love. However, these themes are not of equal importance. Love functions chiefly as an atmospheric counterpoint to the theme of fairyland. A passage from *Baile and Aillinn* (1903) comments explicitly on Yeats's priorities:

> O wandering birds and rushy beds,
> You put such folly in our heads
> With all this crying in the wind,
> No common love is to our mind,
> And our poor Kate or Nan is less
> Than any whose unhappiness
> Awoke the harp-strings long ago.
> Yet they that know all things but know

> That all this life can give us is
> A child's laughter, a woman's kiss.
> Who was it put so great a scorn
> In the grey reeds that night and morn
> Are trodden and broken by the herds,
> And in the light bodies of birds
> The north wind tumbles to and fro
> And pinches among hail and snow?
>
> (VP 190–91)

Yeats concedes that nothing is more important than love, but confesses that he cannot keep his mind on it.

I therefore propose to read these poems, if I may borrow a title from Pope John XXIII, as 'The Diary of a Soul'. They continue the story of Yeats's response to fairyland begun in *The Rose*. The love poems which are interspersed with the fairy poems serve to indicate and generally to explain the changes of mood which advance the main theme, the theme of fairyland.

In *The Rose*, Yeats found himself locked in a vicious circle of aspiration and failure. But now the call of fairyland becomes peremptory. The familiar pattern, in which Yeats simultaneously desires and fears the Otherworld, is not long sustained. Yeats recognises, suddenly as it would seem, that the Otherworld is after all not so Other as he has feared, and that his feeling of *angst* is simply his perception of this world's inadequacy. He trembles on the ambivalent brink for a moment, but then — at last — plunges into fairyland. Yeats's relationship with fairyland, once he is committed to it, assumes a strongly sexual character. His identification with fairyland prompts a desire for the apocalyptic annihilation of this world that is frankly orgasmic. This climax arrives, fades, and approaches again, in a pattern of tumescence and repose. This is not, however, a new vicious cycle, as in *The Rose*. The repetition of the experience is necessary in order that the whole personality in its various moods or personae may be satisfied. That end is achieved, and the figure of the Rose reappears, no longer as a savage goddess, but as a conquered mistress offering her final gift of peace.

I. The Irresistible Call

The Wind Among the Reeds opens with the abrupt cry of 'Away, come away'. 'The Hosting of the Sidhe' is the summons of the fairies to Yeats, Yeats's summons to his readers, and, by virtue of its position, a reciprocal invocation of the fairies. The reader who turns to this poem directly from *The Rose* will notice at once that the languid rhythms of the earlier work are utterly transformed. 'The Hosting of the Sidhe' is not only the fastest of Yeats's poems up to this time, but also the most firmly controlled and deftly manipulated. Though the pace of the poem is apparent at once, the reader does not at first anticipate the effect which it is preparing. 'Niamh calling *Away, come away*' need not have strayed too far from *The Wanderings of Oisin*, until the italicised lines suddenly open up a pattern of regular antithesis, with two emphatic stresses on each side of a strong caesura:

> The winds awaken, the leaves whirl round,
> Our cheeks are pale, our hair is unbound,
> Our breasts are heaving, our eyes are a-gleam,
> Our arms are waving, our lips are apart.
>
> (VP 140)

The effect, of course, is onomatopoeic. One hears the hooves of the horses of the Sidhe. Also, as Allen R. Grossman says, the effect suggests 'uncontrollable energy'.[3] The caesura then disappears and, after a moment's pause, the metre shifts from one basically iambic to one basically anapaestic:

> And if any gaze on our rushing band,
> We come between him and the deed of his hand,
> We come between him and the hope of his heart.
>
> (VP 141)

The uncontrollable energy is released. Onomatopoeically, the horses break from a canter to a gallop. The reader, following the metre, is drawn along with them. The call of the Sidhe is irresistible.

'The Everlasting Voices' is in a metre more akin to those of *The Rose* and is also, at least superficially, a more melancholy poem than 'The Hosting of the Sidhe'. The latter opens with an assertion of violent action, the former with a plea for stillness. However, the poems are more alike than they appear at first glance. In 'The Hosting of the Sidhe', after our attention is first arrested by the call of the Sidhe, we are reminded of the dangers of heeding that call, the same dangers that Yeats spelt out in 'The Seeker' and 'The Danaan Quicken Tree': 'We come between him and the deed of his hand,/We come between him and the hope of his heart.' But this consideration is immediately dismissed. To answer the call of the Sidhe is not to surrender one's hopes and deeds, but to exchange them for superior ones: 'The host is rushing 'twixt night and day,/And where is there hope or deed as fair?' As F. F. Farag points out, the attitude of the poem is summed up in the line 'Empty your heart of its mortal dream': '. . . the poet . . . transvalues the word "dream" so that the world of appearance is the dream, and the world of dream is the reality.'[4]

That the same is true of 'The Everlasting Voices' is immediately apparent from the prose model of the poem, which, as Jeffares indicates, is to be found in *The Celtic Twilight*.[5] Yeats tells of his response to a fiddle played by a man on the train to Sligo:

I seemed to hear a voice of lamentation out of the Golden Age. It told me that we are imperfect, incomplete, and no more like a beautiful woven web, but like a bundle of cords knotted together and flung into a corner. It said that the world was once all perfect and kindly, and that still the kindly and perfect world existed, but buried like a mass of roses under many spadefuls of earth. The faeries and the more innocent of the spirits dwelt within it, and lamented over our fallen world in the lamentation of the wind-tossed reeds, in the song of the birds, in the moan of the waves, and in the sweet cry of the fiddle. . . . It said that if only they who live in the Golden Age could die we might be happy, for the sad voices would be still; but they must sing and we must weep until the eternal gates swing open.

(M 104–05)

Clearly, it is better to sing than to weep. Yeats bids the Everlasting Voices be still because he fears that he cannot answer their call. That is the main difference between this poem and 'The Hosting of the Sidhe'. However, Yeats knows that the voices will not be still for all his bidding. This is emphasised by the cyclical form of the poem. At the end as well as the beginning, Yeats must bid the voices be still, for evidently they will not obey him. 'The Hosting of the Sidhe' likewise begins and ends with 'Niamh calling *Away, come away*'. Her call will not cease. It must be answered somehow, and plainly the hopeless repetition of 'be still' is an inadequate answer.

II. The Recognition of the Moods

Yeats, therefore, finds himself trapped in the classic paradox of the irresistible force and the immovable object. He must but cannot respond to Niamh's call. This paradox is neatly and suddenly resolved by the discovery of 'The Moods':

> Time drops in decay,
> Like a candle burnt out,
> And the mountains and woods
> Have their day, have their day;
> What one in the rout
> Of the fire-born moods
> Has fallen away?
>
> (VP 142)

What exactly Yeats means by the moods emerges clearly from the prose models of this poem, which are both to be found in *Mythologies*, as Jeffares again points out.[6] One, of course, is Winny Byrne's rhapsody on her youth; the other occurs in 'Rosa Alchemica':

> The bodiless souls who descended into [imagined] forms were what men called the moods; and worked all great changes in the world; for just as the magician or the artist could call them when he would, so they could call out of the mind of the magician or the artist, or if they were demons, out of the mind of the mad or the ignoble, what shape they would, and through its voice and its gestures pour themselves out upon the world.
>
> (M 285)

The mood that calls from Winny Byrne is Echtge, a fairy. The moods in 'Rosa Alchemica' are gods or demons. In 'The Moods', Yeats makes no distinction. In *The Wind Among the Reeds* as a whole, he personifies certain moods (or 'principles of the mind') as Aedh, Hanrahan, and Michael Robartes.

The moods can call through the magician or the artist, or they can be called by the magician or artist. In one sense, then, they resemble the Rose. They are both the seeker and the sought. They are what the artist seeks to express, and they are his means of expression. They are, however, always dependent on men for their expression, and in this they differ from the Rose. Though they are ideal, they are not transcendent, like her. She suffers *with* man, but she is not *of* man. The moods, on the other hand, have no *raison d'être* apart from man. They are detached from man inasmuch as 'the individual enters these Moods and passes on'.[7] Alternatively, it is the moods that enter and pass on through the individual. This is the theme of 'The Travail of Passion'. The poem enacts the 'entrance into mortality of the immortal moods'. Grossman comments that 'The origin of all real passion ... is in eternity, and man truly loves only by the consent and participation of what he is not, that is, only "When an immortal passion breathes in mortal clay" '.[8] Thus, the speakers of the poem are the moods themselves. In loosening their hair over the lovers whose sexual act the poem depicts under the metaphor of the Crucifixion, the moods endow them with their own spirit. Still, they are realised only in conjunction with humanity.

'The Travail of Passion' suggests a paradox, however. Though man expresses the moods, the moods in a sense express man. In 'Rosa Alchemica', Michael Robartes says that the moods 'are always making and unmaking humanity, which is indeed but the trembling of their lips' (M 275). This point is crucial, for if the moods are also fairies and gods, that is to say that men and fairies are not so different after all. Furthermore:

Sometimes the mystical student, bewildered by the different systems, forgets for a moment that the history of moods is the history of the universe, and asks where is the final statement — the complete doctrine. The universe is itself that doctrine and statement. All others are partial, for it alone is the symbol of the universal mood we name God.[9]

Thus the Otherwold, in the final analysis, is no other world than this. To enter fairyland is not to go elsewhere but to be more emphatically here. One must, like Owen Aherne, look 'out of the eyes of the angels' ('The Tables of the Law', M 306); one must cease to be 'the trembling of their lips', and become those lips themselves. Of course, this is literally the counsel of perfection. It is to live, as Yeats would later say, in that supernal phase, the Full of the Moon. But at least the barriers are down. The Sídhe may be contemplated (though 'countrymen/ . . . shudder and hurry by'), and their call may profitably be heeded, for perhaps after all, on some strange, triumphal day,

> . . . body and . . . soul
> Too perfect at the full to lie in a cradle,
> Too lonely for the traffic of the world
> [Shall be] cast out and cast away
> Beyond the visible world
>
> ('The Phases of the Moon', VP 374, 375).

III. Earth's Inadequacy

This realisation that the Otherworld is theoretically within reach is accompanied by a renewed awareness of the inadequacy of this world. The poem that most clearly exemplifies this tendency is 'Aedh tells of the Rose in his Heart'. To ascertain the precise nuance of feeling in this poem, one must bear its context in mind. In content, to all intents and purposes, it is identical with 'The Pity of Love' in *The Rose*. Yet this is not, like that, a poem of *angst*. Its import is modified by its position following 'The Moods'. In addition, one word differs significantly between 'The Pity of Love' and 'Aedh tells of the Rose in his Heart'. That word is the transitive verb. In 'The Pity of Love', the details of the environment all *'Threaten* the head that I love' (VP 119; emphasis added); in 'Aedh tells of the Rose in his Heart', they 'Are *wronging* your image that blossoms a rose in the deeps of my heart' (VP 143; emphasis again added). Only vaguely, then, is Grossman correct in saying that 'In *The Wind Among the Reeds* the elements are hostile'.[10] They are not menacing, but inadequate. The material world (which includes Yeats and Maud Gonne themselves) is not worthy of Yeats's ideal image of Maud Gonne. The material world must therefore be remade itself as an ideal Otherworld, so as to match and contain the ideal image:

> The wrong of unshapely things is a wrong too
>   great to be told;
> I hunger to build them anew and sit on a green
>   knoll apart,
> With the earth and the sky and the water,
>   remade, like a casket of gold
> For my dreams of your image that blossoms a
>   rose in the deeps of my heart.
>
> (VP 143)

Yeats no longer hugs his knees and shudders, as in 'The Pity of Love'; he now takes action in the imagination against earth's inadequacy.

IV. Ambivalence

Although this world is thus recognised as inadequate and fairyland as accessible, Yeats still has time for ambivalence. Access to fairyland may be possible, after all, but it is certainly not easy. Owen Aherne lost his soul because he looked out of the eyes of the angels. Is the soul, perhaps, what is lost when the 'mortal dream' is lost? To surrender to the call of Niamh is to take the side of Aengus against the Countess Cathleen.

The contrast between 'The Hosting of the Sidhe' and 'The Everlasting Voices' is itself an example of ambivalence. 'The Host of the Air' and 'The Unappeasable Host' are further examples. These poems are both ambivalent in themselves but also in contrast, as the ambivalence seems weighted in favour of this world in 'The Host of the Air' and in favour of fairyland in 'The Unappeasable Host'. 'The Host of the Air', however, is very much the slighter poem of the two. Yeats tells us that he founded the poem on a ballad which he heard at Balesodare (VP 143), and he does not seem to have added much to it.[11] The only point of interest is the ambivalence expressed in the repeated lines, 'And never was piping so sad,/And never was piping so gay' (VP 144, 145). Since O'Driscoll loses his wife, however, we may suppose that in his eyes the sadness outweighs the gaiety. We are not told Bridget's point of view.

'The Unappeasable Host' also concerns a changeling, or potential changeling, but is very much more subtle. The poem first appeared on its own in *The Savoy* for April 1896, but then in November of that year in *The Senate* as the centre-piece of a story called 'The Cradles of Gold'. In the story, the mother has already been taken for a changeling, but returns at night to suckle her child. She then sings this song while rocking the child in its cradle. Her brother-in-law 'listened with a shudder to the wild air, at whose sound all wholesome desires and purposes were thought to weaken and dissolve, and to the unholy words which pious mothers had ever forbid their daughters to sing'. Eventually the mother is won back from fairyland, but ever after, except when the moon is full, 'her voice was low and her touch chill'.[12] In the story, then, the poem is favourable to the fairies, but only in a context that is the reverse. The brother-in-law, the spokesman of normality, regards the poem as an evil and ill-omened incantation.

The poem itself provokes an ambivalent reaction almost from the first line. The laughter of the Danaan children may seem innocent at first, but begins to acquire sinister connotations in the third line, 'For they will ride the North when the ger-eagle flies' (VP 146). 'Ger-eagle' is the Biblical name for a kind of vulture.[13] It is thus a bird of ill omen. Its heart is 'fallen cold' with cruelty. The Danaan children will ride on its back, and are thus associated with its nature. The North, according to Yeats, is the point where the fairies originate (he may be thinking of the invasion of the Tuatha Dé Danann); but it is also the point where witchcraft and spirits originate.[14] In his note to 'Michael Robartes bids his Beloved be at Peace', Yeats says that he associates the North with 'night and sleep' (VP 808). That which 'rides' on night and sleep is the nightmare. (In 'The Stolen Child', VP 88, the fairies claim to be the cause of evil dreams.) Thus, the fairies have now been associated with everything which is evil from a mortal point of view; but they themselves still laugh.

That fact renders the rest of the poem not only ambivalent but ambiguous. The mother now kisses her wailing child and presses it to her breast. Reading this poem in isolation, one might naturally suppose that mother and child are mortal, in contrast to the Danaan children, and that the mother fears that her child will be taken for a changeling by the evil fairies just described. But in 'The Cradles of Gold' the mother is herself a changeling, and has transferred her allegiance to the fairies. In the poem, she states specifically what she fears, and it is not the North or the Danaan children, but 'the narrow graves calling my child and me', and then:

> Desolate winds that cry over the wandering sea;
> Desolate winds that hover in the flaming West;
> Desolate winds that beat the doors of Heaven, and beat
> The doors of Hell and blow there many a whimpering ghost.
>
> (VP 147)

'Narrow graves' are exactly what the immortal Sídhe do not have to fear; 'the wandering sea' symbolises the instability of human, not of fairy, life; 'the flaming West' symbolises 'fading and dreaming things' (VP 808), but the Sídhe do not fade; the Sídhe inhabit neither Heaven nor Hell, nor are they ghosts. These lines, then, do not represent the horrors awaiting a changeling, but the horrors awaiting one not taken for a changeling. In explicating the poem's final lines, then, Allen Grossman is guilty of an error of emphasis at least. The lines are: 'O heart the winds have shaken, the unappeasable host/Is comelier than candles before Maurya's feet.' Grossman concludes that 'the presence of the host makes impossible the desired relation to the symbol both of comfort and of order' (Maurya); 'The presence of the host invalidates the prayers of the mortal, symbolized by the votarists' candles.' On this reading, the last two lines are ironic or euphemistic.[15] They are not. Neil Grobman, at almost the opposite extreme to Grossman, is closer to the truth. For him, the mother 'compares the furious immortality of "the unappeasable host" . . . who "will ride the North" when mortal things have died with the comfortless, desolate Heaven and Hell of Christianity. . . . the Church can only offer death and a questionable afterlife.'[16] Robert O'Driscoll's position is similar, but he has not forgotten the negative imagery of 11. 3–4. For him, then, the poem expresses 'the uneasy tension between the conventional religion one knows and the unconventional longing one fears'.[17] This is surely correct, as it restores the poem's ambivalence. And yet finally the speaker is not in doubt as to which is comelier between the unappeasable host and the candles before Maurya's feet. 'The Unappeasable Host', then, is a rigorous and honest exorcism of the poet's remaining misgivings, allowing him at last to accept the call of Niamh.

V. Acceptance

The first poem to embody the unambivalent acceptance of fairyland is 'Into the Twilight'. Yeats says himself that he wrote the poem 'to call to myself my courage once again', on the occasion of a serious estrangement with Maud Gonne.[18] This estrangement is reflected in the line 'Though hope fall from you and love decay' (VP 148). Given the date of composition (summer, 1893), it is likely that Yeats was also affected by his feud with Sir Charles Gavan Duffy in the National Literary Society. This may be reflected in the line 'Burning in fires of a slanderous tongue'. These two lines typify the negative characterisation of the real world in 'Into the Twilight'. There is thus no ambivalence about the poem, because this world is firmly rejected. It is in this world that 'God stands winding His lonely horn'. I visualise God, here, as a farmer calling home his cattle, like those 'great black oxen' which, in *The Countess Cathleen*, 'tread the world', and are identified with the years (VPl 169). The image thus portrays God as drawing on the years, or summoning the universe through time to its dissolution.

On the other hand, 'Your mother Eire is always young', and pays no heed to God's lonely horn. In this poem, Eire is the name of the Otherworld. Now, of course, it is the official name of the state, but in 1893 it was almost an anachronism, far more redolent of ancient mythology than of contemporary politics. It thus stands in contrast to the Ireland of bickering nationalists (like Duffy). A time when ancient Eire has become modern Ireland is indeed 'a time out-worn', but Eire persists immortally as the 'other dimension' of Ireland — as fairyland. There is the refuge for an 'Out-worn heart'. The balm that Eire offers appears in the last two lines. The love of this world (unrequited for Yeats) is 'less kind than the gray twilight' of the Otherworld; the hope of this world is 'less dear than the dew of the morn' in that world. This echoes 'The Hosting of the Sidhe's' 'And where is there hope or deed as fair?' (VP 141); but now there is no ambivalence. The question of 'The Hosting of the Sidhe' is a statement in 'Into the Twilight'.

The comparative clarity of 'Into the Twilight' is of great assistance in interpreting 'The Song of Wandering Aengus', a difficult poem. The persona himself occasions the first problem. Many readers assume that he is Angus Óg, but how can the immortal Angus Óg (whose name means 'Angus the Young') be 'old with wandering' (VP 150)? Nonetheless, this poem does bear a faint but probably intentional resemblance to an Early Irish tale in which Angus pines for the love of a girl seen in a dream, until she is finally found for him.[19] That Angus, however, would make a poor persona for Yeats. As one of the chiefs of the Tuatha Dé Danann, Angus Óg has no difficulty in relating to fairyland. Yeats has therefore imagined a mortal, peasant counterpart to Angus Óg.

This Aengus is not a denizen of fairyland, but he is summoned thither by the 'girl/With apple blossom in her hair' (VP 149–50). Critics often read apple blossom in Yeats as a reference to Maud Gonne, because when Yeats first met her, 'Her complexion was luminous, like that of apple blossoms through which the light falls, and I remember her standing that first day by a great heap of such blossoms in the window' (A 82). No doubt the girl in 'The Song of Wandering Aengus' does to some extent represent Maud Gonne. However, Jerome L. Mazzaro points out that apple blossom occurs in poems written before Yeats met Maud Gonne, and has mythological connotations. He cites most pertinently Lewis Spence's *History and Origins of Druidism*, in whch 'the magic apple branch' is called 'a sesame to the land of the immortals', like the Golden Bough in the *Aeneid*, and he reminds us that Ellmann calls apple blossom a symbol of 'the state of blessedness'.[20] In a fairly representative Early Irish story, a fairy woman uses an apple to entice Connla, son of Conn of the Hundred Battles, to Mag Mell.[21] So it is here, of course, but with the irony that this peasant is not Angus Óg or even Connla the Fair. Apple blossom is a summons but not a sesame for him. He has, indeed, grown 'old with wandering/Through hollow lands and hilly lands'. This is an example of the rhetorical figure called hendiadys. Aengus has grown old with wandering through lands of hollow hills, or *sídhe*. But he has not entered them.

Thus far, this poem would seem pessimistic. Many critics believe that it is. But the mood of the last stanza belies this interpretation:

> *Though* I am old with wandering
> Through hollow lands and hilly lands,
> I *will* find out where she has gone,
> And kiss her lips and take her hands . . .

(VP 150; emphasis added). Harold Bloom (for one) believes that the indicative mood is misleading. He believes that Aengus's 'hope is a madness', and that consequently 'There is defeat in the poem'.[22] I would maintain, on the contrary, that the mood of the last stanza can be taken at face value. The strongest indication of this is the place where Aengus's meeting with the girl is to take place. It is a forest of golden and silver apple trees, 'The silver apples of the moon,/The golden apples of the sun'. These are an alchemical symbol, derived, as Grossman has shown, from 'the alchemical reading of Deuteronomy 33: 13–16, Moses' blessing of

Joseph, cited here in the form in which Yeats knew it from Westcott's *Hermetic Arcanum*.

... Blessed of the Lord be his land, for the apples of heaven, for the dew, and for the Deep that liveth beneath: for the apples of fruit both of sun and moon, for the tops of the ancient mountains, for the apples of the everlasting earth.'

What is the significance of this? Grossman suggests that the apples, being metallic, are artificial, and hence symbolise 'a "sinking in" in the mystic sense, upon art as the ground of reality, as itself the superreality'.[23] The meaning of this is somewhat clarified by Lester Conner's suggestion that the silver apples represent fact and the golden apples imagination.[24] The combination of the two then represents fact irradiated by imagination, or imagination irradiated by fact. The forest of apple trees is a world without dichotomies, a world of Truth, where fact and imagination are one. Insofar as fairyland is a land of the imagination, it is equally, under such circumstances, a factual world.

This, one may say, is all very well, but it remains a pious hope. In actuality, this sort of philosophy does not render fairyland any less remote or inaccessible. There is, however, an additional level to the symbolism, which is more psychic and therefore more truly alchemical than the above. On this level, the golden and silver apples represent the same two principles as Aengus and the girl. Robert Langbaum sees Aengus as a Blakean Spectre and the girl as a Blakean Emanation.[25] Their reunion, therefore, symbolises the conclusion of the alchemical Great Work, the achievement of psychic wholeness. This is that looking out of the eyes of the angels that Yeats has determined to be feasible. Thus Aengus will find his girl and enter fairyland.

It should again be noticed, then, that the fairyland where this reunion will take place is a forest of apple trees. Mythologically, this is Manannan's transmarine kingdom Emain Abhlach, or Emain of the Apple Trees. It is not the same fairyland as that of the *sidhe*, represented by 'hollow lands and hilly lands'. That is the fairyland of unfulfilled desire; this is the fairyland of fulfilment. Thus the apple imagery which initiates the quest also completes it. The quest, in fact, is the guarantee of its own success.

VI. The Apocalyptic Cycle

The next group of poems is by far the longest group in the book. It constitutes, in fact, the climax and *raison d'être* of *The Wind Among the Reeds*. These poems are apocalyptic. I had better make clear what I mean by this word. Denis Donoghue, strangely enough, furnishes a fine definition while denying that it applies to Yeats. He cites Jean-Paul Sartre's opinion that the poems of Stéphane Mallarmé arise from a 'resentment against reality, and the poems written in that mood are symbolic acts of revenge: the poet's words are designed to undo the work of the first Creation, the poem being a second and higher version'. However, in Donoghue's view, this is not Yeats's practice. On the contrary, he seeks only 'another country, where the Muse's law is the only writ that runs'.[26] I can see no difference here. An apocalyptic poem is one in which the mundane universe is swept away. It may be replaced by something better, something worse, or nothing at all. This action may be confined to the poet's imagination, or the poet may pray for it in the material world, or both may be the case.

This attitude is not confined to Yeats's poetry. His 'resentment against reality' is at least as much in evidence in his magical writings. The first of his Irish initiation rituals, for instance, includes the words: 'I have given this staff to the fire that it may begin the work of burning the heavens and the earth that there may be nothing but the soul.'[27] In many cases, Yeats's poems are based on occult prose passages where the apocalyptic content is more apparent than it is in the poem. For example. 'The Everlasting Voices' has a considerable pre-history in prose. Its genesis begins in William Blake's 'The Marriage of Heaven and Hell': 'For the cherub with his flaming sword is hereby commanded to leave his guard at the tree of life, and when he does, the whole creation will be consumed, and appear infinite and holy whereas it now appears finite and corrupt.' On this was based the Golden Dawn's ritual of initiation into the lowest, or Zelator, grade of membership:

And Tetragrammaton . . . created Nature that Man, being cast out of Eden, may not fall into the Void. He has bound Man with the Stars as with a chain. He allures him with Scattered Fragments of the Divine Body in bird and beast and flower, and He laments over him in the Wind and in the Sea and in the Birds. And when the times are ended, He will call the Kerubim from the East of the Garden, and all shall be consumed and become infinite and holy.

The verbal similarities between that passage and 'The Everlasting Voices' will not need stressing. Kathleen Raine supposes that Yeats was in fact the author of both works. Notwithstanding his acquaintance with Blake, however, it seems unlikely that he can have composed the Golden Dawn's ritual, for how, then, was he initiated himself? With Edwin Ellis, on the other hand, he did write this commentary on the passage in Blake:

When the Last Judgement has passed over a man he enters that community of Saints who 'are no longer talking of good and evil, or of what is right and wrong, and puzzling themselves in Satan's labyrinth'; but are conversing with eternal realities, as they exist in the human imagination.

This explains in what sense Yeats's apocalyptic poetry is concerned with fairyland, for Grossman remarks that 'The community of saints referred to here is of course analogous to the Yeatsian sidhe and its [sic] many symbolic correlatives'.[28] The world beyond the apocalypse is the community of saints and the community of saints is fairyland. To will the apocalypse is to will admission to fairyland. To destroy the universe in the imagination is to gain admission to fairyland, in the imagination.

Though 'The Everlasting Voices' is at least partially an apocalyptic poem, it is not part of what I call the apocalyptic cycle in *The Wind Among the Reeds*. Even before *The Wind Among the Reeds*, there are other such poems. What distinguishes them from the poems of the apocalyptic cycle is the intensity of the latter's focus. In the case of 'The Everlasting Voices', only members of the Golden Dawn could appreciate its apocalyptic content until scholarship revealed it. Other readers were not even meant to. In other poems, the apocalyptic content is not primary, but an ill-defined extra outside the focus of the poem. This is the case, for instance, with 'The Song of Wandering Aengus'. On the other hand, the poems which I will now consider develop publicly the apocalyptic content of the final stanza of 'The Song of Wandering Aengus'. They constitute by far the most sustained and intense treatment of this theme that Yeats has yet attempted.

VII. 'Mongan laments the Change that has come upon him and his Beloved'

The poems of the apocalyptic cycle obey a sexual as well as a mystical logic. They begin with a literally sexual stimulus, which the two love poems intervening after 'The Song of the Old Mother' are there to explain. The first, 'The Heart of the Woman', portrays Olivia Shakespeare as Eve in a bower of contentment. Yeats himself is the serpent in this Eden, as emerges from 'Aedh laments the Loss of Love'. This poem describes the end of Yeats's affair with Olivia Shakespear, when she realised that he was still in love with Maud Gonne. 'Mongan laments the Change that has come upon him and his Beloved' is the apocalyptic poem that arises from the aftermath of this affair. There is an allusion to the affair in 'I was looking another way' (VP 153). Yeats was distracted from Maud Gonne by Olivia Shakespeare; now that the old passion is renewed, it is, we must gather, more hopeless than ever: 'And now my calling is but the calling of a hound.' The mood of this poem, then, is one of sexual frustration and despair.

The persona, Mongan, contributes another element to the mood. Among mortals, Mongan is the pre-eminent shape-shifter of Irish mythology, and so this poem has about it something like the mood of the Fergus poems in *The Rose*: 'And Time and Birth and Change are hurrying by.' The implication is that unrequited love renders life meaningless. A meaningful life must revolve around a fixed point amid the change. Maud Gonne, the 'white deer with no horns', cannot provide the fixed point for Yeats because, unlike the fish-girl in 'The Song of Wandering Aengus', she is ever in flight and cannot be caught. In plain terms, she does not love him. Consequently, the apocalypse in this poem is negative. If the white deer cannot provide a fixed point, then the 'boar without bristles' must. We shall meet this boar again in 'The Valley of the Black Pig', but for now the note that Yeats appended to the fist printing of 'Mongan laments' explains it adequately: it is 'the ancient Celtic image of the darkness which will at last destroy the world, as it destroys the sun at nightfall in the west'. Thus, this poem would destroy the world and substitute for it nothing. In the broader scheme of *The Wind Among the Reeds*, it provides a *tabula rasa* on which the other, more positive apocalyptic poems can set down their 'fire-born' images.

VIII. 'Hanrahan laments because of his Wanderings'

Though the transition from such a negative apocalypse to a positive one may seem drastic, to Yeats it apparently comes quite naturally. This may be seen from 'Hanrahan laments because of his Wanderings':

> O where is our Mother of Peace
> Nodding her purple hood?
> For the winds that awakened the stars
> Are blowing through my blood.
> I would that the death-pale deer
> Had come through the mountain side
> And trampled the mountain away,
> And drunk up the murmuring tide;
> For the winds that awakened the stars
> Are blowing through my blood,
> And our Mother of Peace has forgot me
> Under her purple hood.
>
> (VP 171)

On the face of it, this poem is almost identical with 'Mongan laments'.

Hanrahan, described in the title as a wanderer, represents 'the simplicity of an imagination too changeable to gather permanent possessions' (VP 803), and so, like Mongan, is characterised by restlessness. The 'death-pale deer', like the 'boar without bristles', are 'fragments of ancestral darkness' (a poor image, since they are pale), and Hanrahan longs 'for the day when they . . . will overthrow the world' (VP 807).

And yet the imagery here is not of 'turning to . . . rest' (VP 153), but of 'The winds that awakened the stars'. Despite Hanrahan's similarity to Mongan, his vision is more penetrating: beyond the darkness, he yearns for an image to arise — 'our Mother of Peace'. In 'The Philosophy of Shelley's Poetry' (1900), Yeats describes the vision of a friend which may well lie behind this poem. In the folds of a 'dark-blue curtain' (corresponding to the 'ancestral darkness' of the poem), Yeats's friend saw a white fawn: 'the seer knew that he would follow the fawn at last, and that it would lead him among the gods' (as in stories of the Fianna). An Hermeticist present said, '. . . I think the fawn is the Morning and Evening Star' (thus a bright image arising out of darkness) (E &I 90). Hanrahan still hopes that when all that impedes the darkness has been destroyed, 'the winds that awakened the stars' may again awaken the Morning and Evening Star, Venus, the Mother of Peace. Hanrahan and Mongan both weary of multitudinous reality, but whereas Mongan seeks obliteration, Hanrahan seeks a single image of perfection.

IX. 'Michael Robartes bids his Beloved be at Peace'

Next in sequence after 'Mongan laments' comes 'Michael Robartes bids his Beloved be at Peace'. Biographically, this poem takes a step back: the 'hair-tent' tells us that we are still with Olivia Shakespear, as this image is nearly always associated with her rather than with Maud Gonne or anyone else.[29] Probably this poem was written before 'Mongan laments'. At all events, it was the first published of the two poems, by an interval of seventeen months. Sexually, on the other hand, experience replaces the frustration of 'Mongan laments', but whether this is a step forward in the narrative sequence is debatable, as the mood which replaces the despair of 'Mongan laments' is scarcely preferable. In any terms, the mood of 'Michael Robartes bids his Beloved be at Peace' is a mood of terror, and given the sexual situation of the poem, therefore, it is not unreasonable to say that we have moved from sexual despair to sexual fear. This mood is further advanced by the position of the lovers, with Yeats (or the male persona) evidently submissive ('Beloved, let . . . your heart beat/Over my heart, and your hair fall over my breast', VP 154). This is normal in the Olivia Shakespear poems (hence the 'hair-tent'), but it is more than usually obvious in this poem. The effect is to impart strongly feminine qualities to the male sexual experience described. Add to this the violence of the opening lines, and the impression that one begins with is one of rape.

This is, nonetheless, an improvement on 'Mongan laments', for internally the poem works out its fears. The abrupt, caesura-dominated rhythms of the opening lines swiftly modulate to a weak caesura in l. 3 and no caesura in ll. 4, 5, and 6. The initial violence, in other words, gives way to a steady sexual rhythm, which in its turn is climatically shattered by the spasmodic rhythm of ll. 7 and 8: 'O vanity of Sleep, Hope, Dream, endless Desire,/The Horses of Disaster plunge in the heavy clay' (VP 154). This rhythm gradually loses itself in longer and quieter rhythms leading to a tranquil conclusion (l. 9 is the only enjambed line in the poem; l. 11 is the only line with seven stresses).

One might easily think, then, that this poem has no need of any nonsexual apocalyptic content. The poem presents itself in sexual terms, confronting and surmounting a sexual difficulty. For many readers, that will be enough. David R. Clark, for instance, considers that 'the cosmic import of the horses is not as impressive as the sexual import, and they simply begin to stand for the lover's sexual excitement or unrest which the lady allays'.[30] This is a very reasonable position, and yet Yeats contributes a note likening the horses to the Púcas (i.e. pookas) and the Fomorians and the horses of Manannan and never mentioning sex (VP 808). The fact is that Michael Robartes, according to Arthur Symons, who was 'tutored by Yeats', represents 'a particular outlook of the consciousness in its . . . intellectual moment'.[31] The sexual experience is not adequate for him without its intellectual commentary.

That commentary converts the sexual experience into another vision of the apocalypse. As Virginia Moore demonstrates, all the levels of significance in 'Michael Robartes bids his Beloved be at Peace' are combined in the symbol of the horse: 'Jung calls the horse a symbol of the libido that 'covers all the unknown and countless manifestations of the will'; a symbol of the wind, which in turn is a symbol of the spirit.'[32] The poem's sexual content is embodied in the horse as a symbol of the libido, while its apocalyptic content is embodied in the horse as a symbol of the spirit. By connecting the horse with the Púca, Yeats reminds us that the apocalypse is a transaction between this world and fairyland. This is also implicit in the horse as a symbol of the wind, as 'certainly the Sidhe have much to do with the wind' (VP 800).

But what is the function of apocalypse in this poem? Plainly, the horses are still another version of the 'boar without bristles' and the 'death-pale deer'. It is the world that they are trampling to bits. And yet the world seems to survive this treatment. The horses are invoked in violence. At the poem's mid-point, they appear to be irresistible: 'O vanity of Sleep, Hope, Dream, endless Desire,/The Horses of Disaster plunge in the heavy clay.' Sleep, Hope, Dream, and endless Desire are four of the immortal moods which are so important in this book, and yet they are threatened by the apocalypse and unable to resist it. It would seem, then, that the apocalypse here is negative, as in 'Mongan laments', but now feared instead of invited.

However, immediately after the failure of the moods to resist the apocalypse, it is dispelled by a mere flick of the head:

> Beloved, let your eyes half close, and your heart beat
> Over my heart, and your hair fall over my breast,
> Drowning love's lonely hour in deep twilight of rest,
> And hiding their tossing manes and their tumultuous feet.
> (VP 154)

The apocalypse, for all its menaces, has thus been invoked only to be banished. It was only a figment of the imagination to begin with. Then why mention it at all? The apocalyptic content of the poem and the apocalyptic significance of the horses still seem irrelevant beside the sexual content.

It is only by remembering that the poem originates in sexual fear that this objection can be answered. It is misguided to attach priority to any of the horses' levels of symbolism. Their ambiguity is their point. '... Love emerges as both the escape from disaster and the disaster itself.'[33] The sexual experience is apocalyptic, but the satisfaction of sexual desire allays the fears at first associated with the experience. As in 'Hanrahan laments because of his Wanderings', an image appears upon the backdrop of nothingness, but this time it is no imagined image, but a restoration of reality: the image of the beloved's hair.

Even now, however, we may justly ask whether such a tortuous path to such a conclusion is not a perversion of the lyric mode. The significance of 'Michael Robartes bids his Beloved be at Peace' is not sufficiently profound to justify the poem's obscurity. Its difficulties arise less from thematic complexity than from thematic imprecision. The fact is that none of the Michael Robartes poems in *The Wind Among the Reeds* can entirely escape a charge of pretentiousness. This one is no exception.

X. 'Hanrahan reproves the Curlew' and 'To my Heart, bidding it have no Fear'

'Hanrahan reproves the Curlew' is still a part of this same group of love poems. From Yeats's own point of view, it is evidently a poem of regret for the loss of Olivia Shakespear: 'Passion-dimmed eyes and long heavy hair/That was shaken out over my breast' (VP 155). From Hanrahan's point of view, the situation is a little more complicated. This poem is actually related to the *Stories of Red Hanrahan*. Grossman, therefore, is correct in his 'suggestion that the cry of the first line of the poem and the cry of the last pertain to two different kinds of love', but surely incorrect in associating the first with 'the seduction of the lost Eden (the Wisdom figure)' (Echtge or Cleena) and the last with 'the obsession of the lost mortal love' (Maive or Mary Lavelle). The word 'wind' in the last line is sufficient to indicate the presence of the fairies, and therefore of Echtge. It is enough that 'the crying of wind' reminds Hanrahan of Echtge, without the curlew reminding him of 'Passion-dimmed eyes and long heavy hair/That was shaken out over my breast.' Hanrahan has enjoyed no such intimacy with Echtge, so these eyes and this hair must belong to Mary Lavelle. Both wind and curlew combine to remind us of 'The Everlasting Voices': 'That you call in birds, in wind on the hill' (VP 141). This poem, like that, then, constitutes 'a banishing gesture, an attempt to restore a protective condition of dream by committing the voice of the infinite emotion to the West, "the place of sunset" and "fading dreaming things" '.[34] Also, Hanrahan speaks of the cry of the plover (a bird of the same family as the curlew) in 'The Twisting of the Rope', and that passage, therefore, sheds some light on this poem:

And one time she heard him telling about white-handed Deirdre, and how she brought the sons of Usna to their death; and how the blush in her cheeks was not so red as the blood of kings' sons that was shed for her, and her sorrows had never gone out of mind; and he said it was maybe the memory of her that made the cry of the plover on the bog as sorrowful in the ear of the poets as the keening of young men for a comrade.

(M 227)

Thus, although the cry of the curlew excites sorrow in Hanrahan, it also reminds him of Deirdre as well as of Mary Lavelle. This is an evasive manoeuvre. Hanrahan would consign his own love affair to the realm of mythology; elevate Mary Lavelle to ideal stature; and so make his memory bearable by making it unreal. Yeats, of course, would do the same for Olivia Shakespeare. This again suggests, if only slightly, an element of the sexual fear that characterises 'Michael Robartes bids his Beloved be at Peace'.

All these elements relate 'The Everlasting Voices', 'Michael Robartes bids his Beloved be at Peace', and 'Hanrahan reproves the Curlew' to 'To my Heart, bidding it have no Fear'. All the elements that have been causes of unrest in the previous poems are now subdued:

> Be you still, be you still, trembling heart;
> Remember the wisdom out of the old days:
> *Him who trembles before the flame and the flood,*
> *And the winds that blow through the starry ways,*
> *Let the starry winds and the flame and the flood*
> *Cover over and hide, for he has no part*
> *With the proud, majestical multitude.*
>
> (VP 158)

This poem is a paraphrase of another passage in the initiation ritual of the Golden Dawn: 'Fear is failure, so be thou without fear. For he who trembles at the Flame, and at the Flood, and at the Shadows of the Air, hath no part in God.'[35] Thus it is fear (including sexual fear) which is to be subdued, and a part in God — an apocalyptic revelation — which is to be won. 'To my Heart, bidding it have no Fear' thus gives reassurance to Michael Robartes. The sexual cycle is to continue and the apocalyptic vision to expand.

XI. 'Michael Robartes remembers Forgotten Beauty'

Michael Robartes, therefore, resumes his place in the sequence after 'Hanrahan reproves the Curlew', this time to remember Forgotten Beauty. It may as well be said at once that this poem, like 'Michael Robartes bids his Beloved be at Peace', is not among Yeats's best. It seems to exist for the sake of its last three lines, which do indeed present a powerful and memorable image:

> Throne over throne, where in half sleep
> Their swords upon their iron knees
> Brood her high lonely mysteries.
>
> (VP 156)

To introduce these three lines, however, Yeats indulges himself in fourteen lines of noun-phrases that seem imitated from the Keats of 'The Eve of St. Mark', and seven lines of images that worked well enough in

The Rose, but by now have become clichéed:

> For that pale breast and lingering hand
> Come from a more dream-heavy land,
> A more dream-heavy hour than this;
> And when you sigh from kiss to kiss
> I hear white Beauty sighing, too,
> For hours when all must fade like dew
> But flame on flame, deep under deep . . .

Nevertheless, the accumulation of noun-phrases marks on important change in Michael Robartes' attitude since he bade his beloved be at peace. 'Michael Robartes is the pride of the imagination brooding upon the greatness of its possessions' (VP 803). In the earlier poem, this brooding was a paranoid thing, a miser's passion. Michael Robartes' eyes were turned outward to what were not his possessions, to the Horses of Disaster that threatened them. Now his eyes are turned inward and he broods with pleasure on what he does possess. In Freudian terms, that is still an anal passion and not entirely healthy, but it does lead back, however ineptly, to the state of ecstasy in which Michael Robartes contemplates the apocalypse. This is no longer a negative and destructive apocalypse. What is revealed when nature is swept away is not the void but Beauty's 'high lonely mysteries', the Platonic Ideals. This is the vision which Hanrahan achieved at his death.

XII. 'The Valley of the Black Pig' (i): The Sexual Content

Unlike 'Michael Robartes remembers Forgotten Beauty', 'The Valley of the Black Pig' wastes no time in inducing a state of ecstasy. The poem begins and ends at the moment of climax. With far more success than in 'Michael Robartes bids his Beloved be at Peace,' the sexual and mystical aspects of the poem are seamlessly united. The symbolism functions equally well on both levels, allowing the speaker to declaim a wisdom that, if sexually inspired, is lifted high above the level of physical sexuality. This poem is at the core of the apocalytpic cycle and is the most important poem in *The Wind Among the Reeds*.

The orgasmic quality of 'The Valley of the Black Pig' is first apparent in its rhythms. The seven words to the left of the caesura in the first line serve basically for a contrast. They establish a quiet and unenergetic mood which is abruptly shattered by the words 'unknown spears/Suddenly hurtle before my dream-awakened eyes' (VP 161). L. 1 is enjambed and so is l. 3, while the comma at the end of l. 2 requires only the slightest of pauses. The entire passage must be read with a single, rapid breath:

> ... unknown spears
> Suddenly hurtle before my dream-awakened eyes,
> And then the clash of fallen horsemen and the cries
> Of unknown perishing armies beat about my ears.

The effect suggests the eruption of enormous potency. This is followed by a sudden exhaustion in l. 5. L. 2 contains two dactyls ('Suddenly hurtle be-'); l. 3 actually contains the foot called in Greek prosody the First Paeon, consisting of three short syllables before one long, practically unknown elsewhere in English ('-men and the cries'); l. 4 contains one anapaest ('-ishing arm-'); l. 5, by contrast, varies its iambic metre only by a spondee in the second foot. In other words, while every irregularity in ll. 2–4 is designed to hasten the rhythm, the sole irregularity in l. 5 is designed to retard it. After this, the poem gradually sinks into physical quiescence, even as the mental afterglow increases.

Symbolically, the 'unknown spears' are obviously phallic. They dominate the first half of the poem. The acoustic imagery 'beating about the ears' strongly suggests the pounding of the blood. The second half of the poem combines images of detumescence with womb or vaginal symbols. The latter are the cromlec and the 'flaming door'. The labourers by the cromlec 'bow down'. Before the flaming door, or setting sun, 'day sinks drowned in dew'. Thus the symbolism follows the prosody in implying a moment of climax between ll. 4 and 5.

XIII. 'The Valley of the Black Pig' (ii): The Tradition

The sexual content of 'The Valley of the Black Pig', though self-sufficient, stands for a ·symbol in its own right of the poem's mystical content. The conjunction of spear and door symbolises orgasm on the sexual level, but on the mystical level the spear may symbolise the soul (as in Blake's 'When the stars threw down their spears'), and the flaming door that goal to which the soul aspires. This is not, of course, one symbol with two different meanings. The mystical experience is like the sexual experience, or is even a higher version of the same thing. The movement of the soul imitates the movement of the body, or *vice versa*, 'For things below are copies, the Great Smaragdine Tablet said' ('Ribh Denounces Patrick' VP 556). For convenience sake, however, we may now put aside the sexual content of the poem. To understand the mystical content, we still need to understand the tradition in which it is couched. What is the Valley of the Black Pig?

Of all the poems in *The Wind Among the Reeds*, this is the one that best justifies Yeats's practice of annotation. What follows is no substitute for Yeats's long and excellent note, but only a commentary upon it. The Black Pig, then, has a triple significance in Irish tradition: on its own, it is some sort of supernatural entity; it is connected with the Black Pig's Dyke, a line of earthworks apparently designed for the protection of Ulster; and it is also connected with the Valley of the Black Pig, the site of a great battle that is the subject of prophecy. I shall begin with the Black Pig itself.

In Ireland the pig has almost always been a creature of ill omen. For instance, the swineherd of Bodb Dearg and his pig were apt to visit mortal feasts, 'and it was said that whatever feast that swineherd would go to, there would blood be shed before it was over'. Pre-eminent among such feasts was the feast at Da Derga's Hostel, 'the night Conaire, the High King of Ireland, met with his death'. The pig at that feast is specifically described as black.[36] When the Tuatha Dé Danann enchanged Ireland to hide it from the invading Milesians, all that the latter could see, in the words of one folk-version of the tale, was 'land, the size of a pig's back . . . and a black back it is'.[37] For this reason, an old name for Ireland was Muc Inis, or Pig Island. There is a possibility, then, that the Black Pig represents Ireland herself under a cursed or enchanted aspect. This might account for its apparition in times of upheaval.

Yeats's seasonal interpretation of the Black Pig probably owes something to Sir Samuel Ferguson, according to whom the Pig did not represent winter, as such, but stormy weather. It was 'a mythical monster, said to have been banished, after the establishment of Christianity, to the Hebridean seas, where his "rootings" may be seen in stormy weather in the hollows of the waves, and his "gruntings" heard from the caverned rocks.'[38] A devil in the form of a black pig raises a furious storm in the folk-tale of 'The Friars of Urlaur'. This story contains one passage that may have a further bearing on Yeats's poem: 'Then came the lightning and the thunder, and everybody thought that it was the end of the world that was in it. There was such a great darkness that a person could not see his own hand if he were to put it out before him.'[39] Is this 'the darkness that will at last destroy the gods and the world' (VP 809)?

Yeats's note attributes a more strictly seasonal symbolism to the Black Pig. This would make the Pig 'a type of cold and of winter that wake in November, the old beginning of winter, to do battle with the summer, and with the fruit and leaves' (VP 809). There is evidence to support

The Wind Among the Reeds as Psychic Narrative

this, although, for the mythographers as for Yeats, the Black Pig of winter seems to overlap with the Black Pig of apocalyptic darkness. There is an anomalous Welsh 'Trystan' in which Arthur arranges that either Trystan or March 'shall have Esyllt while there are leaves on the trees, the other when the trees are leafless'. March 'chooses the leafless period because the nights are then longer'. (It is, in fact, a trap, because March has forgotten the evergreens.)[40] The relevance of this becomes plain when one remembers that the chief Irish counterpart of Trystan is Dearmod, whom 'the black pig . . . killed . . . in November, upon the western end of Ben Bulben' (VP 809). The seasonal symbolism of 'Trystan' is obvious: Trystan is summer and March is winter. However, the story, like the seasons themselves, also has its solar implications. March's preference for the season when 'the nights are longer' should be noticed. Turning again to the parallel Irish myth, John Rhys, whom Yeats cites in his note, held that 'the noble Diarmait, beloved of all, and the grisly Boar were the offspring of one mother: they represent light and darkness'.[41] Though Rhys's interpretations of mythology are generally rejected today, this one appears to be sound. The story of Diarmuid Ó Duibhne is that he is fostered at Brugh na Boinne by Angus Óg at the same time as the son of Roc, the steward of Diarmuid's father Donn. While visiting Brugh na Boinne at one time, Donn is angered to find that Roc's son is treated as well as his own, and he therefore kills the boy. In revenge, Roc turns his dead son to a pig. It is the destiny of this pig to live as long as Diarmuid and to kill him in the end. Angus therefore lays a *geis* on Diarmuid never to hunt swine. Years later, after Diarmuid has eloped with Grainne, the bride of Finn mac Cumhail and counterpart of Yseult, Finn affects a false reconciliation but lures Diarmuid onto Benn Gulban (Ben Bulben), where the Fianna are hunting the Boar of Benn Gulban. In reality, this is Roc's son. The boar kills Diarmuid.[42] The solar interpretation of this myth is strengthened by a list of wedding-guests in a *scéal* called 'The Thirteenth Son of the King of Erin,' which includes 'Diarmuid, son of the monarch of light'.[43] Also, another wild boar in a Fenian tale is turned to 'a beautiful young woman' called Scathach, which means 'The Shadowy One'.[44]

It seems likely that the pig which killed Diarmuid is also the pig which made the Black Pig's Dyke. There is a folk-tale which is clearly a version of the death of Diarmuid even though all the characters have become anonymous. In this, the Black Pig is hunted from Ulster to 'the Valley of the Black Pig, a little vale situated in the townland of MucDuff, in the county Sligo'.[45] The route of this hunt would be bound to follow what is now the Black Pig's Dyke. Eleanor Hull, however, believes that the pig which made this dyke was Cian, the father of Lugh, who is turned to a pig in 'The Fate of the Children of Tuirenn'.[46]

Even though MucDuff (i.e. *muc dubh*) actually means 'Black Pig', there is no general agreement as to where exactly in the Co. Sligo the Valley of the Black Pig is. It is often supposed to be the coastal valley between Knocknarea and Ben Bulben in which the town of Sligo is situated. A battle to be fought in the Valley of the Black Pig against the foreigners, to 'the advantage of the bright Irish', is mentioned in two prophetic lays attributed to Finn mac Cumhail.[47]

The Black Pig is connected with this prophesied battle by more than name. It occasionally appears in the land as a portent of 'serious trouble in Ireland'. In 1918, a black sow with six bonhams appeared at Kiltrustan, Co. Roscommon, following the circulation of 'a long, ill-written, and quite recent prose tract' called the *Prophecy of St. Columcille*. This tract was unusual in foretelling a great massacre of the Irish at the hands of the British. According to Eleanor Hull, the Black Pig and her bonhams were visible only to three small children at Kiltrustan.[48] However, Ernie O'Malley, who served with the I.R.A. in Roscommon during the Tan War, heard rumours of sightings all over the county.[49]

XIV. 'The Valley of the Black Pig' (iii): The Apocalypse

Such, then, is the tradition of the Black Pig. To understand the use that Yeats made of it, it is helpful to remember a remark of Standish O'Grady's, that Irish mythology is to be interpreted, not as history, but as prophecy.[50] The Valley of the Black Pig as a coming battle in which the Gael will expel the Gall is already a projection into the future of the Second Battle of Moytura. In portraying it as 'the battle between the manifest world and the ancestral darkness at the end of all things' (VP 810), Yeats is simply taking this process one stage further.

The first half of the poem presents the apocalypse in a negative light, the second in a positive light. In the first half, the speaker's eyes are 'dream-awakened'. This expression is on the brink of paradox: one must sleep, not awake, in order to dream. This startling word implies that no ordinary dream but a true vision is involved. Yeats speaks in his prefatory note to *The Wind Among the Reeds* of how he experienced, 'sometimes when awake, but more often in sleep, moments of vision, a state very unlike dreaming . . . which seemed always as if it would bring me some strange revelation' (VP 800). The speaker's eyes are opened to behold enormous carnage, a battle apparently without victors. It seems he is awakened only in order to witness defeat and the final darkness.

This prompts the question of who the 'fallen horsemen' and the 'unknown perishing armies' are. Robert O'Driscoll supposes that they are 'those who serve the temporal world'. Since the horsemen are destroyed as the Black Pig is destined to destroy the temporal world, this is extremely plausible. Unfortunately, O'Driscoll couples it with an explication of the poem's second half that is not plausible. In contrast to these horsemen and their fate, he argues, stands 'the still self-sufficiency of artists who, "weary of the world's empires," bow in solitude to the author of eternity'.[51] If artists are self-sufficient, why are they weary? The second half of 'The Valley of the Black Pig' requires a quite different type of explication.

What needs to be noticed is the transition from the first half to the second. Yeats does not simply present a negative apocalypse and a positive apocalypse and invite us to choose one and reject the other. The tradition of the Black Pig is inherently ambiguous, so that any apocalypse associated with it can be transvalued by a simple change of perspective. In terms of seasonal symbolism, for instance, we have seen that the Black Pig represents winter, but O'Driscoll points out that in fairyland the seasons are reversed, so that 'when winter and darkness descend on our world, summer and the light of imagination are awakening in the spiritual world'.[52] The same applies to the Black Pig as a symbol of Darkness. In T. R. Whitaker's view, the Black Pig 'is here obliquely called both conqueror of visible light and ruler of the element of fire'. This conclusion depends to some extent on the unproven assumption that the Black Pig is to be identified with the 'Master of the still stars and of the flaming door', but Whitaker's resolution of the paradox involved is sound and well within Yeats's usual frame of reference: ' "Where there is nothing . . . there is God" — or, as Madame Blavatsky had said, "Darkness, in its radical, metaphysical basis, is subjective and absolute light." Hence the Irish Black Pig becomes the gnostic primal darkness, a paradoxical lightbearer or Lucifer.' In fact, the Black Pig is reminiscent of 'Blake's destructive initiator of a new era, "flaming Orc," whose name, derived from "Orcus," also means "pig" in Irish'.[53]

The Black Pig is thus winter and summer, death and rebirth, darkness and light. But this only identifies the symbolism. It does not tell us, in plain language, the nature of the positive apocalypse. As usual, the negative apocalypse is the destruction of the world and the dissolution of all things in universal darkness. But what is to follow? Yeats does not here, as in 'Hanrahan laments because of his Wanderings' or 'Michael Robartes remembers Forgotten Beauty', provide us with a visual image of the post-apocalyptic state. Indeed, he does not give us any image of the post-apocalyptic state. All of the imagery of the poem's second half pertains to the pre-apocalyptic state, to the here and now. But from it we can, and must, infer what is to follow.

In 'We who still labour by the cromlec on the shore,/The gray cairn on the hill', the cairn is the cairn of Maeve on Knocknarea. The cromlec stands on the Strand of Beltra, between the Ox Mountains and Knocknarea, and was thought by Sir William Wilde to mark the grave of Cúchulainn.[54] William Irwin Thompson quite rightly comments that in contemplating these landmarks Yeats is contemplating Ireland's heroic past,[55] but he mistakes the implications of this. The operative word in l. 5 is 'still'. It is the antiquity rather than the heroism of the past that inspires the mood of the line. It is so long ago, and yet still we labour. Of course, the connotations of 'labour' are negative. Also, our labour is not solely physical. The mind, confined by the five senses, labours in cogitation to elucidate that truth which it would apprehend at once by the 'flight of the alone to the Alone'. It is no wonder that we 'weary of the world's empires'.

In quoting that tag from Plotinus, 'the flight of the alone to the Alone', I deliberately touch upon the Neo-Platonic substratum of this poem. Neo-Platonism is a philosophy which Yeats typically approached through the tradesman's entrance. The area which most interested him was the overlap between Neo-Platonism and the Hermetic and Rosicrucian traditions. In some of what follows, I shall have to rely upon Yeats's general erudition in this field, as the precise extent of his knowledge and instruction cannot be proven beyond a certain point. The Golden Dawn, after all, was a *secret* society.

What is to be done with the world of the five senses? Those who are weary of it, 'when day sinks drowned in dew', bow down to the 'Master of the still stars and of the flaming door'. The key word here is 'dew'. This is its second appearance in the poem. In the first line it may be taken as a 'sign' of 'The region of the darkened West'. This is a function which Yeats specifically attaches to dew in his explication of Blake's 'Little Boy Lost'.[56] As the West is associated with 'fading and dreaming things' (VP 808), the dropping dew of the first line is atmospherically equivalent to 'dreams gather'. Together, the first seven words provide the context for the 'dream-awakening' which transmutes sleep to vision. The second appearance of dew is more literally connected with transmutation, as dew is of alchemical significance. In fact, the importance of dew in alchemy may have been one of the primary secrets of Rosicrucianism, if, indeed, the name of the cult conceals a reference to dew. The word 'Rosicrucian' is generally derived from L. *rosa + crux*, hence 'Rosy Cross'. However, there is an alternative theory that the word is a deliberate pun, hiding behind the obvious derivation a genuine derivation from L. *ros + crux*, hence

'Dewy Cross'. This theory had fallen out of favour, but has been recently revived by Frances Yates, who has noticed that the *Consideratio brevis* of Philip à Gabella (Cassel, 1615), a seminal Rosicrucian work, bears on the *verso* of its title-page the epigraph *De rore caeli et pinguedine terrae det tibi Deus*, 'God give thee of the dew of heaven and of the fatness of the land' (Gen. xxvii, 28). According to Yates, dew is 'a (supposed) solvent of gold',[57] but here she underestimates its alchemical importance. Dew 'burns' the First Matter (earth), making it the Philosopher's Peat. When the Peat has been brought to its 'first perfection' and incinerated, it becomes the Major Leaven. A mixture of the Philosopher's Peat, the Major Leaven, and more dew will indeed dissolve gold, but this is only a step towards the production of the Philosopher's Stone, which of course creates gold by transmuting baser metals.[58] The allusion in 'when day sinks drowned in dew' is not to the dissolution of gold, but to the coction of the First Matter, symbolising the transmutation of the world (common earth) to the imaginative or apocalyptic world made perfect (gold). This is confirmed by one of the sources of Philip à Gabella's *Consideratio*, the *Monas hieroglyphica* of John Dee, a work held in great esteem in magical circles like the Golden Dawn. It too has the epigraph *De rore caeli et pinguedine terrae det tibi Deus* on its title-page, accompanied by a diagram in which 'the theme of the descending dew (*ros*) uniting heaven and earth is visually illustrated'.[59] When day sinks drowned in dew, therefore, the earth is united to the higher realm of being beyond the flaming door.

The flaming door itself invites comparison with the door to fairyland in the side of Ben Bulben that Yeats mentions in *The Celtic Twilight* (M 70), and with the angel with a flaming sword at the gate of Eden, who is dismissed in 'The Everlasting Voices' in order that fallen nature may be redeemed.[60] Like the door in Ben Bulben, the flaming door suggests 'a necessary passageway on the path to another, timeless existence'.[61] In simple terms, however, the flaming door is a metaphor of the sun. This relates it to the Syrian school of Neo-Platonism, which school, being theurgical, was most congenial to the Rosicrucian tradition. In particular, Yeats's image is clarified by the 'Hymn to King Helios Dedicated to Sallust' of the Emperor Julian, commonly called the Apostate.

Yeats may have read Duncombe's English translation of Julian's *Select Works* (1784), though there is no evidence that he did. It is likely that he knew Julian's philosophy at least at second hand, for it would appeal to Madame Blavatsky's circle as well as to the Golden Dawn. For Julian, as for Yeats, the sun is the gateway of souls 'between the visible gods who surround the universe and the immaterial and intelligible gods who surround the Good'. Helios frees men's souls 'from the body and then lifts them up on high to the region of those substances that are akin to the god'. The most remarkable parallel between Julian's 'Hymn' and 'The Valley of the Black Pig' is the method by which Helios frees us from our 'labour by the cromlec on the shore':

> For Plato himself says somewhere that our race was by nature doomed to toil, and so the gods pitied us and gave us Dionysus and the Muses as playfellows. And we recognised that Helios is their common lord, since he is celebrated as the father of Dionysus and the leader of the Muses.[62]

Thus it is through the imaginative arts, symbolised by the Muses, that Helios, the master of the flaming door, delivers us to that state which Nietzsche was to call Dionysian, fifteen centuries after Julian's time.

The image of the 'still stars', on the other hand, probably originates in Dante. Robert O'Driscoll points out the relevance of a passage in Yeats's essay on 'William Blake and his Illustrations to the *Divine Comedy*' (1897): 'Dante, like other mediaeval mystics, symbolised the highest order of created beings by the fixed stars, and God by the darkness beyond them, the *Primum Mobile*' (E &I 133).[63] Again, 'Where there is nothing, there is God'. The stars, like the sun, are an intermediate term between this world and the world of perfection.

The still stars and the flaming door explain why Yeats presents no visual imagery of the post-apocalyptic state. It is because the movement of 'The Valley of the Black Pig' is all away from form and from what can be visually described. This is Yeats's most Dionysian poem. It aspires to an escape into pure, unbounded mental essences. Thus, in the first half, the Black Pig destroys all outward and visible form, leaving only the images and symbols of the mind's eye. Even these are 'drowned in dew,' caught up in the process of transmutation. All images move towards the flaming door, beyond which there are no images at all, but only the white space at the bottom of the page. We have returned to the 'white hush' of 'To Some I have Talked with by the Fire' and 'To Ireland in the Coming Times,' but now without regret. Helios leads the Muses, but in a realm where the imagination is sufficient unto itself, with no compulsion to generate 'Those images that yet/Fresh images beget' ('Byzantium,' VP 498). The poet's labour is finished.

XV. 'The Travail of Passion'

The moment of sexual climax achieved in 'The Valley of the Black Pig' is sustained in a poem which for the second time I must consider out of sequence, 'The Travail of Passion'. Again, the sexual energy of the poem is united with the apocalyptic aspiration. The crucial lines are the last:

> We will bend down and loosen our hair over you,
> That it may drop faint perfume, and be heavy with dew,
> Lilies of death-pale hope, roses of passionate dream.
>
> (VP 172)

Here again dew is alchemical. It is imagined as, literally, the universal solvent, and on this occasion the 'hair-tent' image confirms and enriches the connotations of dew. This particular hair-tent image derives from a line in Villiers de l'Isle Adam's *Axël*, which Yeats quotes in his preface to H. P. R. Finberg's translation: 'O to veil you with my hair where you will breathe the spirit of dead roses.'[64] In the play, this line is the prelude to suicide. Yeats explains in 'The Autumn of the Body' (1898) what he understands death as signifying in *Axël*: Villiers de l'Isle Adam 'created persons from whom has fallen all even of personal characteristic except a thirst for that hour when all things shall pass away like a cloud, and a pride like that of the Magi following their star over many mountains' (E &I 190). Again, then, Yeats combines the sexual 'little death' with the apocalyptic 'great death' which shall obliterate the world and even personality, except for one pure and self-sufficient Mood.

XVI. 'Aedh hears the Cry of the Sedge'

After the climactic mood of 'The Valley of the Black Pig', 'Michael Robartes asks Forgiveness because of his Many Moods', a rather uninteresting and poorly constructed poem, introduces a mood of post-coital triste. In 'Aedh hears the Cry of the Sedge', this mood deepens until it returns to the despair of 'Mongan laments the Change that has come upon him and his Beloved':

> I wander by the edge
> Of this desolate lake
> Where wind cries in the sedge
> *Until the axle break*
> *That keeps the stars in their round*
> *And hands hurl in the deep*
> *The banners of East and West*
> *And the girdle of light is unbound,*
> Your breast will not lie by the breast
> Of your beloved in sleep.
>
> (VP 165)

Surprisingly, this very sad and rather simple poem has been often and drastically misunderstood. Frank Hughes Murphy notes that 'there are *hands* which hurl the banners of East and West into the deep', and concludes that this implies 'a guiding principle behind the destruction, one that must be presumed to outlive that terrible hour'.[65] This would put the poem into the same class as 'Hanrahan laments because of his Wanderings' or 'Michael Robartes bids his Beloved be at Peace'. Allen Grossman is even more sanguine. First, he supplies important information on the banners of East and West: 'The ceremonial chamber, as arranged for the neophyte (O–O) in the Golden Dawn, was dominated by the Banners of East and West, symbolizing the morning and the evening twilight respectively.' Twilight 'is the condition of the uninitiated, the unborn, who awaits in his limbonic state the coming of the light from within and as preparation must learn to master his anxiety'. However, since Grossman reads *The Wind Among the Reeds* as a *sequential* narrative of the neophyte's initiation, he is perversely compelled to regard 'Aedh hears the Cry of the Sedge' as the happiest poem in the book: 'This is the end of initiation, signified by the destruction of the natural order, the dispersal of the twilight, and the unbinding of celestial illumination.'[66] On this reading, then, 'Aedh hears the Cry of the Sedge' is much like 'The Valley of the Black Pig'.

What Murphy and Grossman have both overlooked is the crucial word 'Until'. The happy apocalypse which Grossman describes is projected into an unimaginably distant future. Another word which they have overlooked is 'sedge'. With the help of this word, as Jeffares points out, 'Aedh hears the Cry of the Sedge' is made reminiscent of Keats's 'La Belle Dame sans Merci', with its line 'The sedge is withered from the lake'.[67] Aedh, like that poem's 'knight-at-arms', is paralysed in his hopeless and frustrated condition.

XVII. 'Mongan thinks of his Past Greatness'

Why has the sexual cycle thus returned to its beginning? Is it indeed a cycle, in the sense that the moment of vision or apocalypse, though attainable, is not retainable, but doomed to pass and so return the poet to the condition in which he began? That is possible, but one should bear in mind that 'Aedh hears the Cry of the Sedge' differs from 'Mongan laments the Change that has come upon him and his Beloved' at least in respect of its persona. This seems to imply that there is a cycle for each persona. Each 'principle of the mind' stands in need of its own fulfilment. Rather than extend this cycle of poems to an altogether tedious length, however, Yeats sketches it in with indications of how it would proceed. For instance, Hanrahan's equivalent of 'Aedh hears the Cry of the Sedge' is 'Hanrahan reproves the Curlew'. But a poem that implies the beginning of all cycles is 'Mongan thinks of his Past Greatness'. As a lover, Mongan is in exactly the same position as Aedh:

> I became a man, a hater of the wind,
> Knowing one, out of all things, alone, that his head
> Would not lie on the breast or his lips on the hair
> Of the woman that he loves, until he dies.
>
> (VP 177)

On the other hand, the last two lines recall 'Hanrahan reproves the Curlew' (as well as 'The Everlasting Voices'): 'Although the rushes and the fowl of the air/Cry of his love with their pitiful cries' (in later texts, 'O beast of the wilderness, bird of the air,/Must I endure your amorous cries?'). For all that, Mongan is neither Hanrahan nor Aedh. Still more evidently than in 'Mongan laments', he is this book's equivalent of Fergus:

> I have drunk ale from the Country of the Young
> And weep because I know all things now:[68]
> I have been a hazel tree and they hung
> The Pilot Star and the Crooked Plough
> Among my leaves in times out of mind:
> I became a rush that horses tread:
> I became a man . . .
>
> (VP 177)

Unlike Fergus, however, Mongan does not just drift through an apparently random sequence of incarnations. Rather, his incarnations encompass the other personae of *The Wind Among the Reeds*. Ronald Schleifer associates the hazel tree with Michael Robartes, the rush with Hanrahan, and the man with Aedh.[69] It remains Mongan's tragedy, like Fergus', that he has no fixed personality of his own. However, by the same token, he is the typical man: multifaceted, but changeable, unstable, impure, and unintegrated. Thus, of all personae, he is closest to Yeats himself (and to the reader). As Mongan begins his cycle in despair, so do Aedh, Hanrahan, Michael Robartes, W. B. Yeats, and we ourselves.

XVIII. 'The Blessed'

'Aedh hears the Cry of the Sedge' and 'Mongan thinks of his Past Greatness', then, invite us to imagine other, unwritten poems, in which the whole human personality will be satisfied through its scattered fragments or personae. This strategy is confirmed by 'The Blessed', 'The Secret Rose', and 'Aedh wishes his Beloved were Dead'. Here, the cycle has ended, and satisfaction has been achieved. In the first two of these poems, the symbol of the Rose returns. The meaning is that the long and tormented quest for the Rose is over; she has been found.

The situation of 'The Blessed' recalls that of 'Fergus and the Druid'. Here again we have a supplicant, Cumhal, visiting a hermit, Dathi, to seek wisdom.[70] The wisdom that he learns is superficially very like the wisdom that Fergus learnt: 'And Cumhal saw like a drifting smoke/All manner of blessed souls'; 'And blessedness goes where the wind goes' (VP 167, 168). The difference is that this drifting is no longer perceived as purposeless or meaningless: Dathi 'can *see* where the wind goes/And *follow* the way of the wind'; 'blessedness comes in the night and the day/And whither the wise heart *knows*' (emphasis added). Whereas the Druid is unhappy and communicates only his unhappiness to Fergus, with Cumhal and Dathi the case is the reverse. Dathi smiles 'With the secrets of God in his eyes' and Cumhal's heart is filled with content (l. 20).

Although Dathi is a Christian hermit, not a druid, he is the master of a fairy wisdom. He has learnt to be disengaged like the fairies themselves, those creatures of whim.

> I see the blessedest soul in the world
> And he nods a drunken head.
>
> O blessedness comes in the night and the day
> And whither the wise heart knows;
> And one has seen in the redness of wine
> The Incorruptible Rose,
>
> That drowsily drops faint leaves on him
> And the sweetness of desire,
> While time and the world are ebbing away
> In twilights of dew and of fire.
>
> (VP 168)

This drunkard is most blessed because he is deliberately dissolving with drink the purposefulness that binds him to a futile search, just as the alchemical dew is dissolving the material world that obscures the apocalypse, or Rose. This is the wisdom of the crane in 'The Three Beggars': 'And maybe I shall take a trout/If but I do not seem to care' (VP 297). It is a very unbiblical wisdom: 'Seek not, and ye shall find'.

XIX. 'The Secret Rose'

'The Secret Rose' continues the theme of 'The Blessed'. It is a self-fulfilling prayer. This is particularly apparent at the beginning and the end. The prayer itself is explicit in the first two lines, 'Far off, most secret, and inviolate Rose,/Enfold me in my hour of hours' (VP 169), while the next lines hint that it is already answered:

> . . . where those
> Who sought thee in the Holy Sepulchre,
> Or in the wine vat, dwell beyond the stir
> And tumult of defeated dreams; and deep
> Among pale eyelids, heavy with the sleep
> Men have named beauty.

The hint arises because these types of humanity all include Yeats himself, in one way or another. 'The Holy Sepulchre' refers equally with the tomb of Christ to the tomb of Father Christian Rosenkreuz, in which the Master was found lying incorrupt after 120 years, having attained perfection in death. A reconstruction of this 'event' formed the climax of the Golden Dawn's initiation ritual.[71] Therefore, 'those/Who sought thee in the Holy Sepulchre' are Rosicrucian initiates, like Yeats. 'Those/Who sought thee . . . /in the wine vat' refers back to the drunkard in 'The Blessed'. This drunkard's quietistic, undemanding approach to the Rose is that approach which Yeats now makes his own. The 'defeated dreams' stand for the opposite approach, the struggles of *The Rose*, which Yeats has now put behind him. The syntax shows that those who dwell 'deep/Among pale eyelids, heavy with the sleep/Men have named beauty' include the Rosicrucians and the drunkards, but those chiefly preoccupied with beauty are the artists, who again include Yeats. Thus Yeats has already met the conditions needed for his prayer's fulfilment.

The poem then moves from the general to the particular with a list of individuals whom the Rose has already enfolded, and whom Yeats expects to join. Yeats identifies these individuals in his note. They are the Magi, Conchobar, Cuchullain, Caolte, Fergus, and the hero of William Larminie's 'The Red Pony'. A comparison with the sources shows that Yeats has considerably modified all of these characters for the purposes of 'The Secret Rose'. The episode of Caolte's driving 'the gods out of their liss', in fact, appears to be something that Yeats dreamed. Although he was to allude to the story again in *Diarmuid and Grania* (1900) ('. . . and Caoelte [shall] storm the house of the gods at Assaroe' [VPl 1219]), he was never able to rediscover where he read it.

It is not, as he speculated (VP 814), in Standish O'Grady's *Fionn and his Companions* (1892), nor, so far as I can ascertain, in any work not Yeats's own. The list of figures in 'The Secret Rose' moves from the Christian to the pagan or fairy, from the heroes of faith to the heroes of imagination. The Magi are characters from the New Testament, but the next four are characters from Irish mythology and the hero of 'The Red Pony' a character from folklore. Conchobar, though a pagan king, is remembered for his conversion to Christianity at death, but Cuchullain, though he was posthumously converted, is remembered only for his dalliance with a fairy.

This list of individuals also reiterates in more detail the first six and a half lines of the poem. The 'crowned Magi' are magicians or Rosicrucians. Their claim to peace is that they found the reality of Christ; Conchobar found only the illusion, 'In druid vapour', and, like the earlier Yeats, fell into a 'vain frenzy'; but the Rose enfolds even him, because, like Hanrahan, he purchased his salvation with his death. However, even the Magi for Yeats are always 'unsatisfied'. Although the source of that word, the poem called 'The Magi', was not written until 1913, the idea is already implicit in the story of 'The Adoration of the Magi' (1897). The greater satisfaction belongs to those who derive it from the fairies. Cuchullain, for instance, 'lost the world and Emer for a kiss'. This is no misfortune. The image of losing the world is apocalyptic, and what Cuchullain gains is the kiss of perfection. Caolte's victory is greater yet, for he actually masters the fairies. Fergus remains the ruler of the imagination, as in 'Who Goes with Fergus?' This is symbolised by his bard and clown. But a new element here is that he 'Dwelt among wine-stained wanderers in deep woods'. This again refers us to the drunkard of 'The Blessed'. Fergus is no longer the ruler of restless dissatisfaction, for he has lost all that in the wine-bowl. He who 'sought through lands and islands numberless years' stands for Yeats himself. His search encompasses his previous career and also the figures previously enumerated. As these end with Fergus finding peace at last, so does Yeats find peace.

The last five and a half lines return from the particular to the general:

> . . . . I, too, await
> The hour of thy great wind of love and hate.
> When shall the stars be blown about the sky,
> Like the sparks blown out of a smithy, and die?
> Surely thine hour has come, thy great wind blows,
> Far off, most secret, and inviolate Rose?
>
> (VP 170)

The Rose's hate is the hatred that destroys the world, her love is the love that transfigures it. The image of the sparks indicates the mechanism of the apocalypse. 'As the smith labors at the anvil,' comments Grossman, 'so the poet labors at his art, to bring about a new world which will supplant the old.'[72] Harold Bloom points out the Blakean precedent for the poet-blacksmith metaphor: 'the poet awaits . . . his hour of hours . . . when Los the poet-prophet will come again as Urthona the blacksmith of creation, and the star-world of Urizen shall be blown out and die.'[73] Thus these last lines of 'The Secret Rose', like the first, prophesy the future apocalypse while — reading without the question marks — they affirm its present reality. Again, the Rose is attained.

XX. 'Aedh wishes his Beloved were Dead'

Though it is not the last poem in the book, 'Aedh wishes his Beloved were Dead' adds a final postscript to the narrative of *The Wind Among the Reeds*. The image of the Rose as the mystical, transcendent apocalypse has been brought back and finally assimilated. There remains the image of the Rose as, simply, Maud Gonne. In this poem, Yeats is urging Maud Gonne to see herself as he sees her: 'But know your hair was bound and wound/About the stars and moon and sun' (VP 176). If Maud were dead, she would realise that she is not just a woman but a cosmic presence: the Rose. At present, she does not know. This much, perhaps, but this alone, remains to separate the Rose from her devotee. Death will resolve this problem.

That *The Wind Among the Reeds* closes in such a way is perhaps ominous. The book as a whole represents the solution of many problems for Yeats. The dialogue with the Rose and with the fairies seems no longer a dialogue with the deaf. In fact, it is significant that the book opens with the fairies addressing Yeats, rather than the other way round. Of course, this is all to the good. If we leave out of account *The Shadowy Waters*, which Yeats had begun writing long before he began writing *The Wind Among the Reeds*, we can see that his early obsessions and the symbols of this early anguish are disposed of almost completely with *The Wind Among the Reeds*. The Rose will never again be a dominant symbol. Fairyland will never again be of such importance.

The trouble is that we cannot leave *The Shadowy Waters* out of account. The fact that Yeats was still wrestling with it shows that after all he could not yet forget his problems. The solutions to those problems achieved in *The Wind Among the Reeds* are distinctly makeshift. The apocalypse as a solution to Yeats's mystical or imaginative problems is riddled with problems of its own. The notion that Yeats has attained the Rose, achieved a dialogue with the fairies, and experienced the apocalypse may make good poetry, but it is a rather obvious pretence. *The Rose*, in fact, was more honest in presenting these things as impossible.

As a believed pretence, the apocalypse is playing with fire. To speak of Roses and Black Pigs and death-pale deer and flaming doors is to disguise the fact that one is actually speaking of death. To anyone who genuinely believes that his life in the world is all that separates him from an unimaginable glory, life must be intolerable and death irresistible. Insofar as Yeats's early poetry is a flirtation with that belief, it must be seen as a rough draught for his suicide note. In the end, of course, he did not commit suicide, but he did write the note: *The Shadowy Waters*. It is not a note of despair, but of a sort of triumph — a rather unhealthy sort of triumph. However, *The Shadowy Waters* is also a ritual of exorcism. Afterwards, Yeats could settle into an Apollonian calm.

16. *THE SHADOWY WATERS*: 'WHAT THE WORLD'S MILLION LIPS ARE THIRSTING FOR'

The Shadowy Waters has attracted a great deal of attention in recent years, but none of it has been very favourable. This is one of Yeats's most laboured works, and one of his least successful. Indeed, he wrote himself of the 1900 text that it 'was so overgrown with symbolical ideas that the poem was obscure and vague. It found its way on to the stage more or less by accident . . . and . . . it must have bewildered and bored the greater portion of the audience' (VP1 340). Yeats believed he had overcome these problems in later texts, but there he overestimated his success. In every text, the symbolism is not only excessive and uninteresting, but also indicative of deeper faults. It may be that it engenders these faults, but more probably it only reflects them.

The basic situation of *The Shadowy Waters* is one by now familiar: the inadequacy of this world and the necessity of escape. As in 'The Sorrow of Love', the inadequacy of the world is presented solipsistically. The play seeks a release from this solipsism and finds one. The alternative to solipsism may be defined as fairyland, pure and simple, or as imagination, or as the ground of being. Whatever it is, it is always eclipsed by the shadow of death. The death-wish is the dark side of Yeats's pursuit of the apocalypse, and it could not remain submerged for ever. *The Shadowy Waters* may be read as an attempt to lay this ghost by exposing it to the light of day. Fairyland is revealed as the land of the dead, for better or for worse.

If this were the whole truth, one might condemn the play as morbid, but one could not call it structurally or thematically unsound. The real weakness of the play is that fairyland overshadows the land of the dead as much as the land of the dead overshadows fairyland. Rather than affirm the reality of death, *The Shadowy Waters* seeks continually to evade it. Thus the play is an argument with itself. Yeats continually suggests that fairyland is the land of the dead, and as continually suggests that it is not. In the end, one is left none the wiser. Having been soaked in symbolism to no purpose, one can only conclude that *The Shadowy Waters* is not mystical but pseudo-mystical, and therefore fundamentally pretentious.

I. Solipsism

Like the symbolism of the play, the solipsism is an element which Yeats does reduce through successive revisions, but never eliminates. It dominates this play more than any other of Yeats's works. Indeed, he implies as much himself: 'Sometimes the barrier between myself and other people filled me with terror; an unfinished poem, and the first and never-finished version of *The Shadowy Waters* had this terror for their theme.'[1] The theme extends well beyond the first draught. It is very apparent in a draught written between 1894 and 1896:

> And ⟨now⟩ I find my image upon water
> When I would find a music & a light
> In labouring chariot wheels, or whirling sails
> Or bows of beaten bronze, when galleys drive
> On galleys & the gleaming oar blades break
> ~~Or in the face of friend or enemy~~
> ~~Or deamon of the~~ water
> Or in the face or [of?] friend or enemy
> Or deamons of wind or water.[2]

Forgael's complaint is that his own image — perhaps his Blakean Spectre — interposes between him and any sort of noumenal reality.

In published texts, this solipsism comes to be associated with the word 'dream', transvalued as in 'The Hosting of the Sidhe'. Thus, in the 1900 text Dectora says:

> O! I would break this net the gods have woven
> Of voices and of dreams. O heart, be still!
> O! why is love so crazy that it longs
> To drown in its own image?
>
> (VP 765)

Two pages later she adds: 'The gods hate happiness, and weave their nets / Out of their hatred.' These passages need to be contrasted with the 1907 text:

> And there's no fountain of reality
> But trance alone, that we should be at peace
> Could we but give us wholly to the dreams,
> And get into their world that to the sense
> Is shadow and not linger wretchedly
> Among substantial things

(VPl 332; the 1906 text, VP 230, lacks the first two lines). Superficially, these passages seem contradictory. The gods, to punish us, have trapped us in a world made of our own dreams. That is why love on earth fails of the transcendent quality that Forgael and Dectora seek: it can find only its own image, and not the pure reality of love. And yet the escape from this world is also through dreams.

The contradiction is resolved by the line 'Empty your heart of its mortal dream' in 'The Hosting of the Sidhe', with its emphasis on 'mortal.' Our dreams, as we know them, are only reflections of our dreams as they are, and 'substantial things' are only reflections of our dreams as we know them. That is why, in an early draught, Forgael prays: 'Deliver my heart from shadows of my heart'.[3] To 'give us *wholly* to the dreams' is to find a higher, not a lower, level of reality.

This form of solipsism does provide its own escape clause. The gods are not entangled among the shadows of their hearts, and Forgael and Dectora, though trapped by the gods, are also used by them as mortal bodies for the immortal lovers, Aengus and Edain. This is equivalent to saying that Forgael and Dectora are Aengus and Edain incarnate; or, in Northrop Frye's words, 'the gods who are dreaming them are their own projected selves'. Hence Forgael and Dectora can and do reverse 'the current of reality',[4] or empty their hearts of its mortal dream.

However, this is a solution which creates as many problems as it solves. Forgael and Dectora do not become less dreamy but more so. If this is equivalent to growing like gods, we have only the author's word for it. Even if that is true, Forgael and Dectora are not less subject to the will of the gods than formerly. They have no freedom of choice,[5] and therefore as tragedy *The Shadowy Waters* fails. The play's centre is unacceptably soft. It is all very well for Forgael and Dectora to sail away to dreamland, but one would like to know where and what that is. Without that information, this play is pointless. But that is the information which we do not get. Whether Forgael and Dectora are going to their deaths or going elsewhere is never satisfactorily settled.

II. The *Imram* Tradition

What Yeats provides instead of necessary information is a series of conflicting or ambiguous clues. The most prominent and ambiguous clue is the fact that *The Shadowy Waters* belongs to the tradition of the *imram*, or Otherworld Voyage. A sentence in *John Sherman* suggests that Yeats was inspired by 'The Voyage of Maeldune'.[6] He writes: 'Grey clouds covering the town with flying shadows rushed by like the old and dishevelled eagles that Maeldune saw hurrying towards the waters of life.'[7] These eagles are surely the prototypes of the human-headed birds in *The Shadowy Waters*.

Also relevant is a manuscript in the National Library of Ireland containing 'Notes for a Celtic Order' by Yeats and Annie Horniman. These notes virtually amount to a sketch of *The Shadowy Waters*. They involve 'such things as the Voyage of Life, a ship with a look-out man and helmsman, a wayfarer who is following "the four birds which Aengus made of his kisses, in the desolation of the world. "'[8] The expression 'Voyage of Life' exposes another weakness of this play. It is vague and makes no mention of the destination of that voyage. Traditional *imrama* are also ambiguous in this respect. They do not clearly distinguish between fairyland and the land of the dead. In 'The Death of Synge' (1909), Yeats simply sees no distinction: 'the voyages to Tir-nan-oge' of Early Irish literature, he says, were 'certainly the voyages of souls after death to the their place of peace' (A 343–44). This is not, in fact, an accurate description of most *imrama*. 'The Voyage of Brendan', for instance, is indeed quite obviously a voyage to the land of the dead, but it involves other ports of call along the way, and Brendan remains a live man throughout his voyage. Other *imrama*, like 'The Voyage of Bran', have no inescapable connection with death.

Yeats has couched his play in a tradition that is ambiguous to begin with, and in practice he has maintained that ambiguity. Indeed, Yeats sometimes passes beyond ambiguity to sheer confusion. For example, in the 1900 text of *The Shadowy Waters* Aibric says at one point: 'but our sail has passed / Even the wandering islands of the gods' (VP 749). Two pages later, Forgael says:

> ... I follow the grey wings,
> And need no more of life till the white wings
> Of Aengus' birds gleam in their apple boughs.

Both passages can refer to nowhere else than Emain Abhlach, the transmarine fairyland. How can Forgael hope to find it if he has already passed it? The substitution of Aengus for Manannan as lord of Emain Abhlach may be intended to recall the story of Baile and Aillinn, and so to imply that Emain Abhlach is the land of the dead. Equally, however, it may be forced by the importance of Aengus and unimportance of Manannan in *The Shadowy Waters*, or it may be a mere mistake. It certainly is not proof positive that Forgael is going to his death.

III. The Land of the Dead

On the other hand, there is a good deal of evidence to suggest that the land of the dead is indeed Forgael's destination. A very early draft contains these lines:

> My father I lived in a garden
> away in the south & because of
> evil omens & druids who pres-
> prophesied evil my father hid me
> in a garden in the south amid
> flowers & green boscage & one day
> a prince came but at last
> my lover o one came & we saw
> each other & loved & escaped.[9]

The words are Dectora's, but if one did not know that one would take them for Deirdre's. Yeats was, in fact, plotting *Deirdre* in July 1905, some years after he wrote the lines above, but at the same time as he was rewriting *The Shadowy Waters* and *The King's Threshold* and reading Arthur Symons' article on 'The Ideas of Richard Wagner'. He confessed to being influenced in his rewriting of *The Shadowy Waters* by Symons' article and, because of it, by Wagner himself. The single work of Wagner's that most influenced *The Shadowy Waters* was probably *Tristan und Isolde*, in which Michael P. Goldman, at any rate, finds a dénouement that reminds him of *Axël*. *Axël* in its turn particularly influenced the dénouement of *The Shadowy Waters*. The one thing that *Deirdre*, *The King's Threshold*, *Tristan und Isolde*, and *Axël* have in common is suicide. All except *The King's Threshold*, indeed, involve suicide pacts between lovers. It is not surprising, then, that *The Shadowy Waters* lends itself to exactly the same reading. F. S. Colwell sees the climax of both *Tristan und Isolde* and *The Shadowy Waters* 'as a struggle between the spiritual and material ... resolved, or more properly overwhelmed ... in a medley of night, love, death, and primordial oneness.'[10]

The moment of truth is the cutting of the rope. Dectora addresses it as 'ancient worm, / Dragon that loved the world and held us to it' (VP 251), and Northrop Frye points out that dragons and serpents often symbolise time.[11] Death is the most obvious way of 'breaking' time. As Aibric leaves to cut the rope, he cries:

> The yew-bough has been broken into two,
> And all the birds are scattered — O! O! O!
> Farewell! farewell!
>
> (VP 251)

The stage direction indicates that he is 'half falling into the keen', and well it may, for these are the same words used by the keening sailor at VP 241. In the 1900 text, in which Dectora cuts the rope herself, she says:

> I have cut the rope that bound this galley to ours,
> And while she fades and life withers away,
> I crown you with this crown.
>
> (VP 768)

A few lines later she says, in every text: 'Bend lower, that I may cover you with my hair, / For we will gaze upon this world no longer.' This is a direct echo of the suicide pact in *Axël*, when Sara utters the line 'O to veil you with my hair where you will breathe the spirit of dead roses'.[12]

Even without this information, the imagery of death is surely explicit enough.

There is, in fact, a series of allusions to death throughout the play, but what is most significant about these is their qualification. Forgael begins by speaking of

> ... these waters,
> Where I am rid of life — the events of the world —
> What do you call it? — that old promise-breaker,
> The cozening fortune-teller that comes whispering,
> 'You will have all you have wished for when you have earned
> Land for your children or money in a pot.'
>
> (VP 227–28)

The salient feature of this speech is Forgael's reluctance to use the word he means. 'What do you call it?' he asks, as if he has forgotten the word 'death'. But having said that he wishes to be rid of life, he immediately moderates this to 'the events of the world', and ends up suggesting that he is just a little tired of bourgeois domesticity, of which he can have known little in any case on board a pirate ship. He refuses to face the implication of his remark: 'And yet I cannot think they're leading me / To death' (VP 230). When Aibric flatly confronts him with the reality of his situation — 'It's certain they are leading you to death' (VP 231) — he merely shrugs it off: 'What matter / If I am going to my death?' He then proceeds as if Aibric had not said 'death' at all, but 'fairyland': 'I shall find a woman, / One of the Ever-living as I think' (VP 231). Eventually, Aibric puts the same home-truth to Dectora:

> And if that happiness be more than dreams,
> More than the froth, the feather, the dust-whirl,
> The crazy nothing that I think it is,
> It shall be in the country of the dead,
> If there be such a country.
>
> (VP 248–49)

Challenged to confirm or deny this, Forgael can only answer, like Yeats himself, 'I do not know for certain' (VP 249).

Why this hesitation? Yeats has already used death as the gateway to fairyland in the *Stories of Red Hanrahan*. Why is that more permissible there than here? Because, in every sense, the *Stories of Red Hanrahan* prepare for it and *The Shadowy Waters* does not. Hanrahan might have entered fairyland alive, but failed his initiation, and so spent his life preparing to pass his initiation at death. Forgael and Dectora, on the contrary, make no preparations. They merely sail and die. Similarly, the play itself has prepared for an apocalypse and what occurs, if this reading is followed, is simply a death.

IV. Fairyland

Even an ill-prepared death, however, would be preferable to the incompatible mixture of themes with which *The Shadowy Waters* presents us, for in the face of all the evidence that the land to which Forgael and Dectora are sailing is the land of the dead, there still remains other evidence that it is not. On the lines

> . . . in some island where the life of the world
> Leaps upward, as if all the streams o' the world
> Had run into one fountain,
>
> (VP 249)

Balachandra Rajan comments: 'Here the thrust of the poetry unmistakably suggests that the higher reality is continuous with the lower; the leap upward suggests both the vitality of nature and the aspiration to something above, which completes nature rather than denies it.'[13] Death does deny nature, and though it can be seen as the completion of life cannot be seen as its continuation. If the land at the world's end is meant to be the land of the dead, the details of its description are casually and inconsistently chosen. For example, in the 1900 text we read of the human-headed birds: 'They are sent by the lasting watchers to lead men away from this world and its women to some place of shining women that cast no shadow, having lived before the making of the earth' (VPl 319). If these women have always been alive, they cannot very well be dead.

If Forgael and Dectora are not sailing to the land of the dead, then of course they are sailing to fairyland. Again, the play contains a whole series of hints that they are putting on the fairy nature even as their voyage continues:

> . . . nothing matters
> But laughter and tears — laughter, laughter, and tears;
> That every man should carry his own soul
> Upon his shoulders;
>
> (VP 235)

> The movement of time
> Is shaken in these seas, and what one does
> One moment has no might upon the moment
> That follows after.
>
> (VP 237)

Here is developing that capriciousness which both folklore and Yeats take to be a mark of the fairies who live beyond the nets of good and evil.

When Forgael, posing as 'golden-armed Iollan', tells Dectora 'That the grave-diggers in a dreamy frenzy / Have buried nothing but my golden arms' (VP 243), he in fact suggests that a stock was buried in his place, and that he was therefore taken for a changeling and has thus become a fairy. Dectora certainly believes he is a fairy:

> Is it not true
> That you were born a thousand years ago,
> In islands where the children of Aengus wind
> In happy dances under a windy moon,
> And that you'll bring me there?

At this point Forgael confesses: 'I have deceived you; I have deceived you utterly' (VP 245). But Dectora's response to this is that Forgael's deception has now become the truth:

> What do I care,
> Now that my body has begun to dream,
> And you have grown to be a burning sod
> In the imagination and intellect?
> If something that's most fabulous were true —
> If you had taken me by magic spells,
> And killed a lover or husband at my feet —
> I would not let you speak, for I would know
> That it was yesterday and not today
> I loved him.
>
> (VP 245–46)

The birds — or Forgael — then confirm Dectora's belief that Forgael is bearing her to fairyland:

> *Dectora.* What are they? Unto what country do they fly?
> *Forgael.* To unimaginable happiness.
> ....
> They're crying out, could you but hear their words,
> 'There is a country at the end of the world
> Where no child's born but to outlive the moon.'
>
> (VP 247)

Children would not be born at all in the land of the dead.

V. The Ground of Being

When fairyland is not equivalent to death for Yeats, it is equivalent to a life superior to life, to something like the ground of being. Forgael states early on that he seeks 'The flagstone under all, the fire of fires, / The roots of the world' (VP 227). Whitaker identifies this flagstone with the 'alchemical *lapis* which is source and goal of the manifest world'.[14] The island of the fool may be seen as 'a temporary state of being in a process of becoming, a brief earthly shadow of the state of true being or unity to which the poet aspires'.[15] '. . . The wood of precious stones is "perhaps emotions made eternal by their own perfection".'[16]

This alternative to death works well for a while. It helps to explain the role of Dectora, for instance. She enters the play as Forgael's equal, which is why Forgael is inclined to reject her, but under his influence she becomes 'the Ever-living Woman, the ideal symbol of passion fused with beauty, that Forgael has been seeking',[17] and so becomes his guide to the land of her own heart. It is not Dectora who dies, but only 'Her memories of her previous life and attachments', her lower dreams.[18] This reading seems confirmed by a draught of the play written probably in 1896, and certainly no later than 1899, in which the rose on Forgael's breast and the lily on Dectora's are identified as 'Rose of the world & Lilly of the gods'.[19]

Attractive as it is, however, this reading is not without its problems. John Rees Moore, who advocates it, remarks that Forgael is not at first aware of Dectora's transformation.[20] Stranger still, neither is she. As late as l. 581 (out of 619), she is still begging to be taken home. Her transformation is apparently signalled by the behaviour of the birds in not leaving the ship, but even this is only Forgael's reluctant augury: 'You are not the world's core. O no, no, no! / That cannot be the meaning of the birds' (VP 234–35). In the end, the birds do leave without waiting for Dectora, so it is not clear that they were waiting for her in the first place. Dectora's transformation, like Forgael's, is something that may be implicit but is never plainly shown.

VI. Imagination

All of Yeats's previous work has led us to expect that fairyland will be the realm of the imagination, and so it may be. This is not so much an alternative to the ground of being as the sense in which it is to be understood. Ellmann points out that Forgael's harp, itself the symbol of Yeats's art, has two strains, one that awakens 'dreams of love' and one that awakens 'dreams of a love beyond mortal love'.[21] These two types of love correspond to the two types of imagination. As in *The Wind*

Among the Reeds, Yeats's creative imagination continues to celebrate the possibility of a self-sufficient imagination that generates no images. With his art, Yeats strives to reach beyond those images in which Forgael feels solipsistically entrapped to the ground of being or the imaginative apocalypse. This may be seen in ll. 499–500, which clearly echo 'Aedh tells of the Rose in his Heart': 'I weep — I weep because bare night's above, / And not a roof of ivory and gold' (VP 246). Forgael despises the nullity of his self-created world, and longs for a world of flawless artifice. He is thus the opposite of his mutinous sailors, who care nothing for symbolic ivory and gold, for the treasures of the imagination, but only for tangible treasure, created images.[22]

Unfortunately, there is no way within or without the structure of the play to fulfil Forgael's longings. Yeats is compelled to dodge the problem 'by having the lovers drift off in their private boat over the sea of generation to, again, a *future* union' and a future apocalypse.[23] How that apocalypse is to be achieved is simply not explained.

It would seem that Yeats must have recognised the frustration of his play's intentions in this respect, for the fool exists to bear the responsibility for it. According to a programme note which Yeats wrote for a performance of *The Shadowy Waters* before the Theosophical Congress, this character is simply the 'Fool of the Rath, the fairy fool of modern Irish folklore, from whose touch no man recovers'.[24] In fact, however, the fool in the play owes little to folklore, but a great deal to a figure cooked up by Yeats and his circle in a series of visions spread over at least six years.[25] What emerges from these visions is that the fool is associated with Aengus and Aengus is associated with poetry, ecstasy, and enthusiasm. This should be put beside the fact that it is from the fool that Forgael receives his harp, which is always in Yeats a symbol of art or imagination. It ought to follow that the fool symbolises inspiration, and this seems confirmed by the 1900 text, in which Forgael speaks of 'the fool, who has made the wisdom that men write' (VP 764). Though Forgael thinks himself inspired, however, everyone else has his doubts. Indeed, even Forgael says:

> The fool has made
> These messengers to lure men to his peace,
> Where true-love wanders among his holy woods.

The word 'lure' undermines the supposed benevolence of the fool, and this point evidently is not lost on Dectora, who replies:

> What were true-love among the rush of his streams?
> The gods weave nets, and take us in their nets,
> And none knows wherefore.
>   (VP 764)

Forgael's inspiration, like the 'true-love' which he seeks, may be simply a delusion that makes him serviceable to the fool. On the other hand, of course, it may be genuine. Thomas L. Byrd concludes that 'The Fool of the Wood ... is the irrational element that drives men to madness. The madness, here, however, is madness only to the prosaic mind. For Forgael it is enlightenment.'[26] It is this ambiguity that makes the uncertainty of the apocalypse in *The Shadowy Waters* inevitable. When the inspiration cannot be relied upon, neither can its fruits.

For obvious reasons, this hesitation as to whether death or transfiguration is intended most keenly affects the climax of the play. It is inherent, however, in every part of the play, and even in the prefatory poem, 'I walked among the seven woods of Coole.' This poem hints that the speaker, Yeats himself, is possessed of great but secret wisdom:

> And more I may not write of, for they that cleave
> The waters of sleep can make a chattering tongue
> Heavy like stone, their wisdom being half silence.
>
> (VP 218)

Actually, the poem is an honest though unintentional confession of failure.[27] Yeats may not write of this wisdom because he does not possess it. He has already admitted as much: 'I had not eyes like those enchanted eyes.' He has only 'dreamed' himself surrounded by fairies. Since he cannot give himself wholly to those dreams, he is in the same position as Forgael. Has he forgotten that Forgael's dreams are the condition of error, not of truth? The crucial lines of the poem are ll. 27–40, and they are very weak indeed. The question which they repeat five times is simply whether fairyland is immanent or transcendent. This is a question of considerable relevance, as an immanent fairyland is one that Forgael might hope to find alive. It becomes a test of vision, as in the *Stories of Red Hanrahan*. A transcendent fairyland, on the other hand, he can find only through death. The relevance of this question, however, cannot alter the fact that the philosophical issue raised is elementary and scarcely worth so much attention. This failing is aggravated by the very fact that these lines are written in questions. At its best, the hallmark of Yeats's style is assertion so bold that it defies gainsaying: 'O heart the winds have shaken, the unappeasable host / Is comelier than candles at Mother Mary's feet.' Here, the case is just the reverse. These questions are not rhetorical. They expect no answer. They may be intended to suggest a profound mediation, but all they actually convey is that Yeats does not know how to answer them.

That is true of the play's great question too, the question of whither Forgael and Dectora are sailing when the final curtain falls. There is, of course, nothing inherently wrong about an open ending, but in *The Shadowy Waters* the open ending does not serve to provoke thought but to disguise the paucity of the author's thought. Yeats summarised the ambiguity of the play's ending in *The Arrow*: 'Forgael and the woman drift on alone following the birds, awaiting death and what comes after, or some mysterious transformation of the flesh, an embodiment of every lover's dream' (VPl 340). Death or transfiguration? Yeats seems to suggest that it is up to us to choose, but this is not a fair burden to place on the reader when the play itself is so confused as to suggest that the souls of the dead fly to the land of the immortals.

The play's ending is further damaging to its entire structure. Leonard E. Nathan points out that Forgael resembles Oedipus, Macbeth, and other tragic heroes in founding a scheme of overweening ambition upon an ambiguous oracle. Because he is a tragic hero, however, we expect a tragic play. We expect a form of *nemesis* to follow the *hubris* involved in relying on the oracle. Instead, the play ends as ambiguously as it began, and so thwarts all tragic expectations.[28]

Since *The Shadowy Waters* is a failure, there is no obvious sense in which Yeats can be said to have faced up to the suicidal implications which his work had been generating. It is more as though, having recognised that they exist, he has decided not to face them. Anticlimactic though it is, however, this decision may still be perceived as the response of a fundamentally healthy mind to an obsession which has grown morbid. Yeats appears to have simply lost interest in the concerns which have driven him thus far. From now on, his poetry exhibits a different, more Apollonian mood. From the vantage point of *Responsibilities*, however, he does take time to turn round and bid farewell to the early phase of his career.

17. 'I HAVE NO HAPPINESS IN DREAMING OF BRYCELINDE'

A major change in Yeats's attitude towards poetry and life in general began to occur between the 1900 and 1906 versions of *The Shadowy Waters*. During 1904, Yeats wrote to A. E.: 'I cannot possibly be quite just to any poetry that speaks to me with the sweet insinuating feminine voice of the dwellers in that country of the shadows and hollow nights. I have dwelt there too long not to dread all that comes of it.'[1] He has grown hostile to the fairies. This change of heart evidently occurred early enough to influence a couple of poems in *In the Seven Woods* (1904). Side by side with 'The Happy Townland' in that book we find 'Under the Moon' and 'The Withering of the Boughs', both of which at least make gestures towards a rejection of the fairy faith.

The process of rejection reached completion in *Responsibilities* (1914). In this book, as indeed in *In the Seven Woods*, precisely because the fairy faith is no longer of great importance to Yeats, there are not many poems about it. Those there are constitute an explicit rejection of the fairies and of all those attitudes and issues which they have symbolised or with which they have come to be associated during the early phase of Yeats's career. This shift in Yeats's position is not complacent. He realises and admits that he is perforce giving up much that is valuable along with much that is outworn, and that the universe of his new poetry is meaner than the universe of his old. Like Crazy Jane, however, he realises that a heavenly mansion would be all very well, but a foul sty is home. Like the Magi, for all that, he is unsatisfied. As they have grown weary of Christ, he has grown weary of the fairies, but he still hopes for a rebirth of the supernatural. 'The Magi' itself and 'The Cold Heaven' provide the first inkling of what this is to be. 'The Magi' is the first poem in which the philosophy of *A Vision* begins to emerge, and 'The Cold Heaven' records a mystical experience of a type quite new to Yeats. Indeed, it might well be called Yeats's first genuine mystical experience of any kind: it is a vision, not an hallucination. Yeats discovers that the universe is supernatural in a way that he has never suspected. The cold, bright light of that discovery expels the fairies and makes all symbolism redundant.

I. 'Under the Moon'

'Under the Moon' is a poem that until recently defied any detailed explication, because not all of its allusions had been identified. Thanks mainly to Sheila O'Sullivan, we are now better informed. Brycelinde is the wood where Vivien imprisoned Merlin; Avalon needs no identification and Joyous Isle is sufficiently identified in the text; l. 4 refers to the story of Deirdre, and specifically, it would seem, to the state of Ulster while Deirdre and Naoise were in exile in Scotland; Land-under-Wave refers simply to fairyland; Land-of-the-Tower remains the most obscure allusion in the poem, but Jeffares suggests that it refers to the 'house of glass' in which 'Etain . . . took refuge . . . with Aengus,' according to Yeats's note on *Baile and Aillinn* (VP 188).[2] Lines 9–10 and 13 derive from a long *scéal* called *Eachtra Cloinne Righ na h-Ioruaidhe* (Adventures of the Children of the King of Norway), translated by Douglas Hyde. The hero, Cod, before entering the Forest of Wonders, meets a 'wood-woman, who tells him that her lover has been 'changed to a blue-eyed hawk' by the vindictive daughter of the King of Greece'. Later, in the Forest of Wonders, Cod kills 'a wondrous ox, and two gold horns on him, and a horn trumpet in his mouth', but thereafter, as the poem tells, sees the ox borne before him on a golden bier.[3] Guinevere needs no identification; Branwen features in the *Mabinogion*. She is the daughter of Llyr, of Wales, and wife of Matholwch, king of Ireland, by whom she is mistreated, so causing war between Ireland and Wales. Yeats probably has in mind her utterance, 'Alas . . . woe is me that I was ever born; two islands have been destroyed because of me!' which relates her to Guinevere, the bane of Arthur's kingdom (as well as to Deidre).[4] Line 12 is more or less self-explanatory.

Next one must account for the title of the poem. The moon is mentioned in l. 6 and ll. 17–18. It may also be present symbolically in ll. 9–10. It is possible that the golden horns of the bull are a lunar symbol in the original *scéal*; even if they are not, such an interpretation might well have been suggested to Yeats by Thomas Boyd's poem 'The Brown Bull': 'Awful, upon his brow he hath / The great horns of the moon.'[5] The moon should be taken, I think, in its classical significance, as Juliet's 'inconstant moon', a symbol of mutability. This allows Maud Gonne to enter the scheme of the poem as a fixed point for Yeats's passions, something beyond 'the circle of the moon / That pitches common things about' ('Nineteen Hundred and Nineteen,' VP 428). With her 'irretrievable loss', Yeats's life is reduced to a 'drifting indefinite bitterness'.

The poem's first thirteen lines break down into three sections, ll. 1–4, 5–10, and 11–13, each repeating the same movement and so mimicking a tidal pattern or the phases of the moon itself. Yeats begins with Brycelinde, where Merlin found sleep and relief from his obsession with Vivien; Avalon, of course, is Arthur's place of healing; Lancelot at Joyous Isle likewise found rest, but only 'for a while'. Needless to say, Yeats identifies with Merlin, Arthur, and Lancelot. In the next line he must identify with Conchobar, left alone with his grief after Deirdre has eloped with Naoise.[6] Throughout these four lines, then, there is a gradual diminution of the consolation available.

We then return to images of escape into fairyland. Aengus throwing the gates apart is possibly suggested by the ancient hill-carving of the Long Man of Wilmington, who may be seen either as holding two rods in his hands or as holding open a great door in the side of the hill — a gesture of invitation. Land-under-Wave and Land-of-the-Tower are 'lands that seem too dim to be burdens on the heart', but the emphasis is on 'seem', for in Wood-of-Wonders the apparently vanquished moon (the ox) returns and dispels the illusion of repose.

The destructive queens, Branwen and Guinevere, appear. They seem remote from Yeats, but they are reminiscent of her who

> . . . would of late
> Have taught to ignorant men most violent ways,
> Or hurled the little streets upon the great

('No Second Troy,' VP 256). Niamh, Laban, and Fand, the shape-shifters, reintroduce the theme of mutability, and Yeats then falls victim to it again, being 'changed to a blue-eyed hawk'. Thus the dreams of fairyland that have sustained Yeats's poetry hitherto have now betrayed him. He has 'no happiness in dreaming of Brycelinde'.

II. 'The Withering of the Boughs'

The same theme is stated less emphatically in 'The Withering of the Boughs'. Stanzas two and three again rehearse Yeats's dreams of fairyland. Significantly, they include a dream of 'A king and a queen' — Baile and Aillinn — who found an eternity of love in fairyland. Yeats tells his dreams, and consequently the boughs wither. This is a folk belief which we find also in *The Celtic Twilight* (M 116): 'our dreams lose their wisdom when the sap rises in the trees, and . . . our dreams can make the trees wither.'[7] Yeats tells his dreams on the fairy hill of Slieve Echtge, and so, by making the boughs wither there, Yeats, in effect, makes his dreams wither too. Withered dreams, of course, must be discarded.

III. 'Running to Paradise'

In 'Under the Moon' and 'The Withering of the Boughs', then, we see Yeats parting with his dreams of fairyland, but doing so regretfully. In *Responsibilities*, on the contrary, we see him parting happily with these dreams, as with encumbrances no longer wanted or required. At first sight, an exception might seem to be 'Running to Paradise', a poem superficially rather like 'The Happy Townland'. Discrepancies emerge, however, when we consider the source from which the title derives, which is, as Sheila O'Sullivan has pointed out, a story of St. Brigit:

> One time she was minding her sheep on the Curragh, and she saw a son of reading running past her. 'What is it makes you so uneasy?' she said, 'and what is it you are looking for?' 'It is to Heaven I am running, woman of the veil' said the scholar. . . . Then they said 'Our Father' together, and he was religious from that out, and it was he gave her absolution at the last. And it is by reason of him that the whole of the sons of learning are with Brigit.

Yeats presumably counts himself among the sons of learning, but he has made some changes in the story. As O'Sullivan has again pointed out, the opening line 'As I came over Windy Gap' (VP 300), is derived from a riddle that would have been familiar to many in Yeats's contemporary Irish audience and that begins, 'As I was going through Slippery Gap / I met a little man with a red cap.'[8] A little man with a red cap, is a fairy. Hence, Yeats is not running to the Christian Paradise, but to fairyland. The same fact is further indicated in the final stanza:

> The wind is old and still at play
> While I must hurry upon my way,
> For I am running to Paradise;
> Yet never have I lit on a friend
> To take my fancy like the wind
> That nobody can buy or bind.
>
> (VP 301)

The wind has been associated with the fairies in Yeats's verse since at least 'The Hosting of the Sidhe', but here the association is uneasy, for Windy Gap (a pass in the townland of Carrickhenry, Co. Sligo)[9] is, according to Daniel Hoffman, 'the spot at which the spirits of the dead would appear to a mortal and summon or abduct him'.[10] 'Running to Paradise', then, envisages a similar destination to Forgael's. However, in this poem, Yeats is not half in love with easeful death. Recognising his fantasy's morbidity, he rejects it. He interrupts his journey to 'Paradise' as the runner in the story of St. Brigit interrupts his. Brigit clearly intends a reproach to the son of learning when she stops him, perhaps because, like a suicide, he would take 'out of the hands of God the choice of the time and manner of our death, and by so doing [make] His power the less', as Yeats puts it in 'Out of the Rose' (M 163). The fact that the son of learning becomes religious plainly implies that he was not truly religious before. Having become religious, he does not resume his journey. In the parallel situation of 'Running to Paradise', then, Yeats rejects the pursuit of fairyland and rejects the pursuit of death. The further implications of the Brigit story should not be taken too literally: T. R. Henn considers that in 'The Three Hermits' Yeats rejects holiness as well.[11]

IV. 'The Two Kings'

In 'The Two Kings', yet another retelling of the Edain story, Yeats takes the cancellation of *The Shadowy Waters* a stage further. From this point of view, the most important lines are these:

> . . . With a most masterful voice
> That made the body seem as it were a string
> Under a bow, he cried, 'What happiness
> Can lovers have that know their happiness
> Must end at the dumb stone? But where we build
> Our sudden palaces in the still air
> Pleasure itself can bring no weariness,
> Nor can time waste the cheek, nor is there foot
> That has grown weary of the wandering dance,
> Nor an unlaughing mouth, but mine that mourns,
> Among those mouths that sing their sweethearts' prise,
> Your empty bed.' How should I love,' I answered,
> 'were it not that when the dawn has lit my bed
> And shown my husband sleeping there, I have sighed,
> 'Your strength and nobleness will pass away'?
> Or how should love be worth its pains were it not
> That when he has fallen asleep within my arms,
> Being wearied out, I love in man the child?
> What can they know of love that do not know
> She builds her nest upon a narrow ledge
> Above a windy precipice?'
>
> (VP 284–85)

The first speaker here — Midhir, although unnamed — advocates Forgael's position. Edain's reply is one that did not occur to Aibric or Dectora. Forgael proposes that 'What the world's million lips are thirsting for / Must be substantial somewhere' (VP 229). Aibric, essentially, just denies that this is true. Dectora admits that Forgael speaks the truth, but opts (at first) for what she conceives of as security:

> O carry me
> To some sure country, some familiar place.
> Have we not everything that life can give
> In having one another?
>
> (VP 249)

Edain, on the contrary, accepts Forgael's view that it is earthly love that is insecure because it is subject to time and change and death, but argues that that is all that makes love possible. Yeats is no more sceptical now than ever of the reality of fairyland and of its accessibility, through death if necessary ('Seeing that when you come to the deathbed / You must return' [VP 285]), but his response is no longer enthusiastic. It is not negative either. It is merely indifferent. Fairyland exists, but for the time being earth is more important; for fairyland, Yeats can wait. There is still one more twist to this. As D. S. Savage perceives, the very existence of fairyland ensures that this world is second-rate.[12] In committing ourselves to this world, we should be under no illusion that we are serving a splendid cause.

V. 'The Hour Before Dawn'

'The Hour Before Dawn' constitutes Yeats's clearest rejection of his earlier attitudes. Indeed, it not only rejects them, but parodies them. T. R. Henn has called attention to a relevant passage in 'The Autumn of the Body' (1898): 'Man has wooed and won the world, and has fallen weary, and not, I think, for a time, but with a weariness that will not end until the last autumn, when the stars shall be blown away like withered leaves' (E &I 192–93).[13] In 'The Hour Before Dawn', we find this weary man, Yeats's own dreamy self, snoring away time in the Cave of Cruachan. His philosophy still remains 'Where there is nothing, there is God', and he still awaits God's 'white foot-fall':

> And there's no man but cocks his ear
> To know when Michael's trumpet cries
> That flesh and bone may disappear,
> And souls as if they were but sighs,
> And there be nothing but God left.
>
> (VP 306–07)

The reference to Michael's trumpet, rather than the more conventional

Gabriel's, may be a deliberate recollection of 'The Happy Townland': 'Michael will unhook his trumpet' (VP 215).

This sleeper, then, shares many traits with the early Yeats, but he is made ridiculous by being made literal. He does not dwell 'deep / Among pale eyelids, heavy with sleep / Men have named beauty' (VP 169) — he snores in a hole. As Savage remarks, 'The reversal here in Yeats's implied attitude to 'dreams' is complete'.[14] The dreamer, in fact, is condemned out of his own mouth:

> You cry aloud, O would 'twere spring
> Or that the wind would shift a point,
> And do not know that you would bring,
> If time were suppler in the joint,
> Neither the spring nor the south wind
> But the hour when you shall pass away
> And leave no smoking wick behind,
> For all life longs for the Last Day.
>
> (VP 306)

The dreamer is wishing his life away. Besides being asleep, he is drunk. He is, in fact, the drunkard of 'The Blessed'. This quietistical drunkard has turned his back on life. Frank Hughes Murphy adds that his 'concealment within rocks is especially revealing, since rocks symbolize for Yeats a fanatical resistance to change and, thus, to life itself (as in the later "Easter 1916")'.[15] The drunkard's defence of himself in the lines above — 'You're no better than I am' — hardly justifies his conduct anyway, but even as an accusation is specious. As Henn points out, in longing for spring the beggar wishes the world to abbreviate, not prolong, its winter sleep.[16] When the sleeper disparages the details of nature,

> The lapwing at their foolish cries
> And the sheep bleating at the wind
> As when I also played the fool,
>
> (VP 306)

the beggar answers forthrightly:

> It's plain that you are no right man
> To mock at everything I love
> As if it were not worth the doing.
>
> (VP 306)

He presently begins to give the drunkard 'a great pummelling', but the other has gone to sleep again and he 'might have pummelled at a stone

/ For all the sleeper knew or cared' (VP 307). There is no getting through to those who cut themselves off from the world. Finally, the beggar

> ... prayed and cursed and cursed and fled
> From Maeve and all that juggling plain,
> Nor gave God thanks till overhead
> The clouds were brightening with the dawn.
>
> (VP 307)

Yeats, in his new persona, flees from all the escapist, fairy preoccupations of his early work.

VI. 'The Cold Heaven'

Yeats's rejection of the fairies and the paraphernalia of the fairy faith does not constitute a rejection of the supernatural *per se*. If it did, he could hardly have included 'The Realists' in *Responsibilities*:

> Hope that you may understand!
> What can books of men that wive
> In a dragon-guarded land,
> Paintings of the dolphin-drawn
> Sea-nymphs in their pearly wagons
> Do, but awake a hope to live
> That had gone
> With the dragons?
>
> (VP 309)

'The Magi' demonstrates Yeats's changed perspective on the supernatural. The Magi themselves are like persons whose wish was granted by the 'Master of the still stars and of the flaming door.' They found a Dionysian apocalypse in the Incarnation, and consequently are cast out of the world. Now they desire an Apollonian revelation to call them home again.[17]

Yeats's own Apollonian revelation is embodied in 'The Cold Heaven', a much stranger and more complex poem than many of its exegetes suppose. This is a poem that has particularly suffered from an overemphasis on biographical criticism. T. R. Henn states boldly that 'It is occasioned by the marriage of Maud Gonne to MacBride'[18] (it was first published nine years after that event). To Harold Bloom, it expresses 'torment to the poet who could not sustain his self-annihilating quest for the impossible beloved'.[19] The poem mentions memories 'of love crossed long ago' (VP 316), so Henn and Bloom cannot be entirely wrong. It is worth noticing, however, that Maud Gonne herself, who may have understood Yeats's poetry as well as any of his contemporaries, was far from recognising at once a sort of anti-epithalamion in the poem. On the contrary, she found it necessary to ask Yeats its meaning, 'and was told that it was an attempt to describe the feelings aroused in him by the cold detached sky in winter. He felt he was alone, responsible in his loneliness for all the past mistakes that were torturing his peace of mind.'[20] Yeats said nothing of love, though he was not normally too shy to tell his heart to Maud Gonne. As usual, then, the biographical element in the poem is not its most important aspect.

Indeed, a comparison with 'King and No King' (1909) suggests that the vision of 'The Cold Heaven,' rather than reflecting Yeats's inability to cope with his emotions, as Bloom thinks, utterly transcends and cancels that source of torment. 'King and No King', which is explicitly about Maud Gonne's marriage, includes these lines:

> And I that have not your faith, how shall I know
> That in the blinding light beyond the grave
> We'll find so good a thing as that we have lost?
>
> (VP 258)

This implies that life's emotions are simply not sustained 'in the blinding light beyond the grave'. In 'The Cold Heaven', Yeats, finding himself 'riddled with light' while still alive, passes beyond those emotions. The word 'Until' has been overlooked. Yeats wrestles with his emotions *until*, suddenly, he achieves his moment of vision. Then the light from beyond the grave shines into his life and those emotions fall away.

The nature of Yeats's experience becomes somewhat more clear when the question of what 'the books' are is answered. Balachandra Rajan considers that the books are only 'thrown into the path of the poem to be swept aside by its impetus'.[21] I should say, on the contrary, that the collision of the definite article with the unspecified books demands an explanation. It is equivalent to writing 'Books' with a capital B. Henn suggests that Yeats's reference is to Berkeley,[22] but Jeffares retorts that Yeats had probably not read Berkeley at this time.[23] Ellmann mentions Dante, the *Book of Enoch*, and Ruysbroeck ('whose statement that the mystic ecstasy is "not this or that" Yeats incorporated in one of the lines').[24] *Axël*, certainly one of Yeats's sacred books, appears to have had some influence on 'The Cold Heaven'. In it, the Arch deacon says to Sara, after her renunciation of her religious vows, 'No, you shall certainly not go wandering on the roads like a human being, scattering to the winds what little remains of your soul!'.[25] There is a tale of a cold, half-naked ghost in O'Hanlon's *Irish Local Legends* (which Yeats included in the bibliographies of *Irish Fairy Tales* and *Fairy and Folk Tales of the Irish Peasantry*),[26] while Yeats collected one similar Irish folk-tale himself and mentions in commenting on it a 'cold and naked' ghost in Herodotus.[27] Such books as these, however, are hardly authorities on spiritual matters and so would not seem to merit the dignity of the definite article.

On the other hand, sources both ancient and serious can be found in the Early Irish *Vision of Adamnan* and *Vision of Tundal*. In the first of these, 'certain souls after death' are said to 'pass a restless existence until Judgment on heights and hill-tops, and in marshy places,' attended by their guardian angels. These represent the *mali non valde*.' In *The Vision of Tundal*, these *mali non valde* are said to 'suffer from the effects of rain and wind, hunger and thirst, but . . . are not deprived of light, and . . . go to rest after some years'.[28]

The experience of these ghosts, the *mali non valde*, is obviously very similar to that of the ghost in 'The Cold Heaven'. They are neither in heaven nor in hell, but in a form of purgatory. Too many critics of 'The Cold Heaven' have oversimplified the state described there. For B. L. Reid, the ghost suffers 'the malevolence of the cosmos';[29] for Balachandra Rajan, its suffering is 'frighteningly compounded by the injustice poured on [it] by a malignant universe'.[30] Such judgments overlook the title of the poem: it is 'The Cold *Heaven*', not 'The Cold Hell'. Even the title is paradoxical, however, for in Early Irish literature it is indeed hell that is often said to be cold.[31] Yeats mentions this tradition himself, and if anything rather exaggerates it (VP 795–96). The paradox in his title is certainly deliberate. Harold Bloom offers the rather unconvincing explanation that the cold heaven is 'delight to *antithetical* birds, but torment to the poet . . .'[32] The true explanation surely lies in the purgatorial existence of the *mali non valde*, but with a further twist. Whereas Purgatory is neither Heaven nor Hell, the condition of 'The Cold Heaven' is both simultaneously.

Another word in the poem that receives insufficient attention is 'Suddenly'. In a moment, Yeats's ordinary perception of the sky is rapt to vision. This is a point to be remembered by those who apparently think that the poem derives from an introspective meditation. On the contrary, it records a rending of the veil. For Yeats, this is the veil between life and death. His mind is suddenly awakened, and from this sudden awakening stems his equally sudden emotional storm. He undergoes a period of emotional turmoil side by side with the experience of expanded consciousness.

But as his awareness of enhanced reality grows still more

overwhelming, no room remains for the egotistical indulgence of emotion. Yeats is not merely aware of light, but 'Riddled with light'. The choice of word, 'Riddled', recalls 'riddled with bullets'. The experience is so overwhelming that it is perceived as painful, as a devastating assault upon the self. This is the experience of ego-loss, of the merging of subject and object — hence, again, the appropriateness of 'Riddled', implying interpenetration. From this painful aspect of the experience stem the hellish connotations of the title and the poem. When Yeats considers the soul after death, he again transposes the image, from riddled with bullets or light to pelted with rain: 'stricken / By the injustice of the skies for punishment?' But for the ghost, as for the living man, the pain involved is the price to pay for the access of supreme clarity: 'Confusion of the death-bed over' — hence the heavenly connotations of the title and the poem. In *The Vision of Tundal* such souls 'go to rest after some years'. In every sense of the word, 'The Cold Heaven' records the *ecstatic* process of acquiring serenity. By the title, by the juxtaposition of Yeats's living experience and his speculation about death, and by the parallelism of 'Riddled with light' and 'stricken / By the injustice of the skies', the veil between life and death is rent. The 'blinding light beyond the grave' bursts forth to irradiate life as well as death. Thus, there is no more seeking for fairyland. The black birds of this world are as good as the white birds of the otherworld, for this world, with all its rooks, stands transfigured. There is no need to look elsewhere for supernatural rapture.

VII. Conclusion

During a period of twenty-two years, then, Yeats first longs desperately and hopelessly for fairyland, then persuades himself that his longings are about to be fulfilled, then finally grows tired of those longings and gives them up. In this respect, as in so many others, Yeats was the leader of the Celtic Renaissance. It would not be completely true to say that no fairy tales have come out of Ireland since 1914, but very few have. Even in the case of Lord Dunsany, it is a curious fact that his fairy tales are set in Spain or in 'little countries at the edge of the world' or 'beyond the fields we know,' while *The Curse of the Wise Woman*, which is set in Ireland, has practically nothing to do with the fairies.

Does this correspond to the final extinction of the fairy faith among the people? I would very much doubt it. Before and during my own fieldwork in Co. Sligo I was told repeatedly that the fairy faith no longer existed. As it happened, I was able to find believers with no great difficulty. It is true that old people tend to take the fairies more seriously than the young, and because of this it has been said that the belief will soon be extinct. This is to overlook the fact that the same was being said when today's old people were young themselves. In reality, it always has been the old people who have chiefly maintained the fairy faith.

It is also interesting that in England, where the fairy faith was indeed very close to extinction, there has been a significant revival in this century. I have heard it suggested that this is the reaction of a people that has begun to grow weary of the Industrial Revolution. If that is so, Ireland is likely to follow in due course. I would conclude, then, that the outlook for the fairy faith is very much brighter than is generally supposed. Whether it will find again an exponent of the calibre of W. B. Yeats is in the lap of the gods.

APPENDICES

APPENDIX A: MORTAL PROTÉGÉS OF THE TUATHA DÉ DANANN

Several among the Tuatha Dé Danann are connected more or less obviously, though in varying ways, with certain individual mortals. These connections can sometimes broaden our understanding of the Tuatha Dé Danann. However, the precise nature of the relationship between immortals and their mortal protégés remains problematical. Although the word 'avatar' is often used, it is used rather carelessly. On the other hand, it may be that no more precise term exists. Let us first look at some comparatively easy examples.

I. The Dagda and Angus Óg

The Dagda seems related to two mortal individuals. Surprisingly, neither of these is of great importance in mythology. One is a certain Nuada, the slave of Eoghan Mór, the founder of the Eoghanacht dynasty of Munster. Just as the Dagda built raths for Bres, this Nuada was also 'a famous rath builder'. In him, as in the Dagda, 'was the strength of a hundred, and he would eat the fill of fifty'. Eoghan once moved a huge stone for him, causing a druid to exclaim, 'Noble is thy slave today. O Nauda!' (*Is saér do mogh aníu, a Núadha!*), whence Eoghan acquired his nickname, Mugh Nuadat, 'the slave of Nuada'.[1] Since Eoghan is far more important than Nuada, it seems likely that it was originally he who shared the traits of the Dagda. What is harder to explain is the fact that Nuada shares the characteristics of the Dagda but the name of a quite different member of the Tuatha Dé Danann.

No such problem arises in the case of the monk Constantine, formerly king of Alba. This figure of hagiography, not mythology, is so reminiscent of the Dagda that one thinks of Heine's Gods in Exile or Pater's 'Denys l'Auxerrois'. Constantine is the champion of St. Mochuda, whom he protects with a club like the Dagda's. Like the Dagda, he levels forests and digs trenches. He eats the share of a hundred men until Mochuda sains his mouth, after which he still retains the strength of a hundred. Just as Indech forces the Dagda to eat a huge porridge before the Battle of Moytura, so Constantine is made to eat at one sitting all of his rations left uneaten during a temporary absence, even though some of it is wormy and all mixed unpalatably together.[2]

Angus Óg's protégé is Diarmuid Ó Duibhne. In the Fenian Cycle, Diarmuid is in fact portrayed as Angus' fosterson, but A. H. Krappe thinks he was originally a closer relative. Diarmuid has a mole on his forehead that makes him irresistible to women, and this, Krappe argues, 'would rather betray the hero as a child or an avatar of the god of love'.[3]

II. Manannan

Manannan, like the Dagda, has one clear descendant in hagiographical literature and one protégé in secular literature. The former is St. Scuithin, who, like Manannan, perceives the sea as 'a flowery shamrock-bearing plain', and thus travels to and from Rome across the sea on foot.[4]

Manannan's secular protégé is Mongan, a most mysterious figure. Mongan was a fully historical minor Ulster king who lived well within the Christian era, and yet the stories about him are steeped in paganism and the supernatural, although some at least date from as early as the eighth century, only 100–150 years after his own time.[5] Alfred Nutt argues that the stories actually predate the historical Mongan, and concerned originally a different and unhistorical figure of the same name. Ironically, however, he bases his argument on similarities between the *Mabinogion* and the one Mongan story which is almost certainly much later, not earlier, than the others — perhaps as late as the fifteenth century.[6]

Bran mac Febail, the hero of a famous *imram*, met Manannan riding on the waves, at which time Manannan prophesied to him on the one hand the coming of Christ, and on the other the coming of Mongan. He boasted that Mongan, like himself, would be a great shape-shifter:

> He will be in the shape of every beast,
> Both on the azure sea and on land,
> He will be a dragon before hosts at the onset,
> He will be a wolf in every great forest.
>
> He will be a stag with horns of silver
> In the land where chariots are driven,
> He will be a speckled salmon in a full pool,
> He will be a seal, he will be a fair-white swan.[7]

Appendix A: Mortal Protégés of the Tuatha Dé Dannan

Having been the prophet of Mongan, Manannan in due course becomes his father. His mother is Caintigern, the wife of Fiachna Lurga, or Fiachna Finn, the king of Ulster. When Mongan is three days old, Manannan takes him to be fostered for twelve years in the Land of Promise. It is on his return that Mongan reveals himself as a master of shape-shifting and magic. In a single story, he twice shifts his own shape to that of another person, in one case so convincingly that he has the original executed as an impostor. He also transforms his servant into the likeness of a certain prince and an ugly old woman into the likeness of the prince's beautiful young wife. The old woman's wretched dog and horses he turns to fine ones. Finally, he creates an insubstantial bridge out of nothing.[8]

On one occasion, Mongan conversed with St. Columcille and astonished him with his wisdom. He revealed fairy islands to him, the kingdom of Manannan. He also showed that his shape-shifting ability extended beyond glamour to transmigration, for he spoke of his previous incarnations.[9]

III. The Problem of the Avatar

The relationships of the Dagda, Angus Óg, and Manannan with their protégés are all comparatively straightforward. Complications arise with other mortals and other members of the Tuatha Dé. Take, for instance, the conception and birth of Cúchulainn. In one version of this story, Cúchulainn is first conceived when Dechtire, the sister of Conchobar, swallows a mayfly in her wine at her wedding feast with Sualtim mac Roigh. Afterwards, Lugh appears to her in a dream and reveals that he was the mayfly. Later, Conchobar, not recognising Dechtire, desires to sleep with her. Although there is a clear implication of incest, Dechtire is found to be already in labour and gives birth to a boy. The boy is named Setanta but later acquires the name Cúchulainn.[10]

In an earlier version of the story, Setanta is first born to Lugh and a woman of the Tuatha Dé Danann, but dies while being raised by Dechtire. He is rebegotten by Lugh on Dechtire but aborted, and is begotten for the third and final time by Sualtaim on Dechtire.[11]

When these stories are both considered, it is quite legitimate to say that Cúchulainn has three fathers. He is indeed the son of Lugh. He gives himself that name on one occasion,[12] and in the *Táin* Lugh likewise calls himself the father of Cúchulainn.[13] But it is equally true that Cúchulainn is the son of Sualtaim and Conchobar. Tomás Ó

Cathasaigh argues that Cúchulainn is first of wholly divine parentage (Lugh and the Dé Danann woman), next of mixed parentage, and finally of purely mortal parentage. He is thus a mediator between the divine and the human.[14]

It may be said that this describes the function of an avatar. Krappe (for one) specifically applies the word 'avatar' to Diarmuid Ó Duibhne. Is the word justified, then? I think not. In the first place, of course, only one god properly has avatars, and that is the Indian god Vishnu. If we are to use the word of other gods (let alone of the Tuatha Dé Danann, who are not gods, at least in the Indian sense), we must at all events use it very carefully. All of Vishnu's avatars are born in the flesh to two mortal parents, but informed with the spirit of the god. That may be the case with the monk Constantine, for instance, as his resemblance to the Dagda oversteps the bounds of coincidence although they have no ties of kinship. *Pace* Krappe, it will only be the case with Diarmuid Ó Duibhne if he is *not* the son of Angus Óg. It cannot really be said to be the case with Cúchulainn. Although he does have two mortal parents, he is related to Lugh in more than the spirit. The fact is that he has more than two parents. Also, he is not, during his lifetime, the exclusive embodiment of Lugh, for the two of them appear side by side in *Táin*.[15] Cúchulainn thus conforms more closely to the European concept of the demi-god than to the Asian concept of the avatar. He is of mixed parentage and has an identity quite separate from that of his supernatural father, Lugh.

Even the word 'demi-god' can hardly be admitted, however, if we are reluctant to accord Lugh the status of a god. Can we at least term Cúchulainn Lugh's mortal 'counterpart'? This too, I think, would be inaccurate. In the first place, Cúchulainn has affiliations with Manannan as well as with Lugh. He has a 'concealing cloak . . . made of cloth from Tír Tairngire, the Land of Promise. It was given to him by his magical foster-father.'[16] Although we only ever hear explicitly of Cúchulainn's mortal foster-fathers by name, the combination of a cloak of invisibility with Tír Tairngire strongly suggests Manannan. Furthermore, some apparently say that Culann the Smith was Manannan. He used to live on the Island of Falga, 'that was one of Manannan's places'.[17] As a boy, Cúchulainn acquired his name (which means 'The Hound of Culann') by killing Culann's ban-dog and taking its place until he had trained another, and so Culann was in a sense his foster-father.[18] It was Manannan, also, who taught Cúchulainn the use of his spear, the Gae Bulg, according to one account.[19]

In the second place, Cúchulainn is not by any means Lugh's only 'counterpart'. Finn, in particular, is closely associated with him too. In the modern *scéal* of 'Balor on Tory Island', the father of Lugh is not

Appendix A: Mortal Protogégés of the Tuatha Dé Dannan

called Cian, as in the ancient tales, but Fin, although Fin's father is not called Cumhal but Ceanfaeligh.[20] In another modern *scéal*, a folk-version of the 'Birth of Fin MacCumhail', it is prophesied that Fin will kill his grandfather, just as it is prophesied of Lugh that he will kill Balor.[21] In yet a third such *scéal*, 'Fin MacCumhail, the Seven Brothers, and the King of France', Fin's Helper, Misty, after killing an ogre named Curucha na Gras, tells Fin to put Curucha's head '"on top of the holly bush that's out here above us." Fin put the head on the holly bush, and the minute he put it there the head burnt the bush to the earth, and the earth to the clay.'[22] In the same way, in an old Fenian lay, Lugh puts Balor's severed head in 'a fork of hazel', and its venom splits the tree.

However, at this point, Finn, just like Cúchulainn begins to acquire connections with Manannan as well as with Lugh. The lay continues to say that after fifty years Manannan has the tree felled, and from its wood is made his shield, 'the Dripping Ancient Hazel' (*in Sencholl Snidheach*), which in due course passes into the hands of Finn.[23] Furthermore, Mongan, the protégé of Mannan, revealed on one occasion that he himself was the reincarnation of Finn, and recalled Cailte mac Ronain from the dead to prove it.[24] Thus, with both Cúchulainn and Finn, no sooner have we found clear evidence to relate them to Lugh than we find equally clear evidence to relate them to Manannan. This recalls the peculiarity of the Dagda's secular protégé having the name of Nuada.

Nor is this the end of the problem, for Lugh's 'counterparts', it turns out, are by no means limited to two. If we are to believe all the surmises of scholars, in fact, Lugh has 'been identified with Fionn, Delbaeth, Lugaid Mac Con, Mac Lugdach, Lugaid Laigde (indeed with every mythological character called Lugaid) and Cú Chullain'.[25] Furthermore, on the assumption that 'Lug is the Celtic Sun God', Charles Plummer also finds counterparts of him in the following saints: 'Aed, Boetius (Buite), Cainnech, Carthach, Ciaran of Saigir, Coemgen, Colman Ela, Comgall, Fechin, Finan, Fintan, Ita, Lasrian (Molaisse), Maedoc, Mochoemoc, Mochua, Moling, Molua (Lugaid), Samthann, and Tigernach.'[26] Now this is altogether too much of a good thing. What is more, many of these characters, both saints and pagans, can be found playing independent roles in the same story.

To speak for the moment only of Lugh, then: the case for his having a mortal counterpart in Cúchulainn relies almost entirely on Cúchulainn's parentage; the case for Finn relies almost entirely on late folklore; the case for everyone else mentioned relies on names and on real or imagined solar attributes. This is weak enough under any circumstances, and weaker still when it is remembered that Lugh's own solar character is very far from proven. Furthermore, the likelihood that Lugh has any counterparts is actually diminished by claims that he has so many. The best qualified of his counterparts turn into counterparts of Manannan when too closely questioned. All that remains definitely true is that Cúchulainn is Lugh's son and that Lugh does extend his protection to Cúchulainn. Thus, it is literally true that Cúchulainn is Lugh's protégé. More than that we cannot say. The words 'avatar' and 'counterpart' do not apply.

What is true for Lugh will be true for the rest of the Tuatha Dé Danann as well. However, this is not to deny that stories and attributes proper to members of the Tuatha Dé may sometimes have transferred themselves to mortals. As to why they should do so, there would seem to be no single answer. Sometimes, no doubt, the cause is mere accident, at other times a coincidence of nomenclature. Mongan, however, seems to require more explanation.

In his shape-shifting and his trickery, Mongan is very like Manannan, but he is not Manannan. He is not among the Tuatha Dé, but he is certainly no ordinary mortal. Strangest of all, he is historical. What are we to make of him? The most straightforward answer is provided by the scribe of Standish Hayes O'Grady's 'Fragmentary Annals':

albeit certain dealers in antiquarian fable do propound [Mongan] to have been son to Manannan, and wont to enter at his pleasure into divers shapes, yet this we may not credit: rather choosing to take Mongan for one that was but a man of surpassing knowledge, and gifted with an intelligence clear, and subtle, and keen.[27]

That this is the actual truth of the matter we need hardly dispute, but there have been many other intelligent men who have not been called sons of Manannan, so why Mongan?

A clue may probably be found in 'The Conception of Mongan', where we see druids and clerics acting side by side. This fact is not in itself unique or even remarkable. The druids naturally did not disappear as soon as Patrick set foot in Ireland. In fact, as late as the twelfth century, Giraldus Cambrensis testifies that 'although all this time the Faith has grown up, so to speak, in the country, nevertheless in some corners of it there are many even still who are not bapized, and who, because of the negligence of the pastors, have not yet heard the teaching of the Faith.'[28] But what was running through the minds of the druids during the long decline of their authority? Did they never think of taking steps to reverse the situation by proposing a Messiah of their own to outface Christ? Alfred Nutt thinks not,[29] and James Carney actually thinks that

Appendix A: Mortal Protogégés of the Tuatha Dé Dannan

the story of Mongan's conception was intended 'to explain the Incarnation by parable',[30] but I would maintain that Mongan is precisely the druids' Messiah, sent for Ireland's benefit by Manannan mac Lir. In the Hellenic world, when Christianity was driving the old religion to the edge of extinction, Philostratus produced his Life of Apollonius of Tyana as a would be antidote to the Gospels. Like Apollonius, Mongan is historical. They must be, as the priests of Christ proclaim a Living God. Mongan, according to the 'Fragmentary Annals', died in A.D. 625.[31] Thus his life would very probably coincide with the decisive crisis in Irish religion. (According to Bonwick, druids were 'officially abolished' in A.D. 637, but he seems to confuse druids with *filí*, the legally overprivileged poets.)[32] Probably, at his minor court in Ulster, Mongan made himself the last royal patron of the druids, an Irish equivalent, then, of Julian the Apostate as well as of Apollonius of Tyana. In return, the druids sought to publicise him, like Apollonius, as a miracle-worker and philosopher, a genuine rival to Christ. Of course, a final similarity between the Life of Apollonius and the stories of Mongan is that they are poor substitutes for the Gospels, not least in respect of dignity. Naturally, therefore, the Christian religion prevailed.

APPENDIX B: ADDITIONAL NOTES ON *THE COUNTESS CATHLEEN*

1.

> ... It's this, your honours:
> Because of some wild words my father said
> She thinks you are not of those who cast a shadow.
>
> (VPl 39–41)

Cf. Wood-Martin, II, 297:

An Irish fairy doctor could easily detect if a man had lost his soul. If he had been bargaining with evil spirits the compact was readily detected, as at noonday, and even in the brightest sunshine, his body, demoniacally possessed, cast no shadow.

This tradition is also relevant to Lord Dunsany's novel, *The Charwoman's Shadow* (1926).

2.

> ... A man, they say,
> Loved Maeve the Queen of all the invisible host,
> And died of his love nine centuries ago.
>
> (VPl 55)

Although nine centuries would drastically underestimate the case, the man may be Fergus, who was the lover of Maeve in the *Táin*. However, cf. also *The Celtic Twilight*, M 57–59, or pp. 399–400 above.

It may seem strange that a woman who features in Early Irish literature as a mortal heroine should reappear in folklore as a fairy queen, but she is mentioned as haunting Knocknarea, her burial place, not only in *The Celtic Twilight*, but also in RBÉ SMS 155, p. 487, and Wood-Martin, I, 369. In addition, she haunts Rathcroghan, Co. Roscommon (the ancient Cruachan), where she is supposed to have

Appendix B: Additional Notes on The Countess Cathleen

been waked: Fionán mac Coluim, 'A Tradition About Rathcroghan, Co. Roscommon', *Béaloideas*, 4 (1933), 130. However, in all these instances she may as well be a ghost as a fairy, and in RBÉ SMS 155 she is specifically described as a ghost. A certain person saw her only because he neglected to throw a stone at her cairn (i.e. to build it higher, as a sign of respect). She seems always to be of ill omen, but in *The Celtic Twilight* (M 90) the danger of contact with her seems consistent with the danger of the fairy queen's stroke: in Yeats's time, she brushed a herd-boy with her skirt on Knocknarea, 'He fell down, and was dead three days'.

3.

> I have seen a vision under a green hedge,
> A hedge of hips and haws — men yet shall hear
> The archangel rolling Satan's empty skull
> Over the mountain-tops.
>
> (VPl 153)

In Ancient Ireland it was common practice to decapitate one's slain enemies and roll their heads about or otherwise abuse them. In a comparatively modern recension of Conall Cearnach's Revenge that used to be in Douglas Hyde's possession, Conall finds Cúchulainn's head 'being used as a football by two men near Tara': Wood-Martin, I, 328; Hyde, *Literary History*, p. 352.

4.

> Angels and devils clash in the middle air,
> And brazen swords clang upon brazen helms.
>
> (VPl 165)

The angelomachy for the souls of the dead is an established Irish tradition. Two such fights are described in Adomnan's *Life of Columba* (pp. 477, 485). No body should be keened for three hours after death, so as not to alert the demons while the soul has time to escape: Wood-Martin, I, 309.

5.

> The years like great black oxen tread the world,
> And God the herdsman goads them on behind,
> And I am broken by their passing feet.
>
> (VPl 169)

These lines have been much admired, not least by Ellmann (*Identity*, p. 121). It has not been noticed that they are apparently proverbial, for a very similar expression occurs in Sir Walter Scott's *The Antiquary* (1816; rpt. London: Everyman, 1907), p. 360: 'I'm fain to see ye looking sae weel, cummer; the mair, that the black ox has tramped on ye since I was aneath your roof-tree.' Here the black ox seems to represent sorrow, not time.

NOTES

Introduction

1. Herbert V. Fackler, *That Tragic Queen: The Deirdre Legend in Anglo-Irish Literature*, Sulzburg Studies in English Literature: Poetic Drama and Poetic Theory, No. 39 (Salzburg, Austria: Institut für Englische Sprache und Literatur, 1978), pp. 84–85.
2. James Mac Killop, "'Beurla On It': Yeats, Joyce, and the Irish Language", *Éire-Ireland*, xv, 1 (1980), 140–42.
3. W. B. Yeats, 'Dramatis Personae, 1896–1902', in *Autobiography* (New York: Collier, 1965), p. 295. Lady Gregory had been learning Irish, and had translated a number of Hyde's plays, most of which appeared in her *Poets and Dreamers* (1903). The Coole Edition vol. x has additional plays by Hyde which were previously unpublished. Translations by Lady Gregory of Fr. O'Leary's *Tadg Saor* and *Bás Dalláin* also exist.
4. W. B. Yeats, *Explorations* (New York: Macmillan, 1962), p. 78.
5. Mac Killop, 'Beurla On it', p. 141.
6. W. B. Yeats, *The Variorum Edition of the Poems of W. B. Yeats*, ed. Peter Allt and Russell K. Alspach (New York: Macmillan, 1966), p. 793.
7. W. B. Yeats, *Mythologies* (New York: Collier, 1969), p. 315.
8. Thomas MacDonagh, *Literature in Ireland: Studies Irish and Anglo-Irish* (1916), excerpted in *W. B. Yeats: The Critical Heritage*, ed. A. Norman Jeffares (London: Routledge & Kegan Paul, 1977), p. 198.
9. W. B. Yeats, 'The Trembling of the Veil' (1922), in *Autobiography*, p. 86.

1: Before the Celts Left the Land of Summer

1. Lady Gregory, *Gods and Fighting Men: The Story of the Tuatha de Danaan and of the Fianna of Ireland* (1904; rpt. Gerrards Cross, Buckinghamshire: Colin Smythe, 1970), p. 27.
2. Thomas F. O'Rahilly, *Early Irish History and Mythology* (1946; rpt. Dublin: Institute for Advanced Studies, 1964), p. 76.
3. This section is summarised from the Book of Leinster *Lebor Gabála*, as translated in 'The Conquest of Nemed', in *Ancient Irish Tales*, ed. Tom Peete Cross and Clark Harris Slover (1936; rpt. Dublin: Figgis, 1969), pp. 3–9.
4. Geoffrey Keating, *Foras Feasa ar Eirinn: The History of Ireland*, Irish Texts Society, Vol. IV, ed. & trans. David Comyn (London: David Nutt for the Irish Texts Society, 1902), I, 163, 179; see also Eleanor Hull, *A Textbook of Irish Literature* (Dublin: M. H. Gill & Son, 1906), 1, 13.
5. Francis John Byrne, *Irish Kings and High-Kings* (New York: St. Martin's Press, 1973), pp. 134–35.
6. J. R. R. Tolkien, '*Beowulf*: The Monsters and the Critics' (1936), in *An Anthology of Beowulf Criticism*, ed. Lewis E. Nicholson (Notre Dame, Ind.: University of Notre Dame Press, 1963), pp. 87–88.

7. Gregory, 'The Reign of Bres', in *Gods and Fighting Men*, p. 32.
8. 'The Second Battle of Mag Tured', in Cross and Slover, pp. 45–46.
9. J. F. Killeen, 'Fear an Énais', *Celtica*, 9 (1971), 202–04.
10. Máirín O Daly, ed. & trans., Cath Maige Mucrama: *The Battle of Mag Mucrama*, Irish Texts Society, Vol. L (Dublin: Dublin University Press for the Irish Texts Society, 1975), p. 53; Myles Dillon, ed. & trans., 'The Feast of Dún na nGéd', in *The Cycles of the Kings* (London: Oxford University Press, 1946), pp. 57–64.
11. P. W. Joyce, *A Social History of Ancient Ireland* (Dublin: M. H. Gill & Son, 1920), I, 144.
12. Gwyn Jones, trans., 'Eirik the Red', in *Eirik the Red and Other Icelandic Sagas* (London: Oxford University Press, 1961, pp.154–55.
13. 'Ethnographical Collections from East Greenland (Angmagsalik and Nualik) Made by G. Holm, G. Amdrup and J. Petersen and Described by W. Thalbitzer', *Meddeleslar om Grønland*, 39 (1911), 687–88.
14. Gregory, 'The Reign of Bres', in *Gods and Fighting Men*, p. 32.
15. Thomas Kinsella, ed. & trans., *The Tain* (London: Oxford University Press, 1970), p. 195.
16. Henri d'Arbois de Jubainville, *The Irish Mythological Cycle and Celtic Mythology*, trans. Richard Irvine Best (1903; rpt. New York: Lemma, 1970), p. 56.
17. Alwyn and Brinley Rees, *Celtic Heritage* (London: Thames & Hudson, 1961), p. 40.
18. Katharine Briggs, *A Dictionary of Fairies* (Harmondsworth, Middlesex: Penguin, 1977), p. 179.
19. A. G. van Hamel, 'Partholon', *Revue Celtique*, 50 (1933), 223.
20. The summary of 'The Conquest of Nemed' now resumes.
21. At this point, I begin summarising 'The Conquest of the Fir Bolg', in Cross and Slover, pp. 9–11.
22. T. F. O'Rahilly, pp. 47, 56.
23. De Jubainville, pp. 73n, 81; 'The Second Battle of Mag Tured', in Cross and Slover, p. 43.
24. Lady Gregory, *Visions and Beliefs in the West of Ireland* (1920; rpt. Gerrards Cross, Buckinghamshire: Colin Smythe, 1970), pp. 67, 357.
25. T. F. O'Rahilly, pp. 47–48, 51–54; Barbara Babcock-Abrahams, "'A Tolerated Margin of Mess': The Trickster and His Tales Reconsidered," *Journal of the Folklore Institute*, 11 (1975), 155.
26. T. F. O'Rahilly, p. 205.
27. Byrne, pp. 132–35.
28. I now begin summarising 'The conquest of the Tuatha De Danann', in Cross and Slover, pp. 11–14.
29. Cross and Slover, p. 28.
30. Gregory, 'The Reign of Bres', in *Gods and Fighting Men*, p. 31.
31. 'The Second Battle of Mag Tured', in Cross and Slover, p. 32,
32. Cross and Slover, p. 29.
33. Gregory, 'The Fight with the Firbolgs', in *Gods and Fighting Men*, p. 31.
34. Gregory, *Gods and Fighting Men*, p. 76.
35. Richard Irvine Best, ed. & trans., 'The Battle of Airtech', *Ériu*, 8 (1916), 184.
36. Standish Hayes O'Grady, ed. & trans., 'Death of Crimthann son of Fidach, and of Eochaidh Muighmedoin's three sons: Brian, Ailill, Fiachra', in *Silva Gadelica* (1892; rpt. New York: Lemma, 1970), II, 374.
37. Byrne, pp. 134–35.
38. De Jubainville, *Mythological Cycle*, p. 93.

39 Gregory, *Gods and Fighting Men*, p. 236.
40 Eoin MacNeill, *Duanaire Finn: The Book of the Lays of Fionn*, Irish Texts Society, Vol. VIII (London: David Nutt for the Irish Texts Society, 1908), I, xxxi–ii.
41 I now begin summarising 'The Second Battle of Mag Tured', in Cross and Slover, pp. 28–48.
42 Whitley Stokes, ed. & trans., *Cóir Anmann*, in *Irische Texte*, ed. Whitley Stokes and E. Windische (Leipzig: S. Hirzel, 1897), III, Part 2, 293.
43 This paragraph is summarised from 'The Coming of Lugh', in Gregory, *Gods and Fighting Men*, pp. 38–40.
44 Francis John Byrne, Seminar, Yeats International Summer School, Sligo, Ireland, August 1980.
45 Cross and Slover, pp. 50–58.
46 Máire Mac Neill, *The Festival of Lughnasa: A Study of the Survival of the Celtic Festival of the Beginning of Harvest* (London: Oxford University Press, 1962), p. 5.
47 Gregory, 'The Great Battle of Magh Tuireadh', in *Gods and Fighting Men*, p. 67.
48 'The Destruction of Da Derga's Hostel', in Cross and Slover, p. 116.
49 Lady Gregory, 'The Wedding of Maine Morgor', in *Cuchulain of Muirthemne: The Story of the Men of the Red Branch of Ulster* (1902; rpt. Gerrards Cross, Buckinghamshire: Colin Smythe, 1970), p. 133.
50 Gerard Murphy, ed. & trans. 'The Coming of Laighne Mór', in *Dunaire Finn: The Book of the Lays of Fionn*, Irish Texts Society, Vol. XXVIII (London: Simpkin Marshall for the Irish Texts Society, 1933), II, 222–33.
51 Gregory, 'The Pursuit of Diarmuid and Grania', in *Gods and Fighting Men*, p. 294.
52 A folk-tale and a *scéal* are actually different things, the one told by a *seanchaí*, the other by a *scéalaí*. In some contexts the difference is important, and the terms will therefore be used with precision in this book. A folk-tale belongs basically to the realm of conversation, is short, generally concerns the *seanchaí* himself or his neighbours, and is meant to be believed. A *scéal* belongs to the realm of art, is comparatively long (sometimes very long), is set in a mythical past and often in mythical lands, concerns such personages as the King of Ireland's Son, and defies belief.
53 Dillon, *Cycles of the Kings*, p. 12.
54 I now begin summarising 'The Conquest of the Sons of Mil', in Cross and Slover, pp. 14–27.
55 In the text, this name is variously spelt 'Emer' and 'Eber', but as it is clearly the same person I have standarised the spelling to avoid confusion and to make it agree with Eber Finn (*donn* = 'dark'; *finn* = 'fair').
56 De Jubainville, *Mythological Cycle*, pp. 144–45.
57 'The Intoxication of the Ulstermen', in Cross and Slover, p. 215.
58 Whitley Stokes, ed. & trans., *The Tripartite Life of Patrick with Other Documents Relating to That Saint* (London: Eyre & Spottiswoode for H. M. Stationery Office, 1887), I, 121.
59 *Sídh*, gen. sing. & nom. plur. *sídhe*, = 'fairy hill', sometimes natural but more often an artificial tumulus. *Dun*, *rath*, and Mn. Anglo-Irish 'fort' or

'forth' are often used in the same sense. *Sídhe*, sc. *áes, daoine sídhe*, 'people of the *sídh*', denotes the fairies. To avoid confusion, I write the name of the fairies 'Sídhe' and the plural of *sídh sídhe*.
60 Vernam Hull, ed. & trans., 'De Gabáil in t-Sída', *Zeitschrift für Celtische Philologie*, 19 (1933), 55–58.
61 Gregory, 'Bodb Dearg,' in *Gods and Fighting Men*, p. 77.
62 Proinsias Mac Cana, *Celtic Mythology* (London: Hamlyn, 1970), p. 127.

2. The Ever-Living

1 Cross and Slover, p. 87.
2 S. H. O'Grady, II, 269–85; also in Cross and Slover, pp. 471–87.
3 'The Colloquy with the Ancients', in S. H. O'Grady, II, 115–17.
4 Gregory, 'Finn's Household', in *Gods and Fighting Men*,
5 Cross and Slover, pp. 405–06.
6 Cross and Slover, p. 83
7 Alfred Nutt, 'The Celtic Doctrine of Re-Birth', in *The Voyage of Bran Son of Febal to the Land of the Living*, ed. & trans. Kuno Meyer (1897; rpt. New York: AMS Press, 1972), II, 161.
8 'The Wooing of Etain', in Cross and Slover, p. 92.
9 Cross and Slover, pp. 176–98.
10 Arthur A. Wachsler, 'The 'Elaborate Ruse': A Motif of Deception in Early Celtic Historical Variants of the Journey to the Otherworld', *Journal of the Folklore Institute*, 12 (1975), 35.
11 W. B. Yeats, Note to 'The Secret Rose', in *Variorum Poems*, p. 813.
12 S. H. O'Grady, II, 198–99.
13 Micheál Coimín, *Laoi Oisín ar Thír na n-Óg, or, The Lay of Oisín in the Land of Youth*, ed. Tomás Ó Flannghaile (London: City of London Book Depot, 1896).
14 *Geis*, plur. *geasa*: the usual translation, 'taboo', is not really adequate. In a thesaurus, I would expect to find this word in the company, not only of 'taboo', but also of 'promise', 'obligation', 'supplication', and 'enchantment'.
15 Cross and Slover, pp. 488–90.
16 Gregory, '[Manannan's] Call to Connla', in *Gods and Fighting Men*, p. 114.
17 Eleanor Hull, 'The Development of the Idea of Hades in Celtic Literature', *Folk-Lore*, 18 (1907), 157.
18 Nutt, 'Re-Birth,' II, 147-48.
19 Rees, pp. 322–23, 325.
20 Cross and Slover, p. 588.
21 Alfred Nutt, 'The Happy Otherworld in the Mythico-Romantic Literature of the Irish', in Meyer, *Bran*, I, 161, 327.
22 E. Hull, 'The Idea of Hades,' pp. 157, 158, 160.
23 Gregory, *Gods and Fighting Men*, pp. 252–58
24 Gregory, *Gods and Fighting Men*, p. 318.
25 Whitley Stokes, ed. & trans., 'The Irish Ordeals', in *Irische Texte*, ed. & trans. Whitley Stokes and E. Windisch (Leipzig: S. Hirzel, 1891), III, Part 1, 209.
26 S. H. O'Grady, II, 290–91
27 T. F. O'Rahilly, p. 290.
28 See Myles Dillon, *Early Irish Literature* (Chicago: University of Chicago Press, 1948), pp. 67–8, 112, 116, 118n; Myles Dillon and Nora K. Chadwick, *The Celtic Realms* (New York: New American Library, 1967), p. 154.

Notes to pages 45–49

29 'The Voyage of Bran Son of Febal', in Cross and Slover, p. 589.
30 E. MacNeill, 'Caoilte's Urn', in *Duanaire Finn*, I, 140–49.
31 'The Wooing of Becfola', in S. H. O'Grady, II, 91–93.
32 'The Adventures of Nera', in Cross and Slover, p. 250.
33 'The Adventures of Cian's Son Teigue', in S. H. O'Grady, II, 395.
34 Lady Gregory, 'The Voyage of Brendan,' in *A Book of Saints & Wonders* (1906; rpt. Gerrards Cross, Buckinghamshire: Colin Smythe, 1972), pp. 103–4.
35 Gregory, 'The Voyage of Maeldune', in *Saints & Wonders*, p. 68.
36 Gregory, 'Mochae and the Bird,' in *Saints & Wonders*, p. 99. The *Martyrology of Donegal* quotes a verse agreeing with this but also states on its own authority that the bird 'amused' Mochae for 300 years: Fr. Michael O'Clery, *The Martyrology of Donegal: A Calendar of the Saints of Ireland*, trans. John O'Donovan, ed. James Henthorn Todd and Wiliam Reeves (Dublin: Irish Archaeological and Celtic Society, 1864), pp. 177–79.
37 'The Adventure of Cian's Son Teigue', in S. H. O'Grady, II, 389.
38 'The Adventures of Nera', in Cross and Slover, p. 251.
39 Gregory, *Visions and Beliefs*, pp. 225, 262.
40 Dermot MacManus, *The Middle Kingdom: The Faerie World of Ireland* (Gerrards Cross, Buckinghamshire: Colin Smythe, 1973), pp. 81–86.
41 Mac Cana, *Celtic Mythology*, p. 126.
42 M. Mac Neill, pp. 6–7, 10.
43 Gregory, 'Ilbrec of Ess Ruadh', in *Gods and Fighting Men*, p. 219.
44 Gregory, 'The Coming of Finn', in *Gods and Fighting Men*, p. 144.
45 'The Boyhood Deeds of Finn', in Cross and Slover, pp. 367–68.
46 Gregory, 'The Quarrel with the Sons of Morna', in *Gods and Fighting Men*, p. 325.
47 Gregory, 'Oisin's Children', in *Gods and Fighting Men*, p. 248.
48 Kinsella, pp. 46–50.
49 Gregory, 'The Lad of the Skins', in *Gods and Fighting Men*, p. 161.
50 S. H. O'Grady, II, 333–34.
51 'The Wooing of Etain', in Cross and Slover, p. 92.
52 Gregory, 'The Dream of Angus Og', in *Cuchulain of Muirthemne*, pp. 118–21.
53 Gregory, *Gods and Fighting Men*, pp. 124–36.
54 Cross and Slover, p. 97.
55 Gregory, *Gods and Fighting Men*, p. 225
56 Kinsella, p. 97.
57 S. H. O'Grady, II, 222.
58 Stokes, *Vita Tripartita*, I, 47.
59 E. MacNeill, 'The Enchanted Stag', in *Duanaire Finn*, I, 130–32.
60 'Fafainn,' in Cross and Slover, p. 597.
61 E. MacNeill, *Duanaire Finn*, I, 140–49
62 Gregory, *Gods and Fighting Men*, p. 234.
63 Gregory, *Gods and Fighting Men*, p. 247.
64 'The Wooing of Etain', in Cross and Slover, p. 86.
65 Cross and Slover, p. 402.
66 Cross and Slover, p. 179.
67 Gregory, *Cuchulain of Muirthemne*, pp. 132, 136.
68 W. B. Yeats, *The Variorum Edition of the Plays of W. B. Yeats*, ed. Russell K. Alspach (New York: Macmillan, 1969), p.83.
69 Cross and Slover, pp. 379, 402.
70 Kinsella, p. 142.
71 Cross and Slover, p. 91.
72 Stokes, *Vita Tripartita*, I, 53.

73 'The Pursuit of Diarmuid and Grainne', in Cross and Slover, p. 406.
74 'The Boromean Tribute', in S. H. O'Grady, II, 423.
75 Gregory, 'The Hidden House of Lugh', in *Gods and Fighting Men*, p. 69; 'Cormac's Adventures in the Land of Promise', in Cross and Slover, p. 504.
76 See, for instance, Eunapius, *Lives of the Philosophers and Sophists*, in Philostratus and Eunapius, *The Lives of the Sophists*, ed. & trans. Wilmer Cave Wright (London: Loeb Classical Library, 1921), pp. 368-71, in which Iamblichus produces two boys from springs of water.
77 W. B. Yeats, *Variorum Plays*, p. 916.
78 Cross and Slover, p. 41.
79 Gregory, *Gods and Fighting Men*, pp. 174-75.
80 Cross and Slover, pp. 518-32.
81 'The Destruction of Da Derga's Hostel', in Cross and Slover, p. 100.
82 'The Adventures of Nera', in Cross and Slover, pp. 249-50.

3: Dramatis Personae

1 Francis John Byrne, Seminar, Yeats International Summer School, Sligo, Ireland, August 1980.
2 Katharine M. Briggs, *Nine Lives: The Folklore of Cats* (New York: Pantheon, 1980), pp. 5-7; Briggs, *Dictionary*, p. 90.
3 Count John de Salis, in W. Y. Evans Wentz, *The Fairy-Faith in Celtic Countries* (London: Henry Frowde, 1911; rpt. Gerrards Cross: Colin Smythe, 1977), p. 79.
4 Gregory, 'Aine', in *Gods and Fighting Men*, p. 86.
5 'The Second Battle of Mag Tured', in Cross and Slover, p. 45.
6 Joyce, I, 266.
7 T. F. O'Rahilly, p. 290.
8 Evans Wentz, p. 80
9 W. G. Wood-Martin, *Traces of the Elder Faiths of Ireland* (London: Longmans, Green & Co., 1902), I, 356; Gregory, 'Aine', in *Gods and Fighting Men*, p. 86.
10 Gregory, *Gods and Fighting Men*, p. 182.
11 J. G. O'Keeffe, ed. & trans., *Buile Suibhne (The Frenzy of Suibhne), Being The Adventures of Suibhne Geilt: A Middle-Irish Romance*, Irish Texts Society, Vol. XII (London: David Nutt for the Irish Texts Society, 1913), pp. 23, 164.
12 P. W. Joyce, quoted in Wood-Martin, I, 357.
13 Gregory, 'Aine', in *Gods and Fighting Men*, p. 86.
14 Wood-Martin, I, 357-58.
15 Wood-Martin, I, 358.
16 Briggs, *Dictionary*, pp. 415-17.
17 M. Mac Neill, pp. 151, 186.
18 Stokes, *Cóir Anmann*, p. 355.
19 Nutt, 'Re-Birth,' II, 219.
20 Rees, p. 30.
21 Stokes, *Cóir Anmann*, p. 355.
22 Henri d'Arbois de Jubainville, *Cours de Littérature Celtique* (1883; rpt. Osnabruck: Otto Zeller, 1969), I, 282n.
23 Trans. de Jubainville, *Cours de Littérature*, I, 283n.
24 Marie-Louise Sjoestedt, *Gods and Heroes of the Celts*, trans. Myles Dillon (London: Methuen & Co., 1949), pp. 44-45.
25 'The Second Battle of Mag Tured', in Cross and Slover, p. 47.
26 'The Intoxication of the Ulstermen', in Cross and Slover, p. 229.

Notes to pages 58–65

27 Sjoestedt, p. 19. If the Dagda's name means 'good hand', that may also be thought relevant to abundance.
28 Gregory, 'Bodb Dearg', in *Gods and Fighting Men*, p. 77.
29 Gregory, *Cuchulain of Muirthemne*, pp. 118–21.
30 Gregory, 'Angus Og,' in *Gods and Fighting Men*, p. 83.
31 J. M. Flood, *Ireland: Its Myths and Legends* (1916; rpt. Port Washington, N. Y.: Kennikat Press, 1970), p. 26.
32 G. Murphy, *Duanaire Finn*, II, 370–401.
33 Flood, p. 26.
34 William Leo Hansberry, *Pillars in Ethiopian History*, African History Notebook, Vol. I, ed. Joseph E. Harris (Washington: Howard University Press, 1981), p. 70.
35 Cross and Slover, pp. 82–92.
36 Flood, p. 26.
37 Gregory, 'The Courting of Emer', in *Cuchulain of Muirthemne*, p. 52.
38 Flood, p. 26.
39 Cross and Slover, p. 227.
40 Gregory, 'The Fight with the Firbolgs', in *Gods and Fighting Men*, p. 27.
41 Douglas Hyde, *A Literary History of Ireland* (1899; rpt. London: Ernest Benn, 1967), pp. 114–15.
42 A. G. van Hamel, 'Aspects of Celtic Mythology', *Proceedings of the British Academy*, 20 (1934), 237.
43 'The Death of Finn', in Cross and Slover, p. 432.
44 M. Mac Neill, p. 5.
45 E. Hull, *Textbook*, I, 14.
46 Flood, p. 27.
47 Gregory, 'Fate of the Sons of Usnach' in *Cuchulain of Muirthemne*, p. 99.
48 Cross and Slover, pp. 591–94.
49 Gregory, 'Manannan', in *Gods and Fighting Men*, p. 97.
50 S. H. O'Grady, II, 311–24. In a folk-version of this tale, however, an old beggarman who is equivalent to the churl reveals himself as 'Angus of the Bruff', i.e. Angus Óg: 'The Story-Teller at Fault,' in *Celtic Fairy Tales*, ed. Joseph Jacobs (London: David Nutt, 1892), p. 142.
51 E. MacNeill, 'The Crane-Bag', in *Duanaire Finn*, I, 118–20.
52 Cross and Slover, p. 63.
53 Robert Graves, 'The Crane Bag,' in *The Crane Bag and Other Disputed Subjects* (London: Cassell, 1969), pp. 1–8.
54 Gregory, 'Manannan,' in *Gods and Fighting Men*, pp. 96–97.
55 Francis John Byrne, Seminar, Yeats International Summer School, Sligo, Ireland, August 1980; Briggs, *Dictionary*, pp. 280–81.
56 Flood, p. 25.
57 Joyce, I, 266.
58 Gregory, 'The Landing', in *Gods and Fighting Men*, p. 72.
59 Gregory, 'The Fight with the Firbolgs', in *Gods and Fighting Men*, pp. 29–30.
60 'The Second Battle of Mag Tured', in Cross and Slover, p. 45.
61 'The Adventures of Nera', 'The Cattle-Raid of Regamna', 'The Sick-Bed of Cu Chulainn', and 'The Death of Cu Chulainn', in Cross and Slover, pp. 251–53, 211–14, 191, 338; Kinsella, pp. 98–100, 141–42, 223, 238–39; Gregory, 'The Great Gathering at Muirthemne', in *Cuchulain of Muirthemne*, pp. 242–51.
62 Gregory, 'The Morrigu', in *Gods and Fighting Men*, p. 86.
63 Charles Donahue, 'The Valkyries and the Irish War-Goddesses', *PMLA*, 56 (1941), 1–12; cf. C. Lottner, Postscript to W. M. Hennessy, 'The Ancient Irish Goddess of War', *Revue Celtique*, 1 (1870–72), 55–7.

64 Wood-Martin, I, 359–60
65 See, for instance, 'The Death of Conchobar', in Cross and Slover, p. 343.
66 Some of the issues raised in this chapter, and some members of the Tuatha Dé Danann not mentioned here will be particularly discussed in chapter five. Appendix A discusses the relationship between certain mortals and the Dagda, Angus Óg, Lugh, and Manannan.

4: The People of Peace

1 Gregory, 'The Battle of Rosnaree', in *Cuchulain of Muirthemne*, pp. 231–32; see also James Carney, *Studies in Irish Literature and History* (Dublin: Institute for Advanced Studies, 1955), p. 224.
2 Cross and Slover, pp. 101–02, 122.
3 De Jubainville, *Mythological Cycle*, pp. 67–68.
4 S. H. O'Grady, II, 292–311.
5 Alexandre Haggerty Krappe, 'La Poursuite du Gilla Dacker et les Dioscures Celtiques', *Revue Celtique*, 49, (1932), 106.
6 E. Hull, 'The Idea of Hades', p. 141.
7 G. Murphy, *Duanaire Finn*, II, 114–21.
8 'The Pursuit of the Gilla Decair', in S. H. O'Grady, II, 300.
9 Gregory, *Gods and Fighting Men*, p. 178.
10 G. Murphy, 'The Standing Stones of Ireland', in *Duanaire Finn*, II, 66–99.
11 De Jubainville's position on this issue is peculiar. After leading one to expect that he will identify a Fomorian, he opts for Bile, the father of Mil. The choice of a Milesian is unexpected enough, the choice of Bile even more so: *Mythological Cycle*, pp. 58–59, 126.
12 Carney, pp. 206–10.
13 Hyde, *Literary History*, pp. 49–50n.
14 Käte Müller-Lisowski, 'Contributions to a Study in Irish Folklore: Traditions About Donn', *Béaloideas*, 18 (1948), 151.
15 The epithet *Tetscorach* is of no significance. It means 'possessed of sleek horses'.
16 M. Mac Neill, p. 204. For Donn's other roles, see Müller-Lisowski, pp. 148–63.
17 Byrne, p. 166.
18 Georges Dumézil, *The Destiny of a King*, trans. Alf Hiltebeitel (Chicago: University of Chicago Press, 1973).
19 Cormac mac Cuillenáin, *Sanas Chormaic: Cormac's Glossary*, trans. John O'Donovan, ed. Whitley Stokes (Calcutta: O. T. Cutter for the Irish Archaeological and Celtic Society, 1868), p. 3; see also Rev. Patrick S. Dinneen, *Foclóir Gaedhilge agus Béarla: An Irish-English Dictionary*, 3rd. ed. (Dublin: Educational Company of Ireland for the Irish Texts Society, 1934), p. 953, s.v. *scál*.
20 Robert Kirk, 'A Succinct Account of My Lord of Tarbott's relationes', in *The Secret Common-Wealth* and *A Short Treatise of Charms and Spels*, ed. Stewart Sanderson (Totowa, N. J.: Rowman and Littlefield, 1976), p. 93.
21 Tomás Ó Cathasaigh, 'Between God and Man: The Hero of Irish Tradition', *The Crane Bag*, 2, No. 1–2 (1978), p. 77; 'The Semantics of 'Síd''' *Éigse*, 17 (1977–78), 144.
22 Douglas Hyde, Letter to W. B. Yeats, quoted in the latter's 'Irish Wonders' (1899), in *Letters to the New Island*, ed. Horace Reynolds (Cambridge, Mass.: Harvard University Press, 1934), p. 198; F. F. Farag, 'Oriental and Celtic

Elements in the Poetry of W. B. Yeats 1865–1965: Centenary Essays on the Art of W. B. Yeats, ed. D. E. S. Maxwell and S. B. Bushrui (Ibadan, Nigeria: Ibadan University Press, 1965), p. 47. Yeats does not identify his correspondent by name, but there is no mistaking Douglas Hyde.

5: Dei Terreni

1 'The Colloquy with the Ancients', in S. H. O'Grady, II, 233–38; Gregory, 'The Hound', in *Gods and Fighting Men*, pp. 165–69.
2 Van Hamel, 'Celtic Mythology', pp. 215–16.
3 'The Conquest of the Tuatha De Danann', in Cross and Slover, p. 11.
4 Gregory, *Saints & Wonders*, p. 83.
5 Stokes, *Cóir Anmann*, p. 355.
6 Hyde, *Literary History*, p. 286n.
7 Van Hamel, 'Celtic Mythology', p. 244n.
8 David Fitzgerald, 'Early Celtic History and Mythology', *Revue Celtique*, 6 (1883–85), 205.
9 Whitley Stokes, 'Remarks on Mr. Fitzgerald's Early Celtic History and Mythology', *Revue Celtique*, 6 (1883–85), 369.
10 T. F. O'Rahilly, p. 128.
11 Van Hamel, 'Celtic Mythology', p. 244n.
12 Ward Rutherford, *The Druids and Their Heritage* (London: Gordon & Cremonesi, 1978), p. 95.
13 Byrne, p. 55.
14 Francis John Byrne, Seminar, Yeats International Summer School, Sligo, Ireland, August 1980.
15 Van Hamel, 'Celtic Mythology', p. 215.
16 E. Hull, *Textbook*, I, 9n.
17 Mac Cana, *Celtic Mythology*, pp. 18–19; van Hamel, 'Celtic Mythology,' p. 238.
18 Mac Cana, *Celtic Mythology*, p. 23.
19 Sjoestedt, pp. 14–15, 16.
20 Jan de Vries, *La Religion des Celtes*, trans. L. Jospin (Paris: Payot, 1963), p. 162.
21 Nutt, 'Happy Otherworld,' I, 179.
22 E. Hull, *Textbook*, I, 6, 16, 18.
23 M. Mac Neill, p. 5; E. Hull, *Textbook*, I, 14.
24 Sjoestedt, p. 43.
25 Mac Cana, *Celtic Mythology*, p. 29.
26 Mac Cuilleánin, p. 114n
27 T. F. O'Rahilly, pp. 59, 290.
28 Mac Cana, *Celtic Mythology*, p. 32.
29 David B. Spaan, 'The Place of Manannan Mac Lir in Irish Mythology', *Folklore*, 76 (1965), 185.
30 Byrne, p. 55.
31 Alexandre Haggerty Krappe, 'Nuada à la Main d'Argent', *Revue Celtique*, 49 (1932), 93, 95.
32 Byrne, p. 55.
33 De Jubainville, *Mythological Cycle*, p. 114.
34 Flood, p. 23.
35 Arthur Bernard Cook, 'The European Sky-God. IV. The Celts (p. 1)', *Folk-Lore*, 17 (1906), 30–32.
36 De Vries, p. 162.

37 Sjoestedt, pp. 22, 92.
38 Stokes, *Vita Tripartita*, II, 408–09.
39 Nora Chadwick, *The Celts* (Harmondsworth, Middlesex: Penguin, 1970), p. 170.
40 Cross and Slover, p. 38.
41 Gregory, *Gods and Fighting Men*, pp. 112, 150.
42 James P. McGarry, *Place Names in the Writings of William Butler Yeats* (Gerrards Cross, Buckinghamshire: Colin Smythe, 1976), pp. 18, 62.
43 Rutherford, p. 119.
44 G. F. Dalton, 'The Ritual Killing of the Irish Kings', *Folklore*, 81 (1970), 5, 17–18.
45 S. H. O'Grady, II, 109–11.
46 S. H. O'Grady, II, 171, 186–87.
47 'Scéla Mosauluim', in O Daly, pp. 84–85.
48 M. Mac Neill, pp. 71–73.
49 S. H. O'Grady, II, 232.
50 Cross and Slover, p. 490.
51 S. H. O'Grady, II, 95, 190–91, 260.
52 Stokes, *Vita Tripartita*, I, 101.
53 Gregory, 'Blessed Patrick of the Bells', in *Saints & Wonders*, pp. 50–51.
54 Dillon, *Cycles of the Kings*, p. 13.
55 'The Death of Muircertach mac Erca', in Cross and Slover, p. 522.
56 Cross and Slover, p. 190.
57 Gregory, *Gods and Fighting Men*, p. 178.
58 Stokes, *Vita Tripartita*, I, 91–93
59 Meyer, *Bran*, II, 301–05.
60 Nutt, 'Re-Birth,' II, 160–61; Keating, II, 123.
61 M.Mac Neill, pp. 2–3, 104, 109, 128, 346; Hyde, *Literary History*, p. 85.
62 M. Mac Neill, pp. 171–72.
63 Edward O'Toole, 'The Holy Wells of County Carlow', *Béaloideas*, 4 (1933), 8.
64 Joyce, I, 276–77.
65 Hyde, *Literary History*, p. 90.
66 Mac Cana, *Celtic Mythology*, p. 32.
67 David Fitzgerald, 'Popular Tales of Ireland', *Revue Celtique*, 4 (1879–80), 193–94.
68 Joyce, I, 220.
69 Tomás O Máille, 'Medb Chruachna', *Zeitschrift für Celtische Philologie*, 17 (1928), 146.
70 Joyce, I, 282–83.

6: The Tribes of the Goddess Danu

1 James Bonwick, *Irish Druids and Old Irish Religions* (1894; rpt. New York: Arno, 1976), pp. 33, 107.
2 'The Fate of the Children of Tuirenn', 'The Second Battle of Mag Tured', and 'The Intoxication of the Ulstermen', in Cross and Slover, pp. 51, 54, 57–58; 35–36, 215.
3 Wood-Martin, II, 3.
4 Hyde, *Literary History*, p. 284.
5 Joyce, I, 25–27.
6 From now on, I shall refer to this informant as Dr. A.
7 MacManus, pp. 22–23.

Notes to pages 94–108 301

8 Gregory, *Visions and Beliefs*, p. 260.
9 For evidence and information on this subject, see A. T. Lucas, 'Souterrains: The Literary Evidence', in *Hereditas: Essays and Studies Presented to Professor Séamus Ó Duilearga*, ed. Bo Almqvist, Breandán mac Aodha, and Gearóid mac Eoin (1975; rpt. New York: Arno, 1980), pp. 165–91.
10 Gregory, 'The Fight with the Firbolgs', in *Gods and Fighting Men*, p. 29.
11 This was the opinion of John Rhys, whose dating, however, seems a little reckless. He dates the arrival of the Fir Bolg at c. 600 B.C., by which time he supposes the Milesians to have been already well established: 'Studies in Early Irish History', *Proceedings of the British Academy*, 1 (1903–04), 71–72.
12 S. H. O'Grady, II, 343–45.
13 E. MacNeill, 'The War-Vaunt of Goll', in *Duanaire Finn*, I, 200–08.
14 Wood-Martin, II, 8.
15 Henceforth I will call this informant Mr. B.
16 Evans Wentz, p. 34.
17 Lady Jane Wilde, *Ancient Cures, Charms, and Usages of Ireland* (1890; rpt. Detroit: Singing Tree Press, 1970), p. 179.
18 Gregory, *Visions and Beliefs*, pp. 29–30.
19 Cross and Slover, pp. 34, 57.
20 Elizabeth Andrews, *Ulster Folklore* (1913; rpt. Norwood, Pa.: Norwood, 1975), pp. 11–12, 99.
21 See, for instance, Adomnan, *Life of Columba*, ed. & trans. Alan Orr Anderson and Marjorie Ogilvie Anderson (London: Thomas Nelson & Sons, 1961), p. 343.
22 Cross and Slover, pp. 112–13.
23 Evans Wentz, p. xxiii.
24 Rhys, 'Early Irish History', pp. 79–80.
25 Thomas Johnson Westropp, 'A Folklore Survey of County Clare', *Folk-Lore*, 21 (1910), 187–88.
26 Briggs, *Dictionary*, p. 47.
27 Hyde, *Literary History*, p. 6.
28 Gregory, *Visions and Beliefs*, p. 57.
29 Kirk, p. 55.
30 Gregory, *Visions and Beliefs*, pp. 228–29.
31 Douglas Hyde, *Legends of Saints and Sinners* (Dublin: Talbot Press, n.d.), p. 227.
32 Is this a misprint for *ydor*, corresponding to Gk. ύδωρ?
33 Rev. John O'Hanlon ('Lageniensis'), *Irish Local Legends* (1896; rpt. Norwood, Pa.: Norwood, 1973), pp. 39–44.
34 Evans Wentz, p. 70.

7: The Fairy Faith in Transition

1 Charles Plummer, ed., *Vitae Sanctorum Hiberniae* (1910; rpt. Oxford: Clarendon Press, 1968), I, cxxx.
2 W. B. Yeats, 'A General Introduction for My Work' (1937), in *Essays and Introductions* (New York: Collier, 1968), pp. 513–14. In using this metaphor, did Yeats recall the tapestry in *The Countess Cathleen*?
3 Keating, III, 107.
4 Francis John Byrne, 'The Irish Mythic Background,' 13 Aug. 1980, and Seminar, Yeats International Summer School, Sligo, Ireland, August 1980.
5 Kirk, p. 55.
6 Wood-Martin, II, 4.

7 Pádraig Ó Tuathail, O. S., 'Folk-Tales from Carlow and West Wicklow', *Béaloideas*, 7 (1937), 88.
8 Wood-Martin, II, 3.
9 Evans Wentz, pp. 53, 67, 68, 77.
10 Briggs, *Dictionary*, p. 90.
11 Evans Wentz, p. 47.
12 W. B. Yeats, 'Irish Fairies, Ghosts, Witches, etc.', in *Uncollected Prose*, ed. John P. Frayne and Colton Johnson (New York: Columbia University Press, 1970–76), I, 133; originally published in *Lucifer*, a theosophical magazine, 15 Jan. 1889. Yeats's use of the word 'Sheogue' (in Irish *sidheog*) in a sense confuses the issue, as it is the diminutive of *sídhe*, and hence by definition small.
13 W. B. Yeats, Notes to Gregory, *Visions and Beliefs*, pp. 358–59.
14 R. U. Sayce, 'The Origins and Development of the Belief in Fairies', *Folk-Lore*, 45 (1934), 105.
15 This, too, is mentioned by Yeats (as well as by many others): see 'Ireland Bewitched' (1899), in *Uncollected Prose*, II, 169.
16 W. B. Yeats, *The Celtic Twilight* (1893), in *Mythologies*, p. 44.
17 Andrews, pp. 11, 73.
18 Kirk, pp. 50–51.
19 I was told this by a retired schoolmaster at Ballymote, whom I shall henceforth identify as Mr. D.
20 Wood-Martin, II, 273.
21 Kirk, p. 61
22 G. H. Kinahan, 'Notes on Irish Folk-Lore', *The Folk-Lore Record*, 4 (1881), 109.
23 This is probably connected with Kirk's belief that the fairies change dwellings at the beginning of each quarter (p. 51).
24 MacManus, pp. 111–12.
25 S. H. O'Grady, II, 110.
26 W. Stuart Rogers, 'Irish Lore Collected in Schenectady', *New York Folklore Quarterly*, 8 (1952), 22.
27 Ó Tuathail, p. 88.
28 MacManus, p. 103.
29 Wood-Martin, II, 19.
30 RBÉ SMS 47, p. 159. The acronym stands for Roinn Bhéaloideas Éireann Schoolchildren's Manuscript. Roinn Bhéaloideas Éireann (The Irish Folklore Commission), which is now incorporated with the Department of Irish Folklore at University College, Dublin, possesses a vast collection of these manuscripts, compiled by schoolchildren all over Ireland during the 1930s. I am most grateful to Professor Bo Almqvist and the staff of Roinn Bhéaloideas Éireann for permission to consult these manuscripts and to publish my findings, as well as for the most pleasant and courteous assistance I received in the process.
31 Wood-Martin, I, 213, 218.
32 T. J. Westropp, 'A Study of Folklore on the Coasts of Connacht, Ireland'. *Folk-Lore*, 32 (1921), 122.

8: A First Census of Fairyland

1 RBÉ SMS 158 (Co. Sligo), p. 51.
2 Lady Wilde, *Ancient Cures*, p. 56.

Notes to pages 112–115

3   W. R. Wilde, *Irish Popular Superstitions* (1852; rpt. Totowa, N. J.: Rowman & Littlefield, 1973), p. 13.
4   Lady Wilde, *Ancient Cures*, p. 56.
5   W. R. Wilde, p. 98.
6   Wood-Martin, II, 6.
7   Wood-Martin, I, 188.
8   Ó Tuathail, p. 89.
9   Sean O'Sullivan, 'The Fairy Frog', in *The Folklore of Ireland* (New York: Hastings House, 1974), p. 103.
10 Wood-Martin, I, 188.
11 Mr. D told me that the leprechaun also sits and works on a toadstool, but I suspect that he was recalling illustrations in children's books.
12 Jeanne Cooper Foster, *Ulster Folklore* (Belfast: H. R. Carter, 1951), p. 110.
13 This may be obliquely confirmed by an unusual tradition from Co. Cavan that 'every lone bush marked the resting place of a coffin and that to cut one would bring bad luck': Foster, p. 112.
14 This, too, may be supported in a confused fashion by a sentence in the folk-tale of 'The Three Laughs of the *Leipreachán*': They say that when the Danes were in Ireland, they hid a lot of money in the earth, and only the *leipreachán* knows where it is': Sean O'Sullivan, ed. & trans., *Folktales of Ireland* (London: Routledge & Kegan Paul, 1966), p. 180. It is more probable, however, that the narrator confused the Danes with the Tuatha Dé Danann, as is not uncommon.
15 W. R. Wilde, pp. 59–60.
16 Fitzgerald, 'Popular Tales,' p. 180.
17 John J. Winberry, 'The Elusive Elf: Some Thoughts on the Nature and Origin of the Irish Leprechaun', *Folklore*, 87 (1976), 68.
18 Douglas Hyde, Letter to W. B. Yeats, quoted in the latter's *Fairy and Folk Tales of the Irish Peasantry* (1888), in *Fairy and Folk Tales of Ireland* (Gerrards Cross, Buckinghamshire: Colin Smythe, 1973), p. 75.
19 M. Mac Neill, p. 7.
20 Whitley Stokes, 'Mythological Notes,' *Revue Celtique*, 1 (1870–72), 257; Joyce, I, 271.
21 Joyce, I, 272.
22 Killeen, pp. 202–04.
23 Lady Charlotte Guest, trans., *The Mabinogion* (London: Everyman, 1906), p. 71; cf. Mac Cana, *Celtic Mythology*, p. 28, M. Mac Neill, p. 7.
24 M. Mac Neill, p. 7.
25 Winberry, p. 70.
26 Charles Plummer, ed. & trans., *Bethada Náem nErenn: Lives of Irish Saints* (1922; rpt. Oxford: Clarendon Press, 1968), II, 63.
27 Pádraig Ó Riain, 'Traces of Lug in Early Irish Hagiographical Tradition', *Zeitschrift für Celtische Philologie*, 36 (1977), 151. Ó Riain apparently fails to note the relevance of this to leprechauns.
28 Winberry, p. 64.
29 Thomas Keightley, *The Fairy Mythology* (1850; rpt. New York: Haskell House, 1968), pp. 382–83.
30 Stokes, 'Mythological Notes', p. 257. Winberry proposes *clochan* + *armunn*, which he would translate as 'one who lives near or under a thorn bush' (p. 68). This is even less acceptable than *leipreachán* from *luch* + *armunn*, for similar reasons. P. Ussher proposes *clutharacán*, 'literally "one who lives in the shade" ': 'Waterford Folk Tales', *Folk-Lore*, 25 (1914), 111. This spelling is, in fact, attested.

31 Winberry, p. 64.
32 K. M. Briggs, *The Fairies in Tradition and Literature* (London: Routledge & Kegan Paul, 1967), p. 85.
33 Winberry, pp. 64–66.
34 W. B. Yeats, *Irish Fairy Tales* (1892), in *Fairy and Folk Tales of Ireland*, p. 384.
35 RBÉ SMS 158 (Co. Sligo), p. 61.
36 Hyde, 'Columcille and his Brother Dobhran', in *Saints and Sinners*, pp. 202–03; 'The Soul Cages,' in Croker, p. 199.
37 Briggs, *Dictionary*, p. 290.
38 'The Lady of Gollerus' and 'The Soul Cages', in T. Crofton Croker, *Fairy Legends and Traditions of the South of Ireland* (London: Swan Sonnenschein, n. d. [1906?]) pp. 178, 199. Wood-Martin, who is clearly following Croker, believes this applies only to mer*men*, but there seems no justification for this.
39 Briggs, *Dictionary*, pp. 287–88, 290.
40 Plummer, *Bethada*, II, 61.
41 Hyde, *Saints and Sinners*, pp. 202–03.
42 Briggs, *Dictionary*, p. 288.
43 Plummer, *Bethada*, II, 162–63.
44 RBÉ SMS 158, p. 61.
45 Briggs, *Dictionary*, p. 290; 'The Lady of Gollerus', 'The Soul Cages', and 'The Wonderful Tune', in Croker, pp. 177, 185, 199, 28.
46 RBÉ SMS 157 (Co. Sligo), p. 365; Michael J. Murphy, *Now You're Talking . . .: Folk Tales from the North of Ireland* (Belfast: Blackstaff Press, 1975), p. 95.
47 Hyde, *Saints and Sinners*, pp. 262–63.
48 M. J. Murphy, p. 95.
49 Wood-Martin, I, 375–76.
50 Gregory, *Visions and Beliefs*, p. 19.
51 Stokes, *Vita Tripartita*, I, 131.
52 RBÉ SMS 157, pp. 200, 201.
53 W. B. Yeats, *The Celtic Twilight* (1893), in *Mythologies*, p. 92; Sean O'Sullivan, 'The Conneelys and the Seals', in *Folklore*, pp. 116–19.
54 Patricia Lysaght, '*An Bhean Chaointe*: The Supernatural Woman in Irish Folklore', *Eire-Ireland*, 14, No. 4 (1979), 18, 22.
55 RBÉ SMS 155, p. 628.
56 RBÉ SMS 155, pp. 535–41.
57 Francis John Byrne, Seminar, Yeats International Summer School, Sligo, Ireland, August 1980.
58 Lysaght, p. 20.
59 *Ní túisge an bhean-sídhe ins an teach ná raibh sí deich míle uaidh*: RBÉ SMS 48, pp. 125–26. An anomalous feature of this account is that the banshee is heard keening after the death.
60 Briggs, *Dictionary*, p. 14.
61 Lysaght, pp. 14, 16; cf. D. H. Moutray Read, 'Some Characteristics of Irish Folklore', *Folk-Lore*, 26 (1916), 251.
62 Lysaght, p. 14.
63 Aine's 'clients' include the Desmonds: Francis John Byrne, Seminar, Yeats International Summer School, Sligo, Ireland, August 1980.
64 Quoted by Wood-Martin, I, 364.
65 See above, pp. 53, 54–55.
66 Hyde, *Literary History*, p. 438.
67 Lysaght, p. 13; Ussher, p. 121.

68 Wood-Martin, I, 358–59; II, 141; Briggs, *Dictionary*, p. 14. Both these authorities do note the banshee's connection with the Morrigu, as also do Cross and Slover, p. 613.
69 Foster, p. 17. The others are 'Maeve Roe, the Macquilin banshee who haunts Dunluce Castle, Co. Antrim; . . . Maveen Roe of the Dungannon O'Neills; and Grania or Gramie of the O'Cahans, chieftains of the Roe in Co. Derry.' These are not members of the Tuatha Dé Danann but characters from the Ulster Cycle (Maeve and her diminutive Maveen) and the Fenian Cycle (Grania). 'Roe' (*ruadh*) means 'red-haired'.
70 Sir Walter Scott, *The Heart of Mid-Lothian* (1818; rpt. London: Everyman, 1956), p. 560.
71 Briggs, *Dictionary*, pp. 14, 19; Lysaght, p. 10.
72 Cross and Slover, p. 38.
73 Gregory, 'Fate of the Sons of Usnach' and 'Death of Cuchulain', in *Cuchulain of Muirthemne*, pp. 117, 252.
74 Gregory, 'The Battle of Gabhra', in *Gods and Fighting Men*, pp. 328–29.
75 Niall Ó Dónaill, ed. *Foclóir Gaeilge-Béarla* (Baile Átha Cliath: Oifig an tSoláthair, 1977), pp. 621, 952.

9: A Second Census of Fairyland

1 Gregory, *Visions and Beliefs*, p. 175; Lysaght, p. 14.
2 Lady Wilde, *Ancient Cures*, pp. 60, 124.
3 Cáit Ní Bhrádaigh, 'Folklore from Co. Longford', *Béaloideas*, 6 (1936), 260.
4 Evans Wentz, p. 39.
5 Precisely parallel episodes may be found, among other places, in 'The Witch Transformed: Legend of Cullenagh, Queen's County', in O'Hanlon, pp. 74–82, and Jeremiah Curtin, 'Fin MacCool, Ceadach Og, and the Fish Hag', in *Hero-Tales of Ireland* (1894; rpt. New York: Benjamin Blom, 1971), pp. 477–83. However, in 'The Shee an Gannon and the Gruagach Gaire' the 'wizard hare' does not seem capable of taking human form, and in 'Gilla na Grakin and Fin MacCumhail' the hare is simply a hare: Jeremiah Curtin, *Myths and Folk-Lore of Ireland* (Boston: Little, Brown, & Co., 1908), pp. 114–28, 255–60.
6 See, for example, RBÉ SMS 158, p. 60.
7 Gregory, *Visions and Beliefs*, p. 55.
8 A. C. Haddon, 'A Batch of Irish Folk-Lore', *Folk-Lore*, 4 (1893), 352.
9 Daniel Hoffman, *Barbarous Knowledge: Myth in the Poetry of Yeats, Graves, and Muir* (New York: Oxford University Press, 1967), p. 76.
10 W. R. Wilde, p. 56.
11 Wood-Martin, I, 293; Leland L. Duncan, 'Folk-Lore Gleanings from County Leitrim', *Folk-Lore*, 4 (1893), 184.
12 Foster, p. 64.
13 Haddon, p. 352.
14 Briggs, *Tradition and Literature*, p. 140.
15 See, for instance, W. B. Yeats, *The Celtic Twilight* (1893), in *Mythologies*, p. 87. The motif is used with an ironic reversal in Yeats's poem 'The Collar-Bone of a Hare.' There, it is the mortal world that is viewed from fairyland.
16 Gregory, *Visions and Beliefs*, pp. 290–92.
17 Cross and Slover, p. 268.

18 Gregory, *Visions and Beliefs*, pp. 292–93.
19 Douglas Hyde, ed. & trans., *Beside the Fire: A Collection of Irish Gaelic Folk Stories* (London: David Nutt, 1910), pp. 72–91.
20 Wood-Martin, II, 5, 194.
21 Lady Wilde, *Ancient Cures*, p. 69.
22 RBÉ SMS 156 (Co. Sligo), pp. 30–38.
23 Sean O'Sullivan, 'The Fairy Frog', in *Folklore*, pp. 100–04.
24 Gregory, *Visions and Beliefs*, p. 22.
25 Wood-Martin, II, 117, 141; Gregory, *Visions and Beliefs*, p. 279.
26 W. B. Yeats, Note to 'The Valley of the Black Pig', in *Variorum Poems*, p. 809.
27 Briggs, *Dictionary*, p. 10.
28 Briggs, *Tradition and Literature*, p. 74.
29 Evans Wentz, p. 40.
30 M. J. Murphy, p. 109.
31 Gregory, *Visions and Beliefs*, pp. 278–79.
32 Hyde, 'The Hags of the Long Teeth', in *Beside the Fire*, p. 163.
33 *Deirtear nach feidir d'aon sidheóg dul tar uisce . . . . Deirtear gur tógadh na sidheóga iad*: RBÉ SMS 49, p. 213; cf. Wood-Martin, II, 23: 'Spirits (good, bad and indifferent) cannot cross a stream of running water.'
34 Hyde, 'Leeam O'Rooney's Burial', in *Beside the Fire*, p. 103.
35 Westropp, 'Coast of Connacht', Vol. 29, 310. Westropp adds that in the same locality this function is shared with a white cow, also a ghost, which is 'especially feared'. This is surprising, as the cow sounds like the Glas Gaibhlenn, 'the sacred or fairy milk-white cow' (sometimes with green spots) that is normally the best of omens: W. R. Wilde, p. 70. But perhaps the white cow of Ballycroy belongs to the same herd as 'a great number of white cattle' that once appeared in a valley near Cleanagh, Co. Laoighis. Before vanishing, 'They left tracks of steps seven yards asunder, and the grass was burnt black round the steps': Helen M. Roe, 'Tales, Customs and Beliefs from Laoighis,' *Béaloideas*, 9 (1939), 34.
36 John Messenger, 'Joe O'Donnel, *Seanchai* of Aran', *Journal of the Folklore Institute*, 1 (1964), 210–12.
37 Francis John Byrne, Seminar, Yeats International Summer School, Sligo, Ireland, August 1980.
38 Stewart MacAlister, ed. & trans., 'The Life of Saint Finan', *Zeitschrift für Celtische Philologie*, 2 (1899), 550–64.
39 Whitley Stokes, ed. & trans. 'The Life of Féchín of Fore', *Revue Celtique*, 12 (1891), 347–49.
40 RBÉ SMS 47, p. 159.
41 RBÉ SMS 47, pp. 159–60; Lady Jane Wilde, *Ancient Legends, Mystic Charms and Superstitions of Ireland* (London: Ward & Downey, 1887), I, 182–83; Donal Dorcey, 'Burren's Mysterious Underground', *The Irish Times*, Thursday, 31 July 1980, p. 10.
42 Quoted by Wood-Martin, I, 378.
43 Briggs, *Dictionary*, p. 326; Wood-Martin, I, 55; MacManus, pp. 64, 66.
44 Westropp, 'Coast of Connacht,' Vol. 29, 310.
45 Briggs, *Dictionary*, pp. 326–27. 'The Phooka of Kildare,' in Patrick Kennedy's version, can be found in W. B. Yeats, *Fairy and Folk Tales of Ireland*, pp. 96–98.
46 Wood-Martin, I, 55. This is despite the fact that MacManus derives 'pooka' from '*puc*, a buck goat' (p. 64). I do not find this word in either Dinneen's or Ó Dónaill's dictionary. P. W. Joyce derives 'pooka' from O. N. *púki* 'imp' (I, 272).

Notes to pages 129–136

47 Evans Wentz, p. 53.
48 Wood-Martin, I, 55–56. In Crofton Croker's 'The Crookened Back', the pooka actually rides on its victims, not they on it. It is described as 'a small black goat, only with long wide horns turned out instead of being bent backwards, standing upon its hind legs' (pp. 149–57).

10: The Quick and the Dead

1 Dillon, *Early Irish Literature*, pp. 68–72.
2 Gregory, 'The Voyage of Brendan', in *Saints & Wonders*, p. 106.
3 Reidar Th. Christiansen, 'Some Notes on the Fairies and the Fairy Faith', in Almqvist, mac Aodha, and mac Eoin, p. 97; Wood-Martin, II, 5.
4 M. Mac Neill, p. 205.
5 Evans Wentz, p. 53.
6 Kirk, pp. 56, 57, 93–94.
7 Nutt, 'Re-Birth,' II, 212–13. This tradition is entirely folkloric; it has no foundation in hagiographical literature.
8 Lady Wilde, *Ancient Cures*, p. 76.
9 W. R. Wilde, p. 125.
10 Evans Wentz, p. 47.
11 W. B. Yeats, *The Celtic Twilight* (1893), in *Mythologies*, pp. 70–71.
12 Russell K. Alspach, 'The Use by Yeats and Other Irish Writers of the Folklore of Patrick Kennedy', *Journal of American Folklore*, 59 (1946), 406.
13 W. B. Yeats, *Variorum Poems*, pp. 728–31.
14 W. B. Yeats, *Fairy and Folk Tales of the Irish Peasantry* (1888), in *Fairy and Folk Tales of Ireland*, p. 6.
15 W. B. Yeats, Letter to Katharine Tynan (21 Dec. 1888), in *The Letters*, ed. Allan Wade (New York: Macmillan, 1955), p. 97.
16 Haddon, p. 352.
17 Margaret Dean-Smith, 'Human-Fairy Marriage' (Letter), *Folk-Lore*, 66 (1955), 435.
18 Kirk, p. 58.
19 Gregory, *Saints & Wonders*, pp. 111–12.
20 Evans Wentz, p. 47.
21 Briggs, *Tradition and Literature*, p. 102.
22 Briggs, *Tradition and Literature*, pp. 52–53.
23 MacManus, p. 22.
24 Andrews, p. 73.
25 W. B. Yeats, 'Irish Wonders' (1889), in *Letters to the New Island*, p. 203.
26 Evans Wentz, p. 32. Briggs comments that 'John Graham may have brought the belief, with his name, from Scotland, for it was current in Scotland at the time of the witchcraft trials': *Tradition and Literature*, p. 142.
27 Christiansen, in Almqvist, mac Aodha, and mac Eoin, p. 103.
28 Bryan H. Jones, 'Irish Folklore from Cavan, Meath, Kerry, and Limerick', *Folk-Lore*, 19 (1908), 320.
29 Gregory, *Visions and Beliefs*, p. 58.
30 O'Malley, p. 108; 'Hanlon's Mill', in Croker, p. 250; Lady Wilde, *Ancient Cures*, pp. 163–64.
31 Evans Wentz, p. 71; Hyde, *Beside the Fire*, p. 87.
32 Hyde, 'The Old Woman of Beare', in *Saints and Sinners*, p. 188; Lady Wilde, *Ancient Cures*, pp. 163–64.
33 Hyde, *Beside the Fire*, pp. 87, 186.

34 RBÉ SMS 48 (Kiltartan), p. 132.
35 Evans Wentz, p. 71.
36 Gregory, *Visions and Beliefs*, pp. 232–33.
37 RBÉ SMS 47, p. 195.
38 Kirk, p. 52.
39 Lady Gregory, *Poets and Dreamers: Studies and Translations from the Irish* (1903; 2nd edition, Gerrards Cross, Buckinghamshire: Colin Smythe, 1974), p. 87.
40 See, for instance, RBÉ SMS 155 (Co. Sligo), pp. 277–79, 355–57, 395–96; Hyde, 'Teig O'Kane and the Corpse', in *Saints and Sinners*, pp. 220–38.
41 Curtin, *Hero-Tales*, pp. 41–42.
42 S. H. O'Grady, II, 204–05, 213, 220.
43 Plummer, *Bethada*, I, 128, 151, 164; II, 125, 147, 158.
44 W. B. Yeats, 'The Prisoners of the Gods' (1898), in *Uncollected Prose*, II, 82.
45 W. B. Yeats, 'Irish Wonders' (1889), in *Letters to the New Island*, p. 203, and *The Celtic Twilight* (1893), in *Mythologies*, p. 75.
46 Wood-Martin, I, 78.
47 Briggs, *Dictionary*, pp. 62, 390.
48 Gregory, *Visions and Beliefs*, pp. 68, 70.
49 Briggs, *Tradition and Literature*, p. 120.
50 Gregory, *Visions and Beliefs*, p. 67.
51 Gregory, *Visions and Beliefs*, p. 93.
52 See, for instance, W. B. Yeats, *The Celtic Twilight* (1893), in *Mythologies*, p. 76.
53 Gregory, *Visions and Beliefs*, p. 68.
54 'The Sick-Bed of Cu Chulainn', in Cross and Slover, pp. 176–98.
55 Cross and Slover, pp. 395–96. Lady Wilde states oddly that the fairies have a dislike of hurley, but, as Briggs points out, she is not slow to contradict herself: Katharine M. Briggs, *The Vanishing People: A Study of Traditional Fairy Beliefs* (London: B. T. Batsford, 1978), p. 175.
56 Briggs, *Dictionary*, p. 382, and *Traditional and Literature*, pp. 116–17.
57 Wood-Martin, II, 15; 'The Young Piper', in Croker, pp. 43–54.
58 Croker, pp. 52–54.
59 Duncan, p. 179.
60 W. B. Yeats, 'Away' (1902), in *Uncollected Prose*, II, 268.
61 This was told by an Irish teaching brother at Notre Dame University to W. B. Yeats, and retold by him in a letter from Chicago to Lady Gregory, dated 18 Jan. 1904: Letters, p. 423; see also Gregory, *Visions and Beliefs*, p. 67.
62 Evans Wentz, p. 39.
63 Gregory, *Visions and Beliefs*, pp. 70, 130.
64 Biddy Early's historical existence is beyond dispute. She probably died between 1870 and 1880, although there is some disagreement, partly caused by the fact that altogether three women were named or nicknamed Biddy Early: see Gregory, *Visions and Beliefs*, pp. 32, 35–38, 45–47, 96; T. R. Henn, Foreword to Gregory, *Poets and Dreamers*, pp. 6–7; W. B. Yeats, 'Ireland Bewitched' (1899) and 'Irish Witch Doctors' (1900), in *Uncollected Prose*, II, 173, 224–25; Nancy Schmitz, 'An Irish Wise Woman — Fact and Legend', *Journal of the Folklore Institute*, 14 (1977), 169, 175–76; MacManus, p. 155; and Kinahan, p. 116.
65 See, for instance, Lady Wilde, *Ancient Cures*, p. 76.
66 'Master and Man', in Croker, pp. 114–17; cf. also Lady Wilde, *Ancient Cures*, pp. 68–69.
67 Wood-Martin, II, 151.
68 Lady Wilde, *Ancient Cures*, pp. 41, 68.
69 Wood-Martin, II, 13.

Notes to pages 141–146

70 M. J. Murphy, p. 112.
71 E. MacNeill, *Duanaire Finn*, I, 82, 196.
72 Lady Wilde, *Ancient Cures*, p. 57; Wood-Martin, II, 156.
73 Wood-Martin, II, 176.
74 Wood-Martin, II, 262–63; Louis C. Jones. 'The Little People: Some Irish Lore of Upstate New York', *New York Folklore Quarterly*, 18 (1962), 252.
75 Lady Wilde, *Ancient Cures*, p. 41; RBÉ SMS 155 (Co. Sligo), pp. 478–79; Curtin, 'Mor's Sons and the Herder From Under the Sea', in *Hero-Tales*, p. 48; Kirk, p. 54; Wood-Martin, I, 280, II, 16; Gregory, *Poets and Dreamers*, pp. 92–93.
76 Joyce, II, 211.
77 'The Capture of Bridget Purcell', in Croker, pp. 63–65; Gregory, *Poets and Dreamers*, p. 91.
78 Gregory, *Visions and Beliefs*, p. 77; W. R. Wilde, p. 128; Evans Wentz, p. 49.
79 Wood-Martin, II, 12; Andrews, pp. 26–27; Lady Wilde, *Ancient Legends*, I, 54–56.
80 Wood-Martin, II, 12, 273; Curtin, 'Mor's Sons and the Herder From Under the Sea', in *Hero-Tales*, p. 43.
81 Rees, p. 243.
82 Nutt, 'Re-Birth,' II, 230–31.
83 Sayce, p. 117.

11: The Host of the Air

1 Briggs, *Dictionary*, pp. 108–09.
2 RBÉ SMS 158 (Co. Sligo), p. 51.
3 Foster, p. 67.
4 Lady Wilde, *Ancient Legends*, I. 103.
5 RBÉ SMS 158, p. 61; Briggs, *Dictionary*, p. 290; 'The Lady of Gollerus', 'The Soul Cages', and 'The Wonderful Tune', in Croker, pp. 177, 185, 199, 228.
6 ... *beanín beag a bhí ann agus cóta dearg uirri*: RBÉ SMS 48 (Kiltartan), p. 126.
7 Lady Wilde, *Ancient Cures*, p. 84.
8 Briggs, *Dictionary*, p. 14.
9 Ussher, pp. 109, 121.
10 Lysaght, p. 22.
11 Wood-Martin, I, 354.
12 Foster, p. 17; cf. Lady Wilde, *Ancient Cures*, p. 84, Briggs, *Dictionary*, p. 14, and Ussher, p. 121.
13 Lysaght, p. 22.
14 Evans Wentz, pp. 32, 68. Red trooping fairies in Leinster are also reported by Ó Tuathail, p. 88.
15 Gregory, *Visions and Beliefs*, p. 207.
16 Wood-Martin, II, 4.
17 Evans Wentz, p.74.
18 W. B. Yeats, *Fairy and Folk Tales of the Irish Peasantry* (1888), in *Fairy and Folk Tales of Ireland*, p. 289. A caveat: Yeats's source for this is David Rice McAnally, whom Yeats himself accused elsewhere of inventing his folklore: see *Uncollected Prose*, I, 138–41, and *Letters to the New Island*, pp. 192–204.
19 M. Mac Neill, p. 205.
20 Evans Wentz, pp. 45, 53.
21 Gregory, *Visions and Beliefs*, pp. 235, 246.
22 Andrews, p. 73.

23 Haddon, p. 350.
24 Kirk, p. 55.
25 Gregory, *Visions and Beliefs*, pp. 57, 61, with note by W. B. Yeats, p. 356; see also W. B. Yeats, 'Irish Witch Doctors' (1900), in *Uncollected Prose*, II, 221.
26 W. B. Yeats, 'The Tribes of Danu' (1897), in *Uncollected Prose*, II, 56.
27 Gregory, *Visions and Beliefs*, p. 20.
28 W. B. Yeats, *Fairy and Folk Tales of Ireland*, p. 383, and *Variorum Poems*, pp. 803–04.
29 Briggs, *Dictionary*, pp. 109, 375–76; Devlin A. Garrity, ed., *The Mentor Book of Irish Poetry* (New York: Mentor, 1965), pp. 28–29. By the time she wrote *The Vanishing People* (1978), Briggs had wisely arrived at a position of neutrality: the trooping fairies 'may be evil . . . or they may be harmless and even beneficial' (p. 39).
30 Lady Wilde, *Ancient Cures*, p. 84.
31 Wood-Martin, I, 372–73; II, 147–50.
32 Croker, pp. 27–35.
33 RBÉ SMS 48, pp. 115–16.
34 RBÉ SMS 157, pp. 274–76.
35 Andrews, p. 65.
36 See, for instance, Evans Wentz, p. 54, Andrews, pp. 65–67.
37 L. C. Jones, p. 254.
38 RBÉ SMS 48, pp. 131–32.
39 See, for instance, Andrews, pp. 68–71.
40 Andrews, pp. 3–4.
41 RBÉ SMS 155 (Co. Sligo), pp. 413, 530–32; Wood-Martin, I, 41–42, 80.
42 Briggs, *Dictionary*, p. 385.
43 Ernie O'Malley, *On Another Man's Wound* (1936; rpt. Dublin: Anvil, 1979), p. 108.
44 See, for example, RBÉ SMS 158, p. 173.
45 Plummer, *Bethada*, II, 91.
46 O'Malley, p. 109; Wood-Martin, I, 322.
47 Lady Wilde, *Ancient Cures*, pp. 67–68.
48 Ní Bhrádaigh, p. 264.
49 Mac Manus, pp. 121–26.
50 James MacKillop, 'The Hungry Grass: Richard Power's Pastoral Elegy,' in *The Modern Irish Novel (Excluding Joyce): Papers Presented Before the 1980 American Committee for Irish Studies — Modern Language Association Symposium, Houston, Texas, Dec. 29, 1980*, Research Series, No. 50, ed. Herbert V. Fackler (Lafayette, La. University of Southwestern Louisiana Office of Institutional Research, 1980), p. 5.
51 Mac Manus, p. 130.
52 W. R. Wilde, p. 134.
53 S. H. O'Grady, II, 269–85; Plummer, *Bethada*, II, 63.
54 Keightley, p. 372.
55 RBÉ SMS 155, p. 628; RBÉ SMS 158, p. 51.
56 Winberry, p. 67.
57 Briggs, *Dictionary*, p. 14.
58 W. B. Yeats, *Mythologies*, p. 315. In his note to 'The Host of the Air,' Yeats more accurately substitutes 'host' for 'demons': *Variorum Poems*, p. 803.
59 Yeats does acknowledge this as a distinction that other writers have made: see *Irish Fairy Tales* (1892), in *Fairy and Folk Tales of Ireland*, pp. 341–44, and Note to 'The Host of the Air' (1899), in *Variorum Poems*, pp. 803–04.
60 Gregory, *Visions and Beliefs*, p. 79.

Notes to pages 152–160 311

61 For the facts on the Seelie and Unseelie Courts and the Scottish *Sluagh*, see Briggs, *Dictionary*, pp. 373–74, 419–20.
62 Plummer, *Bethada*, II, 89.
63 Hyde, *Saints and Sinners*, p. 194.
64 W. B. Yeats, *Variorum Poems*, pp. 803–04.
65 Donald Ward, 'The Little Man Who Wasn't There: Encounters with the Supranormal', *Fabula*, 18 (1977), 213.

12: *The Countess Cathleen*: 'Longing for a Deeper Peace'

1 This chapter combines in revised form material from my two essays 'Grown to Heaven Like a Tree': The Scenery of *The Countess Cathleen*,' *Eire-Ireland*, 14, No. 3 (1979), 65–82, and '*The Countess Cathleen* and the Otherworld', *Eire-Ireland*, 17, No. 2 (1982), 141–46. I am grateful to Prof. Thomas Dillon Redshaw and the editors of *Éire-Ireland* for permission to incorporate this material.
    From this point on, the following abbreviations will be used and incorporated, with page-numbers, in the text:
    A = *Autobiography*; E &I = *Essays and Introductions*; M = *Mythologies*; VP = *Variorum Poems*; and VPl = *Variorum Plays*.
2 W. B. Yeats, 'Invoking the Irish Fairies,' *The Irish Theosophist*, No. 1 (15 Oct. 1892), pp. 6–7, quoted by Richard Ellmann, *Yeats: The Man and the Masks* (1948; rpt. New York: Dutton, n.d.), p. 67.
3 Patty Gurd, *The Early Poetry of William Butler Yeats* (1916; rpt. Folcroft, Va.: Folcroft, 1977), p. 8.
4 Thomas Leslie Dume, 'William Butler Yeats: A Survey of his Reading', Diss. Temple University 1949, pp. 57, 91.
5 Ernest Boyd, *Ireland's Literary Renaissance*, 2nd. ed. (1922; rpt. New York: Barnes & Noble, 1968), p. 129.
6 Gurd, p. 11.
7 A. M., 'Mr. Yeats's Poems', Review of *Poems* (1895), *The Bookman*, Dec. 1895, in Jeffares, *Critical Heritage*, p. 89.
8 Dorothy M. Hoare, *The Works of Morris and of Yeats in Relation to Early Saga Literature* (Cambridge: Cambridge University Press, 1937), p. 144.
9 Harold H. Watts, *Hound and Quarry* (London: Routledge & Kegan Paul, 1953), p. 179.
10 Thomas L. Byrd, Jr., *The Early Poetry of W. B. Yeats: The Poetic Quest* (Port Washington, N. Y.: Kennikat, 1978), p. 11.
11 George Sutherland Fraser, *W. B. Yeats*, Writers and Their Work, No. 50 (London: Longmans, Green & Co., 1962), p. 22.
12 Louis MacNeice, *The Poetry of W. B. Yeats* (New York: Oxford University Press, 1941), p. 61.
13 Ellmann, *Man and Masks*, p. 83.
14 W. B. Yeats, *Memoirs*, ed. Denis Donoghue (London: Macmillan, 1972), p. 47.
15 Padraic Colum, Sleeve-notes to the sound recording of *The Countess Cathleen*, featuring Siobhan McKenna, John Neville, *et al.*, Tradition, TLP 501, n.d.
16 Leonard E. Nathan, *The Tragic Drama of William Butler Yeats: Figures in a Dance* (New York: Columbia University Press, 1965), pp. 25–26.
17 Wood-Martin, II, 4.

18 Christopher Marlowe, *Doctor Faustus*, in *The Plays of Christopher Marlowe*, ed. Roma Gill (London: Oxford University Press, 1971), p. 343.
19 W. B. Yeats, *Fairy and Folk Tales of Ireland*, pp. 211–14. Yeats's note also refers to William Larminie's 'The Woman Who Went to Hell', in *West Irish Folk-Tales and Romances* (1893; rpt. Freeport, N.Y.: Books for Libraries, 1972), pp. 188–95. This story was not published until after the first version of *The Countess Cathleen*, and in any case it bears little resemblance to it.
20 Hyde, *Literary History*, pp. 64–65n, 388n.
21 Mac Cana, *Celtic Mythology*, pp. 91–92; Gregory, 'Midhir and Etain', in *Gods and Fighting Men*, pp. 88–96, and 'The High King of Ireland', in *Cuchulain of Muirthemne*, pp. 77–91; 'The Wooing of Etain' and 'The Destruction of Da Derga's Hostel', in Cross and Slover, pp. 82–126; M. Mac Neill, pp. 238–39.
22 W. B. Yeats, *A Vision*, 'With the author's final revisions' (1956; rpt. New York: Collier, 1966), p. 237.
23 Was it a Freudian slip that made Yeats misspell the Countess's name 'O'Shee' in a letter to Father Matthew Russell, 13 July 1889? *Letters*, p. 129.
24 James Stephens, *The Crock of Gold* (1912; rpt. New York: Collier, 1967), p. 12.
25 In this way the swan anticipates the dolphins of 'Byzantium': cf. Alex Zwerdling, 'W. B. Yeats: Variations on the Visionary Quest,' in *Yeats: A Collection of Critical Essays*, ed. John Unterecker (Englewood Cliffs, N.J.: Prentice-Hall, 1963), p. 85.
26 David V. Erdman, annotator, *The Illuminated Blake* (Garden City, N.Y.: Anchor, 1974), p. 290.
27 Cf. *John Sherman* (1891):

The stars, the streams down in the valley, the wind moving among the boulders, the various unknown creatures rustling in the silence — all these were contained within themselves, fulfilling their law, content to be alone, content to be with others, having the peace of God or the peace of the birds of prey:

W. B. Yeats, *John Sherman and Dhoya*, ed. Richard J. Finneran (Detroit: Wayne State University Press, 1969), p. 110.
28 Gregory, *Visions and Beliefs*, p. 221. Yeats was present at this interview. His owls acquired human faces in 1912, but already had human voices in 1892. Lady Gregory began collecting c. 1895.
29 Foster, p. 16.
30 O'Malley, p. 84.
31 Vernam E. Hull, ed. & trans., 'Two Middle-Irish Religious Anecdotes', *Speculum*, 3 (1928), 101–03; O'Clery, pp. 30, 273.
32 S. H. O'Grady, II, 49.
33 Richard Ellmann, *The Identity of Yeats*, 2nd. ed. (London: Faber and Faber, 1964), p. xxi; cf. also Charles Berryman, *W.B. Yeats: Design of Opposites* (New York: Exposition, 1967), p. 61.
34 See George Mills Harper, *The Mingling of Heaven and Earth: Yeats's Theory of Theatre* (Dublin: Dolmen, 1975), pp. 20, 33; Karen Dorn, 'Dialogue Into Movement: W. B. Yeats's Theatre Collaboration with Gordon Craig', and James W. Flannery, 'W. B. Yeats, Gordon Craig and the Visual Arts of the Theatre', in *Yeats and the Theatre*, Yeats Studies Series, ed. Robert O'Driscoll and Lorna Reynolds (Toronto: Macmillan, 1975), pp. 103, 117, 120.
35 Peter Ure, *Yeats the Playwright: A Commentary on Character and Design in the Major Plays* (New York: Barnes & Noble, 1963), p. 21.
36 One of Lady Gregory's informants told her, in Yeats's presence, that the fairies 'have the power to go in every place, even on to the book the priest is using': *Visions and Beliefs*, p. 65. This line was added to *The Countess Cathleen* in 1912.

37 However, Yeats himself points out that his Fergus, who 'gave up his throne that he might live at peace, hunting in the woods,' owes more to Sir Samuel Ferguson's 'The Abdication of Fergus Mac Roy', in *Lays of the Western Gael*, than it does to the Ulster Cycle: W. B. Yeats, 'Plans and Methods' (of the Irish Literary Theatre) (1899), in *Uncollected Prose*, II, 161. In a note to 'The Secret Rose' (VP 814), Yeats says that 'when I wrote . . . "Who will drive with Fergus now"', I only knew him in Mr. Standish O'Grady', but this appears to be a slip.
38 Sister M. Rosalie Ryan's conclusion is slightly different:

A triple effect in setting symbolizing heaven, hell, and earth was evidently intended in the castle scene. At one side of the great hall is 'an oratory with steps leading up to it' . . . . In the back are several arches 'through which one can dimly see the trees of the garden,' a reference to the surrounding powers of evil. At the left is a tapestried wall which surrounds the central part of the stage, the earthly setting of the conflict between powers of good and evil:

'Symbolic Elements in the Plays of William Butler Yeats 1892–1921', Diss. Catholic University of America 1952, p. 34.
39 The distinction between heart and soul would seem to originate in Eastern philosophy. The heart represents the passions. Cf. 'Quatrains and Aphorisms' (1886):

. . . these lines I read
On Brahma's gateway, 'They within have fed
The soul upon the ashes of the heart.'

(VP 734–35)

40 Ure, *Yeats the Playwright*, pp. 19, 26.
41 James Lovic Allen, 'Unity of Archetype, Myth, and Religious Imagery in the Work of Yeats,' *Twentieth Century Literature*, 20 (1974), 92–93.
42 Yeats knew Aleel's experience at first-hand:

I had sometimes when awake, but more often in sleep, moments of vision, a state very unlike dreaming, when these images ['from Irish folk-lore'] took upon themselves what seemed an independent life and became a part of a mystic language, which seemed always as if it would bring me some strange revelation:

Note to *The Wind Among the Reeds*, VP 800.

43 Cf. Henry Goodman, 'The Plays of William Butler Yeats as Myth and Ritual', Diss. Minnesota 1952, pp. 349–50: 'She took upon her self the consequence of sin and suffered, like Christ, the vicarious expiation of the sins of other people. . . . Aleel, it might be said, takes upon himself the *knowledge* of sin, and thus complements Cathleen.'
44 Nathan, pp. 26–27. The tradition that rowan berries are the food of the gods derives from the legend of Innisfree: cf. Yeats's note to 'The Danaan Quicken Tree', VP 742:

It is said that an enchanted tree grew once on the little lake-island of Innisfree, and that its berries were, according to one legend, poisonous to mortals, and according to another, able to endow them with more than mortal powers. Both legends say that the berries were the food of the *Tuatha de Danaan*, or faeries.

45 Allen, 'Unity of Archetype', pp. 92–93.
46 Peter Ure, 'The Evolution of Yeats's *The Countess Cathleen*,' *Modern Language Review*, 57 (1962), 18.

47 Michael P. Goldman, 'The Point of Drama: The Concept of Reverie in the Plays of William Butler Yeats', Diss. Princeton 1962, pp. 96–97; Frank Hughes Murphy, *Yeats's Early Poetry: The Quest for Reconciliation* (Baton Rouge: Louisiana State University Press, 1975), pp. 78–79.
48 Liam Miller, *The Noble Drama of W. B. Yeats* (Dublin: Dolmen, 1977), pp. 3–4.
49 A. G. Stock, *W. B. Yeats: His Poetry and Thought* (Cambridge: Cambridge University Press, 1961), p. 29.

13: The Rose and Her Servants

1 This chapter is chiefly concerned with *The Rose* (1892), *The Land of Heart's Desire* (1894), and *The Secret Rose* (1897), excluding the *Stories of Red Hanrahan*, "Rosa Alchemica," "The Tables of the Law," and "The Adoration of the Magi."
2 George Brandon Saul, 'In . . . Luminous Wind', in *The Dolmen Press Yeats Centenary Papers MCMLXV*, ed. Liam Miller (Dublin: Dolmen, 1968), p. 202.
3 F. H. Murphy, pp. 33–34.
4 A. Norman Jeffares, *A Commentary on the Collected Poems of W. B. Yeats* (Stanford, Ca.: Stanford University Press, 1968), pp. 30–31, 36.
5 Lester Conner, Seminar, Yeats International Summer School, Sligo, Ireland, August 1980.
6 Cf. Walter Pater, *The Renaissance: Studies in Art and Poetry* (1873; rpt. New York: Mentor, 1959), p. 52. Original title: *Studies in the History of the Renaissance*.
7 Stock, pp. 44–45.
8 MacDonagh, *Literature in Ireland*, in Jeffares, *Critical Heritage*, p. 200.
9 Byrd, p. 55.
10 Edwin John Ellis and William Butler Yeats, eds., *The Works of William Blake* (London: Bernard Quaritch, 1893), I, xii; cf. William Blake, 'A Vision of the Last Judgment', in *Poetry and Prose*, ed. Geoffrey Keynes (London: Nonesuch, 1927), pp. 651–52.
11 Ellmann, *Identity*, p. 34.
12 W. B. Yeats, *Memoirs*, pp. 72–73.
13 Goodman, p. 528.
14 This point has been noticed by Ryan, p. 21.
15 Balachandra Rajan, *W. B. Yeats: A Critical Introduction* (London: Hutchinson, 1965), p. 34.
16 Denis Donoghue, 'Yeats: The Question of Symbolism', in *Myth and Reality in Irish Literature*, ed. Joseph Ronsley (Waterloo, Ontario: Wilfrid Laurier University Press, 1977), p. 108. See also Thomas R. Whitaker, *Swan and Shadow: Yeats's Dialogue with History* (Chapel Hill: University of North Carolina Press, 1964), p. 162.
17 Stock, pp. 42–43.
18 McGarry and Malins, p. 48.
19 Cross and Slover, p. 460.
20 Francis John Byrne, Seminar, Yeats International Summer School, Sligo, Ireland, August 1980.
21 Augustine Martin, 'Apocalyptic Structure in Yeats's *Secret Rose*', *Studies*, 64 (1975), 24.
22 Robert O'Driscoll, *Symbolism and Some Implications of the Symbolic Approach: W. B. Yeats During the Eighteen-Nineties*, New Yeats Papers IX (Dublin: Dolmen, 1975), p. 30.

23 Forrest Reid, *W. B. Yeats: A Critical Study* (1915; rpt. New York: Haskell House, 1972), p. 132.
24 In this I differ slightly from George Jay Bornstein, who writes: 'The battle is not a military one between armies but a spiritual one between opposing qualities in human life': 'The Surfeited Alastor: William Butler Yeats's Changing Relation to Percy Bysshe Shelley', Diss. Princeton 1966, p. 67.
25 Stock, p. 45.
26 Giorgio Melchiori, *The Whole Mystery of Art: Pattern and Poetry in the Work of W. B. Yeats* (London: Routledge & Kegan Paul, 1960), p. 116.
27 John Unterecker, *A Reader's Guide to William Butler Yeats* (New York: Noonday, 1959), p. 79.
28 Unterecker, *Reader's Guide*, p. 79.
29 F. H. Murphy, pp. 58–60.
30 Cara Ackerman considers the Rose in this poem comparable with Cleena in 'The Book of the Great Dhoul and Hanrahan the Red' (1897): 'Yeats' Revisions of the Hanrahan Stories, 1897 and 1904'. *Texas Studies in Literature and Language*, 17 (1975), 507.
31 David Daiches, 'W. B. Yeats — I' (1940), in *The Permanence of Yeats*, ed. James Hall and Martin Steinmann (New York: Macmillan, 1950), p. 128.
32 W. B. Yeats, *Letters*, p. 249.
33 Harold Bloom, *Yeats* (New York: Oxford University Press, 1970), p. 112.
34 M. L. Rosenthal, *The Modern Poets: A Critical Introduction* (New York: Oxford University Press, 1960), pp. 37–38.
35 Gurd, pp. 27–28.
36 F. H. Murphy, pp. 57–58.
37 William York Tindall, 'The Symbolism of W. B. Yeats' (1945), in Hall and Steinmann, p. 271.
38 Mary Catherine Flannery, *Yeats and Magic: The Earlier Works*, Irish Literary Studies, No. 2 (Gerrards Cross, Buckinghamshire: Colin Smythe, 1977), pp. 83–84; Daniel S. Lenoski, 'Yeats, Eglinton, and Aestheticism', *Eire-Ireland*, 14, No. 4 (1979), 95.
39 Maurice Beebe, *Ivory Towers and Sacred Founts: The Artist as Hero in Fiction from Goethe to Joyce* (New York: New York University Press, 1964), p. 156.
40 Thomas Parkinson, *W. B. Yeats, Self-Critic: A Study of His Early Verse* (1951; rpt. Berkeley: University of California Press, 1971), p. 14. (In this edition, *W. B. Yeats, Self-Critic* is issued in one volume with the same author's *W. B. Yeats: The Later Poetry*.) Cf. Also Jeffares, *Commentary on Poems*, p. 46.
41 Ellmann, *Man and Masks*, p. 68.
42 Martin, 'Apocalyptic Structures', p. 31.
43 Bloom, p. 115.
44 Edmund Wilson, *Axel's Castle: A Study in the Imaginative Literature of 1870–1930* (1931; rpt. London: Fontana, 1961), pp. 31–32.
45 David Daiches, 'The Earlier Poems: Some Themes and Patterns,' in *In Excited Reverie: A Centenary Tribute to William Butler Yeats 1865–1939*, ed. A. Norman Jeffares and K. G. W. Cross (London: Macmillan, 1965). p. 57.
46 Ellmann, *Identity*, p. 30.
47 Ellis and Yeats, I, 288–9
48 Byrd, pp. 47–48.
49 This is implicit in the poem, but fully explicit in Curtin, 'Cucúlin,' in *Myths and Folk-Lore*, p. 324. Since Yeats himself identifies this as his source (VP 799), it is hard to see why Russell K. Alspach cites Charlotte Brooke's 'Conloch': 'Irish legend in Irish Literature', in *Folklore in Action: Essays for Discussion in Honor of MacEdward Leach*, ed. Horace P. Beck (Philadelphia:

American Folklore Society, 1962), p. 16. However, in many respects George Brandon Saul is quite correct in saying that Yeats's 'version is far from that of Curtin's "Cucúlin" ', a rather barbarous folk-tale in which Cucúlin is actually numbered amongst the Fianna: *Prolegomena to the Study of Yeats's Poems* (Philadelphia: University of Pennsylvania Press, 1957), p. 52.

50 Similar points have been made by Unterrecker, *Reader's Guide*, p. 78, and Janet Frank Egelson, 'Christ and Cuchulain: Interrelated Archetypes of Divinity and Heroism in Yeats', *Éire-Ireland*, 4, No. 1 (1969), 80.

14: 'The Cauldron, the Stone, the Sword, the Spear': Stories of Red Hanrahan

1 W. B. Yeats, *The Secret Rose, Stories by W. B. Yeats: A Variorum Edition*, ed. Phillip L. Marcus, Warwick Gould, and Michael J. Sidnell (Ithaca, N.Y.: Cornell University Press, 1981), pp. 190, 194, 224.
2 Ackerman, p. 507.
3 Ellmann, *Identity*, p. 31.
4 Ackerman, p. 507.
5 Ackerman, p. 509.
6 W. B. Yeats, *Variorum Secret Rose*, pp. 199, 200.
7 W. B. Yeats, 'Ireland Bewitched' (1899), in *Uncollected Prose*, II, 169. David Fitzgerald also mentions a story in which a magician called Nugent performs this trick: 'History and Mythology,' p. 218.
8 Hoffman, pp. 76–77.
9 Maud Gonne, 'Yeats and Ireland', in *Scattering Branches: Tributes to the Memory of W. B. Yeats*, ed. Stephen Gwynn (London: Macmillan, 1940), p. 23.
10 Arthur Edward Waite, *The Holy Grail* (1929), reproduced in his *Pictorial Key to the Tarot* (New York: University Books, 1959), p. vii.
11 See W. B. Yeats, *Memoirs*, p. 125; Gonne, in Gwynn, pp. 23–24. Cf. also Vernam Hull, 'The Four Jewels of the *Tuatha Dé Danann*', *Zeitschrift für Celtische Philologie*, 18 (1930), 73–83.
12 Gwladys V. Downes, 'W. B. Yeats and the Tarot', in *The World of W. B. Yeats: Essays in Perspective*, ed. Robin Skelton and Ann Saddlemyer (Victoria, B. C. : Adelphi Bookshop for the University of Victoria, 1965), p. 68.
13 Gonne, in Gwynn, pp. 23–24. The Sword of Light features in many *scéalta*. It seems to have been Yeat's own intuition that it derives from the Sword of Nuada.
14 Kathleen Raine, 'Yeats, the Tarot, and the Golden Dawn', *Sewanee Review*, 77 (1969), 123–24; Aleister Crowley (The Master Therion), *The Book of Thoth* (1944; rpt. New York: Lancer, n. d.), p. 69.
15 Raine, 'Tarot', pp. 122, 124.
16 Ackerman, p. 521.
17 Here and elsewhere, I refer to the Rider pack version of the Tarot. The Rider pack was designed by A. E. Waite and by Yeats's friend Pamela Colman Smith. Yeats's own Tarot pack was of this design: Downes, in Skelton and Saddlemyer, p. 68; Gertrude Moakley, Introduction to Waite, p. xiii.
18 Raine, 'Tarot', p. 122, quoting Waite.
19 Ackerman, p. 524n.
20 Ackerman, p. 514.
21 Daniel A. Harris, *Yeats: Coole Park and Ballylee* (Baltimore: Johns Hopkins University Press, 1974), p. 190.

Notes to pages 212–226

22 Ackerman, pp. 514–15.
23 Richard J. Finneran, '"Old lecher with a love on every wind': A Study of Yeats' *Stories of Red Hanrahan*', *Texas Studies in Literature and Language*, 14 (1972), 354–55.
24 O'Driscoll, pp. 35–36.
25 Sheila O'Sullivan, 'W. B. Yeats's Use of Irish Oral and Literary Tradition', in Almqvist, mac Aodha, and mac Eoin, pp. 275–76; Ronald Schleifer 'Narrative in Yeats's *In the Seven Woods*', *Journal of Narrative Technique*, 6 (1976), 158. For *The Country of the Young*, which is related to Lady Gregory's *The Travelling Man*, see Hazard Adams, 'Yeats's *Country of the Young*'. *PMLA*, 72 (1957), 510–19.
26 Kathleen Raine, 'Hades Wrapped in Cloud', in *Yeats and the Occult*, Yeats Studies Series, ed. George Mills Harper (Toronto: Macmillan, 1975), pp. 100–01.
27 Andrew Parkin, *The Dramatic Imagination of W. B. Yeats* (Dublin: Gill & Macmillan, 1978), pp. 84, 187.
28 Mary Helen Thuente, *W. B. Yeats and Irish Folklore* (Dublin: Gill & Macmillan, 1980), pp. 212–13.
29 Thuente, p. 211.
30 Gregory, 'Oisin's Children', in *Gods and Fighting Men*, p. 247.
31 W. B. Yeats, 'Swedenborg, Mediums, and the Desolate Places', in Gregory, *Visions and Beliefs*, p. 316.

15: 'The Flaming Door': *The Wind Among the Reeds* as Psychic Narrative

1 He is studied in some detail in Appendix A.
2 Ellmann, *Identity*, p. 302.
3 Allen R. Grossman, *Poetic Knowledge in the Early Yeats: A Study of* The Wind Among the Reeds (Charlottesville: University Press of Virginia, 1969), p. 14.
4 F. F. Farag, 'Oriental and Celtic Elements in the Poetry of W. B. Yeats', in *W. B. Yeats 1865–1965: Centenary Essays on the Art of W. B. Yeats*, ed. D. E. S. Maxwell and S. B. Bushrui (Ibadan, Nigeria: Ibadan University Press, 1965), p. 34.
5 Jeffares, *Commentary on Poems*, p. 52.
6 Jeffares, *Commentary on Poems*, p. 53.
7 Ellis and Yeats, II, 12, quoted by Ronald Schleifer, 'Principles, Proper Names, and the Personae of Yeats's *The Wind Among the Reeds*', *Éire-Ireland*, 16, No. 1 (1981), 72–73. As Schleifer points out, the moods 'derive at least in part from Blake's "external states" '.
8 Grossman, p. 99.
9 Ellis and Yeats, I, 239.
10 Grossman, p. 92.
11 The same theme is found in Child Ballads 4 and 200, 'Lady Isabel and the Elf-Knight' and 'The Gypsy Laddy': Neil R. Grobman, 'In Search of a Mythology: William Butler Yeats and Folklore', *New York Folklore Quarterly*, 30 (1974), 121.
12 W. B. Yeats, *Uncollected Prose*, I, 413–18.
13 Jeffares, *Commentary on Poems*, p. 60.
14 W. B. Yeats, ' "Maive" and Certain Irish Beliefs' (1900), in *Uncollected Prose*, II, 204–05.
15 Grossman, p. 134.
16 Grobman, p. 121.

17 O'Driscoll, p. 53.
18 W. B. Yeats, *Memoirs*, p. 68.
19 Gregory, 'The Dream of Angus Og,' in *Cuchulain of Muirthemne*, pp. 118–21; see also Yeats's poem 'The Old Age of Queen Maeve' (1903). Patty Gurd states with conviction that 'The Song of Wandering Aengus' is based on 'The Dream of Angus Og' (p. 66).
20 Jerome L. Mazzaro, 'Apple Imagery in Yeats' "The Song of Wandering Aengus" ', *Modern Language Notes*, 72 (1957), 342–43.
21 'The Adventures of Connla the Fair,' in Cross and Slover, pp. 488–90.
22 Bloom, p. 126.
23 Grossman, pp. 180–82.
24 Lester Conner, Seminar, Yeats International Summer School, Sligo, Ireland, August 1980.
25 Robert Langbaum, *The Mysteries of Identity: A Theme in Modern Literature* (New York: Oxford University Press, 1977), pp. 164–65.
26 Donoghue, 'The Question of Symbolism', in Ronsley, p. 101.
27 Virginia Moore, *The Unicorn: William Butler Yeats' Search for Reality* (New York: Macmillan, 1954), p. 73.
28 Grossman, pp. 86, 93; V. Moore, p. 144; Raine, 'Tarot', p. 129.
29 John Unterecker, 'The Private Man in the Public Poems', Yeats International Summer School, Sligo, Ireland, 18 August 1980.
30 David R. Clark, *Lyric Resonance: Glosses on Some Poems of Yeats, Frost, Crane, Cummings and Others* (Amherst: University of Massachusetts Press, 1972), p. 37.
31 Arthur Symons, 'Mr. Yeats as a Lyric Poet', *Saturday Review*, No. 91 (6 May 1899), p. 553, quoted by Schleifer, 'Proper Names,' pp. 75–76.
32 V. Moore, p. 446.
33 Clark, p. 38.
34 Grossman, p. 122.
35 Grossman, p. 90. The Ritual of the Fiery Spear, devised by Yeats, also includes the sentence 'He who trembles before the abyss has no part in the gods': V. Moore, p. 79.
36 Gregory, 'Bodb Dearg', in *Gods and Fighting Men*, p. 78; Cross and Slover, p. 102. Yeats's note aptly mentions 'Mac Datho's Pig' as another tale of this type. Fenian parallels listed by G. Murphy are *Feis Tighe Chonáin, Bruidhean Eochaidh Bhig Dheirg*, the Old Irish 'Death of Cúldub,' and the Scottish folk-tale of *Fionn 'an Taigh a' Bhlair-Bhuidhe: Duanaire Finn*, III, 38. See also T. F. O'Rahilly, pp. 122–23, on pigs and haunted or Otherworld feasts.
37 Curtin, 'Balor of the Evil Eye and Lui Lavada', in *Hero-Tales*, p. 301.
38 Quoted by O'Driscoll, p. 58.
39 Hyde, *Saints and Sinners*, p. 128.
40 Rees, pp. 283–84.
41 John Rhys, *The Hibbert Lectures, 1886: Lectures on the Origin and Growth of Religion as Illustrated by Celtic Heathendom*, 3rd. ed. (London: Williams & Norgate, 1898), p. 511.
42 Cross and Slover, pp. 408–12.
43 Curtin, *Myths and Folk-Lore*, pp. 173–74.
44 Gregory, 'The Shadowy One', in *Gods and Fighting Men*, pp. 231–32.
45 Wood-martin, II, 131–32.
46 Eleanor Hull, 'The Black Pig of Kiltrustan', *Folk-Lore*, 29 (1918), 232.
47 E. MacNeill and G. Murphy, *Duanaire Finn*, I, 199; III, 73.
48 E. Hull, 'Kiltrustan', pp. 226–31. Was it only coincidence that the Pig appeared in a village that seems to be named after Trystan?
49 O'Malley, pp. 84–85.

50 Standish James O'Grady, Introduction to *In the Gates of the North* (Dublin: Talbot Press, n. d.), p. ix.
51 O'Driscoll, p. 57.
52 O'Driscoll, p. 60.
53 Whitaker, pp. 58, 307.
54 Kirby, pp. 24–25.
55 William Irwin Thompson, *The Imagination of an Insurrection: Dublin, Easter 1916: A Study of an Ideological Movement* (1967; rpt. New York: Harper & Row, 1972), p. 55.
56 Ellis and Yeats, III, 10.
57 Frances A. Yates, *The Rosicrucian Enlightenment* (Frogmore, St. Albans, Hertfordshire: Paladin, 1975), pp. 76, 77.
58 Armand Barbault, *Gold of a Thousand Mornings*, trans. Robin Campbell (London: Neville Spearman, 1975), pp. 4–8.
59 Yates, p. 76.
60 Lester Conner, Seminar, Yeats International Summer School, Sligo, Ireland, August 1980.
61 F. H. Murphy, p. 79.
62 The Emperor Julian, *Works*, ed. & trans. Wilmer Cave Wright (London: Loeb Classical Library, 1913), I, 377, 417–19.
63 O'Driscoll, p. 57.
64 Rpt. in Marilyn Gaddis Rose's translation of *Axel* (Dublin: Dolmen, 1970), p. xiii.
65 F. H. Murphy, p. 80.
66 Grossman, pp. 89–90, 92.
67 Jeffares, *Commentary on Poems*, p. 75.
68 In 'The Cradles of Gold' (cf. pp. 225–26), Finivaragh admonishes his fairies: 'Did I not tell you to be silent, that I meditate upon the wisdom that Mongan raved out after he had drunk from the seven vats of wine!': W. B. Yeats, *Uncollected Prose*, I, 416.
69 Schleifer, 'Proper Names,' p. 77.
70 These names occur in 'The Crucifixion of the Outcast', but there does not seem to be any significance in that fact.
71 Ellic Howe, *The Magicians of the Golden Dawn: A Documentary History of a Magical Order 1887–1923* (London: Routledge & Kegan Paul, 1972), p. 82. Cf. also 'The Mountain Tomb' in *Responsibilities*, VP 311.
72 Grossman, p. 95.
73 Bloom, pp. 131–32. Bloom adds that this image anticipates 'the smithies of the Emperor in *Byzantium*' (p. 131). Hazard Adams also recognises Blake's influence, but points to 'The Tyger' ('What the anvil?') rather than to Los: *Blake and Yeats: The Contrary Vision* (Ithaca, N. Y.: Cornell University Press, 1955), p. 147n.

16: *The Shadowy Waters*

1 W. B. Yeats, Preface to *Letters to the New Island*, p. xii.
2 Michael J. Sidnell, George P. Mayhew, and David R. Clark, eds., *Druid Craft: The Writing of* The Shadowy Waters (Amherst: University of Massachusetts Press, 1971), p. 106.
3 Sidnell, Mayhew, and Clark, p. 7.
4 Northrop Frye, 'The Top of the Tower: A Study of the Imagery of Yeats', *Southern Review*, N.S. 5 (1969), 870–71. J. R. Moore remarks that, at the

climax of any Yeats play, '"Divine" motivation is substituted for human motivation': 'The Idea of a Yeats Play', in Maxwell and Bushrui, p. 160.
5 Parkin, p. 83.
6 Also, at the same time as he praised Villiers de l'Isle Adam (*La Révolte*, however, not *Axël*, which was a major influence on *The Shadowy Waters*), Yeats disclosed that his favourite among William Morris' prose romances was *The Water of the Wondrous Isles*, itself an English *Imram*. This was on 5 Nov. 1900: John Masefield, 'My First Meeting with Yeats' (1940), in *W. B. Yeats: Interviews and Recollections*, ed. E. H. Mikhail (New York: Barnes & Noble, 1977), 1, 45.
7 W. B. Yeats, *John Sherman*, pp. 78–79.
8 Parkin, p. 187.
9 Sidnell, Mayhew, and Clark, pp. 56–57.
10 Frederick Stewart Colwell, 'W. B. Yeats: The Dimensions of Poetic Vision', Diss. Michigan State 1966, pp. 132, 135; Goldman, p. 34.
11 Frye, p. 860. During the initiation ritual of the Golden Dawn, 'The rope around [the initiate's] waist, the "last remaining symbol of the Path of Darkness," was removed': V. Moore, p. 138.
12 D l'Isle Adam, p. xiii.
13 Rajan, p. 43.
14 Whitaker, p. 273.
15 Byrd, p. 130.
16 S. B. Bushrui, *Yeats's Verse-Plays: The Revisions 1900–1910* (Oxford: Clarendon Press, 1965), p. 9, quoting W. B. Yeats in *The Arrow* for November 1906.
17 John Rees Moore, *Masks of Love and Death: Yeats as Dramatist* (Ithaca, N.Y.: Cornell University Press, 1971), p. 78.
18 Colwell, p. 25.
19 Sidnell, Mayhew, and Clark, p. 188.
20 J. R. Moore, p. 80.
21 Ellmann, *Identity*, p. 83.
22 Goodman, p. 342.
23 Bornstein, pp. 216–17.
24 Sidnell, Mayhew, and Clark, p. 11n.
25 See W. B. Yeats, *The Celtic Twilight*, M 115, *Memoirs*, p. 125, and Letter to A. E. tentatively dated 27 Aug. 1899, in *Letters*, p. 324; George Pollexfen, Letter to W. B. Yeats dated 24 Feb. 1899, in *Letters to W. B. Yeats*, ed. Richard J. Finneran, George Mills Harper, and William M. Murphy (New York: Columbia University Press, 1977), I, 47.
26 Byrd, p. 112.
27 Harris, pp. 14–15.
28 Nathan, pp. 76–77.

17: 'I Have No Happiness in Dreaming of Brycelinde'

1 Quoted by Henn, *Lonely Tower*, p. 108.
2 Jeffares, *Commentary on Poems*, p. 96.
3 Sheila O'Sullivan, in Almqvist, mac Aodha, and mac Eoin, p. 267.
4 Guest, p. 45.
5 Garrity, p. 38.
6 The parallel should not be pushed too far. 'Under the Moon' was first published twenty months before Maud Gonne married John MacBride.
7 Jeffares, *Commentary on Poems*, p. 91.

Notes to pages 270–283

8   Sheila O'Sullivan, in Almqvist, mac Aodha, and mac Eoin, pp. 276, 277; Gregory, 'Brigit, the Mary of the Gael', in *Saints & Wonders*, pp. 18–19.
9   McGarry and Malins, p. 90.
10 Hoffman, pp. 45–46.
11 T. R. Henn, "'The Green Helmet" and "Responsibilities'", in *An Honoured Guest: New Essays on W. B. Yeats*, ed. Denis Donoghue and J. R. Mulryne (London: Edward Arnold, 1965), p. 46.
12 D. S. Savage, 'The Aestheticism of W. B. Yeats' (1944), in Hall and Steinmann, pp. 204–05.
13 Henn, in Donoghue and Mulryne, p. 48.
14 Savage, in Hall and Steinmann, p. 205.
15 F. H. Murphy, p. 131.
16 Henn, in Donoghue and Mulryne, p. 47.
17 Whitaker, p. 66.
18 Henn, *Lonely Tower*, p. 92.
19 Bloom, p. 174.
20 Jeffares, *Commentary on Poems*, p. 146.
21 Rajan, pp. 76–77.
22 Henn, *Lonely Tower*, pp. 93–94.
23 Jeffares, *Commentary on Poems*, p. 146.
24 Ellmann, *Man and Masks*, p. 205.
25 De l'Isle Adam, p. 34.
26 O'Hanlon, pp. 24–25.
27 W. B. Yeats, 'Swedenborg, Mediums, and the Desolate Places', in Gregory, *Visions and Beliefs*, p. 336.
28 St. John D. Seymour, 'The Eschatology of the Early Irish Church', *Zeitschrift für Celtische Philologie*, 14 (1923), 204, 205.
29 B. L. Reid, *William Butler Yeats: The Lyric of Tragedy* (Norman: University of Oklahoma Press, 1961), p. 101.
30 Rajan, p. 76.
31 For instance, the expression 'cold Hell' is used in 'The House of Morna Defend Finn in Hell,' a specifically Christian lay; the Cold Land (*Fuarrdhacht*) in 'The Lay of Beann Ghualann' may well be Hell also: G. Murphy, *Duanaire Finn*, II, 173, 381. Many other examples could be cited from all sorts of literature.
32 Bloom, p. 174.

Appendix A: Mortal Protégés of the Tuatha Dé Danann

1   Stokes, *Cóir Anmann*, pp. 303–05.
2   Plummer, 'The Expulsion of Mochuda from Rahen', in *Bethada*, II, 291–94.
3   Alexander Haggerty Krappe, 'Diarmuid and Grainne', *Folk-Lore*, 47 (1936), 348.
4   O'Clery, p. 5.
5   Francis John Byrne, Seminar, Yeats International Summer School, Sligo, Ireland, August 1980.
6   Nutt, 'Re-Birth', II, 16.
7   'The Voyage of Bran Son of Febal', in Cross and Slover, pp. 593–94. These lines are an obvious influence on Yeats's 'Mongan thinks of his Past Greatness'.
8   'The Birth of Mongan', in Cross and Slover, pp. 546–47; Kuno Meyer, ed. & trans., 'The Conception of Mongán and Dub-Lacha's Love for Mongán', in *Bran*, I, 58–84.

9 Gregory, 'Columcille, the Friend of the Angels of God', in *Saints & Wonders*, p. 33.
10 Gregory, 'Birth of Cuchulain', in *Cuchulain of Muirthemne*, pp. 21–24; 'The Birth of Cu Chulainn', in Cross and Slover, pp. 134–36.
11 Kinsella, pp. 21–23.
12 'The Wooing of Emer', in Cross and Slover, p. 159.
13 Kinsella, p. 142.
14 Tomás Ó Cathasaigh, 'Between God and Man: The Hero of Irish Tradition,' *The Crane Bag*, 2, No. 1–2 (1978), 75.
15 Kinsella, pp. 142–47.
16 Kinsella, p. 150.
17 Gregory, 'Manannan', in *Gods and Fighting Men*, p. 97.
18 'The Boyhood Deeds of Cu Chulainn', in Cross and Slover, pp. 141–42.
19 Gregory, 'Manannan', in *Gods and Fighting Men*, p. 97.
20 Curtin, *Hero-Tales*, pp. 283–94.
21 Curtin, *Myths and Folk-Lore*, pp. 204–20
22 Curtin, *Myths and Folk-Lore*, p. 279.
23 E. MacNeill, 'The Shield of Fionn', in *Duanaire Finn*, I, 134–39.
24 'A Story From Which It Is Inferred That Mongan Was Finn Mac Cumaill', in Cross and Slover, pp. 548–50.
25 M. Mac Neill, p. 10.
26 Plummer, *Vitae*, I, cxxxvi.
27 S. H. O'Grady, II, 425.
28 Giraldus Cambrensis, *The First Version of the Topography of Ireland*, trans. John J. O'Meara (Dundalk, Co. Lough: Dundalgan Press, 1951), p. 94.
29 Nutt, 'Re-Birth', II, 100.
30 Carney, p. 288n.
31 S. H. O'Grady, II, 425.
32 Bonwick, p. 16.

GLOSSARY

Badhb. Royston crow; a name for the Morrigu.
Bile. Tree, especially a sacred tree.
Bolg. Bag, but may have originally meant 'lightning' in the names *Fir Bolg*, *gai bulga*, referring to a people and to the spear of Cúchulainn respectively.
Bruiden, plur. *bruidne*. Hostel; in some contexts also appears to mean 'brawl'.
Caointe. Keening. *Bean caointe*. Keening woman, often used as a term for the banshee.
Cathair. Citadel; chair.
Cenn. Head; top.
Cro. Leap.
Crom. Bent, stooped, leaning. In the names *Crom Cruach*, *Crom Dubh*, 'thunder' and 'maggot' have also been suggested.
Cruach. Mound.
Da. God; hand (?).
Dá. Two; god (?).
Dán. Art, skill. *Áes dána*. The artistic, skilled, or learned professions that were legally privileged.
Dearg. Red.
Donn. Dark.
Dubh. Black.
Eachtra, plur. *eachtraí*. Adventure.
Fear, plur. *fir*. Man.
Fianna. Warriors, militia, comrades-in-arms.
Finn. Fair, pale, white.
Geis, plur. *geasa*. Taboo, obligation, enchantment.
Imram, plur. *imrama*. Voyage.
Óglaech. Warrior.
Ruadh. Red (of hair, fur, etc.).
Scath. Spectre; hero.
Scál. Spectre; hero.
Scéal, plur. *scéalta*. A long, elaborate, artificial folk-tale. *Remscéal*. An introductory story. *Scéalaí*. A teller of *scéalta*.
Seanchaí. A teller of short, anecdotal folk-tales, as distinct from a *scéalaí*.

Sídh, gen. sing., nom. plur. *sídhe*. Natural or artificial fairy hill or mound. (*Áes, daoine*) *sídhe*. The people of the *sídh*, the fairies. *Bean-sídhe* (var. *-síghe*). Lit. fairy woman; banshee. *Leannán sídhe*. Fairy sweetheart; succubus; muse.
Síth. Peace; liable to be confused with *sídh*.
Sluagh. Host, troop.
Tuath, plur. *tuatha*. Tribe.

BIBLIOGRAPHY

Ackerman, Cara. 'Yeats' Revisions of the Hanrahan Stories, 1897 and 1904.' *Texas Studies in Literature and Language*, 17 (1975), 505–24.
Adams, Hazard. *Blake and Yeats: The Contrary Vision*. Ithaca, N. Y.: Cornell University Press, 1955.
——. 'Yeats's *Country of the Young*.' *PMLA*, 72 (1957), 510–19.
Adomnan. *Life of Columba*. Ed. & trans. Alan Orr Anderson and Marjorie Ogilvie Anderson. London: Thomas Nelson & Sons, 1961.
Alderson Smith, Peter. ' "Grown to Heaven Like a Tree": The Scenery of *The Countess Cathleen*.' *Éire-Ireland*, 14, No. 3 (1979), 65–82.
——. '*The Countess Cathleen* and the Otherworld.' *Éire-Ireland*, 17, No. 2 (1982), 141–46.
Allen, James Lovic. 'Unity of Archetype, Myth, and Religious Imagery in the Work of Yeats.' *Twentieth Century Literature*, 20 (1974), 91–95.
Almqvist, Bo, Breandán mac Aodha, and Gearóid mac Eoin, eds. *Hereditas: Essays and Studies Presented to Professor Séamus Ó Duilearga*. 1975; rpt. New York: Arno, 1980. Includes Reidar T. Christiansen, 'Some Notes on the Fairies and the Fairy Faith'; A. T. Lucas, 'Souterrains: The Literary Evidence'; and Sheila O'Sullivan, 'W. B. Yeats's Use of Irish Oral and Literary Tradition.'
Alspach, Russell K. 'Irish Legend in Irish Literature.' In *Folklore in Action: Essays for Discussion in Honór of MacEdward Leach*. Ed. Horace P. Beck. Philadelphia: American Folklore Society, 1962, pp. 12–20.
——. 'The Use by Yeats and Other Irish Writers of the Folklore of Patrick Kennedy.' *Journal of American Folklore*, 59 (1946), 404–12.
Andrews, Elizabeth. *Ulster Folklore*. 1913; rpt. Norwood, Pa.: Norwood, 1975.
Babcock-Abrahams, Barbara. ' "A Tolerated Margin of Mess": The Trickster and His Tales Reconsidered.' *Journal of the Folklore Institute*, 11 (1975), 147–86.
Barbault, Armand. *Gold of a Thousand Mornings*. Trans. Robin Campbell. London: Neville Spearman, 1975.
Beebe, Maurice. *Ivory Towers and Sacred Founts: The Artist as Hero in Fiction from Goethe to Joyce*. New York: New York University Press, 1964.
Berryman, Charles. *W. B. Yeats: Design of Opposites*. New York: Exposition, 1967.
Best, Richard Irvine, ed. & trans. 'The Battle of Airtech.' *Ériu*, 8 (1916), 179–84.
Blake, William. *Poetry and Prose*. Ed. Geoffrey Keynes. London: Nonesuch, 1927.
Bloom, Harold. *Yeats*. New York: Oxford University Press, 1970.
Bonwick, James. *Irish Druids and Old Irish Religions*. 1894; rpt. New York: Arno, 1976.
Bornstein, George Jay. 'The Surfeited Alastor: William Butler Yeats's Changing Relation to Percy Bysshe Shelley.' Diss. Princeton 1966.

Boyd, Ernest. *Ireland's Literary Renaissance*. 2nd. ed. 1922; rpt. New York: Barnes & Noble, 1968.
Briggs, Katharine M. *A Dictionary of Fairies*. Harmondsworth, Middlesex: Penguin, 1977.
——. *The Fairies in Tradition and Literature*. London: Routledge & Kegan Paul, 1967.
——. *Nine Lives: The Folklore of Cats*. New York: Pantheon, 1980.
——. *The Vanishing People: A Study of Traditional Fairy Beliefs*. London: B. T. Batsford, 1978.
Bushrui, S. B. *Yeats's Verse-Plays: The Revisions 1900–1910*. Oxford: Clarendon Press, 1965.
Byrd, Thomas L., Jr. *The Early Poetry of W. B. Yeats: The Poetic Quest*. Port Washington, N. Y.: Kennikat, 1978.
Byrne, Francis John. *Irish Kings and High-Kings*. New York: St. Martin's Press, 1973.
Carney, James. *Studies in Irish Literature and History*. Dublin: Institute for Advanced Studies, 1955.
Chadwick, Nora. *The Celts*. Harmondsworth, Middlesex: Penguin, 1970.
Clark, David R. *Lyric Resonance: Glosses on Some Poems of Yeats, Frost, Crane, Cummings and Others*. Amherst: University of Massachusetts Press, 1972.
Coimín, Micheál. *Laoi Oisín ar Thír na n-Óg, or, The Lay of Oisín in the Land of Youth*. Ed. Tomás Ó Flannghaile. London: City of London Book Depot, 1896.
Colum, Padraic. Sleeve-notes to the sound recording of *The Countess Cathleen*. Featuring Siobhan McKenna, John Neville, et al. Tradition, TLP 501, n. d.
Colwell, Frederick Stewart. 'W. B. Yeats: The Dimensions of Poetic Vision.' Diss. Michigan State 1966.
Cook, Arthur Bernard. 'The European Sky-God. IV. The Celts (p. 1).' *Folk-Lore*, 17 (1906), 27–71.
Croker, T. Crofton. *Fairy Legends and Traditions of the South of Ireland*. London: Swan Sonnenschein, n. d. (1906?).
Cross, Tom Peete, and Clark Harris Slover, eds. *Ancient Irish Tales*. 1936; rpt. Dublin: Figgis, 1969.
Crowley, Aleister (The Master Therion). *The Book of Thoth*. 1944; rpt. New York: Lancer, n. d.
Curtin, Jeremiah. *Hero-Tales of Ireland*. 1894; rpt. New York: Benjamin Blom, 1971.
——. *Myths and Folk-Lore of Ireland*. Boston: Little, Brown, & Co., 1908.
Dalton, G. F. 'The Ritual Killing of the Irish Kings.' *Folklore*, 81 (1970), 1–22.
D'Arbois de Jubainville, Henri. *Cours de Littérature Celtique*. 12 vols. 1883–1902; rpt. Osnabrück: Otto Zeller, 1969.
——. *The Irish Mythological Cycle and Celtic Mythology*. Trans. Richard Irvine Best. 1903; rpt. New York: Lemma, 1970.
Dean-Smith, Margaret. 'Human-Fairy Marriage' (Letter). *Folk-Lore*, 66 (1955), 435.
De l'Isle Adam, Villiers. *Axël*. Trans. Marilyn Gaddis Rose. Dublin: Dolmen, 1970.
De Vries, Jan. *La Religion des Celtes*. Trans. L. Jospin. Paris: Payot, 1963.

Dillon, Myles. *Early Irish Literature*. Chicago: University of Chicago Press, 1948.

——, ed. & trans. *The Cycles of the Kings*. London: Oxford University Press, 1946.

—— and Nora K. Chadwick. *The Celtic Realms*. New York: New American Library, 1967.

Dinneen, Rev. Patrick S. *Foclóir Gaedhilge agus Béarla: An Irish-English Dictionary*. 3rd. ed. Dublin: Educational Company of Ireland for the Irish Texts Society, 1934.

Donahue, Charles. 'The Valkyries and the Irish War-Goddesses.' *PMLA*, 56 (1941), 1–12.

Donoghue, Denis, and J. R. Mulryne, eds. *An Honoured Guest: New Essays on W. B. Yeats*. London: Edward Arnold, 1965. Includes T. R. Henn, ' "The Green Helmet" and "Responsibilities." '

Dorcey, Donal. 'Burren's Mysterious Underground.' *The Irish Times*, 31 July 1980, p. 10.

Dume, Thomas Leslie. 'William Butler Yeats: A Survey of his Reading.' Diss. Temple University 1949.

Dumézil, Georges. *The Destiny of a King*. Trans. Alf Hiltebeitel. Chicago: University of Chicago Press, 1973.

Duncan, Leland L. 'Folk-Lore Gleanings from County Leitrim.' *Folk-Lore*, 4 (1893), 176–94.

Egelson, Janet Frank. 'Christ and Cuchulain: Interrelated Archetypes of Divinity and Heroism in Yeats.' *Éire-Ireland*, 4, No. 1 (1969), 76–85.

Ellis, Edwin John, and William Butler Yeats, eds. *The Works of William Blake*. 3 vols. London: Bernard Quaritch, 1893.

Ellmann, Richard. *The Identity of Yeats*. 2nd. ed. London: Faber & Faber, 1964.

——. *Yeats: The Man and the Masks*. 1948; rpt. New York: Dutton, n. d.

Erdman, David V., annotator. *The Illuminated Blake*. Garden City, N. Y.: Anchor, 1974.

Evans Wentz, W. Y. *The Fairy-Faith in Celtic Countries*. London: Henry Frowde, 1911.

Fackler, Herbert V. *That Tragic Queen: The Deirdre Legend in Anglo-Irish Literature*. Salzburg Studies in English Literature: Poetic Drama and Poetic Theory, No. 39. Salzburg, Austria: Institut für Englische Sprache und Literatur, 1978.

Finneran, Richard J. '"Old lecher with a love on every wind": A Study of Yeats' *Stories of Red Hanrahan*'. *Texas Studies in Literature and Language*, 14 (1972), 347–58.

——, George Mills Harper, and William M. Murphy, eds. *Letters to W. B. Yeats*. 2 vols. New York: Columbia University Press, 1977.

Fitzgerald, David. 'Early Celtic History and Mythology.' *Revue Celtique*, 6 (1883–85), 193–259.

——. 'Popular Tales of Ireland.' *Revue Celtique*, 4 (1879–80), 171–200.

Flannery, Mary Catherine. *Yeats and Magic: The Earlier Works*. Irish Literary Studies, No. 2. Gerrards Cross, Buckinghamshire: Colin Smythe, 1977.

Flood, J. M. *Ireland: Its Myths and Legends*. 1916; rpt. Port Washington, N. Y.: Kennikat, 1970.

Foster, Jeanne Cooper. *Ulster Folklore*. Belfast: H. R. Carter, 1951.

Fraser, George Sutherland. *W. B. Yeats*. Writers and Their Work, No. 50. London: Longmans, Green & Co., 1962.

Frye, Northrop. 'The Top of the Tower: A Study of the Imagery of Yeats.' *Southern Review*, NS 5 (1969), 850–71.
Garrity, Devlin A., ed. *The Mentor Book of Irish Poetry*. New York: Mentor, 1965.
Giraldus Cambrensis. *The First Version of the Topography of Ireland*. Trans. John J. O'Meara. Dundalk, Co. Louth: Dundalgan Press, 1951.
Goldman, Michael P. 'The Point of Drama: The Concept of Reverie in the Plays of William Butler Yeats.' Diss. Princeton 1962.
Goodman, Henry. 'The Plays of William Butler Yeats as Myth and Ritual.' Diss. Minnesota 1952.
Graves, Robert. *The Crane Bag and Other Disputed Subjects*. London: Cassell, 1969.
Gregory, Lady Augusta. *Cuchulain of Muirthemne: The Story of the Men of the Red Branch of Ulster*. 1902; rpt. Gerrards Cross, Buckinghamshire: Colin Smythe, 1970.
——. *Gods and Fighting Men: The Story of the Tuatha De Danaan and of the Fianna of Ireland*. 1904; rpt. Gerrards Cross, Buckinghamshire: Colin Smythe, 1970.
——. *Poets and Dreamers: Studies and Translations from the Irish*. 1903; rpt. Gerrards Cross, Buckinghamshire: Colin Smythe, 1974.
——. *Visions and Beliefs in the West of Ireland*. 1920; rpt. Gerrards Cross, Buckinghamshire: Colin Smythe, 1970.
——. *The Voyages of St. Brendan the Navigator and Stories of the Saints of Ireland Forming a Book of Saints & Wonders*. 1906; rpt. Gerrards Cross, Buckinghamshire: Colin Smythe, 1973.
Grobman, Neil R. 'In Search of a Mythology: William Butler Yeats and Folklore.' *New York Folklore Quarterly*, 30 (1974), 117–36.
Grossman, Allen R. *Poetic Knowledge in the Early Yeats: A Study of* The Wind Among the Reeds. Charlottesville: University Press of Virginia, 1969.
Guest, Lady Charlotte, trans. *The Mabinogion*. London: Everyman, 1906.
Gurd, Patty. *The Early Poetry of William Butler Yeats*. 1916; rpt. Folcroft, Va.: Folcroft, 1977.
Gwynn, Stephen, ed. *Scattering Branches: Tributes to the Memory of W. B. Yeats*. London: Macmillan, 1940. Includes Maud Gonne, 'Yeats and Ireland.'
Haddon, A. C. 'A Batch of Irish Folk-Lore.' *Folk-Lore*, 4 (1893), 349–64.
Hall, James, and Martin Steinmann, eds. *The Permanence of Yeats*. New York: Macmillan, 1950. Includes David Daiches, 'W. B. Yeats — I'; D. S. Savage, 'The Aestheticism of W. B. Yeats'; and William York Tindall, 'The Symbolism of W. B. Yeats.'
Hansberry, William Leo. *Pillars in Ethiopian History*. African History Notebook, Vol. 1. Ed. Joseph E. Harris. Washington: Howard University Press, 1981.
Harper, George Mills. *The Mingling of Heaven and Earth: Yeats's Theory of Theatre*. Dublin: Dolmen, 1975.
——, ed. *Yeats and the Occult*. Yeats Studies Series. Toronto: Macmillan, 1975. Includes Kathleen Raine, 'Hades Wrapped in Cloud.'
Harris, Daniel A. *Yeats: Coole Park and Ballylee*. Baltimore: Johns Hopkins University Press, 1974.
Henn, T. R. *The Lonely Tower: Studies in the Poetry of W. B. Yeats*. New York: Pellegrini & Cudahy, 1952.
Hoare, Dorothy M. *The Works of Morris and of Yeats in Relation to Early Saga Literature*. Cambridge: Cambridge University Press, 1937.

Hoffman, Daniel. *Barbarous Knowledge: Myth in the Poetry of Yeats, Graves, and Muir*. New York: Oxford University Press, 1967.

Howe, Ellic. *The Magicians of the Golden Dawn: A Documentary History of a Magical Order 1887-1923*. London: Routledge & Kegan Paul, 1972.

Hull, Eleanor. 'The Black Pig of Kiltrustan.' *Folk-Lore*, 29 (1918), 226-37.

——. 'The Development of the Idea of Hades in Celtic Literature.' *Folk-Lore*, 18 (1907), 121-65.

——. *A Textbook of Irish Literature*. 2 vols. Dublin: M. H. Gill & Son, 1906.

Hull, Vernam. 'The Four Jewels of the *Tuatha Dé Danann*.' *Zeitschrift für Celtische Philologie*, 18 (1930), 73-83.

——, ed. & trans. 'De Gabáil in t-Šída.' *Zeitschrift für Celtische Philologie*, 19 (1933), 55-58.

——, ed. & trans. 'Two Middle-Irish Religious Anecdotes.' *Speculum*, 3 (1928), 101-03.

Hyde, Douglas. *Legends of Saints and Sinners*. Dublin: Talbot Press, n. d.

——. *A Literary History of Ireland*. 1899; rpt. London: Ernest Benn, 1967.

——, ed. & trans. *Beside the Fire: A Collection of Irish Gaelic Folk Stories*. London: David Nutt, 1910.

Jacobs, Joseph, ed. *Celtic Fairy Tales*. London: David Nutt, 1892.

Jeffares, A. Norman. *A Commentary on the Collected Poems of W. B. Yeats*. Stanford, Ca.: Stanford University Press, 1968.

——, ed. *W. B. Yeats: The Critical Heritage*. London: Routledge & Kegan Paul, 1977.

—— and K. G. W. Cross, eds. *In Excited Reverie: A Centenary Tribute to William Butler Yeats 1865-1939*. London: Macmillan, 1965. Includes David Daiches, 'The Earlier Poems: Some Themes and Patterns.'

Jones, Bryan H. 'Irish Folklore from Cavan, Meath, Kerry, and Limerick.' *Folk-Lore*, 19 (1908), 315-23.

Jones, Gwyn, trans. *Eirik the Red and Other Icelandic Sagas*. London: Oxford University Press, 1961.

Jones, Louis C. 'The Little People: Some Irish Lore of Upstate New York.' *New York Folklore Quarterly*, 18 (1962), 243-64.

Joyce, P. W. *A Social History of Ancient Ireland*. 2 vols. Dublin: M. H. Gill & Son, 1920.

Julian, The Emperor. *Works*. 3 vols. Ed. & trans. Wilmer Cave Wright. London: Loeb Classical Library, 1913.

Keating, Geoffrey. *Foras Feasa ar Éirinn: The History of Ireland*. 4 vols. Irish Texts Society, Vols. IV, VIII, IX, and XV. Ed. & trans. David Comyn and Patrick S. Dinneen. London: David Nutt for the Irish Texts Society, 1902-14.

Keightley, Thomas. *The Fairy Mythology*. 1850; rpt. New York: Haskell House, 1968.

Killeen, J. F. 'Fear an Énais.' *Celtica*, 9 (1971), 202-04.

Kinahan, G. H. 'Notes on Irish Folk-Lore.' *The Folk-Lore Record*, 4 (1881), 96-125.

Kinsella, Thomas, ed. & trans. *The Tain*. London: Oxford University Press, 1970.

Kirby, Sheelah. *The Yeats Country: A Guide to Places in the West of Ireland Associated with the Life and Writings of William Butler Yeats*. Dublin: Dolmen, 1962.

Kirk, Robert. *The Secret Common-Wealth and A Short Treatise of Charms and Spels.* Ed. Stewart Sanderson. Totowa, N. J.: Rowman & Littlefield, 1976.

Krappe, Alexander Haggerty. 'Diarmuid and Grainne.' *Folk-Lore,* 47 (1936), 347-61.

———. 'Nuada à la Main d' Argent.' *Revue Celtique,* 49 (1932), 91-95.

———. 'La Poursuite du Gilla Dacker et les Dioscures Celtiques.' *Revue Celtique,* 49 (1932), 96-108.

Langbaum, Robert. *The Mysteries of Identity: A Theme in Modern Literature.* New York: Oxford University Press, 1977.

Larminie, William. *West Irish Folk-Tales and Romances.* 1893; rpt. Freeport, N. Y.: Books for Libraries, 1972.

Lenoski, Daniel S. 'Yeats, Eglinton, and Aestheticism.' *Éire-Ireland,* 14, No. 4 (1979), 91-108.

Lottner, C. Postscript to W. M. Hennessy, 'The Ancient Irish Goddess of War.' *Revue Celtique,* 1 (1870-72), 55-57.

Lysaght, Patricia. *'An Bhean Chaointe*: The Supernatural Woman in Irish Folklore.' *Éire-Ireland,* 14, No. 4 (1979), 7-29.

MacAlister, Stewart, ed. & trans. 'The Life of Saint Finan.' *Zeitschrift für Celtische Philologie,* 2 (1899), 550-64.

Mac Cana, Proinsias. *Celtic Mythology.* New York: Hamlyn, 1970.

Mac Coluim, Fionán. 'A Tradition About Rathcroghan, Co. Roscommon.' *Béaloideas,* 4 (1933), 130.

Mac Cuillenáin, Cormac. *Sanas Chormaic: Cormac's Glossary.* Ed. Whitley Stokes. Trans. John O'Donovan. Calcutta: O. T. Cutter for the Irish Archaeological and Celtic Society, 1868.

MacKillop, James, ' "Beurla On It": Yeats, Joyce, and the Irish Language.' *Éire-Ireland,* 15, No. 1 (1980), 138-48.

———. '*The Hungry Grass*: Richard Power's Pastoral Elegy.' In *The Modern Irish Novel (Excluding Joyce): Papers Presented Before the 1980 American Committee for Irish Studies — Modern Language Association Symposium, Houston, Texas, Dec. 29, 1980.* Research Series, No. 50. Ed. Herbert V. Fackler. Lafayette, La.: University of Southwestern Louisiana Office of Institutional Research, 1980, pp. 4-24.

Mac Manus, Dermot. *The Middle Kingdom: The Faerie World of Ireland.* Gerrards Cross, Buckinghamshire: Colin Smythe, 1973.

MacNeice, Louis. *The Poetry of W. B. Yeats.* New York: Oxford University Press, 1941.

MacNeill, Eoin, and Gerard Murphy, eds. & trans. *Duanaire Finn: The Book of the Lays of Fionn.* 3 vols. Irish Texts Society, Vols. VII, XXVIII, and XLIII. London and Dublin: Irish Texts Society, 1908-54.

Mac Neill, Máire. *The Festival of Lughnasa: A Study of the Survival of the Celtic Festival of the Beginning of Harvest.* London: Oxford University Press, 1962.

Marlowe, Christopher. *Doctor Faustus.* In *The Plays of Christopher Marlowe.* Ed. Roma Gill. London: Oxford University Press, 1971, pp. 331-400.

Martin, Augustine. 'Apocalyptic Structure in Yeats's *Secret Rose.*' *Studies,* 64 (1975), 24-34.

Maxwell, D. E. S., and S. B. Bushrui, eds. *W. B. Yeats 1865-1965: Centenary*

Essays on the Art of W. B. Yeats. Ibadan, Nigeria: Ibadan University Press, 1965. Includes F. F. Farag, 'Oriental and Celtic Elements in the Poetry of W. B. Yeats'; and J. R. Moore, 'The Idea of a Yeats Play.'

Mazzaro, Jerome L. 'Apple Imagery in Yeats' "The Song of Wandering Aengus." ' *Modern Language Notes*, 72 (1957), 342–43.

McGarry, James P., and Edward Malins. *Place Names in the Writings of William Butler Yeats*. Gerrards Cross, Buckinghamshire: Colin Smythe, 1976.

Melchiori, Giorgio. *The Whole Mystery of Art: Pattern and Poetry in the Work of W. B. Yeats*. London: Routledge & Kegan Paul, 1960.

Messenger, John. 'Joe O'Donnel, *Seanchaí* of Aran.' *Journal of the Folklore Institute*, 1 (1964), 197–213.

Meyer, Kuno, ed. & trans. *The Voyage of Bran Son of Febal to the Land of the Living*. 2 vols. 1895–97; rpt. New York: AMS Press, 1972. Includes two essays by Alfred Nutt: 'The Happy Otherworld in the Mythico-Romantic Literature of the Irish' and 'The Celtic Doctrine of Re-Birth.'

Mikhail, E. H., ed. *W. B. Yeats: Interviews and Recollections*. 2 vols. New York: Barnes & Noble, 1977.

Miller, Liam. *The Noble Drama of W. B. Yeats*. Dublin: Dolmen, 1977.

———, ed. *The Dolmen Press Yeats Centenary Papers MCMLXV*. Dublin: Dolmen, 1968. Includes George Brandon Saul, 'In . . . Luminous Wind.'

Moore, John Rees. *Masks of Love and Death: Yeats as Dramatist*. Ithaca, N. Y.: Cornell University Press, 1971.

Moore, Virginia. *The Unicorn: William Butler Yeats' Search for Reality*. New York: Macmillan, 1954.

Moutray Read, D. H. 'Some Characteristics of Irish Folklore.' *Folk-Lore*, 26 (1916), 250–78.

Müller-Lisowski, Käte. 'Contributions to a Study in Irish Folklore: Traditions About Donn.' *Béaloideas*, 18 (1948), 148–63.

Murphy, Frank Hughes. *Yeats's Early Poetry: The Quest for Reconciliation*. Baton Rouge: Louisiana State University Press, 1975.

Murphy, Gerard. See MacNeill, Eoin, and Gerard Murphy.

Murphy, Michael J. *Now You're Talking . . .: Folk Tales From the North of Ireland*. Belfast: Blackstaff Press, 1975.

Nathan, Leonard E. *The Tragic Drama of William Butler Yeats: Figures in a Dance*. New York: Columbia University Press, 1965.

Ní Bhrádaigh, Cáit. 'Folklore from Co. Longford.' *Béaloideas*, 6 (1936), 257–69.

Nutt, Alfred. See Meyer, Kuno, *The Voyage of Bran*.

Ó Cathasaigh, Tomás. 'Between God and Man: The Hero of Irish Tradition.' *The Crane Bag*, 2, No. 1–2 (1978), 72–79.

———. 'The Semantics of "Síd." ' *Éigse*, 17 (1977–78), 137–55.

O'Clery, Fr. Michael. *The Martyrology of Donegal: A Calendar of the Saints of Ireland*. Ed. James Henthorn Todd and William Reeves. Trans. John O'Donovan. Dublin: Irish Archaeological and Celtic Society, 1864.

O Daly, Máirín, ed. & trans. *Cath Maige Mucrama: The Battle of Mucrama*. Irish Texts Society, Vol. L. Dublin: Dublin University Press for the Irish Texts Society, 1975.

Ó Dónaill, Niall, ed. *Foclóir Gaeilge-Béarla*. Baile Átha Cliath: Oifig an tSoláthair, 1977.

O'Driscoll, Robert. *Symbolism and Some Implications of the Symbolic Approach: W. B. Yeats During the Eighteen-Nineties.* New Yeats Papers IX. Dublin: Dolmen, 1975.

—— and Lorna Reynolds, eds. *Yeats and the Theatre.* Yeats Studies Series. Toronto: Macmillan, 1975. Includes Karen Dorn, 'Dialogue Into Movement: W. B. Yeats's Theatre Collaboration with Gordon Craig'; and James W. Flannery, 'W. B. Yeats, Gordon Craig and the Visual Arts of the Theatre.'

O'Grady, Standish Hayes, ed. & trans. *Silva Gadelica.* 2 vols. 1892; rpt. New York: Lemma, 1970.

O'Grady, Standish James. *In the Gates of the North.* Dublin: Talbot Press, n. d.

O'Hanlon, Rev. John ('Lageniensis'). *Irish Local Legends.* 1896; rpt. Norwood, Pa.: Norwood, 1973.

O'Keeffe, J. G., ed. & trans. *Buile Suibhne (The Frenzy of Suibhne), Being the Adventures of Suibhne Geilt: A Middle-Irish Romance.* Irish Texts Society, Vol. XII. London: David Nutt for the Irish Texts Society, 1913.

Ó Máille, Tomás. 'Medb Chruachna.' *Zeitschrift für Celtische Philologie,* 17 (1928), 129–46.

O'Malley, Ernie. *On Another Man's Wound.* 1936; rpt. Dublin: Anvil, 1979.

O'Rahilly, Thomas F. *Early Irish History and Mythology.* 1946; rpt. Dublin: Institute for Advanced Studies, 1964.

Ó Riain, Pádraig. 'Traces of Lug in Early Irish Hagiographical Tradition.' *Zeitschrift für Celtische Philologie,* 36 (1977), 138–56.

O'Sullivan, Sean. *The Folklore of Ireland.* New York: Hastings House, 1974.

——, ed. & trans. *Folktales of Ireland.* London: Routledge & Kegan Paul, 1966.

O'Toole, Edward. 'The Holy Wells of County Carlow.' *Béaloideas,* 4 (1933), 1–23, 107–30.

Ó Tuathail, Pádraig, O. S. 'Folk-Tales from Carlow and West Wicklow.' *Béaloideas,* 7 (1937), 73–101.

Parkin, Andrew. *The Dramatic Imagination of W. B. Yeats.* Dublin: Gill & Macmillan, 1978.

Parkinson, Thomas. *W. B. Yeats, Self-Critic: A Study of His Early Verse,* 1951; rpt. Berkeley: University of California Press, 1971. In this edition, *W. B. Yeats, Self-Critic* is issued in one volume with the same author's *W. B. Yeats: The Later Poetry.*.

Pater, Walter. *The Renaissance: Studies in Art and Poetry.* 1873; rpt. New York: Mentor, 1959. Original title: *Studies in the History of the Renaissance.*

Philostratus and Eunapius. *The Lives of the Sophists.* Ed. & trans. Wilmer Cave Wright. London: Loeb Classical Library, 1921.

Plummer, Charles, ed. & trans. *Bethada Náem nÉrenn: Lives of Irish Saints.* 2 vols. 1922; rpt. Oxford: Clarendon Press, 1968.

——, ed. *Vitae Sanctorum Hiberniae.* 2 vols. 1910; rpt. Oxford: Clarendon Press, 1968.

Raine, Kathleen. 'Yeats, the Tarot, and the Golden Dawn.' *Sewanee Review,* 77 (1969), 112–48.

Rajan, Balachandra. *W. B. Yeats: A Critical Introduction.* London: Hutchinson, 1965.

Rees, Alwyn and Brinley. *Celtic Heritage.* London: Thames & Hudson, 1961.

Reid, B. L. *William Butler Yeats: The Lyric of Tragedy.* Norman: University of

Oklahoma Press, 1961.

Reid, Forrest. *W. B. Yeats: A Critical Study*. 1915; rpt. New York: Haskell House, 1972.

Rhys, John. *The Hibbert Lectures, 1886: Lectures on the Origin and Growth of Religion as Illustrated by Celtic Heathendom*. 3rd. ed. London: Williams & Norgate, 1898.

———. 'Studies in Early Irish History.' *Proceedings of the British Academy*, 1 (1903–04), 21–80.

Roe, Helen M. 'Tales, Customs and Beliefs from Laoighis.' *Béaloideas*, 9 (1939), 27–50.

Rogers, W. Stuart. 'Irish Lore Collected in Schenectady.' *New York Folklore Quarterly*, 8 (1952), 20–30.

Ronsley, Joseph, ed. *Myth and Reality in Irish Literature*. Waterloo, Ontario: Wilfrid Laurier University Press, 1977. Includes Denis Donoghue, 'Yeats: The Question of Symbolism.'

Rosenthal, M. L. *The Modern Poets: A Critical Introduction*. New York: Oxford University Press, 1960.

Rutherford, Ward. *The Druids and Their Heritage*. London: Gordon & Cremonesi, 1978.

Ryan, Sister M. Rosalie. 'Symbolic Elements in the Plays of William Butler Yeats, 1892–1921.' Diss. Catholic University of America 1952.

Saul, George Brandon. *Prolegomena to the Study of Yeats's Poems*. Philadelphia: University of Pennsylvania Press, 1957.

Sayce, R. U. 'The Origins and Development of the Belief in Fairies.' *Folk-Lore*, 45 (1934), 99–143.

Schleifer, Ronald. 'Narrative in Yeats's *In the Seven Woods*.' *Journal of Narrative Technique*, 6 (1976), 155–74.

———. 'Principles, Proper Names, and the Personae of Yeats's *The Wind Among the Reeds*.' *Éire-Ireland*, 16, No. 1 (1981), 71–89.

Schmitz, Nancy. 'An Irish Wise Woman — Fact and Legend.' *Journal of the Folklore Institute*, 14 (1977), 169–79.

Scott, Sir Walter. *The Antiquary*. 1816; rpt. London: Everyman, 1907.

———. *The Heart of Mid-Lothian*. 1818; rpt. London: Everyman, 1956.

Seymour, St. John D. 'The Eschatology of the Early Irish Church.' *Zeitschrift für Celtische Philologie*, 14 (1923), 179–211.

Sidnell, Michael J., George P. Mayhew, and David R. Clark, eds. *Druid Craft: The Writing of* The Shadowy Waters. Amherst: University of Massachusetts Press, 1971.

Sjoestedt, Marie-Louise. *Gods and Heroes of the Celts*. Trans. Myles Dillon. London: Methuen, 1949.

Skelton, Robin, and Ann Saddlemyer, eds. *The World of W. B. Yeats: Essays in Perspective*. Victoria, B.C.: Adelphi Bookshop for the University of Victoria, 1965. Includes Gwladys V. Downes, 'W. B. Yeats and the Tarot.'

Spaan, David B. 'The Place of Manannan Mac Lir in Irish Mythology.' *Folklore*, 76 (1965), 176–95.

Stephens, James. *The Crock of Gold*. 1912; rpt. New York: Collier, 1967.

Stock, A. G. *W. B. Yeats: His Poetry and Thought*. Cambridge: Cambridge University Press, 1961.

Stokes, Whitley. 'Mythological Notes.' *Revue Celtique*, 1 (1870–72), 256–62.
——. 'Remarks on Mr. Fitzgerald's Early Celtic History and Mythology.' *Revue Celtique*, 6 (1883–85), 358–70.
——, ed. & trans. *Cóir Anmann*. Vol. III, Part 2 of *Irische Texte*. Ed. Whitley Stokes and E. Windisch. Leipzig: S. Hirzel, 1897.
——, ed. & trans. 'The Irish Ordeals.' In Vol. III, Part 1 of *Irische Texte*. Ed. Whitley Stokes and E. Windisch. Leipzig: S. Hirzel, 1891, 203–11.
——, ed. & trans. 'The Life of Féchín of Fore.' *Revue Celtique*, 12 (1891), 320–53.
——, ed. & trans. *The Tripartite Life of Patrick with Other Documents Relating to That Saint*. 2 vols. London: Eyre & Spottiswoode for H. M. Stationery Office, 1887.
Thalbitzer, William. 'Ethnographical Collections from East Greenland (Angmagsalik and Nualik) Made by G. Holm, G. Amdrup and J. Petersen and Described by W. Thalbitzer.' *Meddelelser om Grønland*, 39 (1911).
Thompson, William Irwin. *The Imagination of an Insurrection: Dublin, Easter 1916: A Study of an Ideological Movement*. 1967; rpt. New York: Harper & Row, 1972.
Thuente, Mary Helen. *W. B. Yeats and Irish Folklore*. Dublin: Gill & Macmillan, 1980.
Tolkien, J. R. R. '*Beowulf*: The Monsters and the Critics.' In *An Anthology of Beowulf Criticism*. Ed. Lewis E. Nicholson. Notre Dame, Ind.: University of Notre Dame Press, 1963, pp. 51–103.
Unterecker, John. *A Reader's Guide to William Butler Yeats*. New York: Noonday, 1959.
——, ed. *Yeats: A Collection of Critical Essays*. Englewood Cliffs, N.J.: Prentice Hall, 1963. Includes Alex Zwerdling, 'W. B. Yeats: Variations on the Visionary Quest.'
Ure, Peter. 'The Evolution of Yeats's *The Countess Cathleen*.' *Modern Language Review*, 57 (1962), 12–24.
——. *Yeats the Playwright: A Commentary on Character and Design in the Major Plays*. New York: Barnes & Noble, 1963.
Ussher, P. 'Waterford Folk Tales.' *Folk-Lore*, 25 (1914), 109–21, 227–42.
Van Hamel, A. G. 'Aspects of Celtic Mythology.' *Proceedings of the British Academy*, 20 (1934), 207–48.
——. 'Partholon.' *Revue Celtique*, 50 (1933), 217–37.
Wachsler, Arthur A. 'The 'Elaborate Ruse': A Motif of Deception in Early Celtic Historical Variants of the Journey to the Otherworld.' *Journal of the Folklore Institute*, 12 (1975), 29–46.
Waite, Arthur Edward. *The Pictorial Key to the Tarot*. 1910; rpt. New York: University Books, 1959.
Ward, Donald. 'The Little Man Who Wasn't There: Encounters With the Supranormal.' *Fabula*, 18 (1977), 212–25.
Watts, Harold H. *Hound and Quarry*. London: Routledge & Kegan Paul, 1953.
Westropp, Thomas J. 'A Folklore Survey of County Clare.' *Folk-Lore*, 21 (1910), 180–99, 338–49, 476–87; 22 (1911), 49–60, 203–13, 332–41, 449–56; 23 (1912), 88–94, 204–15.
——. 'A Study of the Folklore on the Coast of Connacht, Ireland.' *Folk-Lore*, 29 (1918), 305–19; 32 (1921), 101–23; 33 (1922), 389–97; 34 (1923), 235–37, 333–49.

Whitaker, Thomas R. *Swan and Shadow: Yeats's Dialogue with History*. Chapel Hill: University of North Carolina Press, 1964.

Wilde, Lady Jane. *Ancient Cures, Charms, and Usages of Ireland*. 1890; rpt. Detroit: Singing Tree Press, 1970.

——. *Ancient Legends, Mystic Charms and Superstitions of Ireland*. 2 vols. London: Ward & Downey, 1887.

Wilde, Sir William R. *Irish Popular Superstitions*. 1852; rpt. Totowa, N.J.: Rowman & Littlefield, 1973.

Wilson, Edmund. *Axel's Castle: A Study in the Imaginative Literature of 1870–1930*. 1931; rpt. London: Fontana, 1961.

Winberry, John J. 'The Elusive Elf: Some Thoughts on the Nature and Origin of the Irish Leprechaun.' *Folklore*, 87 (1976), 63–75.

Wood-Martin, W. G. *Traces of the Elder Faiths of Ireland*. 2 vols. London: Longmans, Green, & Co., 1902.

Yates, Frances A. *The Rosicrucian Enlightenment*. Frogmore, St. Albans, Hertfordshire: Paladin, 1975.

Yeats, William Butler. *Autobiography*. New York: Collier, 1965.

——. *Essays and Introductions*. New York: Collier, 1968.

——. *Explorations*. New York: Macmillan, 1962.

——. *John Sherman and Dhoya*. Ed. Richard J. Finneran. Detroit: Wayne State University Press, 1969.

——. *The Letters*. Ed. Allan Wade. New York: Macmillan, 1955.

——. *Letters to the New Island*. Ed. Horace Reynolds. Cambridge, Mass.: Harvard University Press, 1934.

——. *Memoirs*. Ed. Denis Donoghue. London: Macmillan, 1972.

——. *Mythologies*. New York: Collier, 1969.

——. *The Secret Rose, Stories by W. B. Yeats: A Variorum Edition*. Ed. Phillip L. Marcus, Warwick Gould, and Michael J. Sidnell. Ithaca, N.Y.: Cornell University Press, 1981.

——. *Uncollected Prose*. 2 vols. Ed. John P. Frayne and Colton Johnson. New York: Columbia University Press, 1970–76.

——. *The Variorum Edition of the Plays of W. B. Yeats*. Ed. Russell K. Alspach. New York: Macmillan, 1969.

——. *The Variorum Edition of the Poems of W. B. Yeats*. 3rd. Printing. Ed. Peter Allt and Russell K. Alspach. New York: Macmillan, 1966.

——. *A Vision*. 'With the author's final revisions.' 1956; rpt. New York: Collier, 1966.

——, ed. *Fairy and Folk Tales of Ireland*. Gerrards Cross, Buckinghamshire: Colin Smythe, 1973. Includes *Fairy and Folk Tales of the Irish Peasantry* (1888) and *Irish Fairy Tales* (1892).

——, ed. See also Ellis, Edwin John, and William Butler Yeats, eds.

INDEX

Note. All mythological personages and fairies are indexed under their first names. The works of Yeats are arranged alphabetically by title under his name. Characters that appear only in Yeats's work are not included in this index.

'A. M.', 156, 157
Abcan son of Bicelmos, 93
Abertach, 69
Ackerman, Cara, 206, 315 n 30
Adene, 161, 168
Adomnan: *Life of Columba*, 133, 289
'Adventures of Connla the Fair, The', 42, 43, 87
'Adventures of Nera, The', 86
'Adventures of the Children of the King of Norway, 268
Aed, son of Fidga, 47
Aedh of the Dagda, 56
Aedh, poet of Ulster, 39
Aedh, son of Bodhb Derg, 87
Aedh, son of Eochaidh Lethderg, 137
Aeibhinn (Aoibhell, Aoibheall) of Craig Liath, 119
Aengus, *see* Angus Og
Aibric, 215, 258, 259, 260, 271–72
Aige, 48
Ailill Anglonnach (Ailill of the One Stain), 49, 162
Ailinn (Aillinn), 68, 70, 75, 137, 258, 269
Aillen, son of Midhna, 47
Aillenn, daughter of Bodb Dearg, 88
'Ailne's Revenge', 45
Áine (Anu), 52–55, 66, 72, 82; Chair of Áine, 54
Aine of Knockany, 119
Aine of Lissan, 119
Albion, Giant, 157
Allen, James Lovic, 168, 170, 313 n 41
Allingham, William, 155; 'The Fairies', 147
'Altrom Tige Dá Medar', 131
Amergin, 36, 37, 38
An-Dé (*Andé*), the, 47, 77
Ana (Anann), 53, 63

Andrews, Elizabeth, 97, 109, 134
Angels, 130–131, 160, 167, 168, 201, 224, 245; angelomachy, 289
Angus, son of Aedh Abrat, 41
Angus, son of Bodhb Derg, 87
Angus Og, 36, 37, 41, 48, 49, 58, 61, 66, 68, 71, 72, 82, 116, 130, 161, 162, 167, 169, 172, 183, 224, 227–28, 229, 241, 257, 258, 264, 268, 269, 281–82, 283, 284; 'The Dream of Angus Og', 58
Animals: in Irish folklore, 122–29; psychic powers of, 125
Annals of the Four Masters, The, 89, 91, 116
Aoife, 48, 72
Apollonius, Life of, 287
Apple imagery, 228, 229
Aran Islands prayer, 151
Arkan Sonney, 126
Arthur, King, 268, 269
Artrach, 87
Athairne, 59
Avalon, 268, 269
Avatars, 284

Badb, the, 35, 63, 64, 65, 79
Baile, 68, 70, 75, 137, 269
'Baile in Scáil', 88
'Ballad of True Thomas, The', 55
Balor, 33, 34, 35, 82, 83, 114, 285
'Balor on Tory Island', 284–85
Banba, 37
Banshees, 118–21, 136, 145, 147, 150, 152
Barrie, J. M., 13, 157
'Battle of Tailltin, The', 32
'Battle of the White Strand, The', 50, 54, 71, 88
Be-culle, 35, 50

337

Be-Mannair, 49
Becfola, 45
Bél, 90, 91
'Belated Priest, The', 132
Belgae, the, 30, 32
Benen, 48
Beowulf, 26
Berkeley, Bishop George, 275
Birds, human-headed, 163, 164, 257, 261
'Birth of Fin MacCumhail', 285
Black Annis, 53, 119
Black Dog, 18, 126–27
Black oxen, 289, 290
Black Pig, 126, 239–46, 254
Blake, William, 155, 157, 172, 180, 188, 201, 229, 230, 239, 243, 253, 256; *The Book of Thel*, 198, 210; *Jerusalem*, 163; 'Little Boy Lost', 244; 'The Marriage of Heaven and Hell', 230; 'A Vision of the Last Judgment', 314 n 10; *The Works of William Blake* (eds. Ellis and Yeats), 314 n 10
Blathnait, 40
Blavatsky, Madame H. P., 243, 245
Bloom, Harold, 191, 198, 228, 253, 274–75, 276
Boadach the Eternal, 42, 43
Boar of Ben Gulban, 241
Bodb Derg (Bodbh, Bodhbh Dearg), 34, 35, 48, 59, 71, 86, 87, 103, 110, 240
Bonwick, James, 287; *Irish Druids and the Old Irish Traditions*, 300 n 1
Bookman, The, 156, 199
Book of Armagh, 85
Book of Ballymote, 15
Book of Enoch, 275
Book of Lecan, 15
Book of Leinster, 15, 56, 89, 98
Book of Leinster Dinnshenchas, 89, 91
Book of Lismore, 15
Bornstein, George J., 21, 315 n 24
Boyd, Ernest, 156
Boyd, Thomas: 'The Brown Bull', 268
Bran, The Voyage of, 156
Bran mac Febail, 45, 282
Brandion, 111
Branwen, 268, 269
Brendan, St., 44, 90, 115, 116, 131, 133, 152; Life of, 115, 149, 150, 151, 152; 'Voyage of St. Brendan, The', 133, 258

Bres, 33, 34, 35, 95, 97
Brevarium of Tírecháan, 87
Brí Leith, 59
Brian Boru, 14, 60, 119
'Bricriu's Feast', 124
Brig, 35
Briggs, Katharine M., 28, 53, 99, 126, 134, 138, 145, 152; *A Dictionary of Fairies*, 147, 292 n 18; *The Fairies in Tradition and Literature*, 304 n 32; *Nine Lives: The Folklore of Cats*, 296 n 2; *The Vanishing People*, 308 n 55, 310 n 29
Brigit (Brigid), 63, 64, 81
Brigit, St., 270–71
Bronach of Burren, 99
Brownies, 99, 115, 129
Brycelinde, 268, 269
Buile Suibhne, ed. & trans. J. G. O'Keeffe, 296 n 11
Burials, 136–37
Bushes, lone, 113–14
Byrd, Thomas L., 157, 180, 201, 265
Byrne, Francis John, 83, 133; *The Destiny of a King*, 73; *Irish Kings and High-Kings*, 26, 291 n 5

Caer, 48
Caicer, 37
Cailleach Beirre, 119
Caintigern, 283
Calatin, daughters of, 64
'Caoilte's Urn', 49
Caolte (Cailte, Caoelte, Caoilte), 46, 47, 186, 251, 252, 285
Cards, 208–10, 213; *see also* Tarot, the
Carney, James, 72, 286–87
Cascorach, 87–88
Can Anna, 53
'Cath Cinn Abrad', 115
Cathair Aine, 54
Cathbad, 120
Cathleann, wife of Balor, 34
Cats, 124
'Cave of Cruachan, The', 48
Ceanfaeligh, 285
Celts, 30, 80, 99, 100
Cermat Honey-Mouth, 59, 60
Cethen, 34
Chadwick, Nora, 85; *The Celts*, 300 n 39; (with M. Dillon), *The Celtic Realms*, 294 n 28

Index

Changelings, 137–44, 157, 185, 225, 226
Charms, 141, 142, 182
Christianity, influence of, 106–07, 130–44, 155, 286–87; early Christian texts, 43–44
Christiansen, Reidar, 135; 'Some Notes on the Fairies and the Fairy Faith', 307 n 3
Ciabhan, son of King Eochaid Red-Weapon, 41
Ciach, 36
Cian, 34, 241, 285
Cicul, 28
Cíocal, 26, 27
Clann Morna, 47
Clark, David, R., 234
Cleena, 147, 206, 207, 208, 236
Cliodhna, 119
'Cliodna's Wave', 85
Clockanpooka, pooka of Dun of, 129
Cluantarbh (Clontarf), Battle of, 64
Cluricauns, 115–16, 147, 150, 152
Cnú Dheireoil, 40, 71
Cocks, 125
Cod, 268
Coemgen, St., 137; Solomon's Lives of, 137–38, 143
Coimín, Micheál, 16, 42
Cóir Anmann, 33, 56, 77, 78, 79, 293 n 42
Coirpre mac Rosa Ruaid, 71–72
Cóiste bodhar, 135–36
'Colloquy with the Ancients, The', 41, 47, 48, 77, 86–87, 110, 137, 143, 186, 187
Colman (monk), 152
Colman, King, son of Coirpre, 137
Colman Ela, St., 116
Colum, Padraic, 159
Colum Cille (Columcille, Columba), St., 98, 132, 283; Adomnan's *Life of Columba*, 133, 289; *Prophecy of St. Columcille*, 242
'Columcille and his Brother Dobhran', 116
Colwell, Frederick Stewart, 21, 259
'Coming of Laighne Mor, The', 36
Conaan, son of Faebar, 28, 29
Conair (Conaire) Mór, High King, 36, 51, 68, 161, 162, 240
Connall Cearnach, 289
Conan, 96

Conaran mac Imidel, 96
'Conception of Mongan, The', 286
Conchobar, King, 14, 36, 49, 62, 251, 252, 269, 283
Congal Claen, 64
Conn of the Hundred Battles, High King, 50
'Conneelys and the Seals, The', 117
Conner, Lester, 177, 229
Connla the Fair, 42, 43, 228
'Conquest of Nemed, The', 28
Constantine, monk, former King of Alba, 281, 284
Cook, Arthur Bernard, 83; 'The European Sky-God', 299 n 35
Cormac Conloingeas, 120
Cormac mac Airt, High King, 15, 50, 87
Cormac mac Cuillenáin, 90
Cormac's Glossary, 74
Cows, 129, 142, 149
Craig, E. Gordon, 165, 312 n 34
Credne, 32
Crimthann mac Fidaigh, High King, 32
Crofton Croker, T., 116, 140, 148; *Fairy Legends and Traditions of the South of Ireland*, 304 n 38
Crom Cruach, 89–91
Crom Dubh, 89–91, 132
Cross, T. P., & C. H. Slover, *Ancient Irish Tales*, 42, 292 n 3
Crowley, Aleister, 210; *The Book of Thoth*, 316 n 14
Cruachan, Cave of, 45, 46, 48
Cú, 34
Cúchulainn (Cu Chulainn), 14, 27, 30, 41, 64, 65, 77, 88, 120, 139, 190, 193, 194, 202, 244, 251, 252, 283–84, 285, 286; horses of, 128
Cuckoos, 122
Culann the Smith, 284
Curucha na Gras, 285
Curtin, Jeremiah, 137; *Hero-Tales of Ireland*, 305 n 5; *Myths and Folk-lore of Ireland*, 305 n 5, 315 n 49
Cycles of Early Irish literature, see Fenian Cycle; Mythological Cycle; Royal Cycle, Ulster Cycle
Cycles of the Kings, The, 292 n 10

Dagda, the, 33, 34, 35, 37, 56–58, 66, 78, 80, 81, 82, 120, 281, 282–283, 284; caldron of, 31, 58, 209

Daiches, David, 190, 199
Daily Express (Dublin), 190
Dáire, 71
Dáire of the Songs, 45
Dalton, G. F., 86; 'The Ritual Killing of the Irish Kings', 300 n 44
Danu, people of the Goddess, *see* Tuatha Dé Danaan
Dante Alighieri, 246, 275; *Paradiso*, 178
Danu, 52–53, 55, 56, 77, 142, 177
'Dark Joan', 200
Darkness, 232, 233, 242, 243
Dathi, 250
'Daughter of King Under-Wave, The', 44
Dead, the: Land of, 258, 261, 262; Lord of the, 71–73; Tuatha Dé Danaan and, 67–83
'Dead Coach', 135–36
Dean-Smith, Margaret, 133
'Death of Muircertach, The', 50
Dechtire, 283
Dee, John: *Monas hieroglyphica*, 245
Deer, 48
Deirdre, 61, 62, 176, 189, 208, 236, 259, 268, 269
de Jubainville, Henri d'Arbois, 27, 29, 67–68, 69, 70, 76, 83, 156; *Cours de Littérature Celtique*, 296 n 22; *The Irish Mythological Cycle and Celtic Mythology*, 292 n 16
del Fiore, Joachim: *The Eternal Gospel*, 188
Demons, 160, 161, 163, 165, 167–68, 172, 182
'Destruction of Da Derga's Hostel, The', 48, 68–69, 73, 98
'Destruction of Dinn Rig, The', 86
de Vere, Aubrey, 155
de Vries, Jan, 81, 82, 84; *La Religion des Celtes*, 299 n 20
Dew, 244–45, 246, 247
Diancecht (Dian Cecht), 32, 35, 84
Dianann, 35, 50
Diarmuid (Dearmod, Dermot) O'Duibhne, 36, 40, 44, 49, 71, 203, 208, 213, 241, 282, 284
Dillon, Myles, 45, *Early Celtic Literature*, 294 n 28; (with N. Chadwick), *The Celtic Realms*, 294 n 28
Diodorus, 69

'Disappearance of Caenchomrac, The', 88
Dog of the Tumulus, 127
Dogs, 126–27
Domnann, the, *see* Fir Domnann
Donahue, Charles, 65; 'The Valkyries and the Irish War-Goddesses', 297 n 63
Donchad, O'Brien, 98–99
Donn, 68, 71, 72–73, 75
Donn Cuailnge, 47, 64
Donn mac Midir, 87
Donn of Dubhlinn, 48
Donoghue, Denis, 185, 230
Door imagery, 171; flaming door, 245, 246, 254
Downes, Gwladys V., 209; 'W. B. Yeats and the Tarot', 316 n 12
'Dream of Angus Og, The', 58
Dreams, 256–57
Druids, 85, 92, 196, 202, 286, 287; Druidism and the Church, 106–07
Duanaire Finn, 71, 141, 293 n 40, 293 n 50
Dubh mac Treon, 87
Duffy, Sir Charles Gavan, 227
Dume, Thomas L., 21
Dumézil, Georges, 73, 79, 84
Dun Bolg, Battle of, 64
Dundonians, the, 29, 30
Dunsany, Lord, 277; *The Charwoman's Shadow*, 288

Eachtrai, 41–43; *Eachtra Cloinne Righ na h-Ioruaidhe*, 268; *see also* Adventures
Early, Biddy, 138, 141, 308 n 64
Early Irish literature, Yeats's knowledge of, 19–20
Eber Donn, 36, 37, 87
Eber Finn, 36, 37
Echte, 208, 210, 211–12, 213, 216, 217, 236
Edain, *see* Etain Echraidhe
Edar, wife of, 161
Edinburgh Dinnshenchas, 87
Eibhlinn of Sliabh-Fuaid, 119
Eire, name of, 227
Eithne, 71
Elcmar of Brugh na Boinne, 131
Ellis, Edwin, 230
Ellmann, Richard, 160, 164–65, 181,

Index

197, 199, 207, 244, 228, 263, 275, 290; *The Identity of Yeats*, 312 n 33
Elloth, 29
Elotha, 33
Elves, 85, 88
Emhain (Emain) Abhlach, 61, 110–11, 229, 258
'Enchanted Cave of Keshcorran, The', 96
Eochaid Airem (Airemh), High King, 32, 41, 49, 59, 86, 161, 162
Eochaid Feidlech, 59
Eochaid Lethderg, 137
Eochaidh of the Smooth Joints, 71
Eoghan Bel, 85
Eoghan Mór, 281
Eremon, 36, 37
Eri, 33
Ériu, 37, 64
Ernmass, 53
Esirt, 39
Ethlinn (Ethne), 34
Etain Echraidhe, 40, 41, 48, 59, 161–62, 163, 167, 171, 182, 257, 268, 271, 272; 'The Wooing of Etain', 39, 40, 49, 59
Etain of the Fair Hair, 47, 49
Etan, 37
Ethne the Fair, 88
Evans Wentz, W. Y., 98, 108, 129, 132, 134, 136, 146; *The Fairy Faith in Celtic Countries*, 296 n 3
'Exiles of the Sons of Tuiren, The', 61
'Exile of the Sons of Usnach', 189

Fackler, Herbert, V., 16
Faelan, 137
Fairies: speech, 100–01; traditional immortality of, 107–08; *see also* Fairy faith; Sidhe, the; Solitary fairies; Trooping fairies
Fairy Fair, 134
Fairy faith: in England, 278
Fairy faith, Irish: in general, 105–11; influence of Christianity on, 130–44; transmutation of the, 155; Yeats's rejection of, 267, 271, 274
Fairyland, 13, 41–43; mortals in, *see* Changelings; theme of, in Yeats, 175, 218, 219, 224, 227, 229, 231, 253, 255, 261–65, 269, 270–71, 272, 277; ultramarine fairyland, 61–62

Fairy-mounds, 94
Fairy paths, 109–10
Fairy strokes, 140
Falias, 31
Fall of Man, 157
Fann, 41, 44, 49, 88
Farag, F. F., 221
'Fate of the Children of Lir, The', 48
'Fate of the Children of Tuirenn, The', 34, 63, 97, 241
Fea, 63
Féar gortach, 150
Feara Cúl, 86
Feast of Age, 37, 38, 40, 47, 93
Feast of Tara, 49
Féchin, St., 128
Fedelm the Ruddy, 88
Fenian Cycle, 14, 16, 28, 32–33, 36, 47, 282
Fenians, 168, 171, 187
Feradach, 69
Fergus, 166, 167, 168, 190–93, 194, 201, 202, 205, 249, 250, 251, 252, 288
Ferguson, Sir Samuel, 155, 240; *Lays of the Western Gael*, 313 n 37
'Fiacc's Hymn', 85
Fiacha, 86
Fianna, the, 15, 36, 40, 47, 48, 53, 58, 69, 71, 96, 121, 157, 186, 187, 233, 241
Fiatach Finn, 98
Fiery Spear, Yeats's Ritual of, 318 n 35
Figol, son of Mamos, 85
Finan, St., 128
Findias, 31
Finn mac Cumhail, 15, 36, 38, 39–40, 45, 47, 49, 60, 69, 71, 77, 87, 96, 186–87, 241, 242, 284–85
Finnbennach/Aí, 47
Finneran, Richard J., 213
Finns, 97, 98
Finvarra, 134
Fir Bolg, 14, 29, 30–31, 32–33, 38, 39, 82, 93, 95–96, 131
Fir Domnann, 29, 32
Fishes, 125
Fitzgerald, David, 78, 79, 90, 114; 'Early Celtic History and Mythology', 299 n 8
Flann, 45
Flannery, M. C.: *Yeats and Magic: The Earlier Works*, 315 n 38

Flax, 142
Flood, J. M., 58, 59, 61, 63, 83; *Ireland: Its Myths and Legends*, 297 n 31
Fodla, 37
Foidín Seachrain, 149
Foltlebar, 69
Formorians, the, 14, 26–38 *passim*, 67–68, 69, 82, 93, 97, 131, 234
Forest of Wonders, 268
Foster, Jeanne Cooper, 113, 120
Four Jewels (of the Tuatha Dé Danann), 31, 61, 209, 214, 216
Foxes, 122
'Fragmentary Annals', 287
Fraser, G. S., 158
Frazer, Sir, J. G.: *The Golden Bough*, 72
Freemasons, 92
'Friars of Urlaur, the', 240
Froech, 72
Frogs, 122, 125
Frye, Northrop, 257, 259
Fuamhnach, 161
Funerals, human, 136

á Gabella, Philip: *Consideratio brevis*, 245
Gabhra Lough, 186
Gabriel, 130, 131, 214, 215, 273
Gael, the, 36, 39, 75, 95, 98, 242
Gael, The (New York), 19
Gaileoin, the, 30–31, 32, 33
Gallizenae, 43
Gauls, 80–81
Gearóid Iarla, 55
Ghosts, 133–35, 276
Gilla Decair, the, 69
Giraldus Cambrensis, 27, 286; *The First Version of the Topography of Ireland*, 322 n 28
Gleann na nGealt, 54
Gods: theory of Tuatha Dé Danann as, 76–101
Goibniu, 35, 38, 84; Goibniu's Feast, 88
Gold, 97, 112–13, 183
Golden Dawn, Order of the, 230, 231, 237, 244, 245, 248, 251
Goldman, Michael P., 21, 171, 259
Gonne, Maud, 156, 158, 159, 181, 209, 227, 231, 233, 274–75, 320 n 6, the Rose as, 176, 177, 253; Yeats's image of, 224, 228, 232, 268; 'Yeats and Ireland', 316 n 9
Goodman, Henry, 21
Gorias, 31
Graham, John, 135
Grail Hallows, 209, 212
Grail Quest, 210, 211–12
Grainne (Grania), 36, 49, 203, 208, 241
Graves, Robert: *The Crane Bag and Other Disputed Subjects*, 297 n 53; *The White Goddess*, 63
'Great Gathering at Muirthemne, The', 64
'Great Worm of the Shannon, The', 117
Greeks, 99–101
Gregory, Isabella Augusta, Lady, 16–17, 29, 31, 33, 35, 40, 42–43, 46, 53, 54, 62, 94, 97, 100, 124, 136, 138, 140, 146, 151, 152, 164; and Yeats, 156, 205; *A Book of Saints and Wonders*, 295 n 34; *Cuchulain of Muirthemne*, 293 n 49; *Gods and Fighting Men*, 25, 291 n 1; 'The Hound', 77; *Poets and Dreamers*, 308 n 39; *The Travelling Man*, 317 n 25; *Visions and Beliefs in the West of Ireland*, 292 n 24, 312 n 36
Grian of Cnoc Greine, 119
Grímnismál, 65
Grobman, Neil, 226
Grossman, Allen, R., 220, 222, 224, 226, 228, 229, 231, 236, 248, 253
Guinevere, 268, 269
Guest, Lady Charlotte: *The Mabinogion*, 303 n 23
Gurd, Patty, 156, 157, 194, 318 n 19

Hamilton, Sir Frederick: troopers of, 196, 197
Hanrahan, *see* Red Hanrahan
Hansberry, William Leo, 59
Harbison, Mann, 97
Hares, 123, 126
Harp, symbol of, 263, 264
Hazel wood, 170
Healing powers, 141
Heaven, 168, 171, 172, 276
Heine, Heinrich, 281
Helen, 176, 177, 189
Helios, King, 245, 246
Hell, 168, 169, 171, 172, 276

Index

Henley, W. E., 20
Henn, T. R., 271, 272, 273, 274, 275
Hens, 129, 149
Herfjǫtur, 65
'Hidden House of Lugh, The', 36
Hoare, Dorothy M., 156, 157; *The Works of Morris and Yeats in Relation to Early Saga Literature*, 311 n 8
Hoffman, Daniel, 208, 270; *Barbarous Knowledge*, 305 n 9
Horniman, Annie, E. F., 257
Horses, 234–35
'Host of the air, the', 151–52
'House of Morna Defend Finn in Hell, The' 321 n 31
Howe, Ellic, *The Magicians of the Golden Dawn*, 319 n 71
Hull, Eleanor, 44, 61, 70, 80, 81–82, 241, 242, 318 n 46, n 48
Humans, deformed, 164
Hy-Brasil, 110–11
Hyde, Douglas, 20, 60, 74, 78, 79, 89, 93, 156, 268, 289; *Beside the Fire*, 306 n 19; *Legends of Saints and Sinners*, 301 n 31; *A Literary History of Ireland*, 297 n 41; 'The Old Hag of Dingle', 151, 152

Iaran, 96
imrama, 43–46, 257–58, 282, 320 n 6
Indech, 29, 33, 35, 281
Inishbofin, 111, 146
Innisfree, 180
'Intoxication of the Ulstermen, The', 60, 86, 93
Invasions, Book of, see *Lebor Gabála*
Ir, 36
Irish language, Yeats and, 19–20
Irish magical order, Yeats's plans for, 209
Iron, 95–97
Iruath, 77
Ith, 36

Jeffares, A. Norman, 221, 222, 248, 275
Jewels, *see* Four Jewels
Jones, Louis C., 142; 'The Little People', 309 n 74
Joyce, P. W., 53, 63, 91, 93, 114; 'Fergus O'Mara and the Air-Demons', 151, 152; *A Social History of Ancient Ireland*, 292 n 11

Joyous Isle, 268, 269
Julian, Emperor: 'Hymn to King Helios', 245, 246; *Select Works*, 245, 319 n 62

Keating, Geoffrey, 26, 40, 89, 90, 91, 106
Keats, John: 'La Belle Dame sans Merci', 248
Keening, 118–19
Keightley, Thomas: *The Fairy Mythology*, 303 n 29; 'The Little Shoe', 115; 'The Three Leprechauns', 150
Kennedy, Patrick: *Legendary Fictions of the Irish Celts*, 132
Kermand Kelstach, 90, 91
'Kern in the Narrow Stripes, The', 62, 69
Killeen, J. F., 27
'King of the Lepracanes' journey to Emania, The', 39, 114–15, 150
Kirk, Robert, 105; *The Secret Commonwealth*, 74, 100, 109, 131–32, 133, 136, 146, 298 n 20
Krappe, Alexander, H., 69, 71, 83, 282, 284

Laban, 269
Labraid the Swift, 41
'Laeghaire mac Crimthann's visit to the fairy realm of Magh meall', 45
Laighne Mór, 36
Laigin, the, 31
Lancelot, 269
Land of Promise, 41, 44, 46, 69, 87, 283, 284
Land of the Dead, 258, 261, 262
Land-of-the-Tower, 268, 269
Land of the Young, 42
Land of Virtues, 42
Land of Women, 42, 43
Land-Under-Wave, 44, 268, 269
Land of Boys, 43
Lands of the Living, 42
Langbaum, Robert, 229
Laoi Oisín ar Thir na nOg (*Lay of Oisín in the Land of Youth*), 16, 20, 41–42, 294 n 13
Lapps, 97, 98
Larminie, William: 'The Red Pony',

251, 252; *West Irish Folk-Tales and Romances*, 312 n 19
'Lay of Beann Ghualann, The', 58, 321 n 31
Lebor Gabála, 15, 25, 30, 31, 38, 42, 47, 69, 70, 72–73, 77, 84, 96, 99
'Leeching of Cian's Leg, The', 47
Leprechauns, 18, 39, 40, 98, 108, 112–15, 145, 147, 150, 152
Lespés, Léo, *Les Matinées de Timothée Trimm*, 161
Lewis, Timothy, 30
Lia Fáil, 31, 209
Liban, 41, 44, 49
Lir, 47, 48; Children of, 123
'Little Shoe, The', 115
Little Sidh of the Laughter, The, 109
Llew Llaw Gyffes, 114
Loeg, 88
Loegaire mac Néill, High King, 48, 88
Lord of the Dead, the, 71–73
Lottner, C., 65
Lucian of Samosata, 60
Lucifer, 131
Lugcorp mac Temais, 115
Lugh, 31, 34–35, 40, 46, 47, 49, 57, 60–61, 66, 71, 72, 76, 80, 81, 82, 84, 88, 93, 97, 98, 106, 131, 283, 284, 285; 'counterparts' of, 285–86; leprechauns and, 114, 115, 119; spear of, 31, 61, 209
Lughach of the White Hands, 71
Lughaid Menn, High King, 86
Lugoves, 114
Lunatics, 54
Lynch, Rev. J. F., 54
Lysaght, Patricia, 145, 146; '*An Bhean Chaointe*: The Supernatural Woman in Irish Folklore', 304 n 54

Mabinogion, The, 268, 282
Mac Cana, Proinsais, 38, 82–83, 90; *Celtic Mythology*, 294 n 62
Mac Cecht, 36, 37, 46
Mac Coluim, Fionán: 'A Tradition About Rathcroghan, Co. Roscommon', 289
Mac Cuill, 36, 37, 46
Mac Curtin, Andrew, 72
MacDonagh, Thomas, 20, 180
Mac Firbis, Duald, 32
McGarry, James P., 186; *Place Names in the Writings of W. B. Yeats*, 300 n 42

Mac Gréine, 36, 37, 46
Macha, 63, 64, 65
Macha, wife of Nemed, 25
Mac Liag: *The War of the Gael with the Gaill*, 119
Mac Lughach, 71
MacManus, D. A., 46, 94, 128, 134, 150; *The Middle Kingdom*, 295 n 40
MacNeice, Louis, 158
MacNeill, Eoin, 32; 293 n 40
MacNeill, Máire, 35, 61, 82, 162; *The Festival of Lughnasa* 293 n 46
MacRitchie, David, 97, 98; *Fians, Fairies and Picts*, 92; *The Testimony of Tradition*, 92
Maeldune, 46, 257
Maeve (Maive, Medhbh), 39, 45, 64, 85, 236, 288; cairn of, 244, 288
Mag Mell (Magh Meall), 42, 45
Mag Rath, Battle of, 64
Magi, the, 251, 252, 267
Magnenn of Kilmainham, St.: Life of, 164
Maine Morgor, 49
Mallarmé, Stéphane, 230
Manannan mac Lir, 38, 41, 42, 43, 47, 53, 61–63, 66, 69, 71, 72, 76, 82, 83, 84, 106, 131, 132, 229, 258, 282–83, 284, 285, 286, 287; horses of, 234
Manistrech, Flann, 29
March, 241
Mars Cicolluis, 28
Martin, Augustine, 188, 197
'Math the Son of Mathonwy', 114
Mazzaro, Jerome L., 228
Medhbh, Queen, see Maeve, Queen
Medr, 80
Meilge mac Cobthaigh, King, 48
Melchiori, Giorgio, 189
Merlin, 268, 269
Mermaids, 116–118, 145, 147, 152
Mernoke, 45
Merrows, see Mermaids
Mes Delmann, 32
Meyer, Kuno, 72; (ed. & trans.) *The Voyage of Bran*, 156, 294 n 7
Miach, 32
Michael, Archangel, 189, 272
Mider (Midhir, Midir) of Brí Leith, 39, 40, 48, 49, 59, 66, 78, 72, 80, 82, 87, 161, 163, 271
Midhir Yellow-Mane, 48
Midwives, 138, 139

Index

Mil, Sons of, see Milesians
Mil, Invasion of the Sons of, 36–37, 38
Milesians, the, (Sons of Mil), 14, 28, 36–37, 38, 50, 67, 72, 73, 83, 85, 93, 95, 240
Miller, Liam: *The Noble Drama of W. B. Yeats*, 314 n 48
Mochae, St., 46
Mochaomhog, St., 48
Mochuda, St., 281
Molling, St., 50
Mongan, 218, 232, 233, 249, 282, 283, 285, 286–87
Moore, John Rees, 263, 320 n 4
Moore, Virginia, 234; *The Unicorn*, 318 n 27, 320 n 11
Morc, 28, 29
Morrigu, the, 34, 35, 36, 49, 52, 63–66, 78, 152, 164; names of, 53, 54, 63, 79
Morris, William, *The Water of the Wondrous Isles*, 320 n 6
'Mor's Sons and the Herder from Under the Sea', 145
Mothairén, St., 50
Moytura, First Battle of, 31, 32, 33, 64, 95, 211, 281
Moytura, Second Battle of, 27, 33–36, 37, 60, 64, 120, 242
Muircertach mac Erca, 50–51, 86, 88
Mumain, 137
Murchadh mac Brien, 64
Murias, 31
Murphy, Frank Hughes, 171, 175–76, 189–90, 196, 248, 273
Mythological Cycle, 14, 15, 27, 28, 46, 56, 59, 64, 97

Nanosuelta, 57
Naoise, 61, 62, 268, 269
Nathan, Leonard, E., 160, 170, 266
Nature, Yeats's attitude to, 180–81, 199–201
Nechtan, 83, 84
Nein Roe, 120
Nemain, 63, 64, 65, 81, 120
Nemed, 25–26, 28
Nemedians, the, 14, 28–29, 31, 38, 69
Nennius, 69, 72–73; *Historia*, 15
Neo-Platonism, 177, 244, 245
Neptune, 83, 84
Nera, 45, 46, 51
Niamh Chinn-óir (Niam), 42, 200, 220, 221, 224, 226, 269

Nodens, 80, 84
Nuada (slave), 281, 285
Nuada (Nuadu), King, 32, 33, 34, 35, 78, 79, 81, 83–84, 211; Sword of, 31, 212
'Nurture of the Horses of the two Milk-Vessels, The', 131
Nutt, Alfred, 43, 44, 81, 143, 156, 282, 286; 'The Celtic Doctrine of Rebirth', 294 n 7

Ó Cathasaigh, Tomás, 74, 284
O'Clery, Michael, 78
O'Currey, Eugene, 93
Odin, 57, 81, 82, 84
'O'Donnell's Kern', 62
O'Donovan, John, 82, 119, 128
O'Driscoll, Robert, 188, 213, 225, 226, 243, 246
O'Flaherty, R., 30, 91
Ogma, 33, 35, 59–60, 66, 79, 81, 84
Ogmios, 60, 79
O'Grady, Standish Hayes, 40; (trans) 'Fragmentary Annals', 286; *Silva Gadelica*, 292 n 36
O'Grady, Standish James, 155, 242; *Fionn and his Companions*, 252; *In the Gates of the North*, 319 n 50
O'Hanlon, Rev. John: *Irish Local Legends*, 276, 301 n 33
Oisín (Usheen), 42, 168, 171
'Oisin's Children', 49
'Oisin's Mother', 85
O'Malley, Ernie, 242
Omens, 122
O'Rahilly, Thomas F., 30, 45, 53, 76, 78, 79, 82; *Early Irish History and Mythology*, 291 n 2
Osgar, 121, 217
O'Shea family, 161, 172
O'Sullivan, Sean: *The Folklore of Ireland*, 303 n 9; *Folktales of Ireland*, 303 n 14
O'Sullivan, Sheila, 214, 268, 270
Otherworld, the, 45, 78, 144, 165, 219, 223, 227
Otherworld Voyage (*imram*), 257–58; see also *Imrama*
Owls, man-headed, 163

Pantheon, Irish 81–84
'Paudyeen O'Kelly and the Weasel', 125, 136

Parkin, Andrew, 215
Pater, Walter, 177, 281
Patrick, St., 37, 43, 48, 49, 87–88, 89, 90, 117, 131, 132, 137, 171, 186, 187, 196, 197, 202, 286; *Confession*, 83, 91
Pelagius, 133
Perrault, Charles, 13
Phoenicians, 99–101
'Phooka of Kildare, The', 129
Picts, 98, 99
Pigeons, 122
Pigs, 126
Pipers, 139
Plain of Delight, 42, 43
Plains of Pleasure, 45
Plummer, Charles, 106, 285; *Vitae Sanctorum Hiberniae*, 301 n 1
Pokorny, Julius, 29, 92
Poltergeists, 115
Pomponius Mela, 43
Pookas (púcas), 18, 127, 128–29, 234
Poseidon, 83
Posidonius, 43
Primroses, 142, 182
'Pursuit of Diarmuid and Grainne, The', 40, 49, 139
Pygmies, 98

'Quarrel of the Two Pig-Keepers, The', 47
Quicken, see Rowan

Raine, Kethleen, 215, 230, 'Hades Wrapped in Cloud', 317 n 26; *Yeats, the Tarot, and the Golden Dawn*, 316 n 14
Rajan, Balachandra, 183–84, 261, 275, 276
Redshaw, Thomas Dillon, 21
'Red Woman, The', 32, 49
Rees, Alwyn & Brinley, 28, 43–44, 143
Reid, B. L., 276
Reid, Forrest, 188
Reincarnation, 162
Renan, Ary, 189
Reon, 117
Rhys, Sir John, 29, 30, 98, 241; *Hibbert Lectures*, 156, 318 n 41; 'Studies in Early Irish History', 301 n 11
Roc, 241
Roe, Helen M.: 'Tales, Customs and Beliefs from Laoighis', 306 n 35

Rosenkreuz, Fr. Christian, 251
Rosenthal, M. L., 191, 192
Rosicrucianism, 176, 177, 244–45, 251, 252
Rowan (quicken), 141–42, 143, 144, 170, 182, 313 n 44
Royal Cycle, 14, 15
Ruad-Rofhessa, 56–57
Ruadan, 35
Ruan, Steven, 126
Ruidhe, 86
Russell, G. W. (A.E), 267
Rutherford, Ward, 79, 86
Ruysbroeck, Johannes, 275
Ryan, Sr. M. Rosalie, 21; 'Symbolic Elements in the Plays of W. B. Yeats 1892–1921', 313 n 38
Rymour, Thomas, 55

Sacrifices, 85–86, 91, 143
Sartre, Jean-Paul, 230
Satan, 131, 133
Saul, George Brandon, 174; *Prolegomena to the Study of Yeats's Poems*, 316 n 49
Savage, D. S., 272, 273
Savitar, 82
Scathach, 241
Schleifer, Ronald, 214, 249, 317 n 7
Scotland: distinction between good and bad faries in, 152; fairy faith of, 18
Scott, Sir Walter, 120; *The Antiquary*, 290; *The Heart of Mid-Lothian*, 305 n 70
Scuithin, St., 282
Sea god, role of, 83–84
'Second Battle of Mag Tured, The', 32, 34, 35, 50, 57, 60, 93, 97
Seal-people, 117–18
'Seeker, The', 200
Seelie Court, Scotland, 152
Setanta, 283
Seymour, St. John D., 'The Eschatology of the Early Irish Church', 321 n 28
Shane's Castle, banshee of, 120, 147
Shakespear, Olivia, 231, 233, 234, 236
Shape-shifting, 43, 47–49
Sheridan, Mrs, 100, 146
Shoes, 114

Index

'Sick-Bed of Cu Chulainn, The', 41, 44, 49, 54, 88
Sídh, 74–75, 142–43
Sídhe, the, 18, 88, 92–95, 97–99, 100, 101, 130; domain of, 109–11; immortality of, 107–08; stature of, 108–09
Sídheán an Gháire, 109
Sin, 50–51, 88
Síth, 74–75
Síth Aodha, fairy queen of, 48
Sjoestedt, Marie-Louise, 57, 81, 82, 84; *Gods and Heroes of the Celts*, 296 n 24
Slad, 137
Slieve Echtge, 209, 211, 213, 214, 269
Sluagh Gaoithe, 151–52
Sluagh Sidhe, 151, 152
Smith, Pamela Colman, 316 n 17
Smol, king of Greece, 29
Solitary fairies, 18, 145–46, 147, 150
Spaan, David B., 83
Spear of Lugh, 31, 61, 209
Spence, Lewis: *History and Origins of Druidism*, 228
Sreng, 32, 95
Stephens, James, 155, 163
Stock, A. G., 172, 177, 188
Stokes, Whitley, 78, 79, 82; 'Mythological Notes', 303 n 20
Stone of Destiny, 31, 209
Stray sod, 149
Sualtim mac Roigh, 283
Sucellos, 57, 58, 80
Suibhne Gealt, King, 54, 200
Suicide, 259, 266
Suirge, 37
Sun god, role of, 82–83
Swans, 48, 123, 163
Sword of Light, 209, 212, 316 n 13
Symons, Arthur, 234; 'Mr Yeats as a Lyric Poet', 318 n 31; 'The Ideas of Richard Wagner', 259

Táin bo Cuailgne, 27, 47, 48, 49, 64, 72, 77, 283, 284, 288
Tarot, the, 209, 210–11, 214, 316 n 17
'Teig O'Kane and the Corpse', 100
Teigue son of Cian, 45, 46
Tethra, 42
Teutates, 80
'Thirteenth Son of the King of Erin, The', 241

Thompson, William Irwin, 244
Thor, 57, 81, 84
Thorfinnssaga Karlsefnis, 27
Thorvald, 27
Thuente, Mary Helen, 216; *W. B. Yeats and Irish Folklore*, 317 n 28
Thurneysen, Rudolf, 72
Tighernmas, 40, 89
Tír Fó Thuinn, 44
Tír na nÓg, 42, 45, 46, 110, 128, 144, 162, 163
Tír Tarrngaire (Tairngire), 41, 284
Tolkien, J. R. R., 26; '*Beowulf*: The Monsters and the Critics', 291 n 6
Torinis, Battle of, 28–29
Tory Island, 28, 134–35, 146
Treblann, 71–72
Trees, 165, 170
Trí de danaan, na, 78
Triath mac Faebuir, 72
Tricephalus, 81
Triumphs of Turlough, The, 98
Trooping fairies, 18, 145, 146–49, 150, 152
Trystan, 241
'Tuan, Son of Cairell', 77
Tuatha Dé Danann, 13, 14, 16, 18, 25–112 passim, 106, 109, 130, 170, 177, 150, 226; appearance, 39–40; arrival in Ireland, 31; controversy over divinity of, 76–91; domain, 40–46; Four Jewels of, 31, 61, 209, 214, 216; mortal protégés of 281–320; powers, 46–51; wars of the, 139
Tuathal Maelgarb, 51
Tyr, 81, 84
Tyson: *Philological Essay concerning the Pygmies of the Ancients*, 98

Uillenn Faebarderg, 63
Ulster Cycle, 14, 15, 32, 36, 65, 80, 87
Una of Cnoc Sidhe-Una, 119
Universe: conception of as meaningless, 201–02, 203, 204
Unseelie Court, Scotland, 152
Unterecker, John, 189
Ure, Peter, 165, 168, 171; 'The Evolution of Yeats's *The Countess Cathleen*', 313 n 46; *Yeats the Playwright*, 312 n 35

Ussher, P.: 'Waterford Folk Tales', 303 n 30

Valkyries, 65
Valley of the Black Pig, 241, 242
van Hamel, A. G., 28, 30, 60, 77, 78, 79, 80
de Villiers de L'Islè Adam, J. M. M. P. A., Count: *Axël*, 247, 259, 275, 320 n 6; *Le Révolte*, 320 n 6
Vishnu, 284
Vision of Adamnan, The, 276
Vision of Tundal, The, 276, 277
Vita Tripartita (Tripartite Life of St. Patrick), 87, 88, 89, 91, 293 n 58
Vivien, 268, 269
von Sydow: medical theory on changelings, 143
'Voyage of Bran, The', 43, 44, 62, 258
Voyage of Bran, The, ed. & Trans. Kuno Meyer, 294 n 7
'Voyage of Life', 258
'Voyage of Maeldune, The', 257

Wachsler, Arthur, A., 41
Wagner, Richard: *Götterdämmerung*, 172 *Tristan und Isolde*, 259
Waite, A. E., 209, 210, 316 n 17; *The Holy Grail*, 316 n 10
War-goddesses, Irish, 65
Water-horses, 127–28
Water-wagtails, 122
Waters, Patrick, 129, 131, 146
Watts, Harold H., 157
Weasels, 124–25
'Wedding of Maine Morgor, The', 49
Westcott, Dr. W. W.: *Hermetic Arcanum*, 229
Westropp, T. J., 128–29; 'Coast of Connacht', 306 n 35; 'A Folklore Survey of County Clare, 301 n 25; 'A Study of Folklore on the Coasts of Connacht, Ireland', 302 n 32
Wet-nurses, 138, 139
Whitaker, T. R., 243
Wilde, Jane Francesca, Lady, ('Speranza'), 97, 112, 126, 128, 132, 134, 145; *Ancient Cures, Charms and Usages of Ireland*, 301 n 17; *Ancient Legends, Mystic Charms and Superstitions of Ireland*, 306 n 41; 'Kathleen', 134

Wilde, Sir William, 132, 150, 244; *Irish Popular Superstitions*, 303 n 3
Wilson, Edmund, 198
Winberry, John J., 114; 'The Elusive Elf', 303 n 17
Wind, 270
Windy Gap, 270
Wolves, 163
Wood-Martin, W. G., 54, 65, 111, 113, 129, 146, 160, 288, 289; *Traces of the Elder Faiths of Ireland*, 296 n 9
Wood-of-Wonders, 269
'Wooing of Emer, The', 90
'Wooing of Etain, The', 39, 40, 49, 59
'Wooing of Treblann, The', 71, 73

Yama, 73
Yates, Frances A., 245; *The Rosicrucian Enlightenment*, 319 n 57
Yeats, Susan Mary (Lily), 19
YEATS, WILLIAM BUTLER
apocalyptic writing, 229–31, 238, 242–54; order of celtic mysteries, 209, 318 n 35
Writings:
'The Adoration of the Magi', 20, 151, 152, 252
'Aedh hears the Cry of the Sedge', 247, 248–49
'Aedh laments the Loss of Love', 231
'Aedh tells of the Rose in his Heart', 223–24, 264
'Aedh wishes his Beloved were Dead', 250, 253
The Arrow (ed.), 266
'The Autumn of the Body', 247, 272
Baile and Ailinn, 218–19, 268
'The Blessed', 249–50, 251, 252, 273
'The Book of the Great Dhoul and Hanrahan the Red', 205, 206, 207
'Byzantium', 203, 246
Cathleen ni Houlihan, 206–07, 211, 212
The Celtic Twilight, 132, 221, 245, 269, 288
'The Circus Animals' Desertion', 159
'The Cold Heaven', 267, 274–77

Index

Collected Plays, 20
Collected Poems, 20
The Countess Cathleen, 19, 21, 49, 157, 158–73 passim, 174, 178, 181–83, 188, 190, 192, 194, 224, 227, 288–90
'The Countess Kathleen O'Shea', 161
The Country of the Young, 317 n 25
'The Cradles of Gold', 225, 226
'Crazy Jane on the Mountain', 193
'Crossways', 19, 184
'The Crucifixion of the Outcast', 179–80, 186, 187, 192, 193, 197, 319 n 70
'Cuchulain's Fight with the Sea', 202
'The Curse of the Fires and of the Shadows', 188, 196
'The Danaan Quicken Tree', 199–200, 201, 220
'The Death of Hanrahan', 205, 207, 213, 215, 216
'The Death of Synge', 258
Dierdre, 259
Diarmuid and Grania, 251
'Easter 1916', 273
'The Everlasting Voices', 220, 221, 224, 230, 231, 237, 245, 249
'A Faery Song', 202–3
Fairy and Folk Tales of the Irish Peasantry, 161, 276
Fairy and Folk Tales of Ireland, 304 n 34
'Fergus and the Druid', 191, 192, 198, 201, 250
'The Grey Rock, 206
'Hanrahan and Cathleen, the Daughter of Houlihan', 213
'Hanrahan laments because of his Wanderings', 232–33, 235, 243, 248
'Hanrahan reproves the Curlew', 236, 237, 249
'Hanrahan's Vision', 213, 216
'The Happy Townland', 214, 215, 267, 270, 273
'The Heart of the Spring', 179, 188, 197, 198, 203–04
'The Heart of the Woman', 231
'The Host of the Air', 147, 224–25
'The Hosting of the Sidhe', 200, 219–20, 221, 224, 227, 256, 257, 270
'The Hour before Dawn', 272–74
'I walked among the seven woods of Coole', 265
In the Seven Woods, 267
'Into the Twilight', 163, 227
'Invoking the Irish Fairies', 311 n 2
'Ireland Bewitched', 308 n 64, 316 n 7
The Irish Dramatic Movement, 20
Irish Fairy Tales, 147, 276, 304 n 34
'Irish Witch Doctors', 308 n 64
John Sherman, 121, 257, 312 n 27
'King and No King', 275
The King's Threshold, 259
'The Lake Isle of Innisfree', 181, 199, 201
The Land of Heart's Desire, 180, 181, 182–85, 215
The Letters of W. B. Yeats (ed. A. Wade), 307 n 15
'The Magi', 252, 267, 274
'"Maive" and Certain Irish Beliefs', 317 n 14
'The Man Who Dreamed of Faeryland', 178, 190, 194, 195, 198, 199, 200, 210, 211
Memoirs, 159
'Michael Robartes asks Forgiveness because of his Many Moods', 247
'Michael Robartes bids his Beloved be at Peace', 225, 233–35, 237, 238, 248
'Michael Robartes remembers Forgotten Beauty', 218, 237–38, 243
'Mongan laments the Change that has come upon him and his Beloved', 231–32, 233, 234, 235, 247, 248
'Mongan thinks of his Past Greatness', 248–49
'The Moods', 190, 221–22, 224
Mythologies, 222
'Nineteen Hundred and Nineteen', 268
'No Second Troy', 269
'Notes for a Celtic Order', 257
'The Old Men in the Twilight', 196–97
The Only Jealousy of Emer, 41

'O'Sullivan Rua to Mary Lavell', 218
'Out of the Rose', 177–78, 186, 187, 188, 193–94, 197, 203, 271
'The Phases of the Moon', 223
The Philosphy of Shelley's Poetry', 179, 233
'The Pity of Love', 198, 224
'The Priest and the Fairy', 132
'The Realists', 274
'Red Hanrahan', 205, 208, 216
'Red Hanrahan's Curse', 207, 213, 216
'Red Hanrahan's Song about Ireland', 212
Responsibilities, 19, 158, 266, 267, 270, 274
The Resurrection, 50
'Ribh Denounces Patrick', 239
'Rosa Alchemica', 222, 223
The Rose, 19, 174, 175, 178, 185, 188, 190, 194, 195, 201, 205, 210, 217, 218, 219, 220, 224, 232, 238, 251, 254
'The Rose of Battle', 177, 188, 189–90, 195, 201
'The Rose of Peace', 188, 189
'The Rose of the World', 176, 188, 189, 190, 192–93
'Running to Paradise', 270–71
'The Secret Rose', 250, 251–53
The Secret Rose, 175, 178, 186, 188, 197, 205, 218
'The Seeker', 194, 220
The Shadowy Waters, 19, 21, 157, 164, 215, 253, 254, 255–96, 267, 271
'The Song of the Old Mother', 231
'The Song of Wandering Aengus', 227–28, 231, 232
'The Sorrow of Love', 177, 198, 255
'The Stolen Child', 184, 225
Stories of Red Hanrahan, 19, 20, 21, 204, 205–17, 236, 260, 265
'Swedenborg, Mediums and the Desolate Places', 317 n 31
'The Tables of the Law', 188, 223
'The Three Beggars', 250
'The Three Hermits', 271
'Three Songs to the Same Tune', 193
'To Ireland in the Coming Times', 177, 178, 179, 181, 185, 194, 206, 246
'To my Heart, bidding it have no Fear', 236, 237
'To Some I have Talked with by the Fire', 180, 185, 194, 195, 246
'To the Rose upon the Rood of Time', 178, 179, 201
'The Travail of Passion', 222–23, 246–47
'The Trembling of the Veil', 19
'The Twisting of the Rope', 208, 213, 215, 236
'The Two Kings', 271–72
'The Two Trees', 197
'The Unappeasable Host', 224, 225, 226
'Under Ben Bulben', 193
'Under the Moon', 267, 268–69, 270
'The Valley of the Black Pig', 232, 238–46, 247, 248; apocalypse, 242–46, sexual content, 238–39; tradition, 239–42
Variorum Edition of the Plays of W. B. Yeats (ed. R. K. Alspach), 295 n 68
A Vision, 158, 162, 267
The Wanderings of Oisin, 19, 42, 126, 171, 220
'The White Birds', 176, 203, 204
'William Blake and his Illustrations to the Divine Comedy', 246
The Wind Among the Reeds, 19, 20, 21, 174, 190, 204, 217, 218–83 *passim*, 263–64
'The Wisdom of the King', 188, 191, 192, 196, 197, 198
'The Withering of the Boughs', 267, 269, 270
'Who Goes with Fergus?', 190–91, 192, 252
Yellow Book of Lecan, 15, 65
Yew, 142
Yima, 73
'The Young Piper', 140